SYSTEMS PROGRAMMING FOR SMALL COMPUTERS

SYSTEMS PROGRAMMING FOR SMALL COMPUTERS

DANIEL H. MARCELLUS

Watson School of Engineering
State University of New York, Binghamton

PRENTICE-HALL, INC., Englewood Cliffs, New Jersey 07632

Library of Congress Cataloging in Publication Data

Marcellus, Daniel H. (date)
 Systems programming for small computers.

 Includes index.
  1. Electronic digital computers—Programming.
I. Title.
QA76.6.M3583 1984   001.64'2   83-22951
ISBN   0-13-881664-6
ISBN   0-13-881656-5 (pbk.)

Editorial/production supervision and
   interior design: *Lynn Frankel*
Cover design: *Diane Saxe*
Manufacturing buyer: *Gordon Osbourne*

Cover art: Anonymous sixteenth century German wood-cut.
A vision in which Ezekial perceives the program of the
ultimate system. Courtesy of The Bettmann Archive Inc.,
136 East 57th St., New York, N.Y. 10022

Printed in the United States of America

10 9 8 7 6 5 4 3 2 1

ISBN   0-13-881664-6
ISBN   0-13-881656-5   {PBK}

Prentice-Hall International, Inc., *London*
Prentice-Hall of Australia Pty. Limited, *Sydney*
Editora Prentice-Hall do Brasil, Ltda., *Rio de Janeiro*
Prentice-Hall Canada Inc., *Toronto*
Prentice-Hall of India Private Limited, *New Delhi*
Prentice-Hall of Japan, Inc., *Tokyo*
Prentice-Hall of Southeast Asia Pte., Ltd., *Singapore*
Whitehall Books Limited, *Wellington, New Zealand*

Contents

3. THE SIMPLEST OPERATING SYSTEMS: ROM MONITORS   33

4. ASSEMBLER LANGUAGES   58

5. LINKERS AND LOADERS   91

9. TEXT EDITORS   **170**

10. DESCRIPTION AND ANALYSIS OF HIGH LEVEL COMPUTER LANGUAGES   **203**

11. INTERPRETERS: TINY BASIC   **231**

Contents

APPENDICES

Preface

If you think the business of systems programming is to write good systems programs, then this will be a good book for you. Indeed, it will show you how to construct editors, interpreters, compilers, operating systems, and the like for small computer systems. If you think the business of systems programming is to discuss the characteristics of obscure and elegant abstract machines, and abstruse formal theories of language translators, then this book is not for you, because it doesn't do that.

This book is meant for a first course in systems programming. It has a nontraditional emphasis. What we have tried to do here is collect in one place, the simplest possible examples of all the normal kinds of systems software. These have either been designed for this book or taken from widely known commercial examples. Simple examples are good to learn from. We have tried to delve into their structure enough so that someone could go out and, given enough time and some latitude for learning, he could build that kind of software himself. What we want to elicit from the reader is a certain specific reaction: "Wow, I could do that!"*

The book is also nontraditional in that the software it considers is all for micro-computers, or possibly for minicomputers. We took this approach after noting how daunting it can be to have mainframe principles thrown at you when you are first trying to figure out what really goes on inside the computer. Of course, there is a continuity of common principles connecting the software of all computers—large and small—and that is the core of systems programming, but it is so much easier to teach that core with microcomputers. If you can hold a CPU in the palm of your hand, you tend to have much more confidence that you will be able to understand what it does.

*The pronouns "he," "his," and "him" are used in this text to include both sexes without prejudice.

The organization of the material presented here, i.e., the layout of the topics, is an attempt to imitate what is a very successful way to teach programming in general. You start with a small but potent subset of all the instructions that are in the programming language being taught. When the student is at home with these instructions, successive layers of more specialized and more powerful features can be added in an ordered manner. To bring this strategy to systems programming, the problem is what should be in the various layers. How can we identify a nucleus of important ideas, and then successively elaborate it?

Our ordering principle in identifying layers of features has been total system complexity. To a surprising degree, systems graded on complexity also match the historical development of the subject. Thus our innermost layer corresponds to both the simplest and the oldest types of systems software: ROM monitor type operating systems, assemblers, and program production aids such as macroprocessors and linkers. A layer beyond this one in both historical development and complexity would include more complicated control software such as single user disk based operating systems and program production software such as editors, compilers, and interpreters. Our final layer of complexity, and one which points the way to big systems, includes just one topic—multi-tasking operating systems. If we go any further, our mandate to stay with small systems will have expired.

Along with each of the characteristic software layers, we have introduced the small computer hardware necessary to support the software, so that a total systems picture can be maintained.

Who can use this book? It has been written as a textbook for undergraduates in their first systems programming course. It is a text for the beginning term of the traditional three term computer science sequence in

- Systems Programming
- Compilers
- Operating Systems

It can also be used in short curriculums to introduce the whole area of operating systems, languages, and utilities, if the student only has time for one course. The book has been tested in both these contexts in the author's classes on systems programming at the State University of New York, Binghamton. Finally, the book can be used as a self-learning tool for anyone who has a computer system and wants to know more about it than just how to turn the computer on and off and feed it programs in a high level language.

What about the prerequisites to effective use of this material? To make good use of it, a reader probably should have had courses in a higher level programming language and in assembly language, and enough experience in using a computer so that he appreciates what is in a computer system. Since systems programming is the level at which hardware and software touch, a course on computer hardware would be helpful, although it is not strictly necessary. In addition, we have found that the book is very nicely complemented by any sort of laboratory work with actual microprocessor equipment.

There are some places in the text where it is necessary to show examples in assembly language. For this purpose we have used the language of the Intel 8080. This is not the best microprocessor, and it is certainly not the newest; it is simply the most widely known. For those unfamiliar with the 8080, we have included an appendix to teach about it.

Some potential users may be uncomfortable with this book's main procedure of dissecting examples of different types of software. We do this because we feel that to some extent learning about software is like learning about a car. The main thing you do is take it apart, so that you see how everything works and where everything fits. Certainly at some point it is appropriate to study the aerodynamics of the fuel mixture as it passes through the carburetor, or the thermodynamics of heat exchange following explosions in the cylinder. But no one would do this without a working knowledge of how the car worked as a system. This book is the first stage of that kind of analytic process as applied to computer systems.

Our orientation throughout is intensely practical. An attempt has been made to include only material that is directly useful to producing good systems software. It is easy to talk about being practical, but there is an easy operational principle by which we wish our efforts here to be judged: if you can build it, then you understand it.

ACKNOWLEDGMENTS

The author would like to thank some people who helped get this book in gear. James Van Zee originally introduced the author to the pleasures of small computers. From Professor Melvin Klerer at New York Polytechnic Institute comes the essential idea that systems programming can be taught simply. Paul Davis and Jane Cameron provided valuable advice on various technical matters. Lance Leventhal gave timely encouragement and good advice about the organization of the book. Thanks to Velda Bartek, James Van Zee, and Juan Rodriguez-Torrent for identifying many errors that aren't there anymore. And thanks to Rob Barnaby for WORDSTAR.

DANIEL H. MARCELLUS

1

General Introduction

1.1 WHAT IS SYSTEMS PROGRAMMING?

A computer system is a set of tools that can aid people in performing data processing tasks and in solving computational problems. Some of these tools consist of mechanical hardware and electronic circuits. These are the computer itself and its peripheral equipment such as terminals, printers, disk storage devices, and communications equipment. Other tools are software—the systems programs. These programs knit everything together and make it possible for the user to get down to business working on his problem, without having to learn the complicated but irrelevant details of exactly how the computer system works internally.

Systems programs have two purposes. They make a computer system easy to use for a nonexpert, and they make it possible for the resources of the system to be used efficiently. Systems programs are software that is normally included with a computer system when it is purchased. These programs are typically provided by the manufacturer or by specialized vendors. Some examples are

- Input/Output Subroutine Packages
- Monitors
- Operating Systems
- Assemblers
- Macroprocessors
- Interpreters
- Compilers

- Linking Loaders
- Editors
- Debuggers
- Data Base Managers
- Communications Software

Programmers frequently make a distinction between systems programs and applications programs. Applications are programs that are written by users of computers to solve the problems for which the computers were purchased in the first place. These applications programs use the resources that are provided by the systems software.

A typical large computer today is insulated from its users by layer upon layer of systems programs. Figure 1-1 illustrates this phenomenon. In the environment shown in

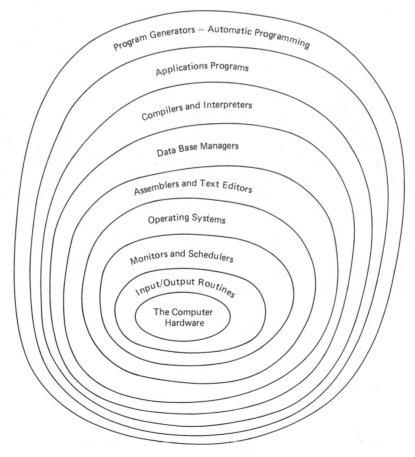

Figure 1-1: **Hierarchies of Systems Software.** The user is separated from the machine by many intervening layers of systems software. Lucky for him!

the figure, someone working in one of the outer shells of programs is apt to be very productive. This productivity will show up when users can make the machine do something useful with relatively few commands. That's what productivity means in the software world. On the other hand, someone working in the outer layers is apt to have only a vague idea of what's happening in the lower level routines between him and the machine. This is the domain of the systems programmer.

1.2 HOW DID THIS TYPE OF SOFTWARE EVOLVE?

Let us now review the evolution of computer systems and the systems programs that grew up with them. Then we will try to establish the place of small computers within this spectrum. The modern computer developed out of engineering requirements for better computation during the era of World War II. The first computers were undoubtedly conceived as extensions of the mechanical calculators with which all engineers of the time were familiar.

During this period, two computational ideas appeared which brilliantly reinforced each other. The first was to try to capture the exact sequence of button pushes someone would use to do a long problem on a mechanical calculator, and keep the sequence electrically in some kind of a machine. Once captured, this "program" could be used over and over on different editions of important data.

This simple idea had another implication. If the instructions were maintained in a machine, then a new style of computation became possible. Looping computations that depended on iteration could now be done easily because new instructions didn't have to be reentered from the keyboard each time control went through the loop. It is quite different trying to do an iterative computation by hand. Capturing the instructions in a machine made iteration feasible.

In 1939, a group at Harvard led by Howard Aiken and supported by IBM began the construction of the first stored program computer. The Mark 1, completed in 1944, maintained instructions electrically in an internal form and permitted looping, as a modern computer does, but it was seriously deficient in two respects. Information was held in electromechanical relays which were very slow. But worse, every time the problem was changed, the machine had to be rewired. The instructions were in the hardware, and rewiring the hardware sometimes took several weeks.

The other crucial idea which defines modern computation was to make a computer in which the hardware was never rewired. It was frozen, but the program was not. Both the data and the instructions, which varied from one problem to the next, were to be maintained as numeric codes in the machine's memory. There was to be no inherent difference between the ways of representing data and instructions. John von Neumann conceived this powerful idea in the late 1940's while working on the ENIAC project. Machines that followed this architecture could be changed for new problems with relative ease. The task of setting up a problem was reduced to producing a program—a sequence of numerical codes that would control the machine. Most of our present day computers are still essentially patterned after the von Neumann type design. They are just much bigger and much faster.

At the beginning of the age of automatic computation, program production was a laborious process. The machine instructions would typically be introduced into the computer's memory by manually setting switches on a front panel for each word to be loaded. Later, programs were put on paper tape. A short loader program would be toggled in from the switches, and that set of instructions would execute and bring in more complicated programs that were on the punched tape.

It must have taken a long time to prepare a program in those days. Correcting the bugs was the hard part. Errors would creep into a program of any length just because machine code is not an easy medium for a human to think in. Even after you found the mistake(s), it took a long time to produce a new version containing the necessary corrections.

This situation was blatantly unsatisfactory, but people quickly found help in being more efficient from an unexpected source—the computer itself. It must have originally been a revolutionary and not very obvious idea to let the computer aid in preparing its own programs. At least two important types of systems programs were developed in this period: the assembler, and the ancestor of the piece of software known today in the small computer industry as the ROM monitor.

An *assembler* is a piece of systems software that greatly aids the rapid and accurate production of programs as compared to writing in machine code. Its development addressed two major problems. The most obvious one was that it was difficult to think in machine code. People began to associate mnemonics with each machine instruction. The mnemonic was an abbreviation for what the instruction did. It is much easier for a human to remember and manipulate programs if they are built from these mnemonics. The earliest assemblers were just translation mechanisms taking mnemonic programs to the equivalent programs in machine code.

The second problem was more subtle. In a program of any length, if you have to make corrections by inserting or deleting code somewhere in the middle of the program, this will ruin many perfectly good instructions at other parts of the program. In particular, it will disturb instructions that refer to particular addresses in the code that are no longer valid because the whole body of the program has been moved up or down in memory to accommodate the corrections. The solution was to write all addresses in the assembler program symbolically, so that on the level of the assembler program itself, nothing would appear to change these addresses, even though the translated machine code would be quite different. Thus in the assembler program, a jump to a certain address would now be written.

```
JUMP    ALPHA
```

instead of

```
JUMP    4128
```

or some other specific memory address. Any time changes were necessary, the code could just be reassembled, and the assembler would figure out all changed addresses automatically.

The *monitor* is the software from which grew the operating systems we know today. It provided a means whereby some sort of electromechanical terminal could be hooked up to control the system. The monitor software implemented a few simple but useful commands, such as to enter a program (in machine code) from the keyboard, to display the contents of the computer's memory, to set a program into execution, to modify an indicated part of memory, and to store or load a program using whatever external medium was available. In the early days, this would have been paper tape or magnetic tape. The monitor made it much more convenient for people to interact with the computer system. In the very earliest computers, some of the monitor functions were built right into the electronics of the computer's control panel. Later, these functions migrated into software.

At about this point, the familiar program production cycle began to emerge. The programmer would create a program, assemble it, try it out, identify errors, make changes, reassemble the program, etc. until he got it right. But how would the program be created in the first place? At this time the principal method was to punch the program on a deck of tabulator cards. After errors were detected, they would be corrected by making new cards and fitting them into the deck at the locations of the errors. The crucial point, though, is that errors were corrected off-line at a card punch rather than with an editor.

With these tools, both software and mechanical, the production and control of programs had arrived at a pretty efficient basis. There are some other tools that extend what you can do with an assembler. They were developed later as people became more familiar with the requirements of the assembly process. The *macroprocessor* is one. It is text processing software that allows a programmer to specify abbreviations that will always stand for certain pieces of code. Thus, if you want the same few lines of code at a number of places in your program, then instead of typing them out each time, you can define a macro and just use the macro name where you need the code. If you then give your text to a macroprocessor, it will remove the abbreviations and insert the text that you wanted at all the appropriate places. A macroprocessor can also be used to introduce code sequences via abbreviations when the general pattern of the code remains the same from one use to the next, but when certain parts of it (usually parameters) have to be set up differently at each occurrence.

As programs got bigger, a need was felt for a way to merge different parts of a big program written by different people. The issue of how to easily incorporate subroutine libraries of commonly used functions is also part of this problem. The solution that emerged was relocatable code that could be processed by *linking software*. It is possible to make an assembler that outputs machine code in which certain of the addresses used by the code haven't been completely determined (because they aren't known at coding time). This is relocatable code. It is used in the following way: All programmers produce their parts of the program as relocatable code. It is the job of the linker to do the final filling in of addresses in all parts of the program so that the modules become executable code and so that they occupy those parts of memory that were planned for them in relation to the whole program.

By the late 1950's, experience was accumulating with big programs written in assembler code, and an alarming fact was becoming known: Programming was very expensive. On large programs, it came to be the norm in industry that a single programmer could produce only about ten statements worth of good code in one working day. This measurement is obtained by dividing the total number of lines of code in the system by the total number of man-days spent in creating it. Time spent for design, coding, debugging, and documentation must all be included. Large systems have thousands of statements of code, so it is easy to appreciate the high cost of programming.

The principal remedies the computer industry has found for problems of programmer productivity have been to develop better programming languages and better programming environments. First let's look at languages. A *compiler* is language processing software that takes a program written in a high level form more or less congenial to a human being and translates it into machine language. Compiled languages can be used at a higher level than assembled languages; that is, a statement in the compiled language does more work. If you write a program in assembler language and the same program in one of the popular compiled languages, like FORTRAN or Pascal, the assembler version will be much longer. It will have on the average somewhere between 3 and 10 times as many statement lines. The amounts of time needed to write the two programs will also be in this ratio. The trend in computer science has been, and continues to be, toward higher and higher level languages. The ultimate will be some kind of programming system that can be accessed with ordinary human language, but that goal is still far away.

Interpreters are another kind of higher level language system. An interpreter executes a program directly from the initial program text prepared by the programmer. There is no intermediate translation into machine code. The interpreter analyzes what each line in the program is asking for and then does it, immediately. Sometimes, an interpretive system is to be preferred over a compiled one because it can make more efficient use of the computer memory. People who are exploring new computer languages frequently will set up interpreters for these languages because they seem to be easier to write than compilers. The disadvantage is that interpreted code executes substantially slower than compiled code.

On-line editing was a key development in making a better programming environment. Of course, the idea here is an extension of the goal of letting the computer aid in program development. An *on-line editor* allows you to type the text of a program on a keyboard device under computer control. Editors also provide ways to access parts of the text, which already exist, in order to make insertions, deletions, or other changes. In order to make this possible, program text is usually stored in the computer memory or on magnetic media accessible to the computer, rather than on cards.

The idea of on-line editing was an early one, but it didn't really catch on for quite a while for several reasons. First of all, punched card input was very effective. Indeed, some still think it has advantages over terminal I/O. Second, it didn't make sense to allow single users to tie up expensive batch computers to do editing. So the real use of on-line editing came after time sharing operating systems on big machines were developed and after small machines became cheap enough for single user applications. This was in the late 1960's.

Assemblers, compilers, editors, macroprocessors, and the like are all *program production software*. As this branch of the systems programming enterprise has been evolving, another separate branch has been growing in parallel. Operating systems are *system control software*. The operating system forms an environment in which program production software and applications programs can run. Parts of a modern operating system will be responsible for moving programs between storage and memory, for finding memory for programs, for giving them access to the CPU (if it is being shared by several programs), for taking care of the interface to the I/O devices, for making it easy to create and use files, and the like.

The *monitor software* on early computers performed functions like those found today in ROM monitors on microcomputers. This is our earliest example of operating-system-like software.

The next developments were *single user batch operating systems* with good file management on tapes or disks. They were like the floppy-disk-based microcomputer operating systems we find today, such as CP/M. Here we have an instance of large computer software of the late 1950's appearing on microcomputers in the early 1970's. This kind of system, thought to be dead by many, was essentially rediscovered after IBM invented the floppy disk in 1972.

A cheap, fast, high capacity, random access device like the floppy changed the character of what a small operating system could do. Now it became possible to load big programs rapidly, as well as to produce programs much more quickly because all the intermediate readings and writings in the program production cycle didn't have to go through transfers to slow tape devices. The character of these operating systems is somewhat like a ROM monitor to which an extensive file system has been added. Most of the operating system's power is given over to loading programs and managing these files.

All of the systems software discussed so far was developed with the objective of making the computer easy to use. After this point, larger and more complex operating systems were designed with an equally important objective in mind: to use the resources of the machine at maximum efficiency.

A great amount of progress in systems programming was made in the early 1960's. The primary development here was the *multi-tasking operating system,* sometimes called a multi-programming system. This is an arrangement whereby a fast CPU is programmed to rotate its attention among a small number of independent tasks that will seem to be executing simultaneously. Typically, the CPU might spend $^1/_{10}$ of a second on Task A, then $^1/_{10}$ of a second on Task B, then $^1/_{10}$ of a second on Task C, etc., and then come back to Task A. Computational progress through all of these tasks will advance simultaneously, although at a slower rate than if a particular task had exclusive possession of the CPU.

Why would we want to do this? The reason multi-tasking operating systems were developed originally was to make batch processing more efficient. Multi-tasking allowed the computation at the heart of a job to be separated from the I/O processes associated with it. I/O had become a serious bottleneck, since it was inherently much slower than computation. With a multi-tasking system, the following pattern of operations became possible. The computer would devote its attention to a small number of batch jobs at once. When one of them came to a point where some I/O was required, rather than wait for it, the CPU would start some special hardware to do the I/O and would switch attention to other of the tasks that were ready for some more computation. When the I/O machinery signaled that it was finished, the CPU would once again begin attending to the first task. On a hardware level, for the first time, a good interrupt system became important to support this kind of processing.

A few years later, around 1967, commercially built *time sharing systems* began to appear. A time sharing system is one wherein some of the tasks in the underlying multi-tasking operating system are devoted to managing terminals through which users can interact with the system. The principal advantage here is in improving programmer productivity by improving the programming environment. Turn-around time can be greatly reduced. A program can be submitted for compilation or assembly from the terminal. If the computer is not heavily burdened, the results will come back in a few minutes and can be viewed immediately. Then an on-line editor can be used to make changes, and the program can be resubmitted. The programmer has the illusion of being in constant contact with the computer. Since many of the mechanical parts of the program production cycle, such as printing and carrying around card decks, are eliminated, the programmer can theoretically get much more work done.

It was also an impressive sales point for a vendor to be able to say, "This machine can simultaneously service 100 terminals." Of course, what was often not said was that, with 100 terminals, everything would be so slow as to make on-line access worthless.

For many years after the introduction of multi-tasking and time sharing, the manufacturers of large computers were in the enviable position of being able to sell relatively inexpensive hardware for huge amounts of money. A crucial point for our discussion is that these sales were made possible by systems software. System control programs allowed large numbers of users to appear to be using a single big computer at one time. It was to arrive in this position that IBM spent, according to one estimate, 5000 man-years developing all the systems programs for the initial family of System 360 computers. We are including here all the operating systems, language processors, and general system utilities. The story of this development is engagingly told in Frederick P. Brook's book *The Mythical Man-Month*.[1]

The multi-tasking multi-user operating system was the last of the classical software innovations in the mainframe world. Since then progress has occurred by taking good hardware and software and making it bigger, faster, more efficient, more reliable, and— to some extent—cheaper.

All of the program production software we have mentioned ultimately found its way to a small computer implementation. This is not true for all the operating system technology. In particular, one common big system type, a computer optimized to run many batch jobs, has no counterpart in the small computer world. However, there are small computer versions of single user disk based operating systems and of multi-user time sharing systems. The small computer versions appeared 10 to 15 years after systems of this kind became common in the most expensive big computers.

---

[1]Frederick P. Brooks, Jr., *The Mythical Man-Month,* Addison-Wesley, Reading, Mass., 1975, p. 31.

1.3 WHY INTRODUCE SYSTEMS PROGRAMMING WITH SMALL COMPUTERS?

The subject of this book is systems programming. The short description we have just had of the evolution of systems programming is the heritage of computer systems of all sizes. Why then does this book propose to focus on small computers? There are four reasons:

1. Small computers lend themselves to teaching. The small computer provides a much more friendly and nonintimidating environment than does a mainframe.

2. Small computers are accessible and inexpensive. In the near future, many schools which could never afford mainframe power will be able to purchase good small computer equipment.

3. The power of small computers is increasing at such a rate that this kind of equipment may even become the predominant computing environment in a few years. If this is so, then surely a study of the programming characteristics and needs of small systems becomes a subject area in its own right.

   There is a metric that can be used to measure the growth in power of the microprocessors that are at the heart of small computer systems. An empirical observation called Moore's Law states that the number of transistors residing on the most complex VLSI chips tends to double every year—and there is no end in sight for this trend. Figure 1-2 shows some microprocessors that provide data in support of Moore's Law. If anything, the later data points suggest that this trend is accelerating.

   Respectable small computer systems have been built using the Intel 8080 as the central processor. The 8080 appeared in 1973 and is constructed from approximately 2000 transistors. Imagine a small computer system built around the Hewlett Packard chip which incorporates 450,000 transistors. Surely, in some respects, it would equal mainframe power.

Processor	Year when available as a real product	Number of transistors
Intel 8080	1973	2,000
Intel 8085	1975	5,000
Intel 8086	1978	25,000
Motorola 68000	1981	70,000
Intel 80286	1982	110,000
Hewlett-Packard Single Chip Processor	1983	450,000

Figure 1-2: Circuit Complexity of Various Microprocessors. Microprocessors are probably the most complex kind of semiconductor chips that are ever manufactured. One measure of their complexity is how many transistors are etched onto the single chip of silicon to make a microprocessor. The data we have are consistent with the hypothesis that the number of transistors on the densest new chips doubles every year.

4. Finally, systems programs for large computers and for small computers are really quite similar; so, except for certain specialized areas, a good appreciation of the field can be obtained from the small systems. We can make an unusual argument in support of this fact. Small systems are not powerful just because they pack a lot of electronic capability into a small package. This is only half of the explanation. The other factor is that there is a continuing trend for small systems to receive more and more software that is like the software which runs on mainframes. In other words, powerful software makes for powerful computers. The little computers now have powerful software. A trickle down effect has clearly been in operation.

Figure 1-3 lists some of the traditional classes of computers and shows what type of software these products had when they were new to the computing scene. For almost all of the software listed under big computers, there is now a micro-computer version that will do the same thing.

Type	Example	Equipment	Software
Single Board Computer	Micro trainers and Evaluation Kits.	Hex Keypad. LED Display. Tape Recorder Interface. Small Memory.	Monitor in ROM.
Micro Computer	Apple-II	64K Byte Memory. 2 Five Inch Floppy Disks. CRT Screen. Keyboard.	Monitor in ROM. BASIC Interpreter in ROM. Single User Disk Operating System Similar to CP/M.
Mini Computer	DEC PDP-11/45	512K Byte Memory. Several Terminals (perhaps 10). Several Hard Disks (perhaps 50 Megabytes).	Multi-user Operating System for Small Scale General Computation or Business Use. Editors, Assemblers, Compilers, Linkers and Loaders.
Mainframe Computer	IBM 370-168	4 Megabyte Main Memory. Many Dispersed Terminals (perhaps 100). Large Tape Drives and Several Thousand Megabytes of Fast Disk Storage.	Large Scale Multiple Purpose Operating System—With Virtual Memory and Dynamic Reconfigurability. Editors, Assemblers, Compilers, Linkers and Loaders, Data Base Managers, Screen Formaters, Extensive Networking and Teleprocessing Software.

Figure 1-3: Typical Systems Software for *Traditional* Computing Environments of Various Sizes. In recent years, even the simplest computers have been acquiring versions of the software traditionally found only on mainframe computers.

In order not to bias this discussion unfairly toward the merits of small computers, we should also point out their present weak points in comparison to big machines. There are microprocessors now that have machine instructions almost approaching the power of mainframe instructions. The clock rates at which these computers run are comparable. We also have asserted that micro systems now have software that is comparable in many essential aspects to large computer software. Does this mean that a small number of microprocessors equals a mainframe in computational power? It does not, at least not for the current generation of microprocessors—the Intel 8086, the Zilog Z-8000, the Motorola 68000, and other 16 bit microprocessors.

Big systems can still sustain a much greater throughput of work than small systems. Why? The larger word size on big computers means that more things can be done in a single instruction. Frequently it will take several 16 bit instructions to equal the power of a 32 bit instruction. In addition, the mainframe usually has much more memory than a micro and has disks that are faster, of greater reliability, and of much higher capacity than similar equipment for small computers. Of course, they cost a great deal. This equipment allows a mainframe CPU to be very efficiently shared among a number of concurrently executing programs in a way that is still impossible for small computers. As a consequence, the computational throughput in big general purpose computers is still 10 to 100 times as great as for the best microprocessor systems of the present generation.

1.4 WHERE IS THE FIELD HEADED?

Certain important topics in systems programming have become almost classical through their development over the last thirty years. The theory regarding these forms is pretty well worked out and when it changes, it is only in small increments. In this category we would include things like the theory of assemblers, compilers, and interpreters for computational languages such as BASIC, FORTRAN, Pascal, or APL. Also fairly well understood is the body of knowledge concerning how to integrate interrupts into an operating system, how to manage disk files, and how to set up a multi-tasking system that uses a single CPU. These kinds of systems account for most of computing as it is done today. They also define a good body of information for a first course in systems programming.

The direction of many of the new areas in systems programming is hardware-driven. New machine architectures with vast computational power and huge memory spaces suggest new types of programs. The following seem to be some of the most important topics:

1. Operating systems for powerful computer systems made from large numbers of independent but closely coupled CPU's. A single chip will contain many of these CPU's. The first use to which this radically new kind of architecture will be applied will probably be computationally intensive engineering work, such as graphics or signal processing. This kind of power may also prove to be the key to real time speech recognition.

2. Concurrent higher level languages. With a language of this type, it is possible to specify right in the programming language that certain parts of a task are to be run in parallel with each other. If the language is properly designed, the same program can then be run without alteration on a multiprocessor configuration or on a single machine with a multi-tasking operating system.

Some other important topics that don't seem particularly hardware-driven also suggest themselves:

3. Automatic programming. Work continues on ways to generate operating systems and compilers automatically and directly from formal descriptions of the software. Similarly, an important goal is to be able to generate application programs directly from an informal description that is close to English.

4. Software lifecycle control systems. This exciting and complex area seeks to have one supervisor program prompt and direct a user through all the stages of constructing and maintaining a program. It will be competent in everything from eliciting initial requirements, to controlling a top-down design hierarchy, to learning by example how it should do certain low level algorithmic tasks, to constructing test cases. It also acts as a secretary, editor, and librarian to keep documentation up to date. This kind of program will be a much needed element in controlling software costs.

In the small systems area, a downward migration of large systems software onto powerful small systems will continue. Two kinds of machines are going to become predominant. First there will be very powerful single user personal computer work stations. This area will keep growing and growing. Users can always use more power if it is available, and users will always want dedicated systems if they can afford them. These kinds of machines will have multi-tasking operating systems, but all of the tasks will be in support of the single user. Certain kinds of systems programs (such as editors) and certain kinds of languages (such as LISP) can run much more smoothly if their work is split up between several concurrent tasks. It is also clear that it will be mandatory to have one of the tasks manage a network interface so that the user will be able to communicate with remote data banks and talk to other computers easily.

Another kind of machine that will become common is a cheap, powerful, multi-user microcomputer system that is essentially comparable in function with today's minicomputers but costs much less. There are many business applications for this kind of setup.

The last trend we wish to mention in small systems software will be a movement in the direction of more portable languages and operating systems. When new processors appear, as they do frequently, it is too expensive to rewrite all the systems software. We can look for new systems software that will be designed for ease of movement to new processors, so that it will not become outmoded, and we can also look for the emergence of automatic translators that will take software written for an older processor and make it workable (although probably not optimized) on a new system.

1.5 MEASURING THE COMPLEXITY OF SYSTEMS PROGRAMS

Our task in this book is to study the more classic types of systems programs, those which have attained some stability in their form. The programs to be discussed here can be considered as benchmarks against which other variants in the same software class can be compared. To aid in this process and to help orient the reader, we now present some complexity statistics that we have collected for some of our programs and for some commercially available programs that are similar to those we describe.

What is complexity? This is a difficult question, but two simple numbers that obviously are related to it are program length and the amount of time required for development. Figure 1-4 shows the size of some benchmark systems programs. All of

	Software	Written in	Length in bytes
1.	A Simple ROM Monitor (as discussed in this book)	8080 Assembler	1.5K bytes
2.	An 8080 Assembler (the CP/M Assembler)	optimized PL/M	8K bytes
3.	A Simple Macroassembler (as discussed in this book)	8080 Assembler	10K bytes
4.	A Single User Operating System (CP/M 1.4)	optimized PL/M	6.5K bytes
5.	A Simple Line Editor (the original CP/M editor)	optimized PL/M	6K bytes
6.	A Simple BASIC Interpreter with built-in editor (as discussed in this book)	8080 Assembler	4.5K bytes
7.	A Full-functioned BASIC Interpreter with arrays and Floating Point Numbers (Applesoft BASIC)	6502 Assembler (similar to 8080)	10K bytes
8.	A Compiler for a Microcomputer BASIC (Applesoft Compiler)	6502 Assembler (similar to 8080)	38K bytes
9.	A Simple Multi-user Operating System (UNIX core resident part)	C	50K bytes
10.	A Complicated Multi-user Operating System (IBM VM/370 core resident part)	370 Macroassembler	400K bytes

Figure 1-4:   Space Complexity of Various Types of Systems Software as Found on Small Systems. The lengths of these programs are probably fairly representative of their relative complexities. Most of the examples are commercial products, and they all have been written by good programmers.

the programs on this list were coded carefully by good programmers. It would probably be difficult to compress their sizes to much smaller than the measurements we give. As a first approximation, the lengths of these programs can be used as an index of their complexity relative to one another.

Notice that some of these programs are written in assembler language and some in various higher level languages. PL/M and C are both high level languages designed for systems programming. They increase programmer productivity, make the code easier to understand, and produce quite tight code. The only penalty incurred is that programs written in languages like these will typically be between one and one and a half times as long as the same program if it were written in assembler code. The trend today is definitely to write systems programs in good higher level languages because typical modern programming environments have plenty of memory. Increase the size of the assembler programs in Figure 1-4 by a factor of perhaps 1.3 for a uniform size comparison.

Time complexity is harder to judge than space complexity because it varies so much with who is doing the programming. An ideal measurement would be to have the same person code all the benchmark examples and record how long each one took. Then the measurements would be internally consistent. Unfortunately, we don't have a set of such numbers. One rule of thumb we can provide concerns mature students with several years of programming experience. Using a high level language and working in small teams (two or three people), they can implement simple editors, assemblers, compilers, and interpreters in a total of 200–400 man-hours. This assumes that they know the system they will work on, that they are provided with a high level design, and that the work is divided among the members of the team.

People who observe the rate of production of programs in different environments know that long programs are inherently different from short ones and big teams of programmers are inherently different from small ones. There are, nonetheless, several suggestive rules of thumb from the study of large project software engineering that we should at least keep in mind. According to Frederick Brooks, it was the experience of the IBM 360 development team, that program production software (such as editors and compilers) is three times as hard to write as applications programs and that system control programs (operating systems) are three times as difficult to write as program production software.[2]

The other useful rule of thumb is that the time required to write a program will increase as a power of the number of lines of code in the program. The relationship will frequently be of the form

$$\text{Total Time} = K * (\text{Lines of Code})^{1.5}$$

The constant K changes in different situations to reflect the inherent complexity of the type of program being developed.

---

[2]Frederick P. Brooks, Jr., *The Mythical Man-Month,* Addison-Wesley, Reading, Mass., 1975, p. 93.

1.6 A PLAN FOR STUDYING SYSTEMS PROGRAMMING

Before we begin looking at specific systems, we would like to suggest a profitable way of thinking about the material in this book. In many technological disciplines, there is a small core of ideas, principles, and systems that really define what the activity is all about and how it should be practiced. An effective core is easy to remember. It acts as an organizing principle for the subsequent acquisition of more complex information. Subsequent layers of information can almost always be understood as extensions, improvements, and elaborations on the basic ideas. A good understanding of the basic ideas is frequently found to be the driving engine behind a technologist's intuition when he tackles new problems. This book is an attempt to organize the central devices in systems programming into such a core.

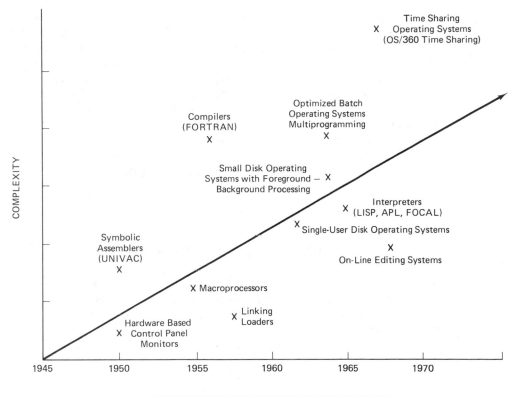

APPROXIMATE TIME WHEN MAJOR USAGE BEGAN
(For some software; original development was much earlier.)

Figure 1-5: The Evolution of Systems Programs. The figure is the rationale for the order of presentation of topics in this book. The trend line will be followed from the oldest and simplest types to more recent specimens which have solved many problems and become complex as a result of it.

In Chapters 2, 7, and 13 we discuss some important types of computer hardware and the low-level I/O programming that is very close to the hardware. We do this because systems programming is the level at which hardware and software touch. These chapters discuss what we have called "the systems environment" for three progressively more complicated classes of computers. The classes are single-board computers, simple microcomputer systems for single users, and larger microcomputer systems capable of providing time sharing for multiple users or tasks.

In our discussion of the systems environment we deal with several questions: What kind of hardware is found at this level? What are its capabilities? What will the interfaces look like where the software touches the hardware? And what will be the character of the input/output programs that manipulate the interfaces? These chapters occur at the beginning, the middle, and toward the end of the book in order to parallel growing software complexity with the underlying growth in hardware capability which makes the software possible.

As mentioned in the preface, the presentation of the material in this book is roughly ordered in terms of complexity and in terms of historical evolution. Thus assemblers are presented before compilers, and single-user operating systems are presented before multi-user systems, as one might expect. We do not separate software along the lines of program production programs and system control as is frequently done. Instead, programs of about the same complexity appear near each other in the discussion. For instance, we have assumed that a single user operating system like CP/M is similar in complexity to a simple language interpreter.

Another view of this issue of complexity and historical evolution is presented in Figure 1-5. This chart shows in a subjective manner how the various topics we will cover are related to one another. The trend line on this graph defines the path we will take in our exploration of them.

STUDY QUESTIONS AND EXERCISES

1. Suggest an index (a single number) that would give the I.Q. of a computer system, or at least reflect its performance. The index should be based on things like word size, instruction execution time, memory size, fast disk space available, etc.

2. Suggest other ways to measure the complexity of a program besides its size and how long it took to create it.

2

The Systems Environment: I

2.1 INTRODUCTION TO SINGLE BOARD COMPUTER SYSTEMS

The very smallest computer systems that you are likely to encounter are the single board computers. By computer system, we will henceforth mean an integrated grouping of processor, memory, I/O devices, and software. Single board computers are frequently sold as learning tools for people who want to study microcomputer architectures or as evaluation kits which are acquired by engineers so they can become familiar with new types of microprocessors.

We are going to study various aspects of single board computer systems in this chapter and the next, because a computer like this is always controlled by an archetypical piece of systems software—the ROM monitor. An ancestor of this kind of program was the progenitor of all operating systems. As such, it is an important starting point in the study of systems programming. In this chapter we will try to get a feeling for the type of hardware and interfaces that exist in the environment of the smallest kinds of computers. We will also look at input/output programming and try to develop a way of looking at I/O interfaces such that a programmer only needs to have a sort of logical picture of a peripheral device and doesn't need to know much about its internal characteristics.

What type of hardware are we talking about at this level? A single board computer will be built around a microprocessor. It will have a small amount of read-only memory (ROM) which will contain the system software. This will usually be one or two kilobytes in length. And there will typically be some larger amount of normal read-write memory (RAM), perhaps eight kilobytes. Finally, the single board computer will have some simple devices for doing input and output operations.

The most common type of input device is a keyboard. It may be a very simple sixteen key numeric pad, or it may be a full typewriter keyboard. Another common input device is the tape recorder. It is not difficult to set up a cheap, easily available audio tape recorder as an input/output device which can be used to load programs into the memory of the computer or record a program from the computer's memory.

There are several common output devices. The very simplest is a bank of lights into which the computer can write binary numbers. Eight lights are required to represent a single byte of output data. Similar output devices are the seven segment displays each of which can display a single decimal digit. It is also common to find, even on the simplest microcomputers, an interface to a printing terminal such as a Teletype machine or to a simple video terminal. Terminals are actually two I/O devices in one. The printer or screen section receives output, and the keyboard produces input. Finally, as mentioned earlier, tape recorders are common output devices for small computers.

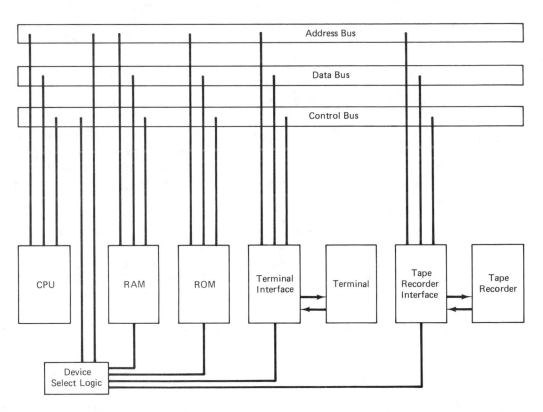

Figure 2-1: Block Diagram for a Single Board Microcomputer. This diagram represents a typical single board computer, either of the micro-trainer type, or of the evaluation kit type, or a very low end computer system with a single enclosure for screen and keyboard and the internal electronics collected on a single printed circuit card. The connectors that are shown are not meant to be single wires. They are data paths. The address bus, for example, is 16 wires in parallel.

The software that can manipulate these kinds of devices, at the lowest level, is very simple. In this chapter we will examine I/O routines that can manipulate the interfaces and send or receive single characters from each of the simple I/O devices to be discussed. Programming of this sort is always done in assembler language. The programs usually are no longer than five or ten lines of assembler code. In the next chapter, we will study a complete design for a ROM monitor. It will make use of the basic I/O routines from this chapter.

The single board computer we are going to discuss will be a rather complex one. We will assume that it has two I/O devices: a simple printing terminal and a tape recorder. The interface electronics for these devices will be included on the board. A block diagram for this kind of computer system is shown in Figure 2-1.

Without software, the system we have been describing will be only a collection of components. The software will make it possible for the keyboard to supply characters to the CPU and for the CPU to put out characters in an ordered way to the display. The software makes everything work together as a system.

This software is called a monitor. The functions that a monitor performs are traditionally to allow programs to be entered into the memory in machine language, to allow portions of the memory to be inspected and modified, to allow a program to be set into execution, and to supervise the loading and saving of programs through some bulk storage device such as the tape recorder. We must now look a little more closely at the hardware interfaces to see how a monitor could accomplish these aims.

2.2   HARDWARE CHARACTERISTICS AND INTERFACING

2.2.1   Interface Ports

All of the interfaces we examine will have a computer side and a device side. The computer side will always consist of a number of locations into which the computer can insert control words, read status, and exchange data. Real-life interfaces are always of this sort. The device side of the interface is a matter for electrical engineers, not system programmers. We will usually represent it by a black box of some sort and go into only a few details of how it operates.

We have something specific in mind when we say the computer can interact "with a number of locations." What are these locations? In the microcomputer world, the eight bit I/O port is a very common and important entity. The computer side of an interface is constructed from ports. You can think of a port as an eight bit addressable register, just like the registers in the CPU, except that it is in external circuitry. Ports can be configured (by the way they are wired) so that they are input only, which means the CPU will only read from them. They can be output only, which means the CPU will only write to one of them. Or a port can be set up for both reading or writing.

The fact that a port is addressable is a consequence of how it is wired into the circuit. Every port will have a number, and ports can be referred to in assembly language programs by their identifying numbers. For instance, let's say we have an interface

containing an input port that can be addressed by the number five. Then the following command in assembly language would cause one byte of information to be transferred from port number five on the interface into the accumulator register of the CPU:

    IN 5

Frequently, a port will correspond to a single chip somewhere on the printed circuit board of the single board computer. In other cases, computer systems will make use of chips specially designed to do I/O interfacing. One of these chips might contain four I/O ports that could be configured in various ways under program control.

It is also common to find port structures built right into large integrated circuits that unite in one place all the acting parts of some complicated function. As an example it is possible to buy single chips each of which can interface a computer to some type of communications line. When such a chip is wired into the overall computer circuitry, it will look to the programmer as though there are several addressable ports there with which he can interact. He will write his programs as if this were so. In actuality, there are no separate ports. They have all been merged into the circuitry of the communications chip.

2.2.2 Keyboards

Let us now look at a simple but representative interface for an input device: the keyboard. Figure 2-2 shows the keyboard interface that we will assume in discussing the ROM monitor. The lines connecting various blocks on the interface diagrams should normally be thought of as data paths of some sort rather than as single wires or particular buses.

The CPU side of the interface consists of two ports numbered 0 and 1. Port 0 is a status port, and it can be inspected by the CPU at any time to see if a key has been pressed and data is ready to be sent to the CPU. Port 1 is a data input port. After a key

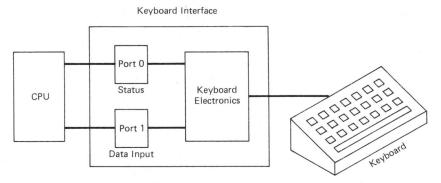

Figure 2-2: A Schematic Keyboard Interface. The keyboard is a simple input device. From the programmer's viewpoint, it can be completely controlled by manipulating two ports. The status port will tell when a character is ready, and the data input port will hold the character until the CPU fetches it.

is pressed, an ASCII code corresponding to the particular key that was pressed will be left in the input port.

A ubiquitous task in the manipulation of I/O interfaces is determining exactly when a transfer to or from the interface should take place. The method we are going to use here is polling. That is, the CPU continually examines a status port until some triggering condition arises. Polling has some problems of inefficient CPU utilization if it is used in high performance, multi-user computers; but for simple systems, it is just fine.

This is a typical input interface. The two port arrangement is quite common. The program that will manipulate the interface need concern itself with nothing about how the keyboard works beyond the details of how and when data will be presented in the two ports. We will consider how to write a program like this in the next section. There is an important point here that should be reemphasized. Interfaces are always going to be like this. The programmer can always think of an interface as a logical abstraction consisting of a number of ports which can be manipulated in specific ways to cause actions in the external world.

Frequently the keyboard will be packaged along with some output device into a terminal. A terminal actually has two separate parts. The keyboard is an input device. The printer or screen is an output device. They only appear to be part of the same module by virtue of the packaging. In our example of a single board computer, we will assume the keyboard and printer are together in a printing terminal.

2.2.3 Simple Character Printers

Now let us examine a simple output interface. An interface for operating the printer part of a printing terminal is shown in Figure 2-3. Again two ports are all that are important to the program that will manipulate the interface. This time, port 2 is a control port and port 3 is a data output port. To operate the interface, characters that are to be printed are placed in the data output port, one by one. When a character is in the output port, then a strobe signal is sent through the control port to cause the printer to accept the character and print it.

The problem of determining when the interface is ready for a transfer occurs with the printer interface just as it does with the keyboard. To appreciate the problem, consider that character printers print a single character at a time and process characters much slower than the computer can provide them. Typical printing rates are from 10 to 50 characters per second, while the computer might be able to access and output 30,000 characters per second. How are these rates to be synchronized? There are many ways to do this. We will use the simplest in this illustration. We will use a timing loop in the CPU so that we never pass characters to the printer at a rate faster than it can accept. If this timing loop interposes between one character transfer and the next, then we can always assume the printer will be ready.

Whatever method we use to decide when to do the transfer, we will still need a printer strobe to communicate this information to the printer. The purpose of a strobe is to establish the precise time at which something is to be done. In this case, it tells the printer circuitry that now is the time to acquire another character and deal with it appro-

Printer Interface

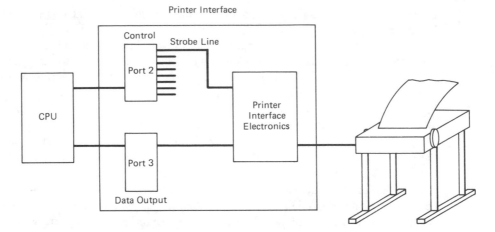

Figure 2-3:   A Schematic Interface for a Character Printer. The character printer is a simple output device. From the programmer's point of view, it can be completely controlled by manipulating two ports. The data output port receives single character data units sent out by the CPU. The control port is used to deliver a strobe pulse to the printer interface electronics to cause it to accept and display a character from the data output port.

priately—i.e., either print it or be controlled by it. The printer is a dumb device. It must be given characters only when it is ready to accept them, and it must be told when to accept them by the strobing mechanism.

A strobe signal is simple yes/no information, and consequently only a single data line is required to carry it. Strobes are generated by writing several words into the control port. Most of the bit positions in those words carry irrelevant information, and they won't be connected to anything. Only a single bit coming out of the port will be electrically connected to form a path along which the strobe can move through the interface. We'll see how this works out later.

Some characters that are sent through the data port are special. They are not printed but instead are interpreted as control information to the printer. The simplest printers will operate something like this. The position of the print head on the paper can be controlled by two special characters. The Carriage Return character will cause the print head to move to the left side of the paper as far as it can go. The Line Feed character will cause the paper moving mechanism to advance the paper by one line. This is equivalent to moving the print head down by one line. There are no other control characters, and no others are necessary. The only other thing the printer does is print a character at the position of the print head when it has been strobed and when data is in the data output port. Then it moves to the right by one character position. If the print head is at the extreme right and no Carriage Return is issued, it will print characters there, one on top of another, until some command moves the print head or the paper. This simple mode of operation is powerful enough to allow a computer to put on the printed page anything that a typewriter could put there.

Simple video terminals are sometimes cheaper than printing terminals, and they are frequently found as input/output devices on single board computers. In this kind of equipment, a television screen replaces the printing section. Both devices, of course, have the keyboard. The very simplest video terminals were conceived as replacements for printers, and they operate in almost the same manner. Instead of a print head moving around over a piece of paper, there is a cursor on the screen that indicates where printing will occur. When a character is transmitted to the terminal, it will appear on the screen at the cursor position and the cursor will move over one space, except at the end of the line. The video terminal will also respond to Carriage Return and to Line Feed just as a character printer does.

A device like this is sometimes called a "Glass Teletype" because it mimics the operation of traditional character printers so well. There are a few differences. There will be at least one more control character, something to initialize the screen—clear it and put the cursor in the beginning position. It is also not really necessary to strobe a terminal of this sort because video display circuitry can be made as fast as computer output circuitry.

Display terminals quickly evolved past the stage of printer replacements. More and more functions were added, activated by control characters. It was found that it was cheap to add functions if the basic circuitry was already there. We will consider the flexible, full-functioned video terminal to be part of the equipment typically found at the next level up in microcomputer systems. For now we want to discuss only simple devices that are very easy to program.

2.2.4   The Audio Tape Recorder for Program Storage

The other interface that we will study on this simple computer is an input/output interface to the tape recorder. It is shown in Figure 2-4. Since the tape is an input and an output device, it would be reasonable for it to have an interface that combines the characteristics of both the two port input interface and the two port output interface that we already looked at. And, indeed, this is what the tape interface is like.

The computer side of the interface consists of four ports: a status port and a data input port, and a control port and a data output port. The first thing that must be done to use the tape is to initialize the interface by sending a byte to the control port to turn the interface on and to indicate if the equipment will be used for input or for output.

To write a character onto the tape, we will put the code for the character in the data output port, and then signal with a control port strobe that the rest of the hardware should accept the character. If a number of characters are being sent in a row, and this will be the normal situation, then before sending each character, the CPU must inspect the status port to determine whether the interface is ready to accept another character. That is, we will used polled I/O. This is necessary because the CPU can ship out characters much faster than the tape recorder can accept them. A typical rate at which this tape system can accept characters would be about 30 per second. An 8080 CPU running at 2 megahertz and looping through a buffer could send the characters out at a rate of perhaps 30,000 per second. So we have a thousandfold rate difference between the inherent capacities of these two devices.

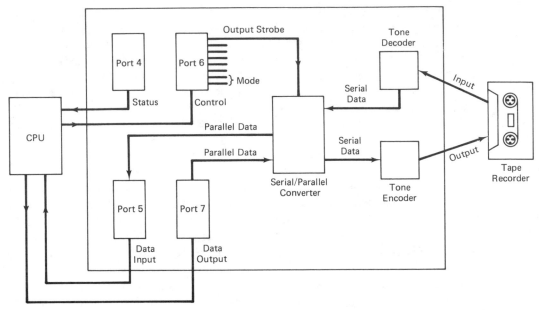

Figure 2-4:   A Schematic Interface for an Audio Tape Recorder. The tape recorder is a simple input and output device. From the programmer's point of view, it can be completely controlled by manipulating four ports. Logically, the interface is used as if it had an input part and a separate output part. The input section is similar in operation to a keyboard interface. The output section is similar in operation to a printer interface.

In order to read characters from the tape, the program must inspect the status port until it sees an indication that a character is ready. Then it can read the character in from the data input port. Again, a typical speed at which the tape can supply characters is about 30 per second.

This interface is considerably more complicated than previous ones in ways that are important to other areas of systems programming, so we will describe what happens inside it in a little more detail.

The data being passed through the interface is represented in three different ways. The first way is as parallel data. Data passed between the CPU and any of the ports is carried by the data bus. This consists of eight wires such that each bit in an eight bit word is placed on one of the wires at the same time. The bits will arrive at whatever port has been addressed all at the same instant, and thus this is a parallel data transmission.

Data is moved from the ports to the serial/parallel converter in parallel mode. When it passes through the converter (in the output direction), it is changed to serial data. That is, the bits composing the data word will be placed one at a time on a single output line. This line can just convey two values—logic one and logic zero—so only one bit can be accepted at a time. We have shown the ports on this interface and the serial/parallel converter as separate blocks. In reality, these devices will be combined on a single chip called a UART (Universal Asynchronous Receiver and Transmitter); however, logically they are separate things.

When a parallel byte is changed to serial format by the UART, several so-called framing bits are usually added to the serial representation of the byte to make its transmission more reliable. The most common way of adding this framing information is according to the asynchronous start/stop format. We will describe how this is done. In this format, the normal state of a serial line is logic one. When a byte is about to be sent down the line, the line will be dropped to logic zero for one bit time to alert the receiver that data is about to be transmitted. This is called the start bit. Next the byte is placed on the line one bit at a time. Two more bits are appended at the end of the data. The first one is a parity bit which will have been set to reflect the parity of the byte that was transmitted. The next and final bit is called the stop bit, and it is always a bit with the value of logic one. Thus we see that in the asynchronous start/stop format, one parallel byte of data is equivalent to eleven serial bits. Figure 2-5 shows how a byte of data will appear over a serial data line. We have described the most common use of this format. But there are variations. The parity can be even or odd, and sometimes there are two stop bits instead of one.

The amount of time during which a bit is applied to the data line is a matter of convention. It is the same for all bits whether they are data bits or framing bits. Inexpensive tape recorders will usually operate reliably if they do not have to record data at rates higher than about 300 bits per second. Some interfaces work at higher speeds, up to perhaps 1200 bits per second, with a corresponding decrease in reliability. Problems in

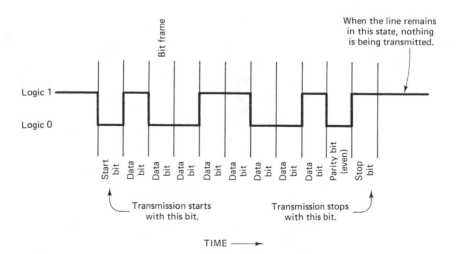

Figure 2-5: The Serial Representation of a Data Byte Using the Asynchronous Start/Stop Format. Each data unit in an asynchronous data stream must carry its own synchronization information. An asynchronous data unit is therefore "framed" by a single start bit and one or more stop bits. The parity bit may be even or odd. There may be one or two stop bits. The data being transmitted here is a byte with the value of 10011001.

using inexpensive tape recorders are caused by great variability in the speed of the tape drive motors, and because the tape itself can stretch.

The data on the tape interface must undergo one more transformation as it passes from CPU to tape recorder. The output from the UART will be in the form of two voltages on a line that correspond to logic ones and logic zeros. An audio recorder cannot absorb information in this form. It records tones, not logic values. Therefore, the last data conversion takes the voltage values on the serial line and converts them to two tones which can be put directly onto the tape recorder. One common standard is that the logic one state will be represented by a tone at 2125 cycles per second and the logic zero state by a tone at 2975 cycles per second. If you play back a tape that has had data recorded on it in this way, you can actually hear the alternating tones that correspond to ones and zeros. Of course, the tones alternate very rapidly.

When data is being input from the tape recorder, all transformations are reversed. The data is first a pattern of tones, then a pattern of logic values on a serial line, and finally parallel bytes appearing at the data input port. The framing bits are only of interest to the UART. It will supply them when data is being output, and it will strip them off and throw them away when data is being input.

The asynchronous start/stop format is used in many places in the computer industry to pass data from one hardware module to another, so perhaps a few more comments about it are in order. It is really a protocol for managing a serial communications line. That line can be between the CPU and some nearby peripheral, or it can be between two modules talking to each other across a telephone connection.

The start/stop format is quite inefficient but also quite reliable in its use of the communications channel. The inefficiency comes from the fact that we must surround every 8 bit unit with 3 or 4 framing bits. So there is as much as 50 percent overhead in transmitting the data. The reliability comes from the fact that the start/stop format is a self-synchronizing format that includes sending frequent synchronization information mixed with the data. This makes the transmission robust.

What is this issue of synchronization? The receiver of digital information on a serial line has two basic problems to deal with: How does he know when the transmitter has begun transmitting, and how does he know when to look at the line in order to pick up the next bit? The first problem is always solved by using some kind of start signal or start character which is a prefix to any transmission. The receiver continually monitors the line and, when it sees this signal, knows data is about to arrive. The other problem is solved with a clocking scheme. The receiver and transmitter have presumably agreed to use a standard transmission speed. Let's say it is 300 bits per second. If the receiver synchronizes itself to the center of a bit period, then it is guaranteed that if it looks at the transmission line every 1/300 of a second, it will receive the next bit that is being sent. A problem arises only if the transmitter is sending bits at a slightly different rate than the receiver is looking for them. The errors are cumulative, so in a long transmission, eventually the receiver would not be able to pick bits off the line correctly. However, in the start/stop format, the transmitter never sends more than 11 bits without giving the receiver a chance to resynchronize itself with the transmission. So errors from mismatch in the sampling clocks are very rare.

2.3 PROGRAMMING WITH SIMPLE INPUT/OUTPUT DEVICES

Now we can consider what it takes to program with a simple printing terminal or a tape recorder given the interfaces that were described in the previous section.

First let's look at the terminal and particularly at its keyboard. Keyboards can be set up to pass data to the CPU with varying amounts of intermediating electronics facilitating the transfer. Very simple keyboards require a correspondingly large amount of software to operate them. On the other hand, some keyboards even have a built-in microprocessor to do housekeeping functions and to make it easy to interface to the CPU. The keyboard on the terminal we will use for our single board microcomputer system will be of the latter sort. There will be helping electronics which will make the software very simple.

There will be a status port and a data input port on our keyboard interface, as on the equipment shown in Figure 2-2. Let us assume that these ports have been set up to work in the following way, which would be a typical interface.

1. Port 0 will be the status port. It will contain the binary number 10000000B when a key has been pressed on the keyboard. It will contain 00000000B otherwise.
2. Port 1 will be the data port. Whenever a key has been pressed, this port will contain the eight bit ASCII code that corresponds to whatever key was selected. It will contain 00000000B otherwise.
3. Both ports will be wired so that after the CPU reads data from either of them, that port will automatically reset and will contain 00000000B.

The simplest way an interface like this could be used is for the CPU to sit in a loop and continuously read the status port until it detected a key press. Then it would read the data input port to bring in the ASCII code identifying what key was pressed. The program that will do this is five lines of assembly language code. It is shown in Figure 2-6.

There is one detail in this program that may not be readily apparent. Data transfer instructions such as MOV or IN do not affect the processor flags. This means that you cannot do a conditional branch right after an input instruction without using an intervening

```
KEYIN:    IN  0        ; READ STATUS PORT
          ANA  A       ; SET CPU FLAGS
          JZ  KEYIN    ; TRY AGAIN IF NOTHING THERE
          IN  1        ; ELSE, TAKE IN DATA
          RET          ; RETURN TO CALLING ROUTINE
```

Figure 2-6:   Program to Input One Character From the Keyboard. These five lines of code are a subroutine that can be called by a program to input one character from the keyboard. The subroutine sits in a loop and will not return until the character is ready. This type of subroutine presupposes a rather intelligent keyboard that can handle the task internally of outputting the correct ASCII code every time a key is pressed.

instruction to set the flags according to the contents of the accumulator. The second line of the program, where the logical AND of the accumulator with itself is formed, will do this for us.

That was simple. Now let's examine programming the other part of the terminal— the printer unit. We will assume that the ports associated with the printer interface have been wired to work in the following way:

1. Port 2 will be the control port. Its function is to pass a signal to the interface electronics to indicate that an ASCII coded character should be taken out of the data output port and processed, either printed or used for control. A signal like this is called a strobe.

2. Port 3 is the data output port and will contain characters sent to the interface from the CPU. These characters can be read by the rest of the interface. If they are display characters, they will go onto the print medium at the current position of the print head. If they are control characters, they will alter the current operation by repositioning the print head.

3. Neither of these ports resets. They latch and hold whatever data the CPU writes into them until the CPU writes in something else.

We need to say a further word about strobing. Just one of the eight lines coming out of the control port is needed for the strobe. Let's assume it is the line connected to the most significant bit. The other lines coming out of the port don't matter and won't be connected to anything.

A strobe signal is normally delivered as a pulse. Figure 2-7 shows a program that will cause a pulse to appear on the output line that is connected to the most significant bit in the port. The pulse is created by ensuring that the line is initially at logic zero, then raising it to logic one, then dropping it again to logic zero. This can be done by writing appropriate words into the control port. The only part of these words that matter is the most significant bits. The width of the pulse can be adjusted easily, if the interface electronics require this, by putting delay loops in the generating program.

```
SPULSE:     MVI   A,00000000B      ; LOAD ZERO IN ACCUMULATOR
            OUT   2                ; SET PORT TO LOGIC ZERO
            MVI   A,10000000B      ; GET A LOGIC 1 FOR MSB
            OUT   2                ; START THE PULSE
            MVI   A,00000000B      ; LOAD ZERO IN ACCUMULATOR
            OUT   2                ; FINISH THE PULSE
            RET                    ; RETURN TO CALLING ROUTINE
```

Figure 2-7:   A Program for Generating a Strobe Pulse at the Control Port. A strobe is a pulse delivered to control circuitry to establish the exact time at which something is supposed to happen. If the strobe line is connected to a port, then the strobe can be generated by writing three successive words into the port. The words must be such as to bring the strobe line to logic zero, then to logic one, and back to logic zero again.

The basic I/O routine with which the monitor software can completely control the printer is a character output routine. It transmits a single character. The same routine may be used for a display character or a control character. The character output routine is shown in Figure 2-8. To use it, the calling program must put the character to be output into the accumulator and then make a call to the output routine. This output routine will put the character in the data output port, delay in a waiting loop for the period of time that the printer needs for one character, and then strobe the control port so that the interface accepts the character.

Notice the way the strobe is delivered in the character output routine: a one is sent and then a zero. The line was not initially established at zero. We are assuming that an initialization routine set it to zero to start with. After that, since all strobes return the line to zero when they finish, a new strobe can count on finding the line in that state.

There are different ways to tell when the printer can accept a new character. The simplest way is to incorporate a delay loop into the code for outputting each character. The delay should be longer than the time it takes to process a character. Since we are dealing with a low performance computer system, simplest is best. An interface capable of higher performance might incorporate another port (a status port), which could be polled to find out when the printer was ready. It also might incorporate a signal line, to be used with the computer's interrupt system, so that the device could be started on one character and would signal when it was ready for another. This kind of interface is complicated. Programming with the interrupt system will be discussed in Chapter 13.

Our last task in this section is to discuss programming the tape recorder interface. Remember that the only thing this interface implements is sending or receiving single characters to or from the tape device. More powerful, and much more expensive, equipment could do other things under computer control, such as rewind the tape, switch between record and playback modes, and search for a particular place on the tape at high speed.

Our interface uses four ports: a control port, a status port, a data input port, and a data output port. We will assume that the ports have been wired to act in the following ways. Please note that the status and control ports have more complicated functions in this interface than in the one for the terminal.

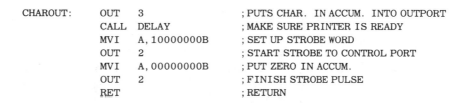

```
CHAROUT:    OUT    3                ; PUTS CHAR. IN ACCUM. INTO OUTPORT
            CALL   DELAY            ; MAKE SURE PRINTER IS READY
            MVI    A,10000000B      ; SET UP STROBE WORD
            OUT    2                ; START STROBE TO CONTROL PORT
            MVI    A,00000000B      ; PUT ZERO IN ACCUM.
            OUT    2                ; FINISH STROBE PULSE
            RET                     ; RETURN
```

Figure 2-8: Routine to Output One Character to the Printer. Three things are necessary to output a character to the printer: establish the character in the proper output port, establish that the printer is ready for another character, and then strobe the interface to accept it.

1. The control port (port 6) must receive an initialization word to turn the apparatus on and set the mode as input or output. In our interface, the control port interprets 0XXXXX01B as meaning turn on and set up for input. The control port interprets 0XXXXX10B as meaning turn on and set up for output. Anything else appearing at any time in the two least significant bits will turn the interface off. The X's represent either 1's or 0's.

2. A strobe to the most significant bit position (MSB) of the control port will cause the interface to take the character from the data output port and write it on tape. Of course, the programmer must make sure the interface is ready before he delivers this strobe. Strobing the MSB of the control port will also clear the data output port after the interface has accepted its character.

3. The status port displays the UART status. The same status words are used whether the interface is in input or output mode. If the status register contains 10000000B, it means the interface is ready, either to accept a new character or to output one. If the status register contains 00000000B, it means the interface is not ready. The status does not clear every time it is read. It will clear in two circumstances. On input, reading the data input port clears both the status port and the data input port. On output, strobing the MSB of the control port will clear the status port and the data output port.

4. The data input and data output ports are straightforward. They are just addressable registers that are intermediate holding areas as data is moved to and from the interface and the CPU. How they reset after use was described earlier.

Once the operation of the tape interface is understood, it is easy to write a program to exchange characters with the tape. Figure 2-9 shows the code needed to do this. There are two initialization routines: one to turn the tape system on in the input mode, and one to turn it on in the output mode. And there is a character input routine and a character output routine. The character input routine waits for a character by polling the status port, and leaves it in the accumulator when it arrives. To use the character output routine, you must put the character in the B register and then call the routine. It will wait until the interface is ready, and then it pushes out the character with a strobe to the control port.

Remember that this interface works with the sort of tape recorder in which tape positioning and setting the recorder to play or record mode must be done by you before the interface can be used.

In this chapter, we have examined simple but effective I/O routines. The movement of data in and out of ports is very simple; the only thing that could introduce complexity, then, is deciding when to do it. We have used two methods: polling and delay loops. These methods are appropriate for systems that can afford to have the CPU tied up with the I/O process from its start to its finish. In later parts of this book, we will discuss two additional I/O structures that add a great deal more complexity to the I/O process but allow the CPU to be doing something else while the process is going on. One of these structures depends largely on hardware (I/O via the mediation of Direct Memory Access equipment), and one depends largely on software (interrupt driven I/O). These things

```
TINITIN:        MVI   A, 00000001B        ; GET INITIALIZATION WORD (IN MODE)
                OUT   6                    ; SEND IT TO CONTROL PORT
                RET

TINITOUT:       MVI   A, 00000010B        ; GET INITIALIZATION WORD (OUT MODE)
                OUT   6                    ; SEND IT TO CONTROL PORT
                RET

TCHARIN:        IN    4                    ; READ STATUS PORT
                ANA   A                    ; SET CPU FLAGS
                JZ    TCHARIN              ; GO BACK IF NOT READY
                IN    5                    ; READ DATA INPUT PORT
                RET

TCHAROUT:       IN    4                    ; READ STATUS PORT
                ANA   A                    ; SET CPU FLAGS
                JZ    TCHAROUT             ; GO BACK IF NOT READY
                MOV   A, B                 ; GET OUTPUT IN ACCUM.
                OUT   7                    ; PUT IT IN OUTPUT PORT
                MVI   A, 10000010B         ; SET UP STROBE WORD
                OUT   6                    ; START STROBE
                MVI   A, 00000010B         ; SET UP STROBE WORD – 2ND HALF
                OUT   6                    ; FINISH STROBE
                RET
```

Figure 2-9:   Tape Input/Output Routines. Before using the tape, the interface has to be established in the input or the output mode. The initialization routines will do that. Characters are brought in by polling a status port to find out when to read the data input port. On output, the status port is also polled to see when the interface is ready. When it is ready, a control strobe causes a byte of data to go from the output port onto the tape.

will be in store for us when we pick up this strand of inquiry later. They are characteristic of more complex systems environments.

With this short introduction to the smallest systems environment behind us, we are now ready to look at the various sorts of software we might find on the smallest computers.

STUDY QUESTIONS AND EXERCISES

1. Assuming a tape recorder that can load data at 300 bits/sec., how long would it take to load a program of 4000 bytes into the computer memory? Remember to include the framing bits with each byte of data. Neglect any header on the front of the program tape. If the tape runs at $1\frac{7}{8}$ in./sec., how long a piece of tape is needed to store the program?

2. Write down the serial sequence of bits that would transmit your last name over a communications line if an 11 bit asynchronous start/stop format were being used with ASCII coded characters. Assume the MSB of the ASCII characters is set to zero. Assume even parity.

3. Write a subroutine that will deliver a strobe pulse to port 1. The strobe should be in the MSB position. It should start at zero, go to one, and come down to zero again. The length of the strobe should be variable according to a parameter that will be input to the subroutine in the accumulator.

4. Write a routine that will output a character string to the printer. It should use the single character output routine that is shown in Figure 2-8. The HL register is to contain a pointer to the first character in the string. We will adopt the convention that the last character in any string will be a dollar sign character which will act as a delimiter.

5. Write a single character output routine for a printer interface in which the interface consists of three ports. Port 1 is a data output port. Port 2 is a status port which should be polled. Port 3 is a control port out of which a strobe should be delivered every time the printer is ready to accept a character. The status port has one in it when the printer is ready, zero otherwise. The control port should be strobed in the MSB position. The status port and data port both clear after the strobe.

6. Write an input routine for a card reader with the following characteristics. There are three ports on the interface: data input (port 1), control (port 2), and status (port 3). The commands that can be given are: turn on (1), turn off (2), transfer next character (3), bring in next card (4), eject present card (5). Upon bringing in a card, the reader itself internally stores all 80 character positions in an internal buffer. Every time it receives a transfer character command, it puts the next character in order onto the input port for reading by the computer. The status port allows the computer to follow what is happening. After a command is issued, the status port will contain zero until the operation reaches a conclusion. Then it will have one for finished or some other code for an exception. For instance, 2 represents that 80 character positions on the present card have already been transmitted, 3 represents no more cards, etc. Write the routine so that it will bring in a card, transfer 80 characters to a buffer in main memory, and then eject the card. The address of the buffer will be in the HL pair.

3

The Simplest Operating Systems: ROM Monitors

3.1 INTRODUCTION: BASIC CONTROL OF A COMPUTER

The ROM monitor is probably the most basic piece of systems software that it is possible to find. It is basic in the sense that it is simple, that it has been around for a long time but is still useful, and that it underlies the operations of a whole class of computers. All very small computers will have a monitor because there must be some software in systems like this that allow you to get a program into the machine and run it. Without a monitor program of some sort, the computer is just a collection of dead hardware. It can't even respond to the pressing of a key on the keyboard, nor can it send characters to a display. The monitor integrates the I/O functions and allows the user to give simple commands to the computer. In fact, the monitor plus the hardware makes a basic computer system. Some people may object to calling a monitor an example of operating system software. But by our definition it clearly is, because we will be thinking of the operating system as the software that allows a computer to be used easily and efficiently. Without a monitor, it can't be used at all.

The functions a simple monitor must perform are easy to enumerate, and they are fairly standard for monitors produced by anyone. The functions are:

1. Load a program into memory (from the keyboard).
2. Display memory to show what program or data is there.
3. Modify some part of memory to correct mistakes, change the program, or insert parameters.
4. Start a program into execution.

5. Save the program on some external storage medium, typically audio tape.

6. Load a program back into memory from external storage.

We will examine closely the design of a monitor that would perform these functions. It will be the most basic software appliance of a small computer.

The monitor forms a baseline for the study of operating systems. As we progress through discussions of various more complicated pieces of software in this book, we will need some measure of the complexity of any given program. We will often use the length of a program as such a measure, because it is easily obtained.

The very simplest monitors, as found on single board computers, are 500–1000 bytes long. They frequently use keypads with a minimal number of keys (perhaps 16) for input. For output, it is common to find a bank of lights that can be turned on or off to represent bit positions. Audio tapes are used for program storage. More ambitious single board computers will be set up to use full keyboards for input, a screen or printer for output, and usually still some form of audio tape for program storage. The monitor for a system like this will typically be 1000–1500 bytes in length.

Microcomputers as full systems (the next step up in hardware) will frequently have ROM monitors. These typically range in size from perhaps 1K to 4K bytes. They implement all the functions mentioned above plus some other ones. For instance, a more advanced monitor might contain the capability to read and write programs onto a disk for external storage. Such a monitor might have the ability to serve as a calculator for hexadecimal arithmetic. It might include features to assemble or disassemble programs. Disassembly means rendering the machine language of a program somewhere in memory into the mnemonics of assembler language, which is much easier for a human to follow. Or a monitor like this might have the ability to set breakpoints and single step the program or otherwise trace its operation. However, even though there are many advanced features, the most crucial ones are the six features mentioned earlier.

How do we get in and out of the monitor program? First of all, small computers universally package their monitors in a few read-only memory chips which are wired into part of the computer's address space. When the computer is turned on, the hardware will typically transfer control to either the first location in memory or the last location in memory (depending on the type of computer). The monitor program should begin at the location to which the program counter will be set when the system is turned on, so that the monitor immediately gets control. The fact that it is in ROM means that the monitor doesn't have to be loaded. It will be immediately available on power-up. Since it is in ROM, it also cannot be destroyed by a bad program written by the user.

One of the things a monitor can do is transfer control to a user program that has been installed in memory. It is easy to do this. The program counter is just set to the location of the first statement in the user program, and the computer is allowed to run. It will process the program. It is important to focus on how such a user program should terminate. If the last statement in that program is some kind of a halt or stop, then, after it has been executed, the system will appear to die. There will be no response to key presses and the display will freeze. This is because the system is doing what you told it to do—it is halting. A better way to terminate a user program is to make the last statement(s) be a jump to the beginning of the monitor program. That way control will go back into the monitor and it will stand ready to receive further instructions about what to do next.

We are now ready to look at a detailed design for a typical monitor. It will be the type of monitor found on an advanced single board computer or on a simple microcomputer system. The peripheral equipment will be a full keyboard, some kind of printing display (either a true character printer or a screen), and an audio tape. The commands we implement will be the six central functions that were mentioned previously.

3.2 THE USER INTERFACE FOR A TYPICAL DESIGN

A very important objective of this book is to think about systems software from a top-down perspective. To be consistent with this viewpoint, we will always begin the discussion of a new piece of software by looking at its user interface. Conceiving the user interface is the same as thinking out all the things you want the system to do and all the ways you want it to behave. The user interface motivates (or should motivate) everything else about the design.

We will now look at the details of one particular monitor. It is a typical monitor and it is like the control software on many small computers being used currently. Whenever the monitor receives control, it will issue a characteristic, recognizable prompt on the output device so you will know that it is waiting for instructions as to what to do next. Whenever it wants instructions from you, it will prompt with

OK-

There are only six commands that can be given to this monitor, and they correspond to the six functions that it can perform. The syntax of the commands is quite rigid. The reason for this is that if the monitor can always expect to get its instructions in a very tightly controlled form, then it will be very easy for us to produce code that can parse the commands in order to understand what they mean. Parsing means analyzing a command string to decide what is being requested by the user.

Here is the command form. Immediately after the monitor prompt, one of six keywords must be typed. This must be followed immediately by a comma. After the comma will come an address or two addresses separated by a "-" character. The last character typed in a command will be a Carriage Return. This syntax will make sense when you see some examples.

We also need to comment about how the user will be expected to enter numbers when they are parts of command lines or further data required by a command. All input data should be cast as hexidecimal numbers, and anything that the monitor displays will also be in this form.

Now let's examine the available commands in the user interface. In what follows, bold printed text represents the part of a command or command dialog that has been generated by the system. Normal printed text is due to the user. The first thing you might want to do is to enter a program in memory. To do this, you must type the ENTER Command, followed by a comma, and then the address at which you want the program to start. Finally you will type the Carriage Return character. All communications with the monitor must end with a Carriage Return. This will be how the monitor can detect that you are finished entering an instruction. If we wanted to enter a program from the keyboard and it would start at location 300, we would type in the following line in response to the monitor ready prompt.

        OK-ENTER, 300

The system will respond by echoing the requested address and "=". After this you may type in the contents of successive locations, one byte at a time as two digit hexadecimal numbers. These bytes should be separated from each other by one or more blanks. The system will use the blanks as delimiters to tell the numbers apart. The last piece of data on a line should be followed by a Carriage Return. This will cause the system to prompt for more data input. At this stage, the user can enter another line of data or terminate the process by typing the word "END". After the monitor system has been given the ending protocol, it will display a message that will indicate the last memory address to have been loaded.

Here is the complete dialog for loading four bytes into memory starting at location 300:

        OK-ENTER, 300
        300=4A 18 20 99
        304=END
        LAST ADDRESS LOADED WAS 303.
        OK-

Another function is displaying memory. In order to display any area in memory, you may type the DISPLAY Command, followed by a comma, followed by the starting address of interest, followed by a dash, and finally followed by the last address you are interested in. For example, to display the memory between the locations 300 and 3A0, we would type

        OK-DISPLAY, 300-3A0

The system will respond by typing the starting address and "=", and then it will list the memory byte by byte with each location shown as a two digit hexadecimal number. When the end of the line is reached, it will wrap around and print a new address and "=" sign to show you how far you have gotten. It will proceed in this way until all the memory asked for has been displayed. If you wish to display just a single location, type a Carriage Return immediately after the first address.

Here is a complete dialog that would display the twelve bytes starting at location 300:

```
OK-DISPLAY,300-30B
300=4A 18 20 99 FF FF 08 07
308=11 00 0F FF
OK-
```

To modify parts of memory, the user must type the MODIFY Command, followed by a comma, followed by a specification of the addresses to be modified. For instance, if we wished to change the memory contents in locations 305 through 310, the command format would be

```
OK-MODIFY,305-310
```

It is also possible to type a Carriage Return immediately after the first address if you want to modify a single location rather than a range. The system will respond to the MODIFY Command by displaying what is at present in memory at the indicated locations. The format will be just the same as for the DISPLAY Command. In fact, internally the DISPLAY Command will be invoked to do the work. After showing what is in the locations of interest, the system will print the starting address followed by " = ". Now you can type in new values for these locations. They should be typed in the same format as for the ENTER Command. In fact, internally, the monitor will branch to the ENTER Command to take care of this part of the work. So MODIFY really has very little to do by itself. The user must remember to terminate the MODIFY process in the way required by the ENTER Command.

To execute a program after it has been installed in memory, the user need only type the GO Command, followed by a comma, followed by the starting address. For instance, if we had installed the program at location 300 and now wished to run it, we would type

```
OK-GO,300
```

Sometimes there will be a problem telling whether the program is executing correctly or even executing at all. There are two ways to investigate the state of a program after using the GO Command. We could have arranged for the program to produce some output on the system output device that could be examined; or, after execution was completed, we could go in with the monitor and inspect memory and see whether a pattern of changes occurred that matched our expectations. Note that control will not go back to the monitor after program execution unless the last statement in the program is a jump to the monitor starting address.

When the user is finished working with a program, he may want to save a copy of it on tape so he can reuse it later. To initiate this process, the user must type the STAPE Command, followed by a comma, followed by an address specification showing the range of memory locations that are to be saved. For instance, to save the program that is in memory between locations 300 and 3FF, the following command line would be used:

```
OK-STAPE,300-3FF
```

In response, the monitor would put the program on tape and come back with the normal system prompt when it was done. With the cheap audio recorders that we are talking about utilizing, the user of the system must manually position the tape and start the recorder in record mode. To have this done under computer control would double the size of the monitor and the cost of all the equipment being used.

The last function we must specify is how to load a program back into memory from the tape. In order to do this, the user must manually position the tape to the correct place and start it in playback mode. STAPE will put a header on the recorded program that will aid in positioning the tape at playback time. We will discuss this later. To bring back the program, the user must type the command LTAPE followed by a comma, followed by the address in memory where the program is to start loading. The reloaded program must go back into the same memory locations that it originally occupied. To load a program from tape that starts at location 300, the user would type

OK-LTAPE, 300

This completes our discussion of the user interface. Our monitor is patterned after a design originally given by G. Gable in *BYTE* magazine.[1] With a user interface firmly in place, we can now proceed to the detailed structure of a monitor that could do the functions that have been outlined. The monitor will be specified in the spirit of top-down design and modular programming. We will show a separate flowchart for each module.

3.3 DATA STRUCTURES USED BY THE MONITOR

The code for the monitor itself and any unchanging data it requires can be put in ROM. Examples of data that don't change would be system parameters such as the number of characters that can be printed on a single line in the display, and the text of messages output by the monitor at various points during its execution.

Any monitor needs a small number of dedicated RAM locations that it can always count on using for pointers, counts, intermediate computational results, and text buffers. In Figure 3-1, we show these particular locations occurring immediately after the part of the address space in which the monitor ROM resides. Collectively these locations are called the Monitor Workspace.

Probably the most important part of this space is a 74 byte line buffer. All the monitor's input is structured in the form of text lines. As the text is being entered, it has to be accumulated somewhere, and the line buffer is where it goes. Whenever a string of text that ends with a Carriage Return has been accumulated in the line buffer, the monitor will always process this material before allowing the user to enter any more. However, since the processing will usually last at most a few milliseconds, the user will not notice this delay.

Why should the length of the line buffer be 74 bytes? This simply enhances the

[1]Gable, G. H., Interact with an ELM, *BYTE*, June 1976, p. 66.

Low Memory

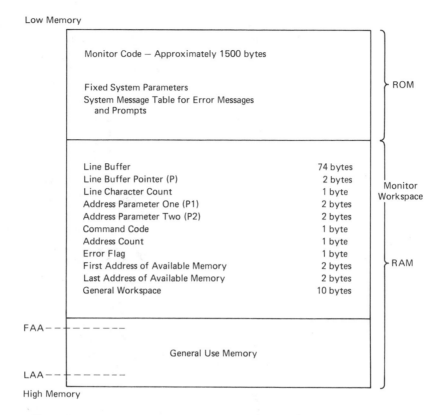

ROM

Monitor Code — Approximately 1500 bytes

Fixed System Parameters
System Message Table for Error Messages
   and Prompts

Line Buffer	74 bytes
Line Buffer Pointer (P)	2 bytes
Line Character Count	1 byte
Address Parameter One (P1)	2 bytes
Address Parameter Two (P2)	2 bytes
Command Code	1 byte
Address Count	1 byte
Error Flag	1 byte
First Address of Available Memory	2 bytes
Last Address of Available Memory	2 bytes
General Workspace	10 bytes

Monitor Workspace

RAM

FAA — — — — — — — —

General Use Memory

LAA — — — — — — — —

High Memory

Figure 3-1: Approximate Memory Layout for the Monitor. The complete monitor consists of a relatively small amount of read-only memory which contains the monitor program and its fixed data, and an associated small extent of read-write memory that the monitor uses for temporary data storage during its work. This is the Monitor Workspace. The rest of the memory is available for anything the user wants.

readability of the display. If we stipulate that no text line can be longer than 74 bytes, then we are assured that there will be no wrap-around of text information from one line to the next. The sum of the number of characters in the longest prompt issued by the system and the longest allowed string of text entered by the user should be 80 characters. This is the number of characters that can be displayed on a single line by most terminals.

What are the other fields in the Monitor's Workspace? A Line Buffer Pointer is maintained in the workspace to be used by the system for entering characters into the buffer. It will always point to the next location in the buffer at which a character can be deposited.

The Line Character Count is maintained for the use of the DISPLAY Command. It is used to keep track of how many more characters can be output without exceeding the width of a screen line.

The two address parameters are meant to receive the one or two addresses that are part of command lines. These addresses will be transformed by the monitor from ASCII digits, which is the way they were typed in, into binary numbers, which is the only numeric form the computer can use. After the transformation, they are stored in Address Parameter 1 and Address Parameter 2. The monitor code also uses these locations as pointers at various times when it has to manipulate addresses.

The Command Code is a one byte code which is filled in with a number from one to six to indicate which of its six possible functions the monitor is working on.

The Address Count Field takes the value one, two, or three depending on how many addresses will be specified as part of the current command. For instance, the STAPE Command must specify two addresses. The GO Command specifies one. The DISPLAY and MODIFY Commands may be used with either one or two addresses. The Address Count Field can take the value three in order to signal this situation of a variable number of addresses. This field contains temporary information that is filled in by the system as soon as a command keyword becomes known. It is used later by the module that has to extract the addresses in a command.

The Error Flag is a location for holding codes that correspond to any errors that might be detected as part of the processing for a command. See Figure 3-2 for the meaning of these various codes.

The Command Code Field has the following usage:
1 = ENTER
2 = DISPLAY
3 = MODIFY
4 = GO
5 = STAPE
6 = LTAPE

The Error Flag Field has the following usage:
1 = Error in Command Decode
2 = Error in Address Decode
3 = Error in Entering from Keyboard
4 = Error in Loading from Tape
5 = Error in Saving to Tape
6 = Request for Nonexistent Memory

The Address Count Field has the following usage:
1 = Expect only one address in this command.
2 = Expect two addresses in this command.
3 = Expect one or two addresses in this command.

Figure 3-2: Codes Used in the Monitor Workspace. Certain fields in the Monitor Workspace take on a range of values depending upon how the processing of a command evolves. The fields that contain multiple code values are shown above.

The First and Last Address of Available Memory (FAA and LAA) are maintained in the monitor workspace for error checking. All of the monitor commands call for manipulations in the computer's memory. If an erroneous address has been given, the monitor may be able to detect it by using these bounding addresses. It might seem reasonable for these addresses to be in ROM. However, then there would have to be a different version of the monitor for every possible memory configuration on the computer. An attractive alternative is to have a single version of the monitor which can test the memory in some way, as part of its initialization, to see how much is there. The results of this test will be kept in the FAA and LAA fields. However, if this is confusing, just imagine that the memory bounds information will be fixed and kept in ROM.

The last locations in the Monitor Workspace are a general purpose scratchpad of 10 bytes. The monitor will always need some dedicated RAM for its own internal processing. For example, doing the conversions from ASCII coded hexadecimal numbers to binary numbers requires some temporary storage, and this part of the workspace is available for it.

3.4 HOW THE MONITOR DECIDES WHAT TO DO NEXT: CONTROL AND PARSING

The top level routine (or driver) for the monitor is shown in Figure 3-3. As you can see, the monitor is just an infinite loop. The monitor solicits a command. The user supplies one. It is put into the line buffer as it is being typed. Then the monitor decodes the command (parses it) and calls an appropriate subroutine to do whatever particular thing has been called for. It is also the responsibility of this top level routine to print any error messages corresponding to errors that may have been detected in lower level routines.

Whenever the top level of the monitor or any of the subsidiary routines need to get a buffer of text from the user, they do this by calling the INPUT Routine, which is shown in Figure 3-4. This routine is much like a primitive editor. It allows the composition of one line of data in any format. Two editing features have been incorporated. One key on the keyboard will be used to signal to the monitor that you wish to discard whatever line is being typed now, and start again. What key is chosen for this is not important; CNTL C would be a good choice. There will also be a key that discards the last character typed or, if you hit it twice, discards the last two characters, etc. What key to use for this is also not important. Any convenient key may be chosen and programmed into the monitor code. The backslash "\" would be a good choice.

It is easy to implement the discard character type of editing. All the program has to do is back up the Line Buffer Pointer by however many characters are to be thrown away. Then the unwanted characters can be typed over in the buffer where the text is accumulating. The program also needs to output an indication of what is happening on the screen so that the user can follow. For instance, suppose the user was typing the word "character" and misspelled the word by typing several k's instead of a t. The error might have been noticed when the following text was on the screen and in the buffer:

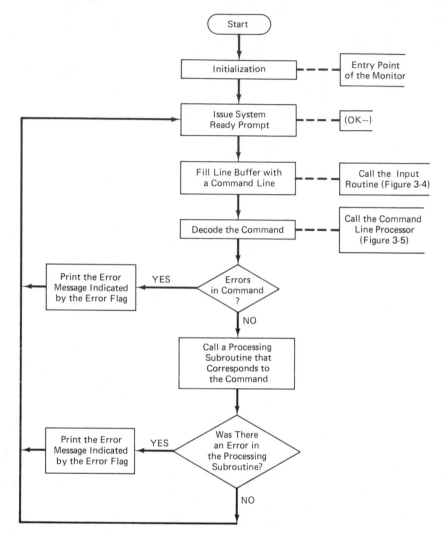

Figure 3-3:   Top Level Driver Routine for a Simple Monitor. This routine administers the monitor at the highest level. It is capable of receiving a command, determining what it means, and calling a subroutine to take appropriate action. With one necessary exception, this routine is the only place in the monitor at which error messages are printed.

```
charackk
```

The user could correct the mistake by completing the word in this way:

```
charackk\\ter
```

This illustrates the type of simple editing that is easy to build into an input routine.

It is even simpler to discard a whole line. All that is necessary is to output some

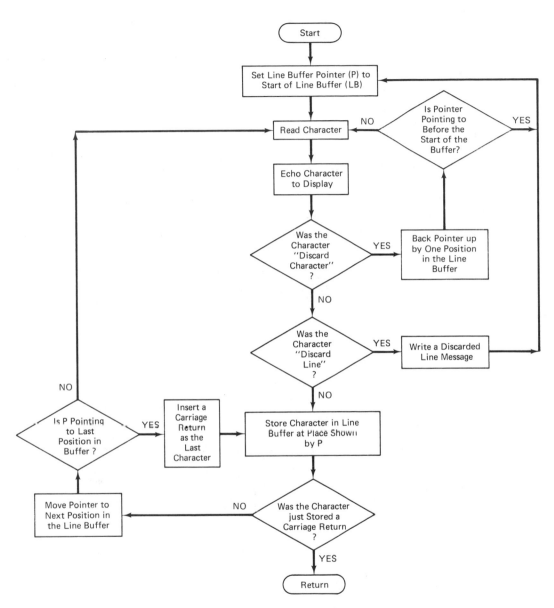

Figure 3-4: The INPUT Routine. The INPUT Routine takes care of all input to the monitor, whether commands or data. It allows the composition of one line of text data in any format. It is also a very primitive editing module.

sort of message, move the display to the next line, and then go back to the beginning of the input module.

One useful feature of the INPUT Routine is an attempt to guard the user from putting more characters into the line buffer than it can hold. The monitor detects when there are 73 characters in the buffer, and in this case, and only this case, it automatically inserts a Carriage Return as the last character and exits as if the user had done it. If the user was about to insert a character other than the Carriage Return, the system prompt at the end of a completed line might alert him to the mistake.

A command is decoded by the routine in Figure 3-5 called the Command Line Processor. The function of this routine is to abstract all relevant information from a command line and store it in preselected locations in the Monitor Workspace. An important transformation is taking place here. The command line has a varying length, depending on the command and its associated addresses. After processing by this module, it is reduced to a fixed length form. Several fixed length fields in the workspace have been filled in with information equivalent to the original command. It is much easier to write a program that deals with fixed length information items than with an entity that varies in length. The importance of this transformation should be emphasized.

The Command Line Processor does its work by calling two subsidiary routines. The Command Parser analyzes the type of command being asked for; and the Address Parser extracts the address or addresses that will be part of the command.

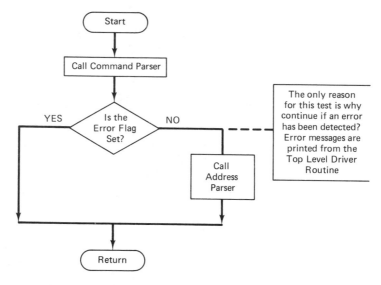

Figure 3-5: The Command Line Processor. The Command Line Processor divides the work of understanding a command into two parts: What is the command, and what are the addresses involved? A subroutine is called to determine the answer to each question. When the Command Line Processor has finished its work, all relevant information from a command line will have been abstracted and loaded into preselected locations in the Monitor Workspace.

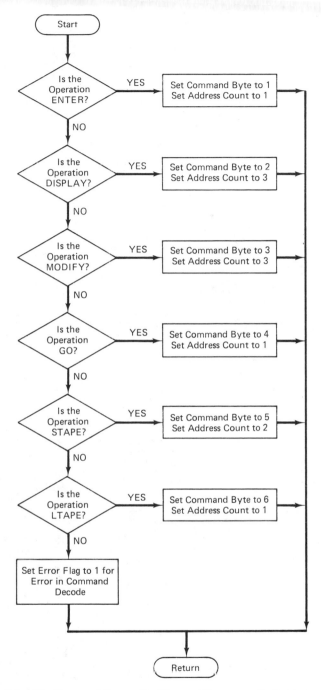

Figure 3-6: The Command Parser. The Command Parser scans the first text appearing in the command to decide which of the six functions is being requested, or to decide whether there has been erroneous input. It also tells the Address Parser how many addresses it should expect to find in the second part of the command.

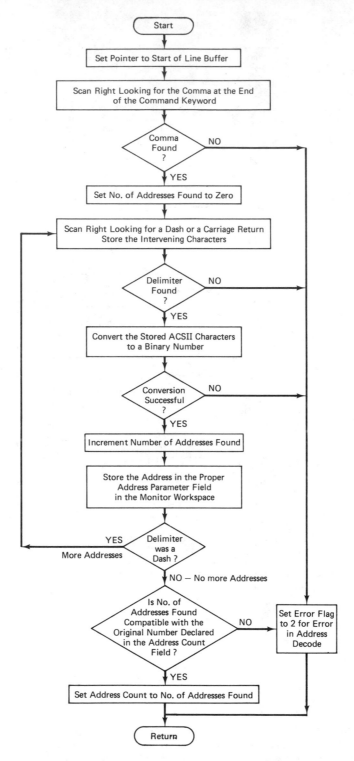

Figure 3-7: The Address Parser. The second part of all commands which the monitor can accept consists of either one or two addresses. The Address Parser isolates these addresses, counts them, converts them to binary numbers, and leaves them in the Monitor Workspace for use in further processing.

The Command Parser is described in Figure 3-6. Its work is very simple. It just has to inspect the first letter of the command to see which one is being referred to. This module will put a code corresponding to the command into the Command Code byte of the monitor workspace. It will also indicate, in the Address Count Field, how many addresses the Address Parser should expect to find as it continues to parse the command line.

The Address Parser is shown in Figure 3-7. It abstracts the addresses by making use of delimiters that are built in as part of a command line. That is, there is always a comma after the keyword; if there are two addresses, they will be separated by a dash; and all commands end with a Carriage Return. If the parser can isolate a character string between two delimiters, then it will attempt to convert this ASCII string into a binary number and store the number in the Monitor Workspace as one of the two Address Parameters. The parser does its work without knowledge of how many addresses will be found in the command. However, it counts how many it finds, and, at the end for error checking, it compares this number to Address Count, which has information about how many it should find. If everything is all right, the number of addresses found is loaded into Address Count so that the DISPLAY and MODIFY Commands will know whether they are dealing with a single address or a range of addresses.

3.5 AFTER TASK IDENTIFICATION COMES TASK EXECUTION

If we focus our attention on the top level routine of the monitor now, we will see that a command has been completely parsed and reduced to the form of fixed length descriptors in the monitor workspace. What happens next is that the monitor will dispatch one of six subroutines each of which is set up to handle one of the six functions the monitor can perform. Let us examine the ENTER Routine first.

The ENTER Routine is described in Figure 3-8. This module supervises loading data from the keyboard. It is really a primitive loader. ENTER works by calling a subroutine MEMLOAD which takes care of inserting a single line buffer into memory. The work of ENTER itself is to function as a driver, to do error checking on the line buffer that is to be loaded, and to detect the end condition. That is, at some point, the user will start a text line with the letters "END". This is how the user indicates that loading is complete. For a long program, control will loop around calling MEMLOAD many times to bring in line after line until the whole program is loaded.

A simpler kind of loading would have had the following kind of pattern. Use Address Parameter One as a load pointer. Start by setting it to the initial loading address. (Actually, command parsing has already done this for you.) Every time a two digit hexadecimal number is typed from the keyboard, convert it to binary and insert it in memory at the location indicated by P1. Then increment the address parameter and go back in a loop to get more input. ENTER is almost this simple. However, we have chosen to use the same routine (INPUT) for all data and command input. Since this routine brings in whole lines of data rather than single two digit hexadecimal numbers, our input loop has to be a bit more complicated. It will have the following form. Get an input buffer.

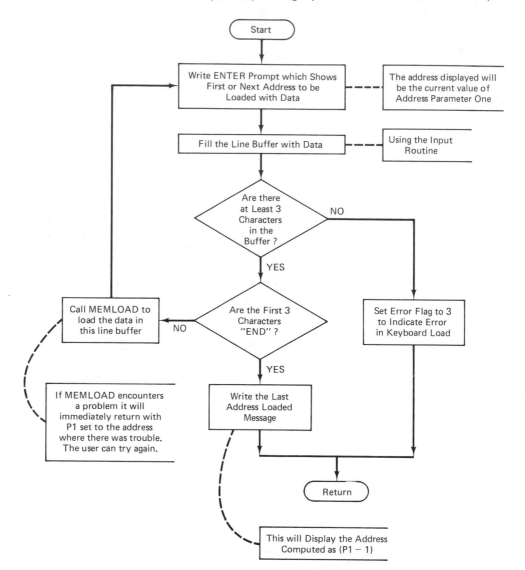

Figure 3-8: The ENTER Routine. The ENTER Routine supervises the loading of data from the keyboard. It is really a primitive loader. It uses two subsidiary routines: INPUT brings in a single line of text, and MEMLOAD installs that line in the proper place in memory.

Convert and load the numbers into memory, one by one, until the input buffer is exhausted. Get another input buffer. Convert and load, etc. That is why ENTER is broken into a driver section and a MEMLOAD section.

The operation of MEMLOAD is described in Figure 3-9. MEMLOAD scans through a single line of input data in the line buffer. The data are in groups of two ASCII bytes

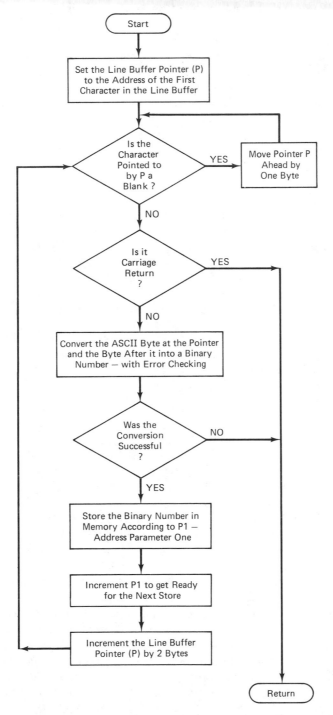

Figure 3-9: The MEMLOAD Subroutine. This routine is responsible for taking a line buffer that is full of two digit hexadecimal numbers separated by blanks and loading the binary image of these numbers into successive locations in memory. It uses Address Parameter One (P1) to indicate where in the memory the data should go.

separated by blanks. MEMLOAD converts these into binary numbers with error checking and deposits them into memory at the position indicated by the pointer P1. This pointer is incremented every time one memory location is filled.

If MEMLOAD detects a problem, such as two characters it can't convert to a valid binary number, then it will exit immediately and pass information describing what has happened back to ENTER. The higher level routine will start its processing anew. It will act as if it had just been called by a command from the keyboard. The address it will regard as the first place to enter data will be the same address as the one at which the loading problem occurred. This mechanism allows the user to write over the bad data and continue loading the program.

The DISPLAY Routine is described in Figure 3-10. This module will list the contents of memory from a starting address to an ending address, both of which are supplied as part of the command. Parsing of the command line will have left the first address in Address Parameter One and the second address in Address Parameter Two in the Monitor Workspace. If the command is only asking for a single address to be displayed rather than a range, the machinery for a range of addresses can still be used if we just set up an ending address which is the same as the starting address.

The DISPLAY Routine is a loop that goes through memory picking up bytes one by one for display, converting the binary numbers to hexadecimal representation, and outputting them. Each time around the loop two conditions have to be tested: Have all the requested bytes been displayed, and have enough bytes been displayed so that a new line should be started? The number of characters that can be printed on a single line of the display is a characteristic of the hardware being used. This number will have been hard coded into the monitor. It is available for use by the DISPLAY module to make sure lines are formatted nicely.

The next two modules are very simple. Figure 3-11 shows the MODIFY Routine. This module works by translating the command (internally) into successive calls to DISPLAY and to ENTER. Thus the present contents of the memory being modified will be listed so the user can inspect them; and then the monitor will go into the mode whereby data is entered from the keyboard.

MODIFY can operate with one or two addresses. However, no work needs to be done on behalf of this variability because the Address Parser takes care of finding how many addresses there are and the DISPLAY Routine can accommodate them either way. The ENTER Routine only needs Address Parameter One. The MODIFY Routine has to copy and save Address Parameter One before calling DISPLAY because DISPLAY uses the Address Parameter as a counter. MODIFY restores it before calling ENTER.

Figure 3-12 shows how the GO Routine is implemented. All that is required is for control to be branched to the location to which Address Parameter One points. Of course, the parsing operation on this command has filled Address Parameter One with the address that the user specified for the beginning of program execution. After a program executes, the monitor does not automatically restart. The user must restart it, by resetting the computer, or by writing his program so that a branch to the monitor is the last statement in the program.

The last two major modules in the monitor implement saving and loading programs

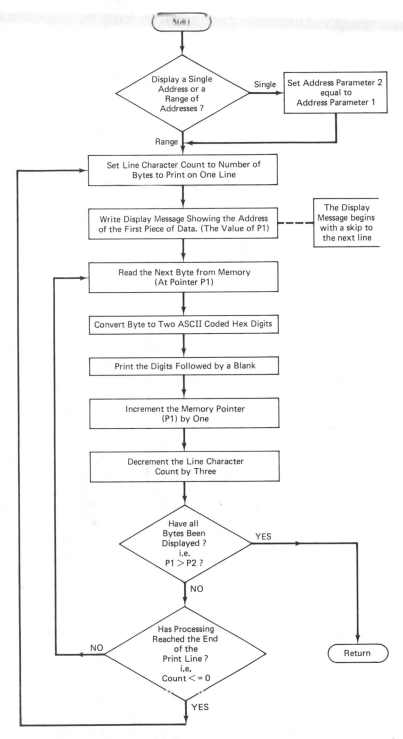

Figure 3-10: **The DISPLAY Routine.** The DISPLAY Routine will list the contents of any single memory location or of a range of memory between any two boundary values. It will begin each line it outputs with an address to show where the current data is coming from. Data is displayed as two digit hexadecimal numbers.

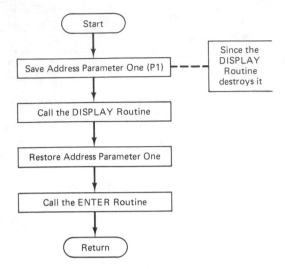

Figure 3-11:   The MODIFY Routine.
This routine allows the user to change the contents of any single location or any contiguous range of locations in memory. The present contents of the locations are displayed before changes are accepted. The internal structure of this command is simple. It is transformed internally into successive calls to DISPLAY and to ENTER.

with the tape drive. Chapter 2 discussed the physical characteristics of these tape files. Now we need to discuss their logical organization. In the microcomputer world, tapes are almost always set up as a lead-in tone, followed by a header, followed by the machine code of the program, and then possibly some sort of trailer for error checking. Several formats are in common use. We will describe the simplest one.

The lead-in tone begins the file. It consists of ten or fifteen seconds worth of data in which every byte is the same. These data bytes will be all ones or all zeros. The typical tape recorder interface converts ones and zeros into two distinct tones. Since the lead-in portion of the tape is all ones or all zeros, this results in a pure tone of a single frequency appearing on the tape recorder. The reason for having this tone at the start of a program file is to help the user position the tape. Remember that the user is responsible, when playing back a tape, for manually positioning the tape to the start of the program file. He can do this by listening to the tape and waiting until he hears the characteristic lead-in tone. The LTAPE routine is written so that the program will be loaded correctly if loading from tape is started anytime during the interval when the lead-in tone is playing.

What is in the header? In this particular example, the header will consist of a marker and some header data. The marker separates the end of the lead-in tone from the rest of the tape. The marker establishes the exact point at which important information begins. It will be some known pattern of data bytes for which the LTAPE program can watch to synchronize itself with the stream of data arriving through the tape interface. For example, a suitable pattern would be two bytes of alternating ones and zeros. Next comes

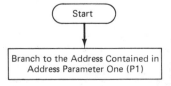

Figure 3-12:   The GO Routine. This routine allows the user to place a program into execution. It is an extremely simple command. The principal result of using it is that the program counter in the CPU will be loaded with whatever address the user has specified. Then the user's program will begin to execute.

the header data. This will be two bytes specifying a load point: the address in memory where loading is to start, followed by two bytes indicating the total number of program bytes that are to be loaded. This completes the header.

The machine code which represents the actual program text follows the header. It may be on the tape in exactly the same order in which it should appear in memory, or there may be addresses and other information interspersed with program text. For our example, we'll assume that the data portion of the tape contains only program text, and that there is no trailer for error checking.

Now we need an example. Figure 3-13 shows the sequence of bytes that would be recorded on the tape to save a twelve byte machine language program. The particular program is of no special consequence. It is just a little code that picks up two numbers from locations in memory and adds them together. Let's suppose that this code has been

Byte Position in File	Content	Usage
1	FFH	Lead-in Tone Byte
2	FFH	Lead-in Tone Byte
•		
•		
•		
299	FFH	Lead-in Tone Byte
300	FFH	Lead-in Tone Byte
301	AAH	Marker Byte
302	AAH	Marker Byte
303	01H	Load Point (High Order Part)
304	00H	Load Point (Low Order Part)
305	00H	Byte Count (High Order Part)
306	0CH	Byte Count (Low Order Part)
307	3A	1st Program Byte
308	00	2nd Program Byte
309	02	etc.
310	47	•
311	3A	•
312	01	•
313	02	
314	80	
315	32	
316	02	
317	02	Eleventh Program Byte
318	76	Twelfth Program Byte

Figure 3-13:   A Tape File Created by the Monitor to Save a Program. This figure shows the sequence of data that must be recorded onto tape to save a simple twelve byte program that adds two numbers together. The file consists of a ten second leader tone, followed by a header with information about where to load the program and how long it is, followed by the machine code of the program itself.

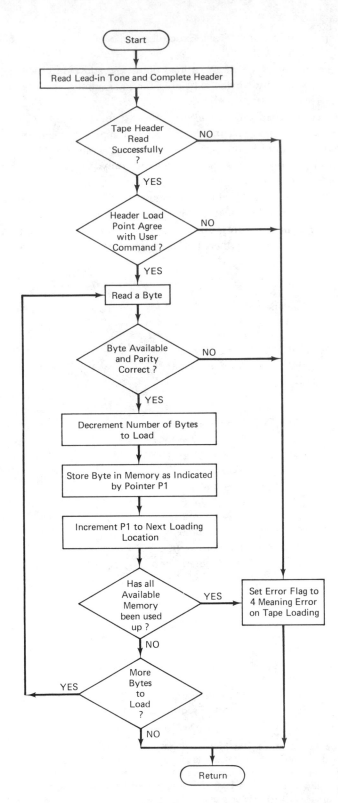

Figure 3-14: The Load from Tape Routine (LTAPE). The Load from Tape Routine allows a user to install a program in memory quickly if he has previously recorded the program on a consumer grade audio tape recorder. The routine reads a header on the tape to synchronize with the data, and to obtain certain descriptive information about the tape. Then it will deposit data coming off the tape byte by byte into successive memory locations.

designed with the intention that it should be installed in memory starting at location 100H.

The LTAPE Routine is described in Figure 3-14. This module is written so that it expects to begin examining data while the lead-in tone is the data that is arriving through the interface. The loading process can actually be fairly simple. The LTAPE module will detect the end of the lead-in tone and then read the header information. Before doing any loading, it will make a check to ensure that the loading point specified in the header is the same as the one given by the user when he issued the LTAPE command. If they are not the same, there is no point in continuing. Let's assume the beginning load point is correctly specified and we can go on to loading. The LTAPE routine will deposit the incoming data, byte by byte, into memory using a load pointer to indicate where to put it. Initially this pointer will be filled with the starting address from the header. It will be incremented every time a byte is installed in memory. We have used the Address Parameter One (P1) field in the Monitor Workspace for the load pointer.

The STAPE Routine is similar to LTAPE in its mechanisms. It is described in Figure 3-15. The user is responsible for positioning the tape and putting the recorder in

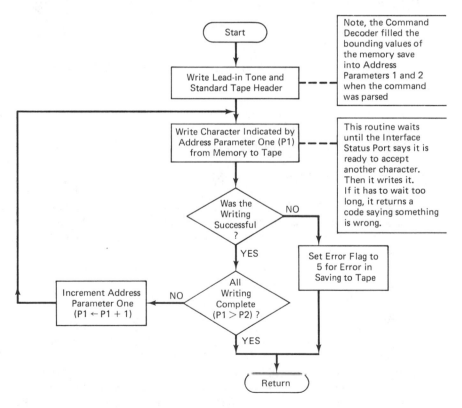

Figure 3-15:   The Save Memory Contents to Tape Routine (STAPE). Programs being saved to tape with this routine are saved in memory image format. There is a lead-in tone and a descriptive header appended on the front of the memory image data bytes.

record mode. Then he will give the STAPE command to the monitor. When control is given to the monitor, the first thing that happens is that a lead-in tone will be written onto the tape. Then the header marker and header data will be written indicating the load point of the program and the number of bytes that will be recorded. These are computed from the two address parameters in the Monitor Workspace that were filled in at initial parsing of the command. Finally, the machine code of the program will be recorded, in the following way: The byte pointed to by Address Parameter One is written to the tape. The address parameter is incremented. A test is made to see whether the required number of bytes have been output. If not, another byte is picked up and passed to the tape until all the memory that was requested has been recorded.

These saving and loading mechanisms are absolutely the simplest possible. They may be inefficient for long programs. Some monitors use more sophisticated schemes in which programs are broken up into small blocks (with size on the order of 128 bytes) and loading consists of installing each block separately in memory. Each block will have its own address. This makes for efficient loading of programs which have some text in low memory and some text in high memory and nothing in between. We will consider these kinds of formats in Chapter 5 which discusses linkers and loaders.

STUDY QUESTIONS AND EXERCISES

1. Why doesn't the MEMLOAD Routine set an error flag when it discovers an invalid conversion? Why doesn't the DISPLAY Routine check for errors?

2. Why is it desirable in a monitor, or any other systems software, to write all error messages from a single place in the program?

3. Write an 8080 assembler language subroutine to convert a two digit ASCII coded hexadecimal representation of a byte into an eight bit binary number. The HL register pair points to the location of the ASCII digits. They are in two successive memory locations with the high order digit coming first. The HL pair points to the high order digit. Return the converted binary number in register B. Return a condition code in the accumulator: 1 for a successful conversion, 0 for no success.

4. A monitor keeps its error messages in a table. A 32 byte area is allocated for each message. The first 32 bytes are for Message 1, the second 32 bytes are for Message 2, etc. No message will actually be 32 bytes long. The last character will be a delimiter, "$", so that the system can tell where each message ends. The message table begins at location 0400H. Write an 8080 assembler language subroutine that has the error message number as input (in the accumulator). Its output is the length of the message, excluding the final delimiter, and this is to be returned in the B register. A pointer to the first address of the message is to be returned in the HL pair.

5. What modifications would have to be made in the ENTER Routine and other parts of the system so that ENTER would count addresses? That is, it would respond to either a single address or a range of addresses just as the DISPLAY Routine does. After this modification, it should no longer be necessary for the user to type "END" to terminate keyboard entry.

6. Suppose you are interested in implementing a SEARCH Command. Its purpose is to scan a range of memory looking for all occurrences of a particular byte. These addresses are printed to the screen as they are found. Suggest what the user interface might look like for this command. Will there have to be any changes in parsing? Write a flowchart for an implementation of the command.

7. Write the flowchart for a new version of the MODIFY Routine that works as follows. Commands are given in the same way as for the present routine except that when the number of addresses specified by the user has been exhausted, the command automatically returns to the monitor driver. The display and change cycle is to work on only a single address at a time. The present contents of the address are shown, and then the user is prompted for new contents by the address and an equals sign displayed on the next line. A Carriage Return typed by the user tells the computer not to change this location but to go on to the next one. The process can be halted after any particular address is processed by typing CNTL C.

8. Suggest a way that a monitor, as part of its initialization, could test the system's memory to find out how much RAM there is and where it is located. This ability would allow one version of the monitor to be used with many different configurations of the computer system.

4

Assembler Languages

4.1 INTRODUCTION: A STEP UP FROM MACHINE LANGUAGE

Assemblers were the first major software aid for program production. They were developed in the late 1940's because of a problem that was apparent to everyone involved with early computers: Human beings are not really very good at writing programs in machine language. A machine program with more than a small number of lines (perhaps 100) is tedious to write and subject to many errors. The patterns of ones and zeros that are natural to machines seem to be unnatural for humans and difficult for them to remember and manipulate in any quantity.

The way out of this difficulty was to invent a new sort of language for expressing programs—assembler language. The new language was close to machine language and yet could be constructed out of words and symbols rather than number codes, so that it was easier for people to use. The whole cycle of program production then became something like this: The programmer writes a program in assembler language. The computer has a special program, called an assembler, which can translate the program written in assembler language into a fully equivalent program written in machine language. This machine language program is now suitable for direct execution on the computer.

Ever since the first assembler was written, one of the major topics in computer science has been this theme of translation from a human-oriented language into machine language. We begin our study of the important area of language translators in this chapter. We plan to take an evolutionary approach. First we'll describe an assembler with the most basic but most important features. Then we'll add more advanced features layer by layer. We'll conclude in Chapter 6 with macroassemblers.

There are two simple but powerful ideas inherent in basic assemblers: mnemonic instructions and symbolic addresses. The first part of the solution to problems posed by machine language was to define and use certain simple mnemonics to stand for the various instructions the machine is capable of performing. If this is done, a program can be written in terms of mnemonics whose names bear some relation to the function of the instructions they stand for. This will make the instructions easier to remember and programs easier to read.

If programs are written in this way, one of the things the assembler has to do is receive symbolic (mnemonic) instructions as input and produce machine code as output. The mechanics of doing this transformation is essentially a table look-up procedure. An operation code table can be maintained which relates every mnemonic instruction specification to its associated machine code.

Symbolic addressing is a more subtle idea. Much of the work in writing a program close to the machine level is in manipulating addresses. Many machine instructions such as calls, jumps, branches, and memory references contain addresses as part of the instruction. The source of the difficulty is that, if a program is modified by adding or deleting code, many of the addresses in the program will also have been changed as a side effect of the primary modification. This is because the program will no longer be of the same length. Data items and branch points could now conceivably be at different places than they were before. So for every modification that changes the length of the program, the programmer must laboriously check and make sure that all his address references are still good. Perhaps he also has to change a large number of them.

Management of address references was such an intolerable problem that programmers began to find ways to automate this process. The technique that emerged was to make it possible to program in a language wherein all addresses could be referred to symbolically, rather than explicitly. The operational implications of this are that the programmer can modify his program as much as he wishes. When he is finished, he reassembles the program (which is a relatively quick operation), and the assembler will figure what all the proper addresses should be.

Figure 4-1 illustrates the idea behind symbolic addressing. The figure shows an assembler program and the corresponding machine code. The program will add up a sequence of small numbers and leave the result in the first memory location beyond the end of the program. We are to assemble the program so that it will appear in memory starting at location 0100H. One byte in memory has the function of saying how many numbers are to be summed, and this byte will be at location 0200H. The numbers to be added will be in the memory immediately after that.

Here is how the program works. It sets up a pointer in the HL register pair to point to where the data is. It brings a count of the data items into register C. Then it proceeds into a loop whereby the data is fetched one item at a time and added to the accumulator. In each pass through the loop the counter is decremented. When the counter hits zero, all the numbers have been added and the answer resides in the accumulator. Finally, we store it into the location at the end of the program using a store accumulator to direct address instruction.

Memory address (hexadecimal)	Assembler code			Machine code (hexadecimal)
	ORG	0100H	; ESTABLISH STARTING POINT	
100	SUB	A	; ZERO ACCUMULATOR	97
101	LXI	H, 0200H	; GET HOW MANY TO ADD	21
102				00
103				02
104	MOV	C, M	; C WILL BE A COUNTER	4E
105	LOOP: INX	H	; POINT TO FIRST NUMBER	23
106	ADD	M	; ADD TO ACCUMULATOR	86
107	DCR	C	; DECREMENT COUNTER	0D
108	JNZ	LOOP	; GO BACK FOR MORE	C2
109				05
10A				01
10B	STA	DEPOT	; ACCUM. TO STORAGE LOC.	32
10C				0F
10D				01
10E	HLT		; PROCESSING DONE	76
10F	DEPOT: DS	1	; ANSWER TO BE PUT HERE	

Figure 4-1: Symbolic Addressing. This program adds up a short series of small numbers and stores the result in the first location in memory beyond the end of the program. The location 0200H contains how many quantities are to be summed. The numbers to be added follow this location in consecutive memory addresses.

Notice the use of symbolic addressing in this program. The instruction at memory address 105 has a label which will be interpreted as the symbolic address of that instruction. The instruction at memory location 108 is a jump which refers to the top of the loop. We could have written this instruction in another way. The jump could have been written with an explicit address:

    JNZ   0105H

There are, however, many advantages to using the symbolic address and letting the assembler figure out what you really mean.

Consider what would happen if it was necessary to insert another statement in the program, say for some sort of initialization, before the start of the loop. All the code following the new statement would be pushed down in memory by a few bytes. This would not affect the translation of most statements, but it could affect those that contained addresses. For instance, the translation of the jump statement as

    C2
    05
    01

would no longer be correct because the address of LOOP would have changed. If symbolic addresses are not used, the programmer will have to inspect all address references that refer to places beyond the inserted statement and probably change them. If symbolic addresses are used, the programmer doesn't usually need to be concerned with the actual addresses to which they correspond. If the program is changed, you simply reassemble it, and the assembler software will recompute all addresses as part of its translation process.

Symbolic addresses make program changes easy. Say we wished to install the whole example program at another location in memory (specified by the ORG statement). Once again the assembler could automatically recompute all the addresses in the program if they were specified symbolically. Otherwise, address computation would have to be done by hand and addresses would have to be explicitly entered into the program by the programmer.

We need to discuss one more feature before we can look at the design of the assembler. As you might expect, we will need a mechanism for giving instructions to the assembler about the way we want it to produce the object code. This is customarily done by including pseudo-operations at various places in the source code. Pseudo-operations look like normal machine code mnemonics, but they are instead instructions to the assembler. Our assembler will utilize five pseudo-operations, examples of which are shown in Figure 4-2.

The function of the ORIGIN pseudo-operation is to tell the assembler where the code that is being assembled will reside in memory when it comes time to execute that code. This is obviously important because many instructions involve addresses and such addresses can only be computed if the assembler knows for what place in memory the machine code is being prepared. This kind of origin statement is referred to as an absolute origin rather than a relocatable origin.

The EQUATE pseudo-operation associates a value with a symbol that is to be used

1. ORIGIN Pseudo-Operation

        ORG   0100H

2. EQUATE Pseudo-Operation

        ALPHA: EQU   000AH

3. DEFINE STORAGE Pseudo-Operation

        ARRAY: DS   100

4. DEFINE CONSTANT(s) Pseudo-Operation

        STOR: DB FFH, '.', 22

Note: The mnemonic used here is DB for consistency
with the Intel assembler. This pseudo-operation
is frequently called DEFINE BYTE.

5. END Pseudo-Operation

        END

Figure 4-2: Basic Assembler Pseudo-Operations. Pseudo-operations are statements that look like normal mnemonics for machine language but instead are interpreted as directions for the assembler. These are the most common ones. More complicated assemblers usually allow the use of several more pseudo-operations which we will not discuss at this time.

somewhere else in the program. It does this by creating an entry in a data structure called the Symbol Table. We'll discuss this important table later on. In the example shown in Figure 4-2, ALPHA would receive the value of 000AH by action of this pseudo-operation.

The DEFINE STORAGE pseudo-operation is used to leave space at specified locations in the machine code so that there is room for tables or a workspace when the program executes. The way the assembler must act after detecting a DEFINE STORAGE instruction is to give the symbol associated with the statement (i.e., the label) a value that is the address where the block of space will appear in the memory. And then it must make sure that that area of memory is left blank and no machine code is translated to appear there.

The DEFINE CONSTANT(s) instruction not only reserves space as DEFINE STORAGE does, but will initialize that space to specified values when the object code is loaded into memory prior to execution. The label associated with this statement receives a value which is the address at which the initialized space will appear in the program to be executed when that program is loaded. The values that the initialized space must assume are listed one by one, separated by commas, after the operation code for this instruction. DEFINE CONSTANT(s) can only specify values that are eight bits wide.

The last pseudo-operation code we will consider now is the END statement. This simply marks the end of the program file. The assembler typically does its work by scanning through the source program line by line and doing some translation operation on each statement. An assembler will usually make several passes over the source code before translation is complete. Encountering the END statement, then, provides a signal that one stage of processing is finished and the next can be begun.

The assembler we will describe here is patterned after the standard Intel 8080 assembler. It is actually a subset of that assembler because the grammar is a bit more restrictive and some pseudo-operations have been left out.

It would be well to describe now what constitutes correct syntax in our rendition of this language. The reader can look at Figure 4-1 for an example. If all the syntactic possibilities in a statement are used, there will be four different kinds of fields in an instruction. The first field will be a label field. The label can be from one to six alphanumeric characters. The first character must be alphabetic. The label must terminate with a colon followed by at least one blank. Next comes an operation field which has an assembler keyword which says what the instruction is about. The operation code mnemonic (opcode) will be separated from any following fields by at least one blank. Next come a number of operand fields (usually one or two) which are separated from each other by commas. The last field is a comment field. It is separated from what comes before it by at least one blank, and it begins with a semicolon. The end of the entire statement is signaled by a Carriage Return.

The label field and the comment field are optional. The other fields are completely dictated by whatever machine instruction or pseudo-operation is being represented. It is also possible to have a line that contains only the comment field. In general, it doesn't matter what column the fields start in, and extra blanks are ignored.

This is the end of our introduction to assemblers. The plan for the rest of this chapter is as follows. All assemblers build tables relating the names and values of symbols in the program being translated. We first describe some characteristic manipulations that must be done on these symbol tables. This is the topic of searching and sorting. Then we will consider how an efficient, simple assembler for the 8080 might be built. Next we begin the process of adding features so as to understand full functioned modern assemblers. We will look at a way to incorporate not just symbolic addresses, but algebraic expressions involving symbols. This will make the operands of many assembler statements computable at assembly time. The final topic in this chapter will be relocatable code. A piece of code that is relocatable can be configured to execute anywhere in memory after it is assembled. At assembly time it is not necessary to say where the code will ultimately be used. This technology has important implications for allowing large programs to be conveniently built up from the work of many people, and for allowing programs to be easily modified.

4.2 SORTING AND SEARCHING IN SYMBOL TABLES

The most important data structure associated with an assembler is the Symbol Table, and all assemblers have one. It will be built, early in the processing, to record the names of all symbols used in the program and the values they are to take. The logical layout of this structure is just two columns with symbols in the first column and values in the second. We'll discuss how the values are determined later. The entities in the first column are the actual text characters that make up the symbol name. For instance, if the name of a symbol is DEPOT, at its position in the first column there will be five ASCII characters (bytes) spelling out this name. For our assembler, we will assume that the value field is two bytes long. We specify this field size because the predominant use of symbols is to stand for addresses, and addresses in most small computers are 16 bits long.

We have been describing the logical layout of the Symbol Table. There can be several different physical implementations of this simple structure in memory. They all have the purpose of allowing particular symbols in the table to be located quickly, since the Symbol Table will be referred to many times during the assembly process. Let's look at how this can be done. We wish to present now a review of several sorting techniques, of the binary search technique for accessing a sorted table, and of the hashed access technique for quickly getting at scatter stored table entries. Sorting and searching is an extensive topic usually presented in courses on data structures. We only mean to give an introduction here.

In many assemblers, the first step to accessing symbol values rapidly is to put the Symbol Table into some kind of order. The easiest thing to do, and one of the most useful, is to put the table in alphabetical order. Then finding a particular symbol can proceed in the same way as finding a name in a telephone book. This procedure is called a binary search, and it depends on having an ordered list of entries.

The binary search procedure for accessing a symbol in any ordered list is as follows. Look at the entry at roughly the middle of the list and compare it with the name you are looking for. If they are the same, stop. Otherwise, the name being sought will lie in one or the other of the halves of the list defined by the first look, and you know which half because of the ordering. Ignore the half of the directory that has been shown not to apply and begin the search procedure again in the remaining half. Continue in this manner, dividing the remaining entries to be searched into relevant and irrelevant halves until the desired name is found or until there is nothing more to search.

Binary searching is very fast. Since the effective table size remaining to be searched is halved on each probe, it is easy to show for a table of size N that not more than LOG_2 (N) trial comparisons are ever required. This many comparisons will either find the search target or determine that it is not in the table. To take an example, searching a table with 16 million sorted entries never requires more than 24 comparisons with the binary search method.

Incidentally, for very small tables it will usually be quicker to search by examining every symbol entry in the table in sequence. This is known as a linear search. Of course, if you're going to look at every entry, the table doesn't need to be ordered. On the average, $N/2$ comparisons will be required to find the search target. However, comparisons aren't everything, and it is easier to program a linear search than a binary search, so there are places where it is very useful. One rule of thumb says that the programming overhead associated with the binary search method makes linear searching the preferred method until tables get to be bigger than 50–100 items.

Many assemblers use binary searches in their symbol tables. So at some point in the processing they must sort the table so that the process of successive division into halves will work. Sorting the table can take a large fraction of the execution time of the assembler, so it is important to choose an efficient sorting method. We will discuss two sorting methods—one that is compact, easy to understand, and easy to implement (Bubble Sort), and one that is very fast (Quicksort).

Most sorting methods run at speeds that are proportional either to $N*N$ or to $N*LOG_2$ (N) where N is the number of items being sorted. Of course, different methods have different proportionality constants which reflect the programming overhead associated with the method.

The Bubble Sort runs at a speed proportional to $N*N$; thus it is quite inefficient for sorting large tables but is good for small tables, and it is very easy to program. The basic idea is to move down the list of items to be sorted making comparisons between each pair of adjacent entries. If those two entries are in the right order, then attention moves one entry further into the list and the comparison is made again. If two entries are examined and they are not in order, then they are switched. After moving this pairwise comparison completely down the list once, the procedure calls for going back and doing it again, and again, until an entire pass is made over the list and no pairs are found out of order. This procedure is called a bubble sort because each pass down the list will serve to move the largest remaining unsorted element to its proper position at the end of the data.

The Quicksort scheme was developed by the English computer scientist C. A. R. Hoare. Quicksort is probably the fastest way to sort a large symbol table. It runs at a speed that is proportional to $N*LOG_2$ (N), and the proportionality constant is relatively small compared to other $N*LOG_2$ (N) sorts. The Quicksort algorithm is most often written recursively, and as a consequence, a modest amount of stack space is required by the procedure in addition to the space needed to store the table being sorted.

A recursive algorithm is one which contains calls to itself as part of the computation, but it calls itself with simpler or shorter arguments than were active at the higher level call. For instance, look at this pseudo-code for a function which can calculate a factorial recursively. Recall that factorial N is equal to $N*(N-1)*(N-2)* \ldots *2*1$.

```
SUBROUTINE FACTORIAL (N)

    IF (N > 1) THEN FACTORIAL (N)  = N*FACTORIAL (N-1)
               ELSE FACTORIAL (N) = 1

RETURN
```

When a procedure calls itself, the original instantiation of the procedure is suspended pending the result of the subsidiary call. During the course of the calculation, a recursive procedure may have been started a number of times and each time been suspended by making a lower level call to itself. In algorithms of this kind, the stack is required to keep track of the environment of the suspended procedure calls. Environment information must be maintained in such a way that suspended procedures can start up again at the proper time and in the proper order when the lower level calls complete their work and begin returning.

Our discussion of Quicksort will assume that the elements to be sorted are arranged in a horizontal row with the front of the list considered to be at the left end. After sorting, the smallest element will be at the left end and the largest element will be at the right end.

There are two steps in the Quicksort algorithm that are repeated over and over. The first step is to choose a so-called pivot element from the list being sorted, and then rearrange the list so that all its elements are in the correct order with respect to the pivot. Elements to the right of the pivot should be larger, and elements to the left should be smaller. This requires considerable ingenuity to do efficiently. After the rearrangement, the position of this particular pivot element will never have to change throughout the rest of the sort. It is now in the proper position with respect to the whole list, even though the other parts of the list will need to be sorted further. Since the position of one element has been finalized, the original problem of sorting the whole list has been broken into two simpler problems: sort the list on the left of the pivot, and sort the list on the right of the pivot. This is where recursion comes in. These subsidiary sorts are the second step in Quicksort. This sorting can be done by restarting the Quicksort procedure on these simpler lists, selecting new pivots and ordering with respect to them, etc.

In order to apply this procedure, the main thing we need is a way to choose a pivot from any given list and a way to rearrange the list efficiently so that all elements to the left of the pivot are smaller than it and all those to the right are larger. Here is what the Quicksort algorithm prescribes. Choose the very first element in the list as the pivot. Now examine the elements from the front of the list one by one until an element is found that is larger than or equal to the pivot. Next, work backwards from the end of the list until an element is found that is smaller than or equal to the pivot. Exchange these two elements. Now continue with this process, working first from the front of the list to find elements larger than (or equal to) the pivot, and then from the end of the list to find elements less than (or equal to) the pivot, and performing interchanges.

When the scanning points finally cross somewhere in the interior of the list, stop the examination. Exchange the first element in the list (the pivot) for the value of the last element that was touched on the scan that originated at the end of the list. Now all the elements to the left of the pivot will be less than or equal to it and all those to the right will be greater than or equal to it.

At this point the original list has been partitioned into two sublists and we can begin the process anew working on them. Eventually the algorithm reaches the situation where all sublists have either one element or no elements. In either case, no more sorting can be done and the whole sort is finished.

Let's look at an example. Say this is a list or table that we wish to sort:

$$7 \quad 1 \quad 4 \quad 18 \quad 2 \quad 20 \quad 3$$

We begin by scanning from the left, looking for an element greater than or equal to the pivot, which is 7. We find 18. Then we scan from the right looking for an element less than or equal to the pivot. The very first element encountered satisfies the criterion. So here are the elements that have been identified so far:

$$7 \quad 1 \quad 4 \quad \underline{18} \quad 2 \quad 20 \quad \underline{3}$$

Since the scanning points haven't crossed, we interchange the elements.

$$7 \quad 1 \quad 4 \quad \underline{3} \quad 2 \quad 20 \quad \underline{18}$$

Now the scan continues from where it left off. The scan from the left finds 20. The scan from the right finds 2.

$$7 \quad 1 \quad 4 \quad 3 \quad \underline{2} \quad \underline{20} \quad 18$$

However, since the scanning points have crossed, we are finished. Now the pivot is exchanged with the scan element that is at the end of the scan from the right, i.e., 2. This is what the list looks like now:

$$2 \quad 1 \quad 4 \quad 3 \quad 7 \quad 20 \quad 18$$

Notice that all the elements to the left of 7 are less than or equal to it, and all those to the right are greater than or equal to it. So 7 is in the proper position with respect to the whole list. It never needs to be moved again as far as this sort is concerned.

$$[2 \quad 1 \quad 4 \quad 3] \quad 7 \quad [20 \quad 18]$$

Our work so far has created two sublists (they are shown in brackets), and each of them can now be sorted further by a recursive application of the procedure we have just demonstrated.

Figure 4-3 shows a trace of the Quicksort algorithm acting on a list of symbols that could be a symbol table of some kind. Each line in this trace is related to the one before it by one interchange of symbols. Underlined elements show the places where scanning has stopped. Brackets indicate sublists that have been created by the partitioning

[FA	MP	AB	QR	AC	PA	RS	DZ	BC	XL	HI]
[FA	BC	AB	QR	AC	PA	RS	DZ	MP	XL	HI]
[FA	BC	AB	DZ	AC	PA	RS	QR	MP	XL	HI]
[AC	BC	AB	DZ]	FA	[PA	RS	QR	MP	XL	HI]
[AC	AB	BC	DZ]	FA	[PA	RS	QR	MP	XL	HI]
[AB]	AC	[BC	DZ]	FA	[PA	RS	QR	MP	XL	HI]
AB	AC	[BC	DZ]	FA	[PA	RS	QR	MP	XL	HI]
AB	AC	BC	DZ	FA	[PA	RS	QR	MP	XL	HI]
AB	AC	BC	DZ	FA	[PA	HI	QR	MP	XL	RS]
AB	AC	BC	DZ	FA	[PA	HI	MP	QR	XL	RS]
AB	AC	BC	DZ	FA	[MP	HI]	PA	[QR	XL	RS]
AB	AC	BC	DZ	FA	HI	MP	PA	[QR	XL	RS]
AB	AC	BC	DZ	FA	HI	MP	PA	QR	[XL	RS]
AB	AC	BC	DZ	FA	HI	MP	PA	QR	RS	XL

Figure 4-3:   A Trace Showing the Use of Quicksort. This figure shows Quicksort working on a list of symbols that are meant to suggest a symbol table. Quicksort has the best average behavior of all sorts that depend on comparisons and exchanges. It works by recursively partitioning a whole list to be sorted into two sublists each of which is in the correct order relative to a central pivoting element. The same strategy is then applied to the sublists until the while list is sorted.

process. Elements that are not enclosed in brackets have reached their final positions. In producing this trace we have made two further assumptions about how the Quicksort algorithm will be programmed. The first is that whenever a two element list is encountered, it will be put in order by a simple comparison. This will be quicker than working a recursive procedure on it. The other assumption is that work will always be applied first to the shortest of the sublists that are extant. The stack space required by the algorithm is minimized if the shorter sublists are sorted first.

Many assemblers develop and maintain sorted symbol tables. We must remember why all this is being done. It is to give rapid access to the values of symbols at varying stages in the assembly process. There is an even faster way to access symbol values which we will describe now and which we will use in the assembler to be built in this chapter. This method stores symbol and value pairs at scattered locations throughout a buffer that serves as the Symbol Table. Symbols can be added to the table and symbol values retrieved by doing a calculation on the name of the symbol which transforms the name into the address where the symbol is to be stored. This procedure is known as hashing.

The first step in designing this kind of symbol table will be to decide the maximum number of symbols it can hold. Let's say it is 2^K. For instance, if $K = 10$, then the table can hold 1024 distinct symbols.

The first step in finding a unique place for a symbol in the table is to convert the name of the symbol into a number that is somewhere in the range between zero and one less than the maximum number of symbols allowed. We will call this just the Symbol Number. The best hashing functions will produce Symbol Numbers scattered haphazardly throughout the acceptable range. They also must have the property that similar names, i.e., names that are clustered, do not produce clustered symbol numbers. The symbol numbers must be scattered so that they are more or less evenly distributed around the whole acceptable range for typical collections of symbol names.

Many functions can be invented to hash in this way. The following is one that works well. Initialize a sum to zero. Add the ASCII code for the first letter in the symbol's name to it. Shift the sum left by one bit position. Add the ASCII code for the next letter in the name to it. Shift the sum left by another bit position. Add the ASCII code for the third letter to it, etc., until all the letters in the name are used up. Then throw away all bits in the sum except the rightmost K bits, and use this result as the Symbol Number.

The Symbol Number is almost an address, but a little more work has to be done with it. The entities we want to store in the Symbol Table are almost always bigger than single byte units. If we want to use the Symbol Number to address four byte units, we can do that by shifting the Symbol Number left by two bits. If we want to use the Symbol Number to address eight byte units, we can shift it left by three bits, etc. The final step in producing an address in the Symbol Table is to add an offset onto the shifted Symbol Number so that the table can be located at any desired starting address in the memory.

For instance, let's say we wanted a Symbol Table that was to begin in memory at location E000H and accommodate 1024 symbols maximum. Let's say eight bytes worth of data are to be recorded in association with each symbol; the first 6 bytes are the ASCII characters of the name (left justified), and the last 2 bytes are the value of the symbol. For purposes of example we'll assume we want to store a symbol with the name DAN and the value F0F0H into the table. Figure 4-4 shows how an address is obtained from this name and shows what is stored at the address.

One problem arises with all hashed access schemes, and that is, what happens if the hashing algorithm applied to two different symbol names yields the same symbol number, i.e., the same address. This situation is called a collision. It can always happen, and the likelihood becomes greater as the table fills up. There are several remedies for this problem. The one that appears best suited to small computers is the rehashing procedure.

If a symbol is being inserted in the table and the address calculation turns up a cell that is already in use, then the Symbol Number must be further manipulated to create another address. If this one is also occupied, we can rehash again until a vacant address is found. Note that whatever procedure we use for rehashing, it must be deterministic so that a particular symbol will always be steered to a particular address, even if several intermediate computations are involved.

The following is a convenient rehashing computation. Take the Symbol Number and shift it left by two bit positions. Add this to the original Symbol Number. Now shift

Computing the Symbol Number:

D	0100 0100
D shifted left	0 1000 1000
A	0100 0001
SUM	0 1100 1001

SUM shifted left	01 1001 0010	
N	0100 1110	
Final SUM	01 1110 0000	= 01E0H
		(This is the Symbol Number)

Computing the Table Address:

Table Address = Symbol Number * 8 + Offset

$$= \quad 01E0H \quad * 8 + E000H$$

$$= \quad EF00H$$

Contents of All Storage Associated with the Symbol DAN

Address	Contents	
EF00H	44H	(ASCII for D)
EF01H	41H	(ASCII for A)
EF02H	4EH	(ASCII for N)
EF03H	—	
EF04H	—	
EF05H	—	
EF06H	F0H	(the symbol's value)
EF07H	F0H	

Figure 4-4:   An Example of Hashed Access to a Symbol Table. This example illustrates the use of a Symbol Table that can accommodate 1024 eight byte entries. It begins at location E000H. Each entry is six bytes for the symbol name and two bytes for the value. A symbol with the name DAN and the value F0F0H is to be inserted into the table.

the sum right by two bit positions and again add on the original Symbol Number. Use the rightmost *K* bits of this ultimate sum as a new Symbol Number. After a new Symbol Number is obtained, it can be converted to an address in the normal way by shifting and adding an offset. Many other rehashing algorithms are possible.

It is important to realize that two processes can go on with a hashed table—inserting and retrieving. When a symbol is being retrieved, the same sequence of address computations will be done as when it was inserted. Each time an address is produced, the name of the symbol at that position must be compared to the name of the symbol we are trying to access. When they are the same, the value can be retrieved and the access is completed. If they are not the same, the access program will have to rehash to the next address. Ultimately the program may hash or rehash to an empty storage location (empty locations must be marked in some way). If this happens, it means the target symbol is not in the table.

We end this section by stating the amazing fact that makes hashing so attractive. The amount of rehashing that needs to be done is really very limited. The number of comparisons that are needed to find an entry depends only on how full the hashed Symbol Table is, not on how large it is. Even when the table is 90% full, only about 2.56 comparisons will be needed on the average to find a symbol's position. The rehashings do not take a long time, and they can always be minimized by making the table somewhat larger than will ever be needed.

4.3   THE BASIC TWO PASS ASSEMBLER

Now we should have enough pieces of information in hand to begin conceptualizing the internal structure of an assembler. An assembler is a language translator. Why can't we just go through the program line by line and translate it? Perhaps we can. Let's look at the details this strategy would require.

Certainly it would be simple enough to translate the following kinds of statements:

```
MOV   A, B
ANA   B
ADD   C
```

They are single byte instructions, and to do the translation, we'd merely have to arrange the mnemonics and the corresponding opcodes in some kind of a convenient table.

Other instructions would require a little more work.

```
MVI   B, 2AH
JMP   4000H
OUT   2
```

These forms have explicit data or address items in the instruction in addition to the opcode. Now the translator would have to do one look-up to get the numerical equivalent of the opcode. Then it would pass the other information in the instruction into the second and third bytes of the resulting code. Remember, 8080 instructions have the opcode in the first byte and any other required information in one or two bytes following the opcode. Still, there is no inherent difficulty here.

Now we must consider symbolic addresses. How would the system translate this type of instruction?

```
JMP   BETA
```

BETA stands for the address of a certain place in the program that is to be jumped to. If the translator knows what BETA means, then translating this instruction is no worse than translating

```
JMP   4000H
```

except that BETA will have to be looked up efficiently in a symbol table. But how would the translator know what BETA means?

Now we reach a central point: how symbol meanings get established in the Symbol Table. There are only two ways. When the code is scanned for translation, the assembler uses a location counter to record the exact location in memory for which the current line of machine code is being prepared. The location counter is set initially to the value specified by the ORIGIN statement. Then, as instructions are translated, the location counter is incremented each time to reflect the number of bytes in each instruction. When the assembler encounters an instruction with a symbol in its label field, it immediately knows what address should be associated with that label. It is the current value of the location counter. Such a statement might look like this

```
DELTA:   CALL   STAT
```

When a statement is encountered with a label, the label is immediately put into the Symbol Table and the associated value is taken from the location counter.

The other route by which symbols get into the table is via the EQUATE statement. EQUATE statements are processed as soon as they are discovered, and the complete and only effect of such a statement is to insert one symbol and value pair into the table.

Unfortunately, not all translations are as easy as our previous examples. Now we come to an inherent difficulty. How can the assembler possibly translate this type of instruction

```
JMP   BETA
```

if it doesn't know what value BETA represents? This might happen because BETA is a label on a statement that is further ahead in the program and has not been scanned yet. This is known as the forward reference problem. It has major consequences for the architecture of all assemblers. Because of the forward reference problem, most assemblers are implemented with at least two passes over the program. The crucial requirement on the first pass is to discover the values of all symbols. Then a second pass can do all the translations as we've outlined earlier. This is the most common pattern of processing for simple assemblers. It is the benchmark for all assembler construction. There is some flexibility as to when translation is done, but symbol values must always be discovered on the first pass.

The assembler we are going to study will be almost as simple as what we have just discussed, but it will be considerably more efficient. We should mention at the outset the two factors which are principally responsible for how fast an assembler can do its work. One is that the Symbol Table should be organized for very fast access, since it will have to be accessed many times. We will take care of this by using a hashed symbol table.

The other factor is that the amount of scanning that must be done by the assembler in the source program should be minimized. By scanning, we mean moving back and forth in program lines to pull out opcodes and operands and other elements upon which a translation is based. The technical term for this process is parsing. It is very time consuming.

We are going to adopt a scheme whereby the source code needs to be looked at only once by the assembler, even though it is technically a two-pass operation. Passes now come to mean a sequential excursion over the program *in some form,* but not necessarily over the source code. Note that an assembler must examine the source code twice if it makes one pass to extract symbols and another pass to translate.

Here is an overview of our assembler. All symbols will be discovered and put into the Symbol Table as part of Pass One. As much of the source code as possible will be translated at this time. This will be perhaps 90 percent of the entire program. Thus, all the opcodes will get translated, but in some places where symbol values are missing, complete translation will not be possible. These places will be marked for more work on Pass Two. Completing the configuration at these sites will be the job of Pass Two. The second pass does not have much work to do relative to the first pass process.

Pass One produces four pieces of output. One, of course, is the Symbol Table. Another is a file of partially configured machine code. This will look like a completed machine code program except that there will be blanks or other place-holder bytes at the locations in the code that will need to receive symbol values later. The place-holders are very necessary. A three byte instruction must be translated as three bytes even if part of the instruction will be altered later.

What other output will we need? We've noted that the locations requiring more work need to be marked in some way. For this we'll use a data structure called the Configuration Table. It forms the basic connection between Pass One and Pass Two. The most reasonable kind of marking would be to record the location in the machine code of every place that needs a symbol value, and the name of the symbol whose value is to be put there. With this table, it is convenient to record the locations as offsets from the front of the machine code file. However, it is not convenient to record the names of symbols in the Configuration Table, because names can be of varying length. So we'll store the names in another data structure and only record pointers to where the names can be found in this table.

Symbol names will be laid down in a String Storage Buffer whenever it is necessary to record them for Pass Two. The buffer has a very simple structure. It is just a long string with the symbol names packed one against another except for a separation character that defines boundaries. Whenever a symbol is placed in the String Storage Buffer, the address of the first character in the symbol is recorded in the Configuration Table Pointer Field.

Figures 4-5A, 4-5B, and 4-5C show the Symbol Table, the Configuration Table, and the String Storage Buffer developed for the example program of Figure 4-1.

In order to keep the assembler simple, let us imagine that as a program is translated, the machine code will be deposited in a memory buffer somewhere in available memory rather than in a file. When assembly is completed, this buffer can be copied to tape or disk and that output will be the assembled program.

Sometimes people are confused about where the machine code is kept when it is being set up, and where it will be when it is executed. These two places have no necessary

A. *Symbol Table*

Symbol	Value
LOOP	0105
DEPOT	010F

B. *Configuration Table*

Pointer to Stored Symbol Name	Insert Value at This Offset
DC00	000C

C. *String Storage Buffer* (the buffer starts at DC00)

Address	Contents	
DC00	44H	(ASCII for D)
DC01	45H	(ASCII for E)
DC02	50H	(ASCII for P)
DC03	4FH	(ASCII for O)
DC04	54H	(ASCII for T)
DC05	5EH	(ASCII for separation
DC06	—	character)
DC07	—	
DC08	—	

etc.

Figure 4-5:   Tables Built by the Assembler. These are the principal data structures built by our simple assembler. During Pass One, these tables are dynamic structures. What is in them will depend on when you look. But after Pass One, all entries have been filled in and there are no more changes in the tables. The Configuration Table controls Pass Two processing. The actual values in these tables correspond to the program in Figure 4-1.

relation to each other and will usually be different. For example, let's say we are assembling a short program that we plan to install in memory at location 0100H when it is to be executed. We have signaled this intention to the assembler by making the first statement in the program be the following:

```
ORG  0100H
```

Figure 4-6 shows what the memory map of a typical small computer might look like after Pass One during the assembly of this program. The figure also shows how the memory would look later, when the program was properly installed in memory and about to be executed. Note that the machine code is in a different place.

Incidentally, the absolute addresses of places in the memory where address configuration must be done on Pass Two can be computed by adding offset addresses from the Configuration Table to the address where the storage buffer for the machine code begins.

We're ready to look at the work of Pass One on a more detailed level. Figure 4-7 shows a flowchart. The assembler works on one program line at a time and is then either

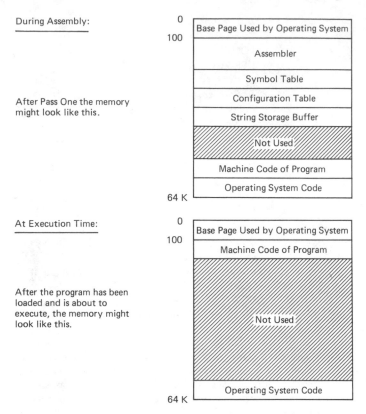

During Assembly:

After Pass One the memory might look like this.

At Execution Time:

After the program has been loaded and is about to execute, the memory might look like this.

Figure 4-6: Memory Maps For an Assembler Program at Two Stages of its Life.
The assembler and all its temporary tables are only in memory when the machine code version of the program is being produced. The place where the machine code is kept while it is being worked on has no relationship to where the code will be when it is finally executed.

finished with it for good or finished with it until some further configuration must be done on Pass Two. The line is brought into a statement buffer; it is parsed, which means the information in the line is abstracted and repackaged in a form suitable for further work; and finally different processing will be done depending upon whether the instruction is a machine instruction or a pseudo-operation. Pass Two is triggered when the END statement is finally detected.

Assembler statements require two classes of processing: processing for machine instructions, and processing for pseudo-operations. If the statement is a normal machine instruction, it is examined to see whether or not there is a symbol in the label field. If there is, this symbol will be hashed into the Symbol Table. Then a subsidiary routine is called to do various table look-up translation procedures and output the machine code. If it is a multi-byte instruction and the operands are all known, the rest of the instruction will be output at this time also. We will discuss the details later.

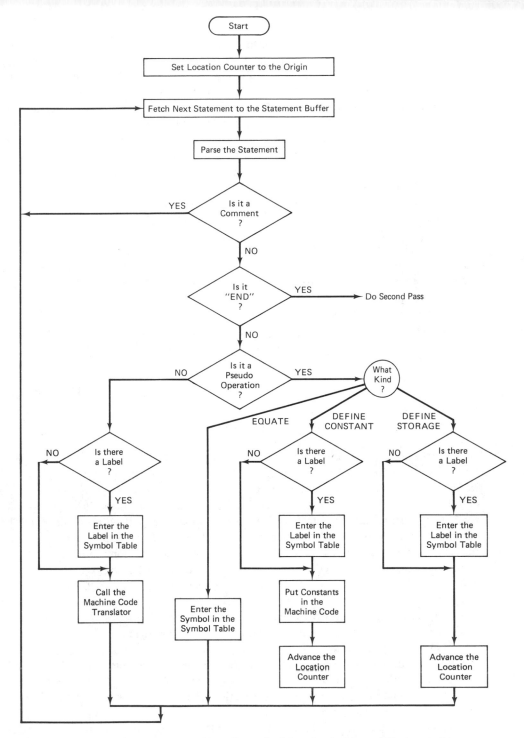

Figure 4-7: First Pass of a Simple Assembler. The work of Pass One in this assembler is to build and complete the Symbol Table and output finalized machine code for all instructions except those which have problems with forward references. Such instructions will be partially translated and marked so they can be dealt with on Pass Two.

On the other hand, if the current instruction is a pseudo-operation, the assembler will branch to processing appropriate for this instruction in the spirit of a case statement. If it is an EQUATE statement, a symbol is immediately put in the Symbol Table. If it is a DEFINE CONSTANT(s) instruction, three things will happen. The label associated with the instruction will be placed in the Symbol Table with the current contents of the location counter used for its value. The constants will be translated and inserted into the memory buffer with the rest of the machine code. And the location counter will be incremented by however many bytes worth of constants were just defined. If we are dealing with a DEFINE STORAGE instruction, the label will be put in the Symbol Table with the appropriate value, and the location counter will be incremented by however many bytes are being set aside for storage use. Sometimes, DEFINE CONSTANT and DEFINE STORAGE instructions are used without labels. In this case, the processing that refers to labels (outlined above) will be bypassed.

There are many binary decision points where questions must be asked about specific parts of the program line that is being assembled. It is the job of the parsing module to recast the information in the program line so that answers to these kinds of questions can be obtained quickly.

What kind of parsing is appropriate here? Since assembler languages are relatively simple, the method of parsing is not the critical thing; almost any method will work. What is of interest is to say what the parser should do and what kind of information it should extract. Operations that involve scanning back and forth in a program line to resolve certain questions of interpretation are very costly in execution time. For instance, an assembler would have to scan a program line to find out whether the keyword was a machine instruction or a pseudo-operation. Later, it might have to scan again to count operands. Ideally, the scanning is all done just once and at one place—that place is the parser.

Let's describe the kind of information the parser should extract and set up in a table (the Parse Table) at the beginning of the work on each line in the program. It would be useful to record several simple pieces of information about some of the fields that could be in the instruction, i.e., the label field, the opcode field, the first two operand fields (note that a DEFINE CONSTANT instruction can have many operands), and the comment field. The information to be recorded is whether the field occurs in this particular instruction, what the address of the first character is, and how long the field is. Other processing modules that need to look at parts of a program line can do so quickly by using this kind of data. It would also be useful to do just enough analysis on the instruction to be able to report two pieces of summary information. The first piece tells whether the instruction is a comment, a normal machine instruction, or a pseudo-operation. The second piece records how many fields are present in this particular instruction.

An ad hoc parser to pull out the kinds of information described here is easily built. It needs to know only what fields are allowed and what their delimiters are. Then, simply by scanning between the delimiters and counting characters and maybe doing a few table look-ups, it can develop the requisite information. Parsing is a ubiquitous topic. We will discuss it in more detail in Chapter 10.

Figure 4-8 shows the details of how a single assembler instruction is translated on

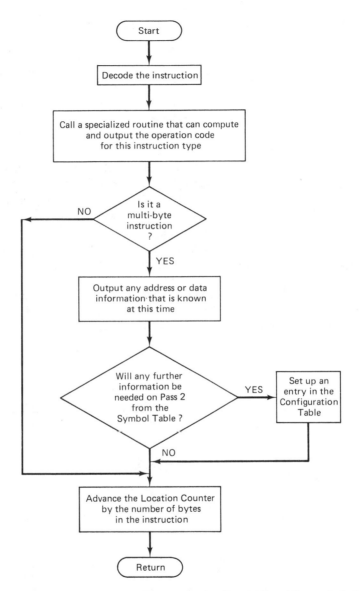

Figure 4-8:   Machine Code Translating Routine (Part of Pass 1 Processing). This routine does the table look-up operations to transform a single mnemonic instruction into the proper operation code. It also outputs any attendant addresses or immediate data that are part of the instruction, if it can. If such information is required but is not accessible, the instruction is marked for further work by leaving an entry in the Configuration Table.

Pass One. It makes sense to partition this translation operation off into a separate subroutine because it is a big and specialized operation. The first thing the flowchart says to do is decode the instruction. This determines which instruction is being translated in such a way that there is a direct operational path for completing the translation. The way we wish to decode instructions is with the aid of a so-called Opcode Translation Table. Figure 4-9 shows part of its layout. Each line in the table relates a type of mnemonic to the name of a specialized routine that is set up to process just that kind of statement. Thus, there is one routine for MOV, another for ADD, another for LXI, another for RET, etc. So the essential ingredient in translation is to search the Opcode Translation Table until the line is found that corresponds to the current statement. This shows the name of a specialized translation routine that is to be used. The translation routine is then called, and it will compute and output the opcode for the current statement.

What kind of search strategy is appropriate for this table? Here is a case where linear search is the best strategy, because there are only 78 different statement types in the 8080 language. Relatively short tables like this can usually be processed quicker with linear search than with binary search. In fact, the search can be made speedy because the most frequently used mnemonics can be put at the front of the table. Five or ten different kinds of mnemonics account for 90 percent of the program lines in most programs. These mnemonics should all be at the front.

We should point out several facts about the translation subroutines. Some of them will be very simple—nothing more than the immediate return of the opcode. Single byte instructions that take no operands are all like this. Other routines will have a fair amount

Mnemonic	Number of bytes in instruction	Subroutine to use for translation
MOV	1	SUB1
LXI	3	SUB2
ADD	1	SUB3
JMP	3	SUB4
CALL	3	SUB5
STA	3	SUB6
LDA	3	SUB7
OUT	2	SUB8
IN	2	SUB9
	•	•
etc.	•	•
	•	•
CMC	1	
XTHL	1	
DAA	1	

Figure 4-9:   The Opcode Translation Table. This table facilitates translating mnemonics to machine codes by allowing the rapid identification of specialized subroutines that know how to work with each mnemonic. The table also records how many bytes are in each instruction. This is important for translating the rest of the instruction beyond the opcode.

of work to do, although it can be done quickly. For instance, there are 63 variations in the Move Statement, all of which get coded differently. Three examples are

```
MOV   M, C
MOV   D, L
MOV   A, E
```

The processing subroutine must use the information returned by the parser to determine which of these variations corresponds to the current statement.

There does not have to be a translating routine for each of the 78 mnemonics. Some groups of mnemonics can easily be served by one composite routine; for instance the nine different kinds of calls are a natural grouping, as are the nine different types of returns.

After an opcode is output, there may be other addresses or data associated with the instruction that can be translated and output at the same time. If so, they are translated. Two examples of where this could be done are an instruction referencing immediate data and an instruction referencing a symbolic address which has already been discovered and is all set up in the Symbol Table ready to go. Two pieces of data are relevant to the decisions the translation machinery has to make: the number of bytes in the instruction, and what is in the last operand field in the instruction as discovered by the parser. This field contains the information governing the rest of the translation.

To finish up the translation, the location counter will be incremented to reflect the number of bytes in the instruction. Finally, if the instruction could not be completely translated, an entry will be made in the Configuration Table reflecting this fact.

Figure 4-10 shows what is required for Pass Two processing in our simple assembler. Pass Two is a loop. Each time through the loop, one of the lines in the Configuration Table is dealt with. The pointer field is used to access a symbol name in the String Storage Buffer. Next, the name is used to retrieve a value from the hashed Symbol Table. Then the value (it is usually an address) is placed in the machine code in the memory buffer at the place shown by the line in the Configuration Table.

After all the lines in the Configuration Table have been processed, the work of the assembler is finished. The assembled code will be in the memory buffer, ready for whatever awaits it. Usually the next thing we will want to do will be to move it into a tape file or a disk file to await further processing by a linker or a loader program.

Let us review once more why we chose to partition the activities between Pass One and Pass Two in the way that we did. The only thing that is absolutely necessary to do on Pass One is to build the Symbol Table. The code could just as well have been output and completely configured on Pass Two instead of most of it on Pass One. Many assemblers work this way. In this case, there would have been no need for us to output a Configuration Table, and the assembler would have been conceptually simpler. However, a substantial penalty would have been paid in the speed of assembly. If the machine code is not output on Pass One, then two complete passes over the source code are required. On each pass, substantial parsing would be necessary: on Pass One to identify symbols and opcodes, and on Pass Two to identify opcodes and operands. Doing parsing two times should be avoided. However, if we get as much of the work as possible done on

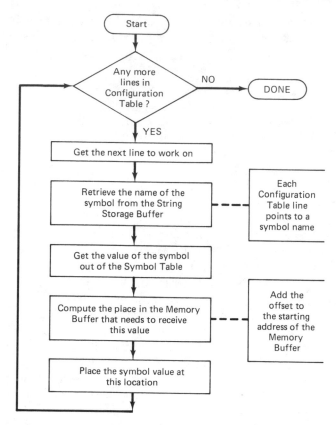

Figure 4-10: The Second Pass of a Simple Assembler. The work of Pass Two is to complete the configuration of the machine code by adding any addresses or other data to the code that was unknown during Pass One.

Pass One, the source code will only have to be looked at and parsed once. Pass Two then becomes very simple. The data it needs are the three tables and the machine code—not the source code.

In order to keep things simple, we haven't shown any error checking in the flowcharts for the basic assembler. The most common kinds of errors will be typing mistakes which make it impossible to parse certain lines in the program, and misused symbols. How would these errors be detected? The parser is an excellent place to check for a number of common errors. The label may be improperly formed; the keyword may be something other than the small set of legal instructions; or an improper set of delimiters may be encountered which would render the fields in the line inseparable. All of these things are easy to detect during the parser's preliminary scan of the program line.

Multiply-defined symbols result from programming errors which attempt to give the same symbol two or more different values in the Symbol Table. If an EQUATE statement is being translated or a statement with a label is being translated, and the assembler finds that the symbol in question is already in the Symbol Table, then something is wrong. The system should give an error message about doubly defined symbols. Any errors of this sort will be detected during Pass One as the Symbol Table is being built.

The other common symbol error is an undefined symbol. If we are trying to translate an instruction with a symbolic operand and find that the symbol is not in the Symbol Table, this is a case of an undefined symbol. In the assembler as we have outlined it, all undefined symbols will be discovered during Pass Two when they are looked up to complete the configuration of instructions that were not finished on Pass One.

4.4 ADDING SYMBOLIC EXPRESSION CAPABILITY

More complicated assemblers will normally allow the use of an expression as the operand of any instruction. An expression is an algebraic combination of symbols and integers. Why would you want to do this? Let's consider some examples. You might want to leave a variable amount of space in a program for insertion of a table that would be built at execution time. The amount of space might depend on the size of a record with which the program was dealing and the number of records. In this case you could set aside space for the table as follows:

```
ALPHA:  DS  NRECORD*RECSIZE
```

Presumably the variables corresponding to the number of records and the record size would be defined somewhere else in the program, probably by EQUATE statements.

It adds some element of adaptability to a program if the amount of storage for a table can be computed rather than explicitly stated. This feature would allow the vendor of a business program to easily produce several different versions of his program that were customized for small, medium, and large businesses. By setting NRECORD with an EQUATE statement at the front of the program, before doing an assembly, he could control table sizes to be appropriate for the intended users.

As another example, suppose the programmer wanted to access information that was contained in the fourth element in an array. He could do it with the following code, which includes an expression:

```
LXI  H, ARRAYSTART + 3
MOV  A, M
```

There are many legitimate and useful applications of expressions in assembly language programming. Most of the expressions are very simple forms such as

```
ALPHA*BETA + DELTA
```

or

```
ALPHA + BETA
```

but sometimes it is desirable to be able to evaluate more complex expressions. What we want to do now is think of how the assembler must be modified to accommodate this additional capability.

It is necessary to specify exactly where expressions will be allowed. Let us say expressions can be the arguments of EQU and DS pseudo-operations, and they can specify the address or data operand in any two or three byte 8080 machine instruction. It does not turn out to be useful to compute the fields associated with one byte instructions.

What forms will expressions be allowed to take? Most assemblers do not allow general algebraic forms with many parentheses to specify the order of evaluation. The penalty for this much generality is much computational overhead associated with finding out what the expression means and checking it for errors. Assemblers usually require a more constrained format which results in easier evaluation. A very common way to do it is to specify that expressions may consist of any number of terms linked by plus or minus signs. A term is a string of symbols and integers linked by multiplication or division operations. Some examples of valid expressions are

```
ALPHA/10  +  BETA*GAMMA*DELTA  -  4

X/Y*R  -  P/Q
```

This kind of loose description is not enough to define unambiguously what an expression means. We must also know the order of evaluation. It is always assumed with these kinds of forms that all terms are to be evaluated first and then they are to be combined together according to the plus or minus signs that link them. We also need some conventions about the order of evaluation within terms. In general, the multiplication and division within a term can give different answers depending on the order in which the operations are carried out. Therefore the most common usage is to specify that the value indicated by a term will be whatever the result would be of evaluating the term moving from left to right and doing the operations in the order they occur. The programmer in assembly language must write expressions such that they will make sense when they are subjected to this or whatever other evaluation procedure his assembler uses.

Should we add expression evaluation to Pass One or Pass Two of our assembler? Pass One allocates memory spaces and outputs operation codes. Clearly there has to be expression evaluation on Pass One because a very common use of expressions is to set up variable length tables. All memory allocation must be completed by the end of Pass One, so that the Symbol Table can be completed. Thus, the expression which says how much space to leave for the table must be evaluated at that time. A variable length table was the intent of our first example:

```
ALPHA:  DS  NRECORD*RECSIZE
```

On the other hand, there are some cases where expressions cannot be evaluated until the second pass because some symbol which is part of that expression is undefined. The symbol may be undefined because it is a forward reference. Our example of referencing an array element could be of this sort:

```
LXI   H,ARRAYSTART + 3
MOV   A,M
```

The routine whose responsibility it is to evaluate expressions must be callable, then, in either Pass One or Pass Two, as circumstances dictate. It will be quite a complicated routine, not because of the evaluation algorithm itself, but because of the need to check for errors and the need to decide whether to do the work on Pass One or Pass Two.

Since it would be wasteful to charge into an expression on Pass One and try to evaluate it only to find that the value of some symbol is missing, we will adopt the strategy of leaving as much expression evaluation until Pass Two as is possible. This won't disturb the overall division of responsibilities between Pass One and Two greatly, because in practice only a small fraction of lines in a program will involve expressions. Whenever the expression evaluator is called, the first thing it should do is decide whether the work is to be done now or later. On Pass One all work can be postponed except when the expression is the argument of an EQUATE or a DEFINE STORAGE statement.

Let's suppose the evaluator routine has decided that the work must be done now. Evaluation is complicated enough that it makes sense to scan the expression twice: once to see if it is properly formed and all the symbols are defined, and once to evaluate it. Our strategy of looking symbols up on the preliminary error finding pass implies that these symbol values should be saved somewhere to prevent the need to look them up again on the evaluation pass.

Let's turn to the evaluation process itself. There are probably many algorithms for doing this. An algorithm that makes only one pass through the expression, that never backs up, and that requires just three storage registers for its operation is shown in Figure 4-11. The storage registers are called TERM, RESULT, and OPERAND.

The basic idea is to scan through the expression left to right and build up the value of each term, one at a time, in a storage location. This can be done by properly initializing the storage location and then doing multiplications and divisions against that location in the order in which these operations occur. When a plus or minus is discovered, it means a complete term value has been built up, so it can be added onto RESULT. Then the storage location for TERM is reinitialized, the scan continues, and the value of the next term is built up, etc. The storage holder for terms should be initialized to plus or minus one depending on the sign that prefaces this part of the expression.

The flowchart for this algorithm frequently asks for "the next token." In the context of these expressions, "the next token" means either the next operator or the value of the next operand that will be discovered as the scan moves through the expression.

There are more potent and systematic ways to evaluate expressions if they are in general algebraic form with parentheses defining the order of operations. We will study these methods in Chapter 11. To use them in assemblers, however, would be overkill.

We should point out several potential difficulties in doing the arithmetic implied by the expression. The final result must fit in either an 8 bit quantity or a 16 bit quantity depending on what assembler statement is being translated. In a complicated expression, the intermediate results may overflow the size of a number that can be maintained in a 16 bit register. The designer has two options: to watch for this and declare it an error if

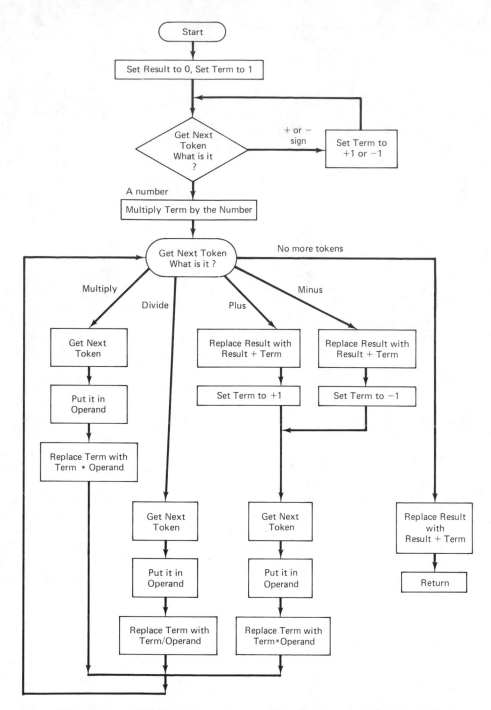

Figure 4-11: An Algorithm for Evaluating Simple Expressions. This algorithm can evaluate expressions formed by terms connected with plus or minus signs. A term consists of symbols or numbers connected by multiplication or division. No parentheses are allowed. The order of evaluation is always left to right.

it occurs, or to do all the arithmetic with extended precision. For instance, all numbers could be assumed to be 32 bit integers and be packed down into an 8 bit or 16 bit frame at the end of the computation. Either of these approaches is a significant complication.

The other potential difficulty is in number representation. We really would like arithmetic that gives results as positive numbers between zero and 65,535. However, the underlying two's complement machinery of the CPU is constructed to regard 16 bit numbers as lying between $-32,768$ and $+32,767$. Again, a good remedy is to use extended precision arithmetic where the range of numbers is greater, and then repack the answer so that it is in the proper form for its intended usage.

Expressions that are to be evaluated on the second pass must be detected and marked in some way on Pass One. The easiest way to do this is to expand the usage of the Configuration Table. Recall that this table identifies all the places in the code where addresses have to be inserted, after the values of the addresses have been determined. We can in addition require the table to mark all those places that have an expression which must be evaluated before the number needed to configure the code can be determined.

The Expanded Configuration Table would perhaps look as in Figure 4-12A. The pointer column and the offset column are there as in the original version. Before, when an unknown symbol was discovered, its name would be copied to the String Storage Buffer and the pointer field would be used to record where the name was stored. Now we want to expand this usage so that the complete text of expressions that are to be evaluated on Pass Two will be copied into the String Storage Buffer. Their position in this buffer will also be recorded by the pointer field of the Configuration Table. Figure 4-12A shows an example of a Configuration Table that is keeping track of some expressions. Figure 4-12B shows how the String Storage Buffer would look in this case.

We have added a new column to the Expanded Configuration Table. The purpose is to record the type of configuration that is required. There are four possibilities. The first possibility is a single symbol which must be packaged into the second and third bytes of an instruction. An example would be all the places where an address is needed, but where it is not ready because of forward references. For completeness, we should now take account of a second kind of single symbol configuration: one in which the data is packed down into the second byte of a two byte instruction. An example would be instructions such as

```
OUT   ALPHA
MVI   A,BETA
```

This usage is less common than the normal situation of address configuration. What about expressions? Once again there will be cases where the result of expression evaluation should be packed in one or in two bytes. This information should be recorded when the entry is first made into the Expanded Configuration Table.

The work of Pass Two is still to process the Configuration Table line by line and add parts of instructions to the code at those places that need further configuration. Single symbol configurations will be handled as we described previously except that the symbol

Pointer to Stored Symbol Name or Expression	Type of Configuration	Insert Value at this Offset
DC00	symbol-2bytes	000A
DC06	symbol-1byte	0023
DC0C	expression-2bytes	0027
DC12	expression-1byte	0042
DC1A	symbol-2bytes	0049
etc.		

Figure 4-12A: Expanded Configuration Table. If an assembler allows expressions, there will be more work to do on Pass Two. In addition to its normal usage, the Configuration Table must record all places where expressions have to be evaluated to produce numbers in order to finish the configuration of instructions.

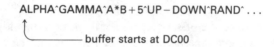

ALPHA^GAMMA^A*B + 5^UP – DOWN^RAND^ . . .

⎿————— buffer starts at DC00

Figure 4-12B: The String Storage Buffer With Expressions. The String Storage Buffer normally stores the names of symbols that will have to be looked up on Pass Two. It is little extra work to use the buffer for the additional function of recording the text of expressions that have to be evaluated on Pass Two. This type of recording eliminates the need for a second look at the source code.

value may now be packed into either one or two bytes. When a line in the table indicates expression evaluation, here is what will happen. The pointer into the String Storage Buffer will be used to retrieve the actual text of the expression. It will be passed to an expression evaluation routine like the one shown in Figure 4-11. This routine will reduce the expression to a single number using data from the Symbol Table. Finally the number will be inserted in the machine code at the place indicated by the offset field, and it will be inserted in either one or two bytes depending on what is coded in the Type of Configuration Field. By the end of Pass Two, all code is configured.

4.5   ASSEMBLER CODE THAT CAN BE RELOCATED

An absolute assembler will translate assembler language into machine language that is configured to fit in only one area in memory. And that area begins with the address that was specified on the ORIGIN statement which is the first statement in the program. It is also possible to assemble code in a way so that you don't have to specify at assembly time where it will be placed in memory. There are certain advantages to this which will be explored later. This is called relocatable code. It will be incompletely configured code in the sense that some more address information will have to be added to the code at the point when it is to be installed in some specific area in memory.

Instructions that contain direct addresses are the ones that must be dealt with in a special way if code is to be relocatable. All other instructions will be translated just the same with absolute or relocating assemblers. The 8080 instructions that specify direct addresses are

```
LDA
STA
LHLD
SHLD
JMP and all conditional jumps
CALL and all conditional calls
```

Let us explore why direct addresses are important. The 8080 code for a jump instruction is one byte for the operation code (C3) followed by two bytes which specify a 16 bit address to be transferred to. Examine the jump instruction in the example program shown in Figure 4-1. Actually this is a variant of the simple jump instruction, because the jump will be taken only if the result of executing the previous instruction was nonzero. This particular program was assembled starting at location 0100H. The address part of the jump instruction is 0105H. If the whole program had been assembled to start at location 0300H, then the address in the jump instruction would have been 0305H. If the program had been assembled to start at location, 0400H, then the jump address would have been 0405H, etc. Instructions which use direct addresses are sensitive to where the code will ultimately lie in memory. If you are assembling a program with a relocatable origin, that means you don't know where it is going to be in memory. It could be anywhere. So it will be impossible to complete the configuration of any instructions that use direct addresses during such an assembly.

The way direct addresses can be accommodated is to have the assembler fill the address bytes with the relative address of the target location that is being referred to. The relative address means the number of the byte at the place being referenced relative to the start of the program. This address will be constant no matter where the program is ultimately installed in memory. However, when the program is ultimately loaded, some piece of software will have to come in and change the relative address to an absolute address because the 8080 only understands absolute addresses. It is very simple to make this change. All that must be done is to add the address of where the program is being loaded to every location in the program that needs to specify a direct address. This will convert all the relative addresses to correct absolute addresses.

Very few changes are necessary in order for the assembler to output relocatable code. A new pseudo-operation must be specified at the start of the program to tell the assembler to produce relocatable code. That pseudo-operation is usually indicated by

```
RORG
```

The assembler will react to this by outputting a new table in addition to the normal machine code that is the final assembler output. It will do the assembly with everything else just the same as if you had asked for an absolute assembly of code that was to start at location 0. If we start the code here, all direct addresses that are produced by the assembler will automatically be correct relative addresses.

The additional table will be called the Direct Address Table. It will record the locations in the machine code that will require further work when the code is loaded. In fact, all the further work that is required will be to add the starting location of the program onto all of these locations. Actually, doing this final work is the job of the linking loader, but in order that this may be done later on, the assembler must output a Direct Address Table of some sort to show the linking loader where to act.

How should we prepare the Direct Address Table? Probably the easiest way is to add a module to the Machine Code Translator that is part of Pass One. The translator is shown in Figure 4-8. When the table look-up operation is done to get the opcode for an instruction, the table can be checked to see whether the instruction involves a direct address (i.e., put another column in the Opcode Translation Table). If it does, the value of the location counter can be output immediately into a file or a memory buffer that will become the Direct Address Table. If it is output at this time, the Location Counter will have the same value as the offset address in the machine code of the place we want to mark as a direct address.

The example program of Figure 4-1 could have been specified as a relocatable assembly by changing the first statement in the program to RORG. The machine code

Memory Address (hexadecimal)		Assembler Code		Machine Code (hexadecimal)	
		RORG		; SET RELOCATABLE ORIGIN	
00		SUB	A	; ZERO ACCUMULATOR	97
01		LXI	H, 0200H	; GET HOW MANY TO ADD	21
02					00
03					02
04		MOV	C, M	; C WILL BE A COUNTER	4E
05	LOOP:	INX	H	; POINT TO FIRST NUMBER	23
06		ADD	M	; ADD TO ACCUMULATOR	86
07		DCR	C	; DECREMENT COUNTER	0D
08		JNZ	LOOP	; GO BACK FOR MORE	C2
09					05
0A					00
0B		STA	DEPOT	; ACCUM. TO STORAGE LOC.	32
0C					0F
0D					00
0E		HLT		; PROCESSING DONE	76
0F	DEPOT:	DS	1	; ANSWER TO BE PUT HERE	

Figure 4-13:   An Example of a Relocatable Assembly. This program is the example of Figure 4-1 assembled so that the code will be relocatable. Most of the machine code is just the same as in the program of Figure 4-1; however, statements involving direct addresses now produce different code. The machine code from this relocatable assembly is exactly the same as what would be produced if the assembler had been told to do an absolute assembly at location 0000H.

would look just the same except for the statements that reference LOOP and DEPOT. Figure 4-13 shows this program assembled with the relocatable origin. The Direct Address Table that would result from this assembly is shown in Figure 4-14.

Offset Locations of
All Direct Addresses
0009
000C

Figure 4-14: An Example of the Direct Address Table. This table identifies the locations in a program where direct addresses occur. The locations are recorded relative to the start of the machine code. To relocate the program, the loading point address must be added on to all these locations. This particular table would have been generated by the assembly shown in Figure 4-13.

STUDY QUESTIONS AND EXERCISES

1. Assume you have been given the task of writing a one pass assembler. It will be a true one pass assembler in that after each source code line is scanned and processed, nothing more ever needs to be done on behalf of that line. No further configuration is allowed. You are told that the program input will always be suitable for this kind of processing. In what way(s) must programs to be used with the one pass assembler be written more restrictively than normal assembler programs? Write a flowchart showing the processing that must be done by the one pass assembler.

2. Disassembly means working backwards from a machine code program in an attempt to recreate the original assembler program. Could a disassembler totally recreate the original program? Think up a disassembly algorithm and try your algorithm on a real program. Where would it fail? Write a flowchart for a disassembler.

3. In the Appendix of this book, Figure A-3, there is a short program that finds the minimum element in a small array. Assume that this program is to be given a relocatable assembly with an RORG. Answer the following questions about it:
   (a) List the machine code image of the program as developed by the assembler after the first pass.
   (b) Generate the Symbol Table, Configuration Table, and String Storage Buffer for the first pass of the program assembly.
   (c) List the memory content in hexadecimal that would be developed for the entire assembled program after the second pass.
   (d) Show the Direct Address Table for this program.

4. It is sometimes easy to become confused over exactly when an expression will be evaluated. Write an assembly language program fragment in which the expression "ALPHA + BETA" is evaluated at assembly time. Write another assembly language program fragment in which "ALPHA + BETA" is evaluated at execution time. The expression doesn't have to be used

for the same purpose in each case. You can assume ALPHA and BETA are stored or represented in any place that is convenient to your examples.

5. Write a detailed flowchart for a statement parser that will operate on a line of 8080 assembler program text and produce the kind of output described in the book.

6. Estimate the average time (in terms of the number of instructions executed) that it would take an assembler to do the assembly of just one line in a short program such as the examples given in this chapter. Justify your estimate. Which instructions could be translated quickly? Which would take a long time?

7. Write a 16 bit subtraction subroutine for the 8080 processor. The routine should be such that the number in the DE register pair is subtracted from the number in the HL register pair and the answer is left in the HL pair. Use 2's complement representation for all numbers. A routine similar to this will be necessary for the use of the expression evaluator in the assembler.

8. Get a listing for a large assembler program written in 8080 and analyze the program to find the frequency of usage of the different statement types.

9. Imagine that we want to translate opcodes (i.e., the first byte in an 8080 instruction) solely by a table look-up procedure with no special translating routines. How would the table be searched? How would the search key be constructed? What would be the impact on the other parts of the processing as we have outlined it?

10. Think about the machine code translating module used on Pass One. After the opcode has been output, outline the logic the program has to use to decide whether it can translate the remaining parts of the instruction. What data structures does it consult for the information it needs to make this translation? How does it make the translation?

5

Linkers and Loaders

5.1 INTRODUCTION: HANDLING LONGER PROGRAMS

Relocation and linking are two sides of the same coin. In this introduction we have to consider why you would want to link code, generally how you could do it, and what burdens this requirement will make on the output of an assembler. Next, we will discuss in detail the implementation of a linker that could work in conjunction with the 8080 assembler we have been examining. Then we will discuss how to integrate prewritten program libraries into a program being developed. We will conclude with a look at several strategies for loading completely configured programs.

Most programs of any size are not submitted all at once to an assembler. Instead, the program will be constructed of modules, and each module will receive a separate relocatable assembly. Modular programming is very desirable. It allows the work to be divided up among a team of programmers, and it enhances the testability of the program. If each of the parts can be completely tested in isolation from the main program, the chances that the whole thing will work without many bugs are good. The reason for small, testable modules is that programmers have found empirically that the amount of testing required increases exponentially with the length of the program for many types of programs.

At some point all the parts will have to be integrated together, and perhaps combined with some standard routines from some other source (like a program library) and then installed in memory. This task of integrating the modules together is called linking. The linking and installing in memory will frequently be done at one time by the linking loader, although the two processes are distinct. We need to concentrate now on what additional pieces of information an assembler must supply in order for its modules to be linked later on.

The need for linking arises because statements in one module may refer to locations in another module, and we are presuming these modules have been assembled separately. The programmer will need to tell the assembler explicitly which symbols in a module submitted to the assembler refer to symbols that are in other modules. Otherwise, the assembler would think there were errors in what it was assembling, because it wouldn't discover values for some of the symbols in the normal course of the assembly. When a statement in one module refers to a symbol which is associated with another module, it is called an external reference. The programmer will need to declare all external references at the start of each module, with a new pseudo-operation. If module A refers to symbols ALPHA and GAMMA which mark locations in another module, then one of the first statements in module A will have to be

        EXTERNAL   ALPHA, GAMMA

Likewise, it will be necessary for the programmer to identify explicitly any symbols in a module that will be referred to from outside, from another module. These are called entry points. For example, if the module being assembled contains a statement labeled by BETA, and this statement will be referred to from outside, then BETA needs to be declared by still another pseudo-operation as an entry point.

        ENTRY   BETA

If a module is going to be linked later on, it will have to furnish, as part of its output, information on all external references and entry points associated with the module. It can do this by outputting an Entry/Externals Table along with each module in addition to the normal assembler output. This table will use a line for each symbol. On that line will be the name of the symbol, whether it is an entry point or an external reference, and where the symbol appears in the code. If it appears in several places, there will be one table line for each appearance. For entry points, where it appears in the code means the number of the first byte in the instruction identified by the entry point label. For external references, where it appears in the code means the number of the first byte where an address should be inserted when the external reference is resolved (i.e., a value is found for the symbol).

How this table is used to determine absolute addresses at the places where they are needed and how the code can be prepared for loading will be discussed in the next section. The reader can examine Figure 5-2 to see an example of the Entry/Externals Table.

5.2   THE LINKING PROCEDURE

The input to the linker will consist of three kinds of output from each module being linked. There must be a file that has the machine code in relocatable form. There will also be two tables. The Direct Address Table indicates the relative address in the machine code of all places that require the insertion of direct addresses when the program is ultimately installed in memory. The Entry/Externals Table gives the relative address of all places where an entry point appears or where an external reference is made. A code will indicate whether the associated symbol is an entry or external reference. The table dedicates one line to each symbol, and if the symbol occurs in several places, there will be a line for each occurrence.

The linker can keep all its tables and various versions of the evolving code in memory, or they can be stored on the disk. This is a design decision that depends on the hardware environment in which the linker will be used. We have decided to keep as much of the intermediate information on disk as possible, and perhaps make more passes through the code than necessary, for the following reason. Small computers, without memory mapping hardware, typically have an address space of about 64 kilobytes. If we have the operating system, plus the linking loader, plus linker tables, plus intermediate results, plus the code being configured, all in memory at the same time, then the size of the program we can ultimately link may become severely limited. Because of these considerations we decided to implement the linker in three passes with only such files and tables being in memory at any time as are absolutely necessary.

Now we are ready to describe what happens on the various passes. As the description evolves, please refer to the example in Figure 5-1. Here we have three 8080 programs that were assembled as separate modules. The first module is a main program. It does very little. It calls a subroutine which executes and returns a single byte in the accumulator. The main program then outputs that byte to port one. The second module is the subroutine that is called by the main program. Its function is to find the maximum value in an array of one byte numbers. The third module is the array of numbers on which the rest of the program works. The first position in the array says how many numbers there are. The following positions contain the numbers. Incidentally, the third module only contains data structures. There is no executable code in it.

The tables output during separate assemblies of these modules are shown in Figure 5-2.

There are three kinds of symbols in these programs that are important for linking. They are local address variables, externals, and entry points. Local address variables are symbols that are used in such a way that their definitions and all references to them occur in the same module. The local address variables will be dealt with according to the simple techniques we studied previously in connection with relocation. No linking is required, but an offset will have to be added onto each of the local direct addresses when it is known where the module that contains them will be loaded. This is the standard relocation procedure. It is customary, however, to coalesce this function into the linker. In Figure 5-1, the local address variables are all in the module called MAXFIND. They are called LOOPST, SWCH, NOSWCH, and LOOPEN. Two of these variables are never referred to in the code. They are there only for the convenience of the programmer in understanding what the program does.

Linking will begin with the linker ascertaining, in some way, what modules you want to link, and where you want them loaded. The user will be able to specify to the

Text of Program One		*Relative Location*	*Relocatable Code*
	; PROGRAM MAIN		
	RORG		
	EXTERNAL MAXVAL		
	CALL MAXVAL	0000	CD 00 00
	OUT 1	0003	D3 01
	HLT	0005	76
	END		

Text of Program Two		*Relative Location*	*Relocatable Code*
	; PROGRAM MAXFIND		
	RORG		
	ENTRY MAXVAL		
	EXTERNAL DATANB, DATA		
MAXVAL:	LDA DATANB	0000	3A 00 00
	MOV B, A	0003	47
	DCR B	0004	05
	LXI H, DATA	0005	21 00 00
	MOV A, M	0008	7E
LOOPST:	INX H	0009	23
	CMP M	000A	BE
	JP NOSWCH	000B	F2 0F 00
SWCH:	MOV A, M	000E	7E
NOSWCH:	DCR B	000F	05
LOOPEN:	JNZ LOOPST	0010	C2 09 00
	RET	0013	C9
	END		

Text of Program Three		*Relative Location*	*Relocatable Code*
	; PROGRAM DATASET		
	RORG		
	ENTRY DATANB, DATA		
DATANB:	DB 3	0000	03
DATA:	DB 4	0001	04
	DB 1	0002	01
	DB 10	0003	0A
	END		

Figure 5-1: Three Modules to be Linked. These modules illustrate three types of symbols: local, external, and entry, each of which must be handled differently during relocation and linking.

linker separate load points for modules or, alternatively, that they will be squeezed together, one after another, from some given starting point.

Here is what happens on Pass One. The linker passes over all routines and adds the appropriate load points to all direct addresses that reference local symbols. Then it writes the altered code back to disk. The only places where our example code would be altered would be in the 16 bit words that start at relative locations 000C and 0011 in the

A. Direct Address Tables. No Direct Address Tables would be generated for Programs One and Three. These programs contain only entries and external references. The Direct Address Table for Program Two is shown.

Relative Address
000CH
0011H

B. Entry/Externals Tables

Symbol	Type	Program	Relative Address	
MAXVAL	External	MAIN	0001H	Table for Program One
MAXVAL	Entry	MAXFIND	0000H	Table for Program Two
DATANB	External	MAXFIND	0001H	
DATA	External	MAXFIND	0006H	
DATANB	Entry	DATASET	0000H	Table for Program Three
DATA	Entry	DATASET	0001H	

Figure 5-2:   Tables Generated by the Assembler for Three Example Modules. The most general sort of relocating assembler will output tables that identify two sorts of direct addresses that must remain unconfigured at assembly time. Local address variables that are direct addresses and external references cannot be configured until the code is linked.

MAXFIND routine. These places must ultimately contain the direct addresses of local symbols NOSWCH and LOOPST. Pass One completes all processing that has to be done to service local symbols.

The other thing that Pass One has to do is to copy all of the Entry/Externals Tables from all the modules one after another into a memory buffer, so that all the information will be there simultaneously. We need to use all these tables together in order to resolve external references. We will call this table the Augmented Entry/Externals Table because some more columns will be added to it beyond the information that was present in the Entry/Externals Tables put out by the assembler.

Between Pass One and Pass Two, the Augmented Entry/Externals Table will be completed. As part of doing this, all external references will be resolved. When the table is being built, the entries will be put together in one part and the externals will be collected in another part. If the program hasn't made an error, for every external listed in the table there will be a corresponding entry. Actually, several external references may map to one entry because references to the same external location may have been made in a number of places. For example, let's say BETA is an external symbol in a particular module. Perhaps the module contains ten separate subroutine calls to BETA in different places. They look like this:

        CALL   BETA

The assembler will then detect ten external references, and it will generate ten lines in the ENTRY/EXTERNALS Table for the module.

        The load points for the modules and the Augmented Entry/Externals Table now contain all necessary information about the meaning of symbols. At this point, it is implicit. During processing to complete the Augmented Entry/Externals Table, it is made explicit. It is best to consider an example to see how this may be done. Figure 5-3 shows the Augmented Entry/Externals Table as it would look after coalescing all the symbol references from all the modules. Let us focus on the symbol named DATA. It is an entry point in the DATASET module, and it is an external reference in the MAXFIND module.

        Figure 5-3B shows the Augmented Entry/Externals Table after it has been com-

A. The Augmented Entry/Externals Table (Before Processing)

Symbol	Type	Program	Relative Address	Load Point	Value of the Symbol
MAXVAL	ENTRY	MAXFIND	0000H		
DATANB	ENTRY	DATASET	0000H		
DATA	ENTRY	DATASET	0001H		
MAXVAL	EXTERNAL	MAIN	0001H		
DATANB	EXTERNAL	MAXFIND	0001H		
DATA	EXTERNAL	MAXFIND	0006H		

B. The Augmented Entry/Externals Table (After Processing)

Symbol	Type	Program	Relative Address	Load Point	Value of the Symbol
MAXVAL	ENTRY	MAXFIND	0000H	1020H	1020H
DATANB	ENTRY	DATASET	0000H	5000H	5000H
DATA	ENTRY	DATASET	0001H	5000H	5001H
MAXVAL	EXTERNAL	MAIN	0001H	N.N.	1020H
DATANB	EXTERNAL	MAXFIND	0001H	N.N.	5000H
DATA	EXTERNAL	MAXFIND	0006H	N.N.	5001H

Note: N.N. means not needed,

Figure 5-3:   Table Manipulations to Resolve External References. All external references are resolved between Pass 1 and Pass 2 using this table. Everything about entry points is known at this stage of linking. For every external reference in the table, there is an entry point. This coupling allows sufficient address information to be developed for all the external references.

pletely filled in. Let us assume that we have told the linker that MAIN will be loaded at location 1000H, MAXFIND will be loaded at 1020H, and that DATASET will be loaded at location 5000H. The load point of DATASET plus the relative address of DATA in the procedure where it is an entry point indicate the actual address associated with this symbol: 5001H. We will call this the value of the symbol DATA. Once this value is determined, it can also be written into the table on the line where DATA is cited as an external. It will be written into the last column. This information is what we need to resolve an external reference and complete the configuration of the code at one point in program two. We have now determined what address was being referred to by this line in the MAXFIND program:

```
LXI   H,DATA
```

Let's review the processing in the Augmented Entry/Externals Table one more time. The first thing that happens is that the entry section is completely filled in. All the symbols in the entry section were labels in the code. What we are really doing at this point is establishing an absolute address to associate with each of these labels. And this is easy to do. In every case, it is the relative address of the label plus the starting address (load point) of the program it is in. This address is the value of the symbol that is being used as a label. Now we are in a position to resolve the external references in the second part of the table. All we have to do is copy symbol values for all the symbols in the upper part of the table into the last column for the same symbols in the lower part of the table. These values are the numbers that will ultimately be inserted in the machine code at the sites of external references.

In Pass Two, the processing by the linker is very simple. It must go through the Externals part of the Augmented Entry/Externals Table and do some processing for each line. All that is required is for it to pick up the number that is in the Value of Symbol Field and write it into the actual code for this module at the position in the code indicated by the relative address. To pick up our example again, the number 5001 must be inserted into the code for program MAXFIND at the relative address 0006.

In Pass Three, the linked modules must be combined into one file that is suitable for being installed in memory by a loader. Several different formats are possible corresponding to a trade-off between programming ease and loader efficiency. Almost all loadable files begin with a header containing summary information. This is followed by a mixture of program code and address information showing where the code should be installed. Occasionally, the file will end with a trailer of some sort that is used for error checking.

There are three common formats for files which contain programs ready to be installed by the loader. Let's examine their characteristics:

1. Every byte of data has an address associated with it which specifies where to put that byte in memory. Thus the whole program file consists of a series of address-data units. The virtue of this format is that it can be installed in memory by a very simple loader. It is also obviously very inefficient with respect to the amount of disk or tape storage space it requires.

2. The file consists of a sequence of bytes that is the exact memory image of how the program will look in memory. Associated information kept in the header will be the loading point and the number of data bytes in the file. This format may be inefficient if the program is located in several widely separated locations in memory. It also has poor error checking properties because the unit of code on which checking is done (i.e., the whole program at once) is too big.

3. The program is broken up into blocks each of which has an associated load point, byte count, and a checksum for local error checking. This is a superior format for most uses.

The format we are going to use for program loading is the third version. The loadable file will consist of a header followed by a number of variable length blocks. The header for the whole file contains two pieces of information: the name of the file including an extension for file type, and the number of blocks in the file. A block has the following structure: the first piece of information is the load point, which is the address at which the code should start in memory. The next piece of information is the number of bytes of information in this particular block. After this comes an exact disk image of the code as it will be in memory. The feature that defines a block is that it is one continuous stretch of code. If there are any embedded holes, places that don't belong to the program, or long, uninitialized tables, then the block should end before this region begins and a new block should begin after the region ends. The last item in the block is a checksum for error detection.

Pass 1:   Adds load points to local variable direct
                addresses in the code. Coalesces entries
                and externals all together to begin the
                Augmented Entry/Externals Table.

Between Pass 1 and Pass 2:
                All external references are resolved. To
                do this, the Augmented Table is com-
                pleted. Actual Addresses for all entries
                are copied into the Value of Symbol fields
                for the externals.

Pass 2:   External reference direct addresses are
                inserted into the code for each module.

Pass 3:   All modules are read one more time and
                formatted into a loadable program file.

Figure 5-4: Summary of the Pass Structure of the Linker. In order to be able to link long programs, the linker is implemented in a number of passes so that the minimum amount of memory is taken up by systems software overhead at any time. The basic task of the linker is to complete the code for several kinds of direct addresses that are still unconfigured at link time.

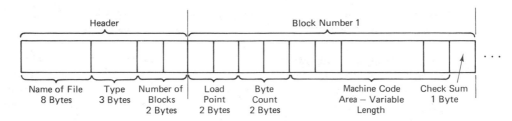

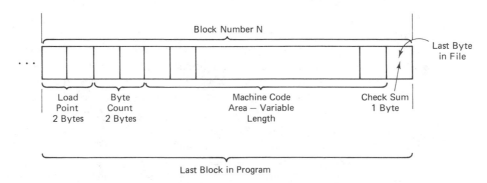

Figure 5-5:   A Loadable Program File. A file consists of an identifying header followed by a number of variable length blocks. Each block has all the code that goes into a particular contiguous area in memory. The typical block size is several hundred bytes.

There is an easy way to use the checksum. As each block is being formatted by the linker, all the data in the block will be added up. The low order byte of that sum can be used as the last piece of data in the block. This data is the checksum. When the loader installs the block in memory, it will recompute the checksum. If everything is all right, the recomputed checksum will agree with the one originally recorded in the block.

Figure 5-4 summarizes all the linking operations we have been discussing. Figure 5-5 depicts the layout of a loadable program file. In a later section of this chapter, we we will consider what a loader can do with a file like this.

5.3 LINKING WITH PROGRAM LIBRARIES

Frequently, certain standard routines that many users will want to access are collected together in a library. An example would be routines for floating point operations, exponentiation, and trigonometry that were meant to be used with assembly language programs. The library contains the normal relocatable image of each module, i.e., machine code in relocatable form, the Direct Address Table, and the Entry/Externals Table. How can a programmer access these modules? It is usually very easy. When the user assembles his program modules, he takes no notice of the library routines that he will need, except that the names of these modules appear as external references in some of the user's programs. At linking time, the linker will automatically pick up any library modules that are needed.

How is this done? Between Pass One and Pass Two, the linker tries to resolve all external references and complete the Augmented Entry/Externals Table. If there is an external reference for which no entry can be found in the modules supplied by the user, then there are two possibilities: either it is an error, or the reference corresponds to an entry point in a subroutine in a standard library that is part of the system and accessible to users.

To accommodate this second possibility, we need to specify some more processing between Pass One and Pass Two. If any external reference can't be found, the linker must search through any libraries that are part of the system to see whether the module is there. In some systems, the linker will automatically search all libraries. In others, the user must tell the linker which specific libraries to examine. If a needed module is found in the libraries, several things will have to be done. Basically, the module needs to be brought to the same form as all of the user submitted modules. This means the system must calculate a load point for the new module and configure the direct addresses in it. Then the code can be appended to the file of user modules, and the new entry and externals information can be merged into the Augmented Table.

After a complete scan through all the library modules, the linker should restart the standard processing that attempts to complete the Augmented Entry/Externals Table. A problem may arise here. Even if the library is sufficient to resolve all references, several passes through the library may be necessary because the new modules that are picked up may have unresolved external references themselves. This calls for some iteration. Eventually a scan will have been made in which nothing new is picked up from the library. If there are still unresolved externals, the program is in error. Otherwise, we can go on to Pass Two.

All other processing can proceed as we have already discussed. Where library modules will be kept and the operational details of how to coalesce them with the user modules can greatly affect system efficiency. This must be carefully considered in the actual design of a system.

5.4   THE LOADING PROCEDURE

How the loading phase works depends in detail on the output of Pass Three from the linker. If we wished to have the very simplest loader possible, then we would have set the linker up to output three bytes of information for every byte to be loaded into memory. The first two bytes would specify an address, and the next byte would specify what should be loaded into that address. If we use this structure, a loadable program file consists of a great many of these three byte units prefaced by a count stating how many units there are in the program. The loader itself is extremely simple. It is a loop in which addresses are read and data deposited in those addresses until a count is satisfied. Bootstrap loaders are frequently like this. A bootstrap loader is a very simple loader whose only

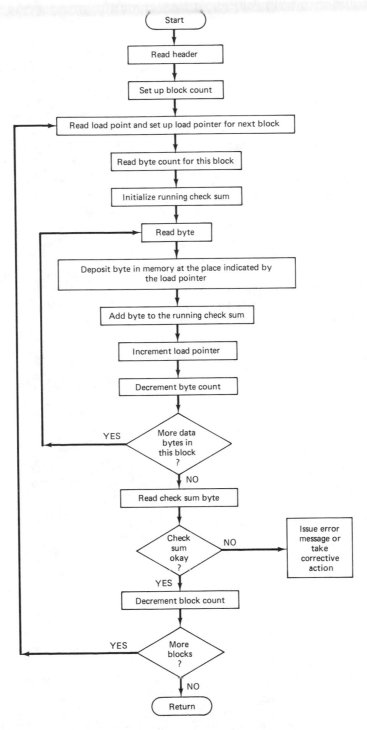

Figure 5-6: A Simple Loader That Uses a Blocked Program File. This program implements an efficient kind of loading where the program to be loaded consists of a series of blocks of code, each of which has an associated starting address, byte count, and checksum.

function is to get a more complex loader into the machine. The more complex loader then loads the rest of the system. If you had to toggle a loader into computer memory from the switches on a front panel (as was the case with some early machines), you would want it to be very simple.

A loader for the straight memory image type of program format was discussed in Section 3.5 when we were looking at the design for a ROM monitor.

The loader we will need to go with the linker we studied in this chapter requires a loadable program file in the form of variable length blocks where each block represents one contiguous region in memory. The file structure is shown in Figure 5-5. The character of the loading is the same as before but a little more complicated. There are two loops. The outer loop counts which block is being loaded. The inner loop handles a particular block. There is another count and a load point in each block. Since we are dealing with a contiguous area of memory, the only address that needs to be specified is the beginning address. The code is loaded sequentially from that address toward the high end of memory. While each block is being loaded, its checksum is being recomputed. If the stored checksum and the one just computed don't agree, the loader may just issue an error message and stop, or it may take corrective action such as trying again on that particular block. Figure 5-6 shows the details of this kind of loader.

STUDY QUESTIONS AND EXERCISES

1. Consider the following nonsense program:

```
                RORG
                ENTRY   BETA
                EXTERNAL ALPHA, OMEGA
        BETA:   LXI    H, 41H
                SHLD   GAMMA
        DELTA:  POP    PSW
                STA    ALPHA
                CALL   OMEGA
                JMP    DELTA
        GAMMA:  DS     2
                END
```

   (a) By hand, assemble the program into the machine code that would result from a relocatable assembly.
   (b) What places in the machine code will require more configuration when the code is linked? Describe the kinds of configuration that will be required in each instance.

2. In 8080 relocatable assemblies, are there any symbolic addresses used in program lines that will appear in neither the Direct Address nor the Entry/Externals Table? Do any addresses appear in both tables?

3. What kind of error checking should our linker have? During or between what passes should error checks be inserted?

4. Construct three "dummy modules," one of which comes in with programs from the user, and two of which are in system libraries. With these modules, show how it could be necessary for a linking system to go through the processing at the end of Pass One several times before all external references were resolved. The modules need contain no actual code, only declarations.

5. Design the dialog for a user interface through which a user could give instructions to a linking loader of the type discussed here.

6. Many microprocessor instruction sets contain the "jump relative" instruction. When translated to machine code, this instruction consists of an opcode followed by a one or two byte field that represents a displacement. The effect of executing the instruction is to add the displacement, whatever it is, to the current value of the program counter. In doing an assembly, what account has to be taken of this instruction, in order for the resulting code to be relocatable?

7. An executable program is stored on tape in the following format: a ten second lead-in tone, two marker bytes, two bytes that give the count of the total number of program bytes that will be installed in memory (let's say it is n), and finally n data units. Each data unit consists of 3 bytes; the first two bytes specify a loading address, and the next byte is the data that is to go there. Write the flowchart for a loader that would read this tape, load the program, and transfer control to it.

6

Macroprocessors

6.1 INTRODUCTION: EXPANDING THE USEFULNESS OF LANGUAGES WITH MACROS

Before we say what macros are, let's consider some of the places where macros can be easily and profitably applied:

1. To expand a standard programming language with new statements.
2. To quickly implement a special purpose application language.
3. To allow a software package to be easily customized to a particular hardware environment.
4. To facilitate the operation of language translation software systems such as compilers.

The kind of software structure that is capable of all this power is really something very simple. A macro is a statement in one language that can be used to refer to one or a group of related lines of code in another language. Stated another way, the macro name can be considered an abbreviation which stands for some related lines of code. Macros are most frequently found in association with assembler languages, although some of the more complicated higher level languages have them too. For instance, PL/1 has a macro capability.

The idea of using a consistent abbreviation to stand for a set of program lines is deceptively simple, but, if a few related features are added, macros become very useful. The most common features, in addition to this abbreviation idea, are parameter substitution and conditional assembly. Parameter substitution means that the code that corresponds to the macro can be configured with changeable parameters which are mentioned as part of the process of invoking the macro. Conditional assembly means that not all of the macro code has to be used. Different parts can be used as circumstances dictate.

In this chapter, we will demonstrate the various features of a simple macroprocessor and discuss how one could be implemented.

6.2   FEATURES OF MACROPROCESSOR SYSTEMS

In order to appreciate how the fabulous applications mentioned in the introduction have been set up, we need to discuss in detail some of the common features found in macro-processing systems. All our examples will consider macroprocessors in relation to as-semblers, but the reader should feel free to generalize to any other system where that seems useful. In fact, macro systems are easy to set up, so you can expect that they will have been implemented in almost any environment where there is anything to gain by it.

The most basic of the macro features is the so-called *copy-code* facility. Let us imagine coding an assembler program in which we find in a number of places that we always use the same sequence of instructions. The copy-code idea is to somehow associate an abbreviation with the set of statements that are always the same, and write the ab-breviation instead of the statements where appropriate. In order to make this useful, there would also have to be some piece of software that would process our assembler program and produce a new program in which the proper code was substituted for the corresponding abbreviation. This is just a kind of text manipulation operation, and the software that will do this is called a *macroprocessor*.

Some standard terminology can be introduced now. The abbreviation is called the *macro name*. When it appears in a program that consists of a mixed grouping of assembler statements and abbreviations, each abbreviation is referred to as a *macro call*. A macro can be called simply by using its name at the places where text should be inserted. The standard group of assembler statements, which are represented by the abbreviation, to-gether with a few extra things form the *macro definition*. The process of taking a source program consisting of a mixture of abbreviations and normal program statements and substituting code for the abbreviations is called *macro expansion*. Figure 6-1 shows what is involved during a macro expansion.

Macroprocessors can be separate, stand-alone text processing programs that are not integrated with any other software entity. But they are most frequently found in association with one of the standard language translation programs such as an assembler or a compiler. If an assembler begins with a stage of macro processing, it is called a macroassembler. From here on all our comments should be viewed in the context of the macroassembler. A normal assembler requires two sequential passes over the code in some form in order to do its work. If the assembler has macro capability, this usually means the whole assembly process will require three passes. The first pass is used for macro expansion.

The copy-code feature is the most basic of many things that macroprocessors can do, and yet it is very useful. We now are in a position to demonstrate how copy-code

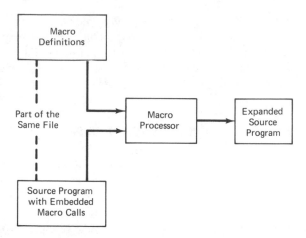

Figure 6-1:　Macro Expansion on a Source Program. Macroprocessing can be viewed solely as a text manipulation operation. The program given to the macroprocessor will contain certain standard abbreviations called macros. The macroprocessor will insert the lines of code for which each abbreviation stands into the original program at the point where the abbreviations occur. This process is called macro expansion.

can be used to expand a standard programming language with new statements. The INTEL 8080 processor has no machine instruction to change the sign of a number in the accumulator. Using macros, we can add such a statement to the language. Let's call the new statement

　　COMP

meaning form the two's complement of whatever is in the accumulator. Of course the 8080 instruction set has the capability to do this job; it's just that it takes more than one statement to do it. A sequence of two statements in 8080 code that will complement the accumulator is

　　CMA
　　INR　A

The first statement forms the one's complement of the accumulator, and the second adds one to that to form the two's complement.

　　In a sense, we have added a new statement to the language. When we write an assembler program, we are free to use the new statement any time it is necessary to change the sign of the accumulator. After the program is all written, it will be given to a macroassembler for processing. In the first pass over the code, the macroassembler will substitute the two lines of code given above for every place where we have used the new statement. This produces another program, then, that is equivalent to our original program but is slightly longer. After it has done this, the macroassembler proceeds to assemble the program in the normal manner. Every place in the code where we have used the new statement is termed a macro call.

The same code is ultimately executed every time a macro call is made in a program, although there are multiple copies of it in various places in the program. Another commonly used term for this type of code is an in-line subroutine.

We haven't explained yet how the macroassembler will know how to expand the new statement. The file that is given to the macroassembler for processing will have two parts: the program part, which is assembler code and macro calls, and the definitions part, which shows how macros are to be expanded. Figure 6-2 shows a typical format for a macro definition. It is the definition for the example macro we have been discussing. The definition begins with the keyword MACRO and ends with the keyword MACEND. The second line is called the *prototype*. It shows the macroprocessor how a call to this macro will look. The rest of the lines are called the *template*. They show the code that is to be substituted for the macro call during the expansion phase. Each line in the definition is numbered beginning from line number one.

Another useful feature which is a little more complex than copy-code is the *parameter substitution* facility. Since it is easy to implement, almost all macro systems have it. Parameter substitution was invented because programmers realized that it is frequently not enough to copy out an unvarying block of code when the macro is expanded. It is often very useful to make some changes in the operands of the statements that are being copied; and it is useful to be able to specify those changes as part of a macro call.

We can motivate this idea best with an example. Let's say we now wish to extend the 8080 language further with another statement. This statement will be able to form the 2's complement of any register, not just of the accumulator. Figure 6-3 shows what the macro call would look like, what the definition would be, and how the expanded code would look for a particular case. In this case a call to the macro of the form

    NEG   B

will output code to change the sign of the contents of the B register. But we could output different code from the same macro to change the sign of the C register, if we had used

    NEG   C

Definition		Explanation
1	MACRO	This is called the header.
2	COMP	This is called the prototype.
3	CMA	This is called the template.
4	INR A	
5	MACEND	This is called the trailer.

The macro indicated by this definition will change the sign of whatever number is in the accumulator (Intel 8080).

Figure 6-2:   An Example of a Macro Definition. We are viewing the macro as an abbreviation for a number of program text lines. The macro definition is a standard form that states what the abbreviation is, how it is used, and what it stands for.

The reader may notice a slight problem with this version of the register changing macro. If you see it, don't worry. We will attend to it soon.

The essential idea in parameter substitution is that the macro definition contains dummy parameters. These are the variable or variables that appear as operands on the prototype line. These dummy variables have no fixed meaning in the definition. They are only place holders. What they mean in any specific expansion is determined by matching the variables mentioned in the macro call against the dummy variables shown in the prototype. The macroprocessor automatically does this at macro expansion time.

A macroprocessor that can do only copy-code and parameter substitution is still quite a powerful tool. Here is an interesting application that can be supported through the use of these features. An easy way to set up a special purpose language is to decide

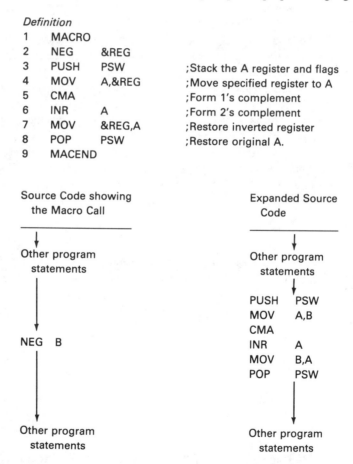

Definition
```
1   MACRO
2   NEG     &REG
3   PUSH    PSW        ;Stack the A register and flags
4   MOV     A,&REG     ;Move specified register to A
5   CMA                ;Form 1's complement
6   INR     A          ;Form 2's complement
7   MOV     &REG,A     ;Restore inverted register
8   POP     PSW        ;Restore original A.
9   MACEND
```

Source Code showing the Macro Call	Expanded Source Code
Other program statements	Other program statements

	PUSH PSW
	MOV A,B
	CMA
	INR A
	MOV B,A
	POP PSW

NEG B	
Other program statements	Other program statements

Figure 6-3: Example of a Macro with Parameter Substitution. The purpose of the code generated by this macro is to change the sign of a number in any of the 8080's registers. It does this by outputting a certain standard unit of code, called the template. This template will also be configured at a few specific points, through the process of parameter substitution, with the name of a register.

on a set of statements for the language and only choose statements such that each statement can be set up as a macro call. Then a program in this system would consist entirely of a series of macro calls. There are a number of languages of this sort. The IBM product CICS is probably the best known. This system consists of a set of macros that can be used to enter information into and retrieve information from a data base and to easily format a terminal screen to aid in these operations. Of course the parameter substitution idea here is crucial because a language needs a way of representing variable data.

The last feature we would like to examine in our introduction to simple macroprocessors is conditional assembly. It will frequently be desirable to define a big macro in such a way that when it is expanded only part of the macro is copied out into the source code. Which part is copied out will be under the control of one of the parameter values that form part of the macro call. Parameter substitution gave us some flexibility, but combined with *conditional assembly,* it will enable us to generate heavily tailored and customized code in response to just one macro call. Incidentally, conditional assembly is usually found in connection with a macro capability, but in some systems, it is present as a feature of the assembler even if there are no macros.

Let's examine how a conditional assembly can be specified. The lines in the macro are numbered, to facilitate the conditional assembly. There will be a special statement that can be inserted in the definition at any place where we wish to control whether some stretch of code will be used or bypassed. The syntax of this statement is like an IF statement in a higher level language. That is, there is a clause that has a Boolean expression that the macroprocessor evaluates to get an answer of true or false. If the result is true, macro expansion will continue at a line number that is given as part of the conditional assembly statement. If the expression is false, macro expansion will ignore the conditional assembly statement and simply proceed to copy out code in the usual sequential order. So conditional assembly affects the copy-code feature of a macro system, causing only certain parts of the code to be copied out rather than all of it.

The conditional assembly statement in the version we are going to use has the form

```
8     CONMB(&C>2), 15
```

The number that begins the line is simply a line number. All statements in a macro definition are numbered. CONMB means Conditional Macro Branch. It is a keyword that tells the macroprocessor that this is a control statement rather than code to be copied out. The Boolean expression in parentheses is what must be evaluated to a result of true or false. At macro expansion time this obviously can be done because the dummy parameter &C will have been given a value, and that value will or will not be greater than two. If it is greater than two, the macroprocessor skips over all code in the macro definition up to line 15. It then continues expansion starting at line 15 in the definition. If &C is not greater than two, then macro expansion will continue with the next line which will be line 9.

In our version of conditional assembly, Boolean expressions are restricted to the form of a dummy parameter, or an integer constant, or a single ASCII character on either side of the relational operator. The relational operators permitted will be greater than, less than, and equals.

To show the usefulness of conditional assembly, we will give two examples. The first one is an extension of a previous macro we examined which could change the sign of a number in one of the 8080's registers. As we mentioned, there is a problem with the code shown in Figure 6-3. It won't work for the accumulator. Saving and restoring the program status word will overwrite any sign changing in the accumulator, so we have to be a little more clever. Conditional assembly allows us to detect a reference to the accumulator as a special case. The macro definition shown in Figure 6-4 is what we need to handle this problem. The macroprocessor, using this definition, will copy out one section of the template for the accumulator and another section for the other registers. Incidentally, the Boolean expression in line 10 of the macro may look peculiar, but it is correct. This expression is a way to cause an unconditional jump to a new line during macro expansion. Certainly $(1 = 1)$ always evaluates to TRUE, and this is what makes the branch unconditional. It will always be taken.

Our second example of conditional assembly arises in connection with implementing a compiler. Later we will learn how to make a compiler. A compiler is software which takes a program written in a high level language like FORTRAN or BASIC or PL/1 and translates it into the assembler language of some particular machine. One common way to do compilation is to translate each statement in the higher level language into a macro call (or perhaps several macro calls) that can then be expanded by a macroassembler into normal assembly language. The syntax of higher level language statements is frequently quite flexible; that is, the statement, if it is used in different ways, may require quite different sequences of assembler statements to be generated. Conditional assembly makes it easy to do this.

Definition

```
1      MACRO
2      NEG      &REG                       ; THIS IS HOW A CALL WILL LOOK.
3      CONMB           (&REG=A),11         ; DETECT SPECIAL CASE.
4      PUSH     PSW                        ; STACK THE A REGISTER AND FLAGS.
5      MOV      A,&REG                     ; MOVE SPECIFIED REGISTER TO A.
6      CMA                                 ; FORM ONE'S COMPLEMENT.
7      INR      A                          ; FORM TWO'S COMPLEMENT.
8      MOV      &REG,A                     ; RESTORE INVERTED REGISTER.
9      POP      PSW                        ; RESTORE ORIGINAL ENVIRONMENT.
10     CONMB           (1=1),13            ; END NORMAL PROCESSING.
11     CMA                                 ; SPECIAL CASE PROCESSING, 1'S COMP.
12     INR      A                          ; FORM 2'S COMPLEMENT OF A.
13     MACEN D
```

Figure 6-4: Example of a Macro with Parameter Substitution and Conditional Assembly. This is a macro that can be used to generate code to change the sign of a number in any of the 8080's registers. Changing the sign of the accumulator is a special case because the code saves and restores the PSW at its beginning and ending. This feature would wipe out any change of sign in the accumulator. The macroprocessor detects a call to change the sign of the accumulator and treats it as a special case. Conditional assembly allows us to output the code shown in Figure 6-2 when servicing the accumulator and the code shown in Figure 6-3 for all other registers.

We will consider the translation by a compiler of just one statement in the language TINY BASIC. This is the statement that controls looping. Every loop in a TINY BASIC program begins with a particular type of statement and ends with another type. There are two ways to begin a loop and they are shown in the following code:

```
FOR  I = 1  TO  100
```

or

```
FOR  I = 1  TO  N
```

The first statement specifies that the code that follows will be looped through 100 times. The second statement specifies that the loop will be traversed N times. This type of higher level language statement upon compilation translates into about 8 lines of assembler code, but the code for the two variants is significantly different. However, all the compiler has to do to handle this is look at the statement and then set up one macro call to specify what assembler code will be output. One of the parameters passed by the compiler to the macro will be a variable that takes the values 1 or 2 so as to tell the macroprocessor which part of the template code to output. The other parameters that are passed into the macro will be the name of the loop counter variable (I), the ending value (100 or N), and the value of a count that is incremented by 1 every time the compiler encounters a loop. The starting value doesn't need to be passed, since these loops always start with the value one. Figure 12-9 shows the definition of the macro for the looping statement. The reader can examine this definition to see how conditional assembly allows for two different pieces of code to be output to account for the two variants of the higher level language instruction.

To conclude this section, we address a question that always comes up in any discussion of macros. Beginners in systems programming frequently are confused about when you would use a subroutine and when you would use a macro in a program. Indeed, as we have stated, a macro is sometimes called an in-line subroutine. Here are some examples bearing on this problem. For certain low level applications it takes more code to set up a subroutine call than it does to put the code for the function in line with a macro. In this case, a macro certainly would be used. If parameters have to be passed to the subroutine, sometimes even a 5 or 10 line macro is still more efficient with regard to memory usage.

The other clear case for macro usage is for those situations in which we need to output highly customized code by some conditional assembly process. Let's take the example of a manufacturer who needs to make an I/O package for a computer system he produces. Perhaps the system comes in a wide range of sizes. If the I/O package was a standard subroutine that could be called in a variety of ways, it would have to be very big. In fact, the subroutine would have to contain enough code to service even the largest possible variant of the computer system. And this same huge subroutine would be installed on all the manufacturer's systems — even the little ones. A better solution would be to have a standard I/O macro associated with all these systems. Then, when an operating system was being generated for a particular system, only the parts of the I/O macro that were relevant would be expanded, and only those relevant parts would become part of the operating system.

6.3 THE DESIGN FOR A SIMPLE MACROASSEMBLER

Macroprocessing is really a text manipulation operation that is usually a prelude to something further, like assembly. We now discuss how to set up a macroprocessing first stage for an assembler. It can be regarded as an additional enhancement to the type of assemblers we were looking at in Chapter 4.

The macroprocessor stage must receive as input a file containing macro definitions at the front followed by the text of the program. This will normally be a mixture of assembler language statements and macro calls. The output will be a file containing only assembler language statements; i.e., all the macro calls will have been expanded. This file is now ready for processing by a normal type assembler. Figure 6-5 shows the top level operation of a macroprocessor that will do this.

The first thing to do is to read the macro definitions into someplace in memory reserved for them. These definitions will be referred to often, and it will not be desirable to have to retrieve them from disk every time. Next the processor begins reading the input file line by line. If it discovers a normal assembler statement, it immediately transfers this to an output file that it is building. On the other hand, if a macro call is discovered, the processor will call a routine whose responsibility it is to expand single macros appropriately.

Figure 6-6 shows the macro expanding routine. There must be a way of relating the dummy parameters in the macro definition to the actual parameter values they will take on during any specific expansion. A parameter table will be built to service this need. First the macro expander will find the definition associated with the current macro call. Then, all that needs to be done is to form a number of pairs where each pair has a dummy parameter and an associated value for all the parameters mentioned in the macro definition. The table does not need to have a complicated structure. In fact, it is quite sufficient just to use a simple linear array, that is, a number of successive memory locations, and write the pairs into the array one after another. The members of a pair should be separated by some special symbol. We will use the slash.

As an example of a parameter table, let us consider a macro call that looks like this:

```
ALPHA   2,C,14
```

and let us suppose the prototype portion of the macro definition looks like this:

```
ALPHA   &1,&2,&3
```

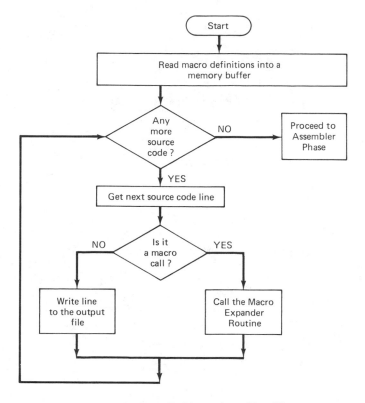

Figure 6-5:   A Macroprocessor Front End for an Assembler. When a macroprocessor is used as the first stage in an assembly, it collects the macro definitions into one place and then goes through the program line by line and makes appropriate code substitutions for all macros it discovers. Its output is pure assembler code.

The parameter table could be implemented as a simple character string that would be constructed in the following manner:

```
&1/2&2/C&3/14
```

In this case, the ampersand denotes the start of a parameter pair. The slash separates the members of a pair. And the buffer would be terminated with some distinctive character such as a Carriage Return. Certainly this is the simplest type of symbol table we will ever see, and yet it is sufficient. Any time the program needs to find the value of the real parameter that should replace a particular dummy, the table can be searched linearly. It is so small that the answer will be found quickly.

After the parameter table is established, macro expansion can begin. The lines in the macro definition will be copied out one by one, configured with real parameters, and

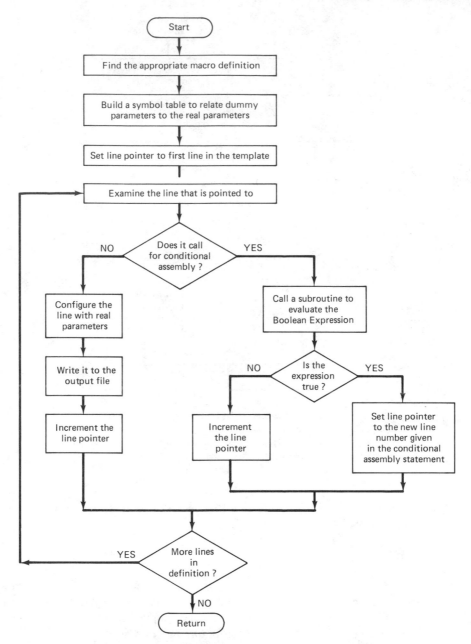

Figure 6-6:   A Macro Expander Routine with Parameter Substitution and Conditional Assembly. This routine does the work of translating a single macro call into an equivalent sequence of assembler statements. The code produced by different calls to the same macro can be highly customized. Specific parameters can be inserted at marked places in the code, and it is possible to control which parts of the definition will be expanded on any given macro call.

written to the output file. The line currently being worked on will be identified by a line pointer. As each line in the definition is examined, it will be determined if the line calls for conditional assembly. If it does not, the line is expanded in normal fashion. If it does, then a subsidiary routine will be called which has the sole function of inspecting the Boolean expression in the line and deciding whether it evaluates to a value of true or false. The Boolean expression will usually be written in terms of dummy parameters, so real values will have to be substituted before it can be evaluated. If the expression turns out to be false, expansion continues at the next line in the definition. If it turns out to be true, then expansion proceeds further along in the code at the line number given in the conditional assembly control statement.

At the top level at least, these are the steps that need to be taken to implement a macroprocessor of considerable power. Other processors are more powerful, but a great deal can be done with just the three simple features of copy-code, parameter substitution, and conditional assembly. We will return and see a powerful use of macroprocessors later, when we consider how to build a simple compiler.

STUDY QUESTIONS AND EXERCISES

1. Structured assembly language is the result of attempts to bring the blessings of structured programs to assembler code. It can be done with macros. Describe the usage and write the macro definitions for macros that could be used as "new statements" in an assembler language in order to implement these structured control constructs:

    (a) IF—THEN—ELSE

    (b) DO WHILE

2. Write a macro to increment the instruction set of the 8080 to incorporate 16 bit subtraction. Make the syntax parallel as much as possible to the 16 bit addition routine that is a normal instruction.

3. Assume you are in a programming environment where it is desirable to save all the registers upon entry to a subroutine and restore them upon exit. Write ENTRY and EXIT macros that could be called upon to do this job.

4. A subroutine that is used at many places in a program needs to be set up in a certain way before it can be called. It requires its first parameter to be in register B, its second parameter in register D, and its third parameter (a 16 bit number) to be in the HL register pair. The subroutine is named ALPHA. Write a macro that could be used to set up this subroutine call.

5. Design a block of assembler code that can take the most significant 4 bits of any of the 8 bit registers on the 8080 and shift those bits into the right half of the register. The left half is then to be filled with zeros. Write a macro definition for this block and then write the same block as a subroutine. Assume that the subroutine will find a code on the top of the stack that will indicate to it which register to work with (choose the code yourself).

6. Flowchart a module that could evaluate the allowed types of Boolean expressions as they occur in conditional assembly control statements.

7. Flowchart a module that could search the macroprocessor's symbol table (we called it a parameter table) and return the real value associated with any dummy parameter. How does this task compare with accessing the symbol table in an assembler?

8. Discuss what changes would be necessary in the macro expansion routine (Figure 6-6) if calls to other macros were permitted inside macro definitions.

7

The Systems Environment: II

7.1 INTRODUCTION TO POWERFUL SINGLE-USER MICROCOMPUTER SYSTEMS

The full function personal computer defines the next computer system environment we wish to discuss. This type of system will employ one of the standard microprocessors as the central processing element. The high end machines in this group are beginning to use 16 bit microprocessors; the medium and low end machines use 8 bit processors. The most typical memory size is on the order of 64 kilobytes with some memory in RAM, some in ROM. The newer machines have greater addressing ranges and are appearing with memories several times as big as the traditional 64 kilobyte unit. This class of computer will also have some kind of flexible video display unit. It will frequently have a cheap dedicated printer. Most important, it will have a floppy disk storage subsystem.

More memory and the floppy disk are the key hardware elements that separate this kind of computer system from simpler variants. The key software element is a single-user disk operating system such as CP/M. With these tools, for the first time, areas appear in which the small stand-alone computer can perform better than a terminal which shares some part of a mainframe. Perhaps this is the proper operational criterion for finding the computers that occupy the next step up in complexity of the systems environment.

What can these small computers do? The equipment is still cheap enough that many people purchase a personal computer with just one application in mind or to run a particular piece of purchased software. Word processing is a dominant application that small computers do very, very well. Small business accounting and record keeping is another. Business planning as done with spread sheets, PERT charts, and various graphical presentations of data is a third successful application. The capability certainly exists for a computer in this range to be used very profitably in education, although lack of software has held this back. It can be used in any area where there is a large amount of material requiring rote learning, from foreign languages to arithmetic. Personal computers will increasingly be used as work stations in computer networks. In this configuration, sometimes they emulate terminals in order to communicate with larger computers in the networks, and sometimes they act as general purpose stand-alone computing elements. Beyond these generic applications, there are also many special purpose applications such as doing engineering mathematics, or controlling machines or processes in a factory. The author feels that new applications will keep being invented, and that for the time being, the available systems capability has outdistanced available applications programs.

Of the peripherals found with computers in this range, the disk is by far the most complicated to program. Disk manipulations will occupy large parts of standard systems programs. The only other device at this level with any complexity in its programming is the video display. The bulk of this chapter will be given over to understanding how to use the floppy disk. But we will spend some time discussing displays because their hardware features will directly govern the quality of editing or word processing software that can be produced for any given system.

Let's consider some general characteristics of the floppy disk. First, where did it come from? Floppy disks were brought into the marketplace by IBM around 1972. IBM was looking for a way to make data entry operations more efficient, and the floppy was their answer. The standard way to do data entry at that time was to use mechanical keypunches and tabulator cards. Any company with a large volume of customer transactions had rooms full of keypunchers engaged in transferring information from customer documents to punched cards. Making this process more efficient would mean making it faster and getting rid of the cards. Cards are reliable, durable, and easy to understand, but they are not compact. Cards always tend to accumulate in such quantity that storage becomes difficult and expensive.

The floppy disk was to be the solution. One diskette has the thickness of a piece of cardboard, and it is packaged in a plastic envelope that is square and eight inches along a side. Yet each of these diskettes in original form could hold the equivalent of several boxes of tabulator cards. Electronic systems that passed data directly from a keyboard onto a magnetic medium could also work somewhat faster and were certainly much quieter than mechanical keypunches.

Floppy disks successfully addressed some of the traditional problems of data capture from keyboards. However, they ultimately provided the basis for two kinds of electronic systems that are probably much more important; and this was not foreseen at all when the diskette was originally developed. They made powerful, single-user personal computers possible. They also created the word processing industry.

How does the floppy disk work? Inside the plastic envelope that protects the disk, there is a circular piece of flexible plastic coated with material on which magnetic recording can be done, just as on a piece of recording tape. Data is organized on the diskette in tracks and sectors. The original IBM diskettes used 77 concentric tracks each of which could store 3300 bytes of data. Tracks further from the center were recorded less densely so that the amount of data on any track would be uniform. Each track is subdivided into

26 sectors. Any sector on any track can be individually accessed by the floppy disk machinery. Since each sector can store 128 bytes, the total storage capacity of the diskette is

$$\text{Storage Capacity} = 77 * 26 * 128 = 250,000 \text{ bytes (approximately)}$$

Figure 7-1 shows what a floppy disk looks like and gives some summary information.

The diskette is a random access storage device. This means that any sector on the recording surface can be accessed in a small amount of time. A tape, on the other hand, is a sequential access device. If the read/write head is positioned near the start of the tape and data is desired which is near the end, then practically the whole tape will have to be wound past the head before the data can be positioned. This is very time consuming. The mechanism of accessing a sector using the floppy disk works in the following way. The disk rotates at 6 revolutions per second. The read/write head will be moved in or out along a radius of the circle until it is positioned at the correct track. Then the disk will be allowed to rotate until the desired sector is properly positioned with respect to the read/write head, and then the data transfer will take place.

A floppy disk subsystem gives a microcomputer many advantages:

1. Programs can be loaded from memory image disk files perhaps 50 times faster than with standard tape operations.

2. Better systems software, such as compilers and assemblers, can be written in a disk environment. These programs typically take a source file, which is the program, and make a number of passes over the file, transforming it until a machine language object program is produced. If the program is of any size, there is no room to keep the intermediate files in memory. They must be kept on some sort of external storage. If multipass software has to keep intermediate results on tape, the whole process is so cumbersome that few people would ever use it. But disks are well suited to processing that requires multiple passes over files.

3. Better system software increases programmer productivity.

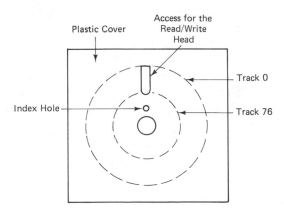

Index Hole

Plastic Cover

Access for the
Read/Write
Head

Track 0

Track 76

Figure 7-1: Demographics of the Floppy Disk. The standard soft-sectored disk has 77 tracks. Each track is divided into 26 sectors. Each sector can record 128 bytes. The capacity of the whole diskette is approximately 250,000 bytes or the same as 3,000 punched cards.

4. Disks are more reliable than tapes. This has made it possible for one person to write a program and then distribute it to many other users. The disk has become a medium for reliable program distribution.

5. There are certain kinds of file operations, very common in business applications, which require random access files. Diskettes made it possible to do these things with a microcomputer.

There are a few other pieces of information that are desirable to mention here in order to set up the context for floppy disk based software. It is often necessary to estimate the speed with which certain data can be accessed. Several things affect this. Rotational latency is the time it takes for a sector to rotate into the proper position after the head has been moved to the correct track. The diskette rotates six times a second, so there will be one rotation every 167 milliseconds. Another factor is the track positioning time. A typical time to move the read/write head from one track to the next is 45 milliseconds. These two factors combine to determine how long it will take to access any particular sector. The average time to access a randomly positioned sector somewhere on the disk is in the neighborhood of one second.

The original IBM diskettes were soft-sectored and could store about 250,000 bytes of useful data. Soft-sectored means that in addition to data, other information is recorded with the data, and this information can be read to aid the disk controller in positioning the read/write head. Other diskette technologies have developed and are now common. Hard sectoring refers to the practice of punching holes along one circumference of the circle at the boundaries of sectors. A sensor can detect these holes and thus can easily find the sectors.

The storage capacity of diskettes has tended to double every few years. A double density recording format is now common which records information more densely. Each disk using double density can store approximately 500,000 bytes. If a drive is used that can access both sides of the diskette, then the capacity is doubled again. Other technologies are beginning to push the storage capacity even higher. However these systems begin to be quite sensitive to dust in the air, mechanical alignment, etc., and they are not as robust as the original technology. A trade-off must be established.

It is also a most curious thing that almost all of these new technologies are incompatible with one another. There are no standards except the original IBM 3740 format. This means that if you and I are using the same software on two different computer systems, the chances are that I can't produce a disk file on my system and hope to have your system read it, unless we're using exactly the same kind of disk equipment. When information absolutely must be transferred from one type of system to another on diskette, the users will usually arrange that both systems can read and produce 3740 type disks.

7.2 HARDWARE CHARACTERISTICS AND INTERFACING

7.2.1 Floppy Disks

Let us now direct our attention to the original soft sectored low density technology, since it is the basis for all others, and inquire more deeply into the mechanisms of recording.

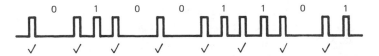

Figure 7-2:   An Example of Frequency Modulation Recording. This figure illustrates the type of digital recording used in the IBM 3740 disk format. The basic recording unit is one clock pulse followed by one data pulse. The pulses checked from below are clock pulses. They define a window within which a data pulse may or may not appear. The data being represented here is the hexadecimal byte 4D.

The tape system that we discussed in Chapter 2, recorded data as a varying pattern made by two audio tones. With the disk there are no tones. Information is recorded digitally. This means that all the read head will see on playback is a sequence of pulses. A strictly controlled amount of time is allocated to each pulse. The presence of a pulse in this time period is equivalent to a one, and the absence is equivalent to a zero. Thus it is digital recording. Time registration is maintained by writing a clock pulse in front of every data bit. There are 16 real or implicit pulses associated with every byte that is recorded. Eight are clock pulses, and the rest are data pulses. They are interleaved. However, remember that a zero bit is indicated by the absence of a data bit following the clock bit for this bit position. This recording technique is called frequency modulation. Figure 7-2 shows the way a particular byte of data would be represented if it was in this format.

Now that we have seen the recording method, let's examine the layout of a single sector of data on the diskette. User recorded data will only represent about two thirds of the data along any given track. The rest of the information is for the use of the controller so that it can position randomly to any sector. For instance, 188 bytes total are required to store the amount of data that the user thinks of as a sector, which is 128 bytes. This data is formatted in six fields with the following lengths:

ID Address Mark	1 byte
Track/Sector ID	6 bytes
ID Gap	17 bytes
Data Address Mark	1 byte
Data (including 2 byte checksum)	130 bytes
Data Gap	33 bytes
Total:	188 bytes

When the controller sees the ID Address Mark, it knows that a new sector is starting. The Track/Sector ID field uniquely identifies the sector that is about to begin. The Data Address Mark indicates that data is about to start. The Data field contains the data which is being recorded. There are 2 bytes tacked on the end of it to aid in error checking. The two gap fields contain nothing. They are there to allow the controller electronics and the computer software some time to make decisions before the next field with substantive information spins into reading position. This is also a place where the mode of the recording head can be changed from read to write, or visa versa. Since electrical transients might be developed by this operation, producing local magnetic fields, it's best to do this in a region of the disk where there is no data.

We have discussed recording formats, and the layout of data on a disk. Now we need to consider the operation of the disk controller. This complicated piece of electronics interfaces to the computer on one side and to the disk drive on the other. In general, it will be able to accept a few simple commands from the CPU which are enough to accomplish all the activities we have been talking about. A typical set of commands that could be given to a simple controller are the following:

1. Select Disk Drive 1
2. Select Disk Drive 2
3. Select Disk Drive 3
4. Select Disk Drive 4
5. Set Up DMA Registers
6. Return Current Sector Address (1-26)
7. Return Current Track Address (0-76)
8. Move Head In One Track
9. Move Head Out One Track
10. Move Head To Track Zero
11. Read Current Sector
12. Write Current Sector

The Select Disk Drive commands are necessary because the system might have multiple drives. A simple controller can only refer to one at a time. DMA stands for Direct Memory Access. It is a procedure for transferring data directly between the controller and the main memory without the help of the CPU. We will discuss it later. The next commands allow the CPU to find out exactly where (at what address) the read/write head is currently positioned. The commands which follow allow the CPU to control the positioning. The last commands control reading and writing after the proper sector has been positioned to.

A typical interface between the CPU and controller is shown in Figure 7-3. The Status Port returns status in conjunction with various commands. And sometimes it contains the answer to a query from the CPU. For instance, if the command was Return Sector Address, this data would become accessible in the Status Port. The Control Port is the place where command codes are sent to activate the various functions of the controller. There are two DMA registers which have the sole function of receiving a 16 bit address from the CPU.

Virtually all disk drives use the DMA process. A DMA device is like a separate CPU with some specialized and useful properties that relate to data transfer. It has the capability of shutting the CPU down for short periods of time, seizing control of the system buses, and making data transfers between memory and an external device without any intermediation by the CPU.

DMA is implemented totally in hardware. There is no software burden besides starting the process. Consequently it is very popular with programmers. In the context of disk reads, all a user must do is supply the DMA device with an address in memory

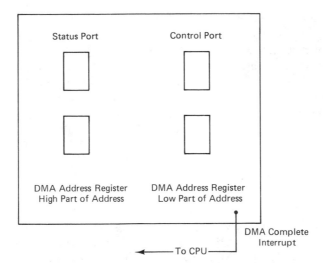

Figure 7-3:   A Typical Disk Controller Interface. The programmer's view of as complicated a piece of electronics as the disk controller is still just a matter of a few ports and attendant rules for manipulating them.

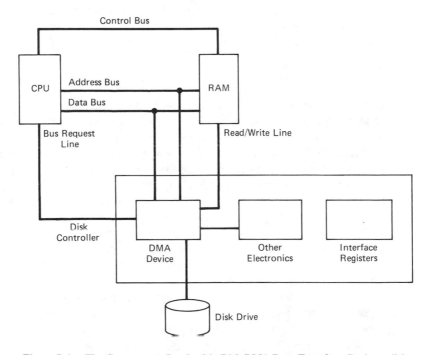

Figure 7-4:   The Components Involved in Disk DMA Data Transfers. During a disk read, when the DMA device has a byte, it will disconnect the CPU, put the proper address on the address bus, put the byte of data on the data bus, and strobe the memory to cause it to accept the data. Then it gives control back to the CPU, which continues operation with no way to know that a few cycles of its operation were stolen.

where the data is supposed to go, and then start it. The CPU can now go about its business doing any other computation it chooses. Sometime later, it will inspect a port or receive an interrupt signal indicating that the DMA is finished. What this means is that a whole sector of information will have been taken from the disk and that it now resides in 128 bytes of main memory at the location that was specified to the DMA device. A disk write does the same kind of transfer but in the opposite direction. DMA devices nowadays are implemented on single chips, and they will be found as built-in components on disk interfaces. Figure 7-4 shows some of the data paths and devices that are important in DMA based data transfers.

Let us now review the whole procedure of a typical read or write sequence. The first thing is that the I/O program must position the read/write head to the proper track. It does this by requesting the current track address, which will appear in the Status Port, and giving commands through the Control Port to move the head until it is at the proper track. Then the DMA registers will be set up with the main memory address to or from which you want the transfer to proceed. Next the disk is positioned to the proper sector. This is purely a passive process of waiting until the proper sector rotates under the read/write head. Of course, there will be a loop in which the Status Port is continually interrogated to get the addresses of current sectors as they pass under the head. Finally, when the proper sector makes its appearance, the program will issue a Read Current Sector or Write Current Sector command. From there the disk controller hardware takes over. It determines the exact time to begin the transfer and then moves 128 bytes, each at the proper time, using its built-in DMA device.

7.2.2 Video Displays

There is great variety in the display units found on microcomputer equipment. The largest natural division is probably between displays with graphics capability and those whose principal function it is to display characters. We will not discuss the graphics types. They are more expensive; the hardware is complex; and the programming would lead us off into a specialized area outside of the mainstream of systems programming.

Another natural division develops around the utilization of internal memory within video displays. All video displays have internal memory of the same sort used by computers. Codes for displayable characters are stored in this memory, and mapping hardware continually scans through the memory creating a picture on the screen that reflects what character codes have been stored. A complete memory to video mapping is done on the order of 30 times a second. The basic procedure for changing what is on the screen is to change what is in the memory.

The division we wish to examine stems from the fact that with some displays, the computer can treat the memory in the video unit almost as an extension of its own. In other units, the video display memory is relatively inaccessible to the computer. We will call these two types memory mapped displays and dedicated memory displays, respectively.

Dedicated memory displays were developed earlier. The oldest types of video terminals were conceived as replacements for printing terminals. The cursor on the screen simulated the print head on the printer. Looking at the screen, you would see the same type of operation as if you looked at a roll of paper being printed. A terminal like this would typically receive characters for display, one at a time, through some kind of line connecting to the computer. The terminal would be set up to interpret some of the characters it received as control codes rather than as information to be displayed. This kind of device could do only a few things: output a character at the cursor position, return the cursor to the beginning of the line (carriage return), and move to the next line (line feed).

The internal memory associated with this type of display had the capacity for holding however many characters you could see displayed on the screen at one time. For instance, a standard screen size is 24 lines which are 80 characters wide. The ASCII code for each character is stored in one byte, so the internal memory would be 1920 bytes long. The only trouble was that the memory couldn't be manipulated from the outside very well. It could only display a record of what characters had been shipped down to the terminal— much like a printed roll of paper.

The next step in the evolution of these terminals was to give them more control codes and more memory. Frequently, the terminal could hold the 1920 bytes of text and perhaps several times more than this. More text could be held than was to be displayed on a single screen. There were control code commands to do things like position the cursor anywhere on the screen, insert text at the cursor position by moving all the other text over, move the text apart to open up blank lines at any place in the body of the displayed text, and scroll the text up or down. This kind of capability is obviously useful for good text editing software.

Figure 7-5 shows a typical repertoire of commands for a modern dedicated memory terminal. There is a control code for each command. Logical agility is required to execute so many commands. Because of this, these terminals usually incorporate a microprocessor.

A dedicated memory terminal can be quite good for editing, but it has an Achilles heel—its speed. There will be either a serial or parallel interfacing line linking the terminal to the computer, and it will not be able to transmit data very fast. The highest rate customarily used is 9600 bits per second. If you are attempting to scroll through a large amount of text or trying to position to a point remote from the present location in the text, you will notice problems with the speed. All the intervening text characters will have to be transmitted down to the terminal one by one. In such a situation, the speed of the display comes to be governed by the speed of the line linking it to the computer.

From the standpoint of editing, there is an even better kind of display to have. We'll call it a shared memory or memory mapped display. In this case, the display is really connected directly to the processor's bus in the same way as other close-in peripheral equipment is connected. The video hardware and the computer share some of the computer's memory as the place characters to go on the screen are kept. It is called the screen memory. This is a very desirable situation. If the computer wants to change what is displayed on the screen, it simply needs to write characters into appropriate parts of its own memory. This can be done very quickly. The video hardware is set up to scan the screen memory continuously and convert the characters it finds there into an appropriate video image. This is done automatically and requires no intervention from the CPU.

Cursor Control:
Move Cursor Left
Move Cursor Right
Move Cursor Up
Move Cursor Down
Home Cursor
Clear Entire Screen
Carriage Return
Line Feed
New Line
Put Cursor in Window
Move Cursor to Coordinates
Tab Set
Tab Clear
Move to Next Tab

Display Control:
Scroll Up One Line
Scroll Down One Line
Display Previous Page
Display Next Page

Editing:
Line Insert
Line Delete
Character Insert
Character Delete

General Purpose:
Ring Bell
Lock or Unlock Keyboard
  (from remote)
Enable or Disable Key Clicks
Enable or Disable Margin Bell

Screen Formatting:
Give attributes to Screen Windows
  (Text from computer goes into
  the present active window.)
Define Window
Protect a Field of Text
  (so it can't be erased)
Underline Field
Reverse Video Field
Blinking Field
Half or Double Intensity Field
Set Window Active or Inactive

Mode Control:
Block Mode or Normal Mode
Display Status Line
Send Description of current
  terminal set-up
Receive Commands for remote
  terminal set-up
Set-up Programmable Function Keys

Transmission Control:
Send/Receive a Character at a Time
Send/Receive a Line at a Time
Send/Receive a Field at a Time
Send/Receive a Whole Page at a Time
Remove Blanks From Transmissions

Figure 7-5: A Typical Command Repetoire for a Modern Dedicated Memory Video Terminal. Video Terminals with an internal display memory not accessible to the computer tend to be set up to respond to large numbers of control codes or escape sequences. These are codes that are interpreted as instructions to the terminal rather than as data. Shown here is a typical set.

With a shared memory set up, scrolling is extremely easy to implement. Sometimes, the screen memory can be moved. In this case, to scroll is just a matter of changing a pointer in order to move the window that the video hardware uses to define what part of main memory it will display. If the screen memory can't be moved, the processor will have to adjust what characters are there to give the appearance of scrolling. This will involve doing block moves of characters from one part of the memory to another. Inserting text is easy, too, because the processor doesn't have to worry about what the display is doing or send commands to control it. It simply has to shift data within its own memory to open up space for the new text. Indeed, most of the things you might want to do with a shared memory display can be accomplished by moving characters around with normal programming instructions. There is no complicated command repertoire.

Dedicated memory and shared memory displays are both common in small microcomputer systems today. Both can give good service, although a shared memory system is easier to work with for systems programmers, and it is quicker. Computers such as the Apple II and the TRS-80, which have one big internal printed circuit card with all the basic circuitry on it, tend to use shared memory display techniques with a CRT tube integrated right into the computer unit. Bus-oriented computers, such as most S-100 bus systems, tend to have external terminals of the dedicated memory type.

Currently, there is no standardization as to how to give commands or as to what function to expect from a given command in any of the types of displays we have discussed. Therefore, there is no uniform programming methodology we can describe for any of them.

7.3 PROGRAMMING IN A MORE POWERFUL HARDWARE ENVIRONMENT

More memory and the capabilities of the floppy disk define a new hardware environment for microcomputers. Programming for the disk will be at the heart of a new software environment. What we want to do now is look at an example of this kind of programming. We will examine a routine which can read any sector on the disk if furnished with the track and sector address. Remember that track addresses go from 0 to 76, sector addresses from 1 to 26. This is clumsy, but it is part of the IBM 3740 standard. We will show the code for this routine, rather than a flowchart, so that a comparison can be made with our earlier examples of I/O routines.

The Read Sector Routine follows the general procedure described in the last section for reading and writing. The structure of this software will be that of a driver that sets things up and several subsidiary routines that do the actual work. The example program for reading a disk sector contains many instances where codes are written into the Control Port. We are assuming that the available commands and the corresponding number codes are the same as the list of twelve commands we gave in the last section.

The disk interface is exactly the same interface discussed in the last section. There is a status port, a control port, and two ports to receive a DMA address. We are assuming that the names of these ports, which are used in the code of SREAD, are equated somewhere else in the program to the actual numbers of the ports involved. These numbers are ultimately determined by the way the ports are wired into the interface. Machine code, as produced by an assembler, does not contain any names. All names must be rendered into numbers.

The driver routine is named SREAD. It calls another routine, SETUP, which positions the read/write head to the proper track and supplies the DMA machinery with the address in main memory to which the data will be transferred. We will assume that the track and sector addresses are supplied to the Read Sector Routine, by whatever higher up program is calling it, through memory locations called TRAKADDR and SECTADDR. These will have been set up before SREAD is called. The desired address for the DMA machinery will also have been set up previously in the memory locations called DMAHI and DMALO. The SREAD routine is shown in Figure 7-6.

After SETUP has done its work, the driver routine enters a loop where it will try up to 10 times to read the indicated sector by using the routine called GETSC. A

```
SREAD:      PUSH  B              ; SAVE MACHINE ENVIRONMENT
            PUSH  D
            PUSH  H
START:      LDA   SECTADDR       ; PUT SECTOR ADDR. IN REG. E
            MOV   E, A
            LDA   TRAKADDR       ; PUT TRACK ADDR. IN REG. D
            MOV   D, A
            CALL  SETUP          ; POSITION TO TRACK AND SET UP DMA
            MVI   B, 09H         ; SET UP TRY COUNTER
GS;         CALL  GETSC          ; ATTEMPT TO READ SECTOR
            CPI   01H            ; EXAMINE COMPLETION CODE
            JZ    OKAY           ; IF OKAY, THEN EXIT
NOTOKAY:    MOV   A, B           ; TRY AGAIN? GET TRY COUNTER
            ANA   A              ; SET CONDITION FLAGS
            JZ    NOGO           ; HAVE WE DONE ENOUGH?
            DCR   B              ; NO, DECREMENT TRY COUNTER
            JMP   GS             ; TRY AGAIN
NOGO:       MVI   A, 02H         ; ENOUGH TRIES, SET ERROR CODE
            JMP   RT             ; GO TO EXIT
OKAY:       NOP                  ; A WILL CONTAIN 1, SIGNALLING SUCCESS
RT:         POP   H              ; RESTORE MACHINE ENVIRONMENT
            POP   D
            POP   B
            RET                  ; RETURN
```

Figure 7-6: The Sector Read Driver Routine, SREAD. This routine can be called to read any sector on the disk. Prior to the call, the track and sector address and the DMA address must have been set into the memory locations reserved for this purpose. SREAD calls a subsidiary routine to get to the correct track and to set up the DMA device. Then it tries up to ten times to read the requested sector using the GETSC routine.

completion code will be returned in register A when the driver routine has finished its work. It will return the number one for a successful read/write or two for a failed read/ write. Failures may occur if the read/write head has become misaligned or if dust or grease have altered the surface of the disk where the data was, or if stray fields have scrambled the magnetization. We must distinguish between hard failures and soft failures. A soft failure is one that can be recovered from by just trying again.

Now we need to look at the principal subsidiary routines that are called from the driver. The SETUP routine positions to the proper track by the following procedure. It reads the current track address and compares it to the desired address. If they are the same, positioning is finished. If they are not the same, a command is given to move one track in the correct direction. This sequence is repeated until the head arrives at the right track. SETUP also establishes a starting address for the sector transfer in the DMA machinery. This code is shown in Figure 7-7.

The routine GETSC does its work by sitting in a loop and inspecting the addresses of the sectors passing by the read/write head until the proper one appears. Then it sends the read current sector command to the controller and waits until the read operation

```
SETUP:    MVI    A,07H       ; REQUEST TRACK ADDRESS
          OUT    CNTLPRT     ; SEND COMMAND
          NOP                ; ALLOW TIME FOR RESPONSE
          IN     STATPRT     ; READ TRACK ADDRESS
          CMP    D           ; IS POSITION CORRECT?
          JZ     SETDMA      ; YES, POSITIONING DONE
          JP     MOVOUT      ; NO, TOO CLOSE TO CENTER
          JM     MOVIN       ; NO, TOO CLOSE TO RIM
MOVOUT:   MVI    A,09H       ; SET UP TO MOVE OUT 1 TRACK
          OUT    CNTLPRT     ; SEND COMMAND
          CALL   DELAY       ; ALLOW TIME FOR MOVE
          JMP    SETUP       ; CHECK POSITION AGAIN
MOVIN:    MVI    A,08H       ; SET UP TO MOVE IN 1 TRACK
          OUT    CNTLPRT     ; SEND COMMAND
          CALL   DELAY       ; ALLOW TIME FOR MOVE
          JMP    SETUP       ; CHECK POSITION AGAIN
SETDMA:   LDA    DMAHI       ; LOAD DMA ADDRESS
          OUT    HIADDR      ;    (HIGH PART)
          LDA    DMALO       ; LOAD DMA ADDRESS
          OUT    LOADDR      ;    (LOW PART)
          MVI    A,05H       ; MAKE DMA ACCEPT ADDRESS
          OUT    CNTLPRT     ; SEND COMMAND
          RET                ; RETURN
```

Figure 7-7:   The Track Positioning and DMA Preparation Routine, SETUP.
This routine positions the read/write head to the proper track and sets the proper memory address into the DMA apparatus for the upcoming transfer.

```
GETSC:      MVI   A, 06H        ; SET UP READ SECTOR ADDRESS COMMAND
            OUT   CNTLPRT       ; OUTPUT IT
            NOP                 ; ALLOW TIME FOR RESPONSE
            IN    STATPRT       ; INPUT ADDR. FROM STATUS REG.
            CMP   E             ; COMPARE WITH DESIRED ADDR.
            JNZ   GETSC         ; CYCLE UNTIL IT MATCHES
            MVI   A, 0BH        ; SET UP READ COMMAND
            OUT   CNTLPRT       ; SEND IT
            NOP                 ; ALLOW TIME FOR RESPONSE
RSTAT:      IN    STATPRT       ; READ STATUS FOR COMPLETION CODE
            ANA   A             ; SET CONDITION FLAGS
            JZ    RSTAT         ; GO BACK IF NOTHING HAPPENED
ENDGSC:     RET                 ; RETURN, COMPLETION CODE IS IN REG. A
```

Figure 7-8:   The Low Level Sector Read Routine, GETSC. This routine waits for the proper sector to go by and then issues the read command to the controller. It returns a completion code that is furnished by the controller for result monitoring.

completes. Then it takes the completion code provided by the controller and returns it in the A register to indicate its own success or failure. Let us assume that this particular controller returns zero to mean transfer in progress, one to indicate success, and two to mean that something went wrong. The GETSC routine is shown in Figure 7-8.

There is no really critical timing that must be furnished by the software. The controller takes care of it. After GETSC identifies the proper sector, it has plenty of time to issue the read command. It is interesting to compare the time for a typical CPU instruction (2 microseconds) and the speed at which data moves by the read/write head. At the rotational speed of a floppy disk, it takes 666 microseconds between the reading of a sector address and when the data field starts. Within the data field, each byte is under the read/write head for 37 microseconds.

In the next chapter we will be studying the single user operating system called CP/M. This important piece of software also has disk read routines. For those of you who may have read ahead, we want to make it clear that SREAD is not a CP/M routine. The CP/M routines are written according to a different format, but the way in which they do their work will be very similar to the way SREAD operates.

In addition to floppy disks, we introduced several types of flexible video displays in this chapter. They are also characteristic of the systems environment of powerful single-user microcomputer systems. We will not now discuss programming the various types of displays. It is not difficult. Programming is just a matter of knowing the repertoire of commands your own particular display will accept (there can be a lot), and making judicious use of them. There is no standard, and every display is different. We will consider the interaction of the display capability with one important type of systems software in Chapter 9 when we study editors.

STUDY QUESTIONS AND EXERCISES

1. Imagine that you are using a disk just as a speedy version of a tape drive. Write a flowchart for a program that will save the image of a program in memory into a series of consecutive physical sectors on disk. The disk sectors are numbered in the IBM floppy disk format. The program will be told the memory boundaries of the region to be transferred and it will be told at which physical sector to begin the transfer.

2. Single-user disk based operating systems frequently have a set of basic I/O routines (BIOS) that they use to communicate with disk, printer, and terminal. Estimate the size of this package (lines of code or bytes) if it consists of character input and output routines for the printer and terminal, and sector input and output routines for the disk. For comparison, compute the size of a similar I/O package for a board level computer of the kind that was discussed in Chapter 2. The actual I/O routines that were exhibited in that chapter and this one should be the basis of your estimate.

3. Compute the approximate recording density in bits per inch along the innermost and along the outermost tracks of an IBM standard floppy disk. Assume the innermost track corresponds to a radius of 2 inches and the outermost to a radius of 3 inches.

4. You are familiar with the numbering of physical sectors on a disk track. In addition to this, the CP/M operating system uses another numbering system called logical sectors. Figure 8-11 will show you how these entities are laid out along a disk track. Write an 8080 subroutine that is given a logical sector number in the accumulator and that returns with the corresponding physical sector number in the accumulator. Use the CP/M standard sector layout.

5. Estimate the amount of time it would take a microcomputer to scroll the whole display up by one line in the following three situations. The display is a shared memory display in which the screen window can be moved. The display is a shared memory display that can't be moved. A dedicated memory terminal is being used in which the internal memory is the same size as the maximum number of characters that can be displayed on the screen. The terminal receives information from the CPU over a serial line operating at 300 bits per second.

6. Write a subroutine that could be called by a word processor every time it wanted to start a new paragraph at the end of some text on a terminal screen. To start a new paragraph means to return the carriage, to go down two lines, and to go in five spaces. Assume that the terminal receives commands through port number two. Some relevant codes for this particular terminal are

Carriage Return	CNTL-A
Line Feed	CNTL-B
Cursor Right	CNTL-C
Cursor UP	CNTL-D
Cursor Down	CNTL-E

8

A Single User Disk Based
Operating System: CP/M

8.1 INTRODUCTION: CREATING AN ENVIRONMENT FOR SOFTWARE

An operating system is a collection of software tools that allows a user to produce programs quickly and use the resources of a computer easily and efficiently. Let's consider a typical small computer disk operating system. It can be viewed from several perspectives.

For the naive user, the operating system will appear as though it is a "load and go" machine. That is, the user can tell the system the name of a program he or she wants to run (probably written by someone else), and the system will quickly find that program, load it into memory, and execute it. The disk makes this operation fast.

An application programmer will probably view the system as a convenient environment in which to use several major systems programs, such as editors, assemblers, or compilers, that she uses to do her work. This work will be in support of the end uses of computers: accounting packages, graphics programs, engineering calculations, games, and the like.

The systems programmer, who must write the editors, the assemblers, and compilers, will have a different view of the machine. In addition to all the things already mentioned, he will view the system as a set of independent I/O routines (perhaps 30) which he can call from his programs to move information to and from the surrounding hardware. Some of these routines will be extensive. For instance, a computer at this level almost always has software primitives to manage a file system on the disk. Files are the result of the most complicated kind of I/O the system is likely to do. In addition, the systems programmer will be keenly aware of the operations of the user interface program whereby a user can give commands to the system, and of the mechanism whereby programs are loaded into memory and started into execution.

The primary new feature that an operating system has at this level, that simpler computers will not have, is a file system. A file is a collection of related data items called records. A record frequently corresponds to an individual case, observation, or instance in a collection of data that contains many cases. Each record in the file normally has the same format.

Files are a natural outgrowth of the way people have always handled manual forms. After all, we are used to keeping personnel information organized with one index card (record) per person, or billing information with one bill (record) per customer, etc.

The file idea also simplifies certain kinds of programming. A file is a logical construct that programmers can deal with fairly easily and that is independent of the underlying hardware of the disk. This independence is very important. Files as they are normally used, allow a programmer to deal with record X which is part of file Y. The alternative would be simply to write a list of data items directly to the disk. In the general case, where the size of a data item doesn't correspond to the size of a disk sector, and where the string of data might be allowed to start anywhere on the disk, access can be very difficult. Programs would have to go through a great deal of calculational gymnastics just to locate where a particular piece of data in the file is stored. To avoid these problems, perhaps 4 kilobytes worth of code in the operating system will be dedicated to managing files and thereby making disk accesses easy for the user.

In this chapter, we will examine the internals of one very influential small disk operating system—CP/M. This software comes from Digital Research, Inc. of Pacific Grove, California. CP/M is probably the most widely used operating system in the world, if one gives every computer—micro and mainframe—an equal count. We hope that by examining this one system in detail, we will leave the reader with a sense of what is easy and what is hard, what is necessary, and what is desirable in a small operating system.

CP/M is a single-user operating system. This means that the user has the computer all to himself. The original CP/M makes no attempt at multiprogramming or time sharing. All programs written to operate under CP/M do all the operations that they require serially: The program does its input, then some calculation, then more input, then more calculation, then output, etc. All of these things are done one at a time. There is no interleaving of operations. There will always be operating systems organized along this pattern, but in the future they will be realized on more and more powerful machines.

The original 8 bit version of CP/M consists of a number of modules, which are shown in Figure 8-1. They fall roughly into four categories: a System Control Module, the I/O Control Modules, the Program Production Modules, and the System Utilities. The System Control Module is called the Console Command Processor. One of the things it does is interface with the user. The user tells the system what to do by typing a command line. This is a single line of text, entered from the terminal, which contains information such as program names, file names, and other parameters. The Console Command Processor controls the inputting of this line; then it decides what's being called for, loads an appropriate program, and sets it into execution.

Module name	Function performed
Console Command Processor (CCP)	System Control
File Management System (BDOS)	Input/Output Control
Low Level I/O System (BIOS) Editor Assembler Linker Debugger	Program Production
Peripheral Interchange Program (PIP)	System Utility for Manipulating Files

Figure 8-1:   High Level Modules in CP/M. These modules correspond to the major divisions in the CP/M system.

The I/O Control modules are a set of independent subroutines that can handle high level file oriented I/O requests to the disk subsystem and also low level, character by character I/O to slow devices like printers and terminals.

The Program Production Modules consist of an editor, an assembler, a linker, and a debugger. These are all standard types of systems software. Except for the debugger, they are discussed in other sections of this book.

The System Utilities are gathered together in one big module called the Peripheral Interchange Program. This module can do many operations on files, such as copying and concatenating. It can also move files from one device to another; for instance, from the disk to the console or to the printer.

Some parts of CP/M are in memory all the time. Other parts are called off the floppy disks as they are needed. The designers of CP/M selected a relatively small set of very useful functions and packaged them in a way that doesn't use a great deal of resident computer memory. The part of CP/M that is in memory at one time is about 6.5 kilobytes in length. This is an acceptable and necessary number when you consider that this operating system was made to be used with a generation of computers that can address a maximum of 64 kilobytes. If CP/M had required 40 kilobytes of resident memory storage, for example, there wouldn't have been any room for user programs.

The file handling that CP/M supports is its most sophisticated feature. CP/M files can be accessed both sequentially and randomly. Sequential file access means accessing records in a file one after another in linear order. Random access implies that all the records in the file are numbered and you can specify exactly which one you want.

One unusually advanced feature is dynamic allocation of disk space for growing files. What this means is that when you create a file, you don't have to specify your plans for its usage at the same time. You don't have to say how long it is going to be. Here's how this feature works. When you write the first record, the system gives the file a small amount of disk space. As you write additional information into the file, the system will find more space for it as space is needed. Furthermore, the new space can come from any free area of the disk. It doesn't need to be contiguous to the area already being used for the file.

The original CP/M was limited to processors that can execute the 8080 instruction set, that is, the Intel 8080, the Intel 8085, and the Zilog Z-80. The reason for this is that the operating system itself is written in PL/M which is Intel's system programming language. In spite of this limitation on processors, the operating system is in wide use.

To what does CP/M owe its success? Probably the biggest factor is that it is easy to adapt the system to many environments. On the hardware side, it can be easily configured to run on almost any hardware system that incoporates an 8080 type processor. The software is also adaptable. There is a procedure whereby the user can do something equivalent to adding individualized special purpose commands to the operating system.

CP/M has really made it possible for many small computer manufacturers to enter the business. It only takes a couple of man-years to develop the hardware for a new small computer. The software can take much longer. New manufacturers frequently avoid this problem by investing the several months it takes to get CP/M running on their specific kinds of hardware. Then a great deal of software becomes instantly available.

Much software has been written by independent vendors that will execute within the CP/M environment. The concept of using an operating system as an environment is important. It means a programmer can write a program in a generalized manner that will execute on many different computer systems, as long as they support CP/M. In a program, any time it is necessary to do input/output or file operations, the programmer can call on a CP/M routine in a standard manner. Since the system supports CP/M, the programmer knows he or she can count on a set of standard system routines being accessible. These routines can always be accessed in one standard way, but their internals will be different depending on the underlying equipment.

It is possible to find a version of almost any computer language that will run on a microcomputer under CP/M. There are versions of FORTRAN, BASIC, Pascal, COBOL, LISP, etc. In addition, there are many utilities such as communications packages and data base managers. And the CP/M environment is the host for many specialized applications programs. Probably the best known are various word processing systems and business planning systems. Software builds up rapidly if the user community can agree on a standard environment.

The version of CP/M that we are going to focus on in this chapter is the original version 1.4. Later versions are more complex but add no features which represent new concepts. CP/M 1.4 imposed a constraint on the kinds of disks that a system could use. Only one sort was supported, the IBM 3740 eight inch floppy disk standard. This disk is single-sided, single density, and very reliable. It is also, by virtue of use on early CP/M systems, the only real disk standard that exists in the microcomputer world today. Even though it doesn't store very much information (250 kilobytes), there is still a compelling reason to use it. Files can be easily exchanged with other users of CP/M type computers.

Where do we go from here? Our plan in Chapter 8 will be to explore the details of this operating system in a bottom-up fashion. That is, we will first look at the system memory layout and at the lowest level I/O routines (BIOS) on which everything else depends. With that in place, we can fruitfully discuss file management issues for small systems in general. Then we will discuss the particular file management system used by CP/M (BDOS), which happens to float on top of the BIOS layer. Next we study the loading and command operations at the very top (CCP), which use the file system.

Ultimately, we will be in a position to appreciate a look at features that have been found useful for newer and more elaborate single-user disk operating systems.

That is the plan for this chapter. The goal is to have the reader come to feel that a small operating system is not intimidating. Rather, it is a structure that any mature and self-sufficient programmer could create, given enough time and necessity.

8.2 MEMORY USAGE IN CP/M

This operating system is arranged so that part of it is always in memory and part of it is brought in only when needed. All of the I/O routines and the Console Command Processor stay in memory. They occupy perhaps the last 6.5 kilobytes of the address space, although the actual size will vary from system to system.

There is another section of memory which is always used by the system but which is a data structure rather than code. This is the System Tables and Buffers Area in the first 256 bytes of memory. This area contains a 128 byte I/O buffer that the system uses in making transfers to and from the disk. It also has several locations in which the addresses of various parts of the system are written. Any program can use these to do an indirect address reference to get into various system modules. The locations that function like interrupt traps in the 8080 are also in this area. CP/M makes no use of the interrupt system but leaves most of these areas blank in case a sophisticated user wishes to manipulate them. A complete picture of CP/M's memory usage is shown in Figure 8-2. The first 256 bytes in memory is called the base page. CP/M usage of the base page is diagrammed in Figure 8-3.

So the system has fixed uses for certain areas at the beginning and at the end of memory. Everything in between is available for programs written by the user or for the program production modules of the system, such as the editor, or the assembler. This intermediate region is called the Transient Program Area and it is approximately 59 kilobytes long.

The size of various versions of CP/M realized on different equipment may vary. Therefore certain crucial boundaries between modules cannot be counted on to occur at particular addresses. CP/M refers to these boundaries instead by name. For instance, the start of the Transient Program Area is called TBASE. The starting address of the Console Command Processor is called CBASE. And the starting address of BDOS is called FBASE.

The hardware of the 8080 processor mandates that certain locations in the processor address space are special. The reset location is special. For instance, when the reset line on the processor is made active, it will cause the program counter to be set to 0000H, and it will cause the machine to start executing instructions. CP/M always ensures that the first three address locations in memory contain a three byte instruction which says jump to the beginning of a system initialization routine. Therefore, after a reset, this jump is the first thing to be executed. The effect is to initialize the system and transfer control to the Console Command Processor.

There are other special locations that are associated with the interrupt system. The

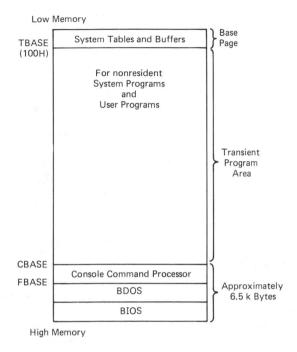

Low Memory

Figure 8-2:   CP/M Memory Layout. CP/M reserves locations at the bottom and top of the memory space for system use. The areas in between can be used for programs.

8080 processor is built so that whenever there is an interrupt, external hardware can insert a single extra instruction into the stream of instructions that the CPU would normally be processing. The instruction comes from outside the normal processor-memory system. It comes from some hardware whose only purpose is to administer the interrupt process. When the 8080 receives an interrupt, it will pull a word off the data bus (furnished by the external hardware) and use that as the next instruction to execute. There is a special one byte instruction, the Restart instruction, RST, that was put in the 8080 instruction set for use in this context. Normally the instruction fed in from outside upon an interrupt will be a Restart. This instruction operates just like a subroutine call, except that the instruction is one byte long instead of three, and it only allows you to access a subroutine in some special memory locations. It causes the program counter to be put on the stack and control to jump to one of the following locations. The specific location desired can be coded as part of the instruction.

```
0000H
0008H
0010H
0018H
0020H
0028H
0030H
0038H
```

Memory location (hexadecimal)	Field length (decimal)	Contents
0000H	3	Jump instruction to the WBOOT system initialization routine. Programs can jump to this location to get back to the Console Command Processor.
0003H	1	The IOBYTE—defines system I/O configuration.
0004H	1	Current Default Drive Number.
0005H	3	Jump instruction to BDOS. Programs make the standard entry to the I/O package by making a subroutine call to this location.
0008H	40	For use of Restart instructions. CP/M does not use these locations.
0030H	16	Reserved for future use of the system.
0040H	16	A scratch area reserved for use by the BIOS module for intermediate computations.
0050H	12	Reserved for future use of the system.
005CH	33	Default File Control Block—the CCP loads the descriptor for a file request here. If additional files are requested, their FCB's go at the front of the TPA Area.
007DH	3	Reserved for future use of the system.
0080H	128	Disk buffer—used for I/O transfers with the File Management System.

Figure 8-3: **CP/M Base Page Layout.** The lowest 256 memory addresses are reserved by CP/M for special operating system uses. This is the System Tables and Buffer Areas.

A normal way of using the interrupt system would be for external hardware to feed in different variants of the Restart instruction corresponding to various interrupt causing events in the external world. For instance, there might be an external clock, and every time this clock ticked, the processor would learn about it because the interrupt hardware would feed in a Restart instruction to location 0008H. There might be a switch somewhere in the computer system such that we wanted to know immediately every time it was closed. It could be arranged that the interrupt hardware would send in a Restart instruction to location 0020H whenever this happened, etc.

If the interrupt system is being used, it is normally a part of system initialization to write different jump instructions into each of the restart locations. These jumps can be used to route control to appropriate interrupt handlers which are written by the user and which are located somewhere else in the system. Interrupt handler code is very problem specific. It depends in detail on what external events may be signaling the computer. In any event, CP/M leaves all the restart locations free except for the lowest one, so that the user can manipulate the interrupt system if desired. We will discuss the details of writing interrupt handlers in Chapter 13.

8.3   THE LOWEST LAYER OF INPUT/OUTPUT ACTIVITIES (BIOS)

The I/O control modules of CP/M are organized very simply. They are principally a collection of subroutines that can be called by other parts of the system or by programs written by the user, in order to do basic I/O operations. They are very similar to the I/O drivers we studied in Chapters 2 and 7.

There are two layers in this I/O system. One part, the BDOS, deals with basic operations you might want to do on disk files, for example, manipulating the file directory, or reading a particular record in a file. The other part, the BIOS, is distinguished in two ways from BDOS. First of all, the I/O activities occur at a lower level. There is no file oriented I/O. Instead there are certain basic activities like transferring a single character to a printer or reading a particular addressed sector off a disk. The other distinguishing feature is that the BIOS routines are the only part of the CP/M system that changes from one computer system to the next. All higher layers stay the same. However, there must be some level in the operating system where we take account of the fact that we are using a printer made by manufacturer A rather than a different sort made by manufacturer B. The BIOS is the level at which this is done. The routines in the BIOS package are called I/O primitives because all I/O commands, however complicated, ultimately come down to sequences of these basic operations.

The BIOS routines are why CP/M can fit on many different kinds of computer systems. All that the vendor of a new computer system has to do to get software for his machine, if he uses an 8080 type processor, is to write a set of BIOS routines that interface his hardware to the CP/M system. All the rest of the operating system then becomes immediately available, and all the user programs which have been written to run in a CP/M environment become available for his machine. Thus, the vendor can achieve the blessings of standardization.

The BIOS is the interface between this operating system and the hardware. The routines that must be in the BIOS package and the exact procedure by which they can be invoked are all rigidly specified in the CP/M system. However, the way to write the internals of these routines is up to the producer of the particular computer system. There is room for some exotic programming in the BIOS. A good variant can run considerably faster than a poor one.

There are fifteen subroutines in the BIOS package. Six of them deal with I/O to slow devices like terminals, printers, and paper tape punches. Seven more deal with I/O to a faster device, the floppy disk. In addition there are two other routines that are used as part of initializing the system. They are not for I/O at all. Figure 8-4 displays the names of the routines that make up BIOS and states their functions.

Initialization Routines

BOOT	—	Subroutine to bring up a cold system.
WBOOT	—	Partial reinitialization on a warm system.

Slow I/O Routines

CONST	—	Checks if a character is ready at the console.
CONIN	—	Reads in a character from the console.
CONOUT	—	Outputs a character to the console.
LIST	—	Outputs a character to the listing device.
PUNCH	—	Outputs a character to the punch device.
READER	—	Inputs a character from the reader device.

Fast I/O Routines

HOME	—	Moves head to track 0 on the selected disk.
SELDSK	—	Identifies which disk drive to use.
SETTRK	—	Identifies desired track number for an access.
SETSEC	—	Identifies desired sector number for an access.
SETDMA	—	Prepares DMA device for a data transfer.
READ	—	Reads the sector indicated by SETTRK and SETSEC.
WRITE	—	Writes the sector indicated by SETTRK and SETSEC.

Figure 8-4: Subroutines in the BIOS Package. These I/O primitives are the basis for all I/O done in the CP/M system. They are used by other I/O modules higher up in the operating system, and they may be used directly by applications programs. The code in these modules is the only part of CP/M that varies from one system to the next if the hardware is different.

There are two ways for a program to make use of the routines in the BIOS package. One way is to access a jump table that is the very first code in the BIOS. The beginning of BIOS is set up as shown in Figure 8-5. For an example, let's say you want to use the CONST routine. Notice where it is in the jump table. If the beginning address of BIOS happened to be equated to a variable called BBASE, elsewhere in the program, then you could run the CONST routine with this line of code:

```
JMP   BOOT
JMP   WBOOT
JMP   CONST
JMP   CONIN
JMP   CONOUT
JMP   LIST
JMP   PUNCH
JMP   READER
JMP   HOME
JMP   SELDSK
JMP   SETTRK
JMP   SETSEC
JMP   SETDMA
JMP   READ
JMP   WRITE
```

Figure 8-5: Jump Table Control Structure in BIOS. This data structure is the very first code in the BIOS module. It will route control to the proper subsection for a specific I/O task.

```
CALL  BBASE + 6
```

All of the routines end with a RET statement to transfer control back to the user code.

There is a standard for passing data back and forth between user programs and the I/O routines. One or two byte data or addresses being passed in should be right justified in the DE register pair. Data being returned will be presented in the A register if it is a single byte, and in the A and B register if it is two bytes. The high order part will be returned in B.

There is an easier way to use most of the BIOS routines and all of the BDOS routines. Ninety-nine percent of the I/O in user programs will be done as follows: CP/M allows you to access I/O routines by placing an identifying number for the desired routine in register C, setting up the other registers as described above to pass in other information, and executing a subroutine call to address 0005H. The three bytes beginning at location 5 are always used by CP/M to contain the following code:

```
JMP  BDOS
```

So, for most I/O routines, it is possible to activate them by setting up a function number, and any data or address parameters in the registers, and then calling a single entry point. There is a mechanism at the beginning of BDOS that will immediately route control to any of a large group of I/O routines irrespective of whether they reside in BDOS or BIOS. We will have more to say about using this mechanism in Section 8.6 when we discuss BDOS.

Figure 8-6 shows a small assembly language program that will print a message on the console. It makes use of a BDOS command that will print a string of characters. As part of the setup, the routine is identified as I/O routine number nine, which is the standard CP/M identification. The address of the buffer containing the string is passed in the register pair DE. There is one other convention associated with the usage of this routine: the string must end with the dollar sign character.

```
; DEMONSTRATION PROGRAM FOR ACCESSING BDOS
; PROGRAM WRITES A TEXT STRING TO THE CONSOLE
; USES STANDARD CP/M I/O ROUTINE NO. 9.
          ORG   100H        ; CODE STARTS AT BEGINNING OF TPA
BDOS:     EQU   5           ; ESTABLISH BDOS JUMP ADDRESS
          MVI   C,09H       ; SET UP NUMBER OF I/O ROUTINE
          LXI   D,PBUF      ; SET UP ADDRESS OF BUFFER
          CALL  BDOS        ; ENTER BDOS
          JMP   0           ; RETURN FROM PROGRAM TO CP/M
PBUF:     DB    'HELLO$'     ; THIS IS THE TEXT STRING
          END
```

Figure 8-6: A Demonstration Program Using the Standard Access into the I/O Package. This demonstration program prints a message on the console screen. It uses one of the BDOS routines (9) which can output a text string. A call must be made to the entry point of BDOS to activate this routine.

8.4 *PHYSICAL AND LOGICAL I/O OPERATIONS*

It has come to be accepted practice in operating system design for there to be a level of indirection between the I/O devices mentioned in high level I/O calls in user programs and the devices that ultimately perform this I/O. This means the high level program will direct I/O to some device with an abstract name such as the LIST device. The operating system will intercept the call and direct it to and configure it for a specific piece of hardware. We call what the high level program does making a logical I/O call.

The reason for constructing a real I/O operation out of at least two layers is as follows. It allows the system to be easily reconfigured with little or no required changes in user programs that are already written. For instance, let's say I am doing word processing. If I have a long document file that I want to send to a line printer when I am editing it, and to a high quality character printer when I am finished, a logical I/O capability presents a convenient way to do this. In my program, I would write the code so that I simply send all I/O to the LIST device. But when it comes time to print the document, I would give a command to the operating system that tells it whether to associate the high speed printer or the high quality printer with the list device.

The linkage between a logical and a physical device will occur somewhere deep in the operating system just before the real I/O is done. There will be a table, linking the two, that is configured to reflect the current arrangement of I/O devices at any particular installation. The IOBYTE in CP/M is a primitive implementation of this concept.

CP/M is designed to work with a floppy disk and a few other low speed devices. These devices may be standard items like terminals, paper tape punches, or readers, Teletype machines, or various kinds of printers. It is also fairly easy, given the interface electronics, to make CP/M work with other more unusual I/O devices such as optical character readers, bar code readers, card readers, and modems. The system can also be configured with a normal audio tape recorder as an I/O device, although it is uncommon to see setups like this.

On the logical level, besides the disk, CP/M recognizes four logical devices: the console, the reader, the punch, and the list device. Four mappings can be made to physical devices for each logical device. A particular byte on the base page in memory (the address is 0003H) is used to keep track of the mappings that apply at any given time. It is called the IOBYTE. Two bits are allocated to each logical device. Figure 8-7 shows the kinds of mappings that the system will keep track of. One of the routines in BDOS can be used to change the current value of the IOBYTE.

Let's consider again how we would set things up to be able to switch several different kinds of printers in and out of the system. The burden of doing this would fall on the BIOS routine with the function of transferring a character to the LIST device. This routine would have to be written in such a way that whenever it was entered, it first would inspect bits 6 and 7 in the IOBYTE. Then depending upon what it found there, it would branch internally to one of up to four different printer handlers. That's all. Applications programs, or CP/M commands, can have variability in their output by manipulating this underlying structure. Anytime an applications program needs to change a printer, it can do so by properly setting the indicators in the IOBYTE.

Console Field (bits 0, 1)

    0   —   Console assigned to a TTY (Teletype machine)

    1   —   Console assigned to a CRT (cathode ray tube—
                 screen terminal)

    2   —   Batch mode, paper tape is console input and
                 paper tape punch is console output.

    3   —   User defined console device (UC1)

Reader Field (bits 2, 3)

    0   —   Reader is the TTY paper tape reader

    1   —   Reader is a high speed paper tape reader

    2   —   User defined reader device (UR1)

    3   —   User defined reader device (UR2)

Punch Field (bits 4, 5)

    0   —   Punch is the TTY paper tape punch

    1   —   Punch is a high speed paper tape punch

    2   —   User defined punch device (UP1)

    3   —   User defined punch device (UP2)

List Field (bits 6, 7)

    0   —   List device is the TTY printer

    1   —   List device is the CRT screen

    2   —   List device is the line printer

    3   —   User defined list device (UL1)

Figure 8-7:   Usage of the Fields in the IOBYTE. The fourth byte on the base page is called the IOBYTE. It is used to keep track of the current relationship between the logical devices used by the operating system and the real physical devices to which they correspond. Bits are numbered from zero to seven starting at the left end of the byte.

8.5 FILE CONCEPTS IN CP/M

8.5.1 Overview of What the System Does with Files

All file systems have similar objectives and similar constraints. When the reader sees the kind of design trade-offs that were made with CP/M, hopefully it will be easy to conceptualize the operations of other systems. Let's pause now and inventory the kinds of things we might want to know about the internals of any computer file management system.

Here are some issues that need to be addressed:

1. What kind of mass storage devices can the system use—hard disks, floppy disks, tapes, etc.?

2. What kind of files does the system have? Can we access a file sequentially? Can we access it randomly? Any other way?

3. How big can a file be?

4. How many files can a disk (or other system media) hold?

5. What is the record size? Can the size of a record be changed? Is it possible to have several record sizes in the same file?

6. What kind of directory must be maintained for file access?

7. How do user programs interface with the file system?

8. How are files laid out on the storage media? If a disk is used, are the parts of a file contiguous, or can they be scatter stored at various free locations on the disk?

9. Is a file given all its space when it is defined initially, or can it acquire space on demand as the space comes to be needed?

10. What part of the directory structures related to managing files are kept on the storage media and what part in memory?

11. How does the system map down from a logical description of a record in a file to a determination of where that information is actually stored?

12. What happens to the file if the system crashes?

Here is an overview of how CP/M 1.4 handles these matters. Of course, the only storage media in the original CP/M system is the IBM type 3740 floppy disk. CP/M files can be used sequentially like a tape, or it is possible to direct the system to specific records. This is a basic random access mechanism. A file can be up to about 250 kilobytes in length. There can be a maximum of 64 files on a disk. Of course, the combined lengths cannot exceed the total amount of space available. The record size in a CP/M file is fixed, and it is the same as the size of a sector on the floppy disks that are being used—128 bytes. Every record in a file corresponds to a particular physical disk sector, although this correspondence may change as files are created, destroyed, or moved around.

The system uses a file directory to record all relevant information about its files. It is contained in 16 sectors in a system area at the beginning of the disk. Space is reserved in the file directory for up to 64 entries, whether they are used or not. The system uses 32 bytes of storage to keep track of each file. It's amazing that 32 bytes is enough, because keeping track of a file means knowing its name, where it starts, how long it is, what sectors are associated with the file, and what order they are in. The 32 bytes which contain the system's description of a particular file are called a File Control Block (FCB).

The common file operations are creating a file, opening or closing it, reading or writing a record, and possibly deleting the file. Positioning to particular records are part of the read and write operations. All of these things can be done from a user program by making calls to certain of the BDOS routines that are provided with CP/M.

Considerations of where files are stored on the disk, how they acquire space when they are expanding, and how the system knows which logical record corresponds to which physical sector are all quite complicated and ingenious. They are at the heart of any file system. We will examine these implementation strategies later.

To complete our overview, let us consider some of the things that may happen when the system uses a file. Imagine that a program is trying to read a particular record.

The first thing that must be done is to open the file. What this means is that all of the directory information describing the file is copied from the disk directory and installed in some convenient location in memory. Actually, the File Control Block itself is copied into memory. Any time that changes are made to the file, they will be recorded in a suitable fashion in this File Control Block. When the program is finished with the file, the altered File Control Block, as it now exists in memory, will be copied back into the disk directory. This is known as closing the file. If this procedure is followed invariably, at the conclusion of editing operations, the directory will always have a true and current representation of every file it describes.

In order to read a particular record, the program must write the number of the record into the File Control Block, and then call the Read Record routine in BDOS. This routine will determine the proper sector, position to it, read it, and transfer the data into a 128 byte system buffer. The buffer is located at a standard location in memory so that the calling program can get at the data after the transfer. A similar procedure is used to write a particular record in a file. When the program is finished, it must close the file. Once again, this is a procedure in which the memory File Control Block is copied back into the disk directory.

8.5.2 Directory Manipulations

The file directory on CP/M disks always occurs in the same place. It is contained in the first 16 sectors of track two. To put the directory in perspective, we should mention here what is on the rest of the disk. Track 0, sector 1 has a cold start loader that is used to bring the system into memory initially. The rest of tracks 0 and 1 contain the code for the memory resident part of the CP/M operating system. The next sixteen sectors contain the directory, as we have indicated. All the rest of the disk is free to be used for files.

The File Control Block (FCB) data structure is at the heart of any discussion about CP/M files because it represents all the summary information that needs to be maintained about the file. There are really two versions of the File Control Block in CP/M: a version that is kept in the disk directory, and a version that is slightly altered and transferred to memory to control the file when it is being actively used. Figure 8-8A shows the usage of the various fields when an FCB is on the disk. The same FCB when it has been put in memory is shown in Figure 8-8B. The memory version is one byte longer than the disk version.

Creating a file is equivalent to getting a File Control Block for it established on the disk directory. A user program can do this by setting up a partially filled-in FCB in some available memory buffer and then making an appropriate call to one of the subroutines in BDOS. It doesn't matter where the buffer is. Any free space that is 33 bytes long will do. The program that is creating the file must place zeros in the buffer and then write the name and type of the file into the proper fields. The parts of these particular fields that are not used should contain blanks. The name should be right justified in its field, and the type should be left justified in its field. Next, the user program must put

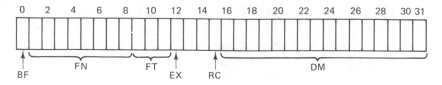

Field	Position	Usage
BF	0	Busy/free byte. Indicates whether this directory entry is in use. 00 for in use (busy), 'E5' for free.
FN	1–8	File Name, right justified, automatically padded with blanks on the left.
FT	9–11	File type, three character extension.
EX	12	File extent, normally set to zero except for long files.
	13–14	Not used.
RC	15	Record count: number of records used in this extent.
DM	16–31	Disk Allocation Map. Shows clusters owned by file and sectors in use within the clusters.

Figure 8-8A: The File Control Block (Disk Version). This data structure contains all the information the system needs to know about a named file that is less than 16 kilobytes long. For longer files, one FCB is required for each 16 kilobyte extent. This is the way the FCB looks when it is part of the disk directory and is describing an inactive file.

the address of the buffer into the DE register pair, put the number 22 in the C register, and make a call to BDOS. The Create File routine, which is part of BDOS, will then read the memory buffer and establish a corresponding entry in the disk directory for this new File Control Block.

Each File Control Block can record all necessary information on up to 16 kilobytes of a file. If the file becomes longer than this, another File Control Block must be created for the next 16 kilobytes of the file. The system will do this automatically. The Extent Field in the FCB records which part of a long file the FCB controls. Extent 0 is for the first 16 kilobytes; Extent 1 is for the next 16 kilobytes, etc. If necessary, up to 16 extents can be associated with a single file. The length of such a file would be nearly 256 kilobytes, which is the entire capacity of the diskette.

The Disk Allocation Map field and the Next Record field contain data that allow the system to make a correspondence between a particular record in a particular named file and a track and sector address which specifies exactly where that record is on the disk. We will discuss these fields more extensively in the next section.

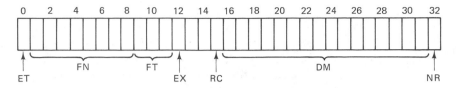

Field	Position	Usage
ET	0	Entry type, not used in CP/M 1.4.
FN	1–8	File Name, right justified, automatically padded with blanks on the left.
FT	9–11	File type, three character extension.
EX	12	File extent, normally set to zero except for long files.
	13–14	Not used.
RC	15	Record Count: number of records used in this extent.
DM	16–31	Disk Allocation Map. Shows clusters owned by file and sectors in use within the clusters.
NR	32	Next record number for reading or writing.

Figure 8-8B: The File Control Block (Memory Version). This data structure contains all the information the system needs about a named file that is less than 16 kilobytes long. For longer files, one FCB is required for each 16 kilobyte extent. This is the way the FCB looks after it has been installed in memory by an OPEN command as preparation for using a file.

8.5.3   Dynamic Space Allocation

A sophisticated feature that CP/M implements is to award space to a growing file dynamically. In some systems, when a file is created, you must specify exactly how long it will be. This is hard if you don't know. Not so with CP/M. The protocol of this operating system is that, when a file is created, it is given no space at all. Later, it will acquire space in small increments when it needs it.

When you first begin to write into a file, it is assigned one kilobyte worth of space at any convenient location on the disk. The one kilobyte unit corresponds to eight 128 byte sectors. This unit is called a cluster. The clusters are uniquely numbered. All space allocation by the system is done in terms of clusters.

After the user program writes eight records into the first cluster owned by the file, there will be no more space. When the program attempts to write a ninth record, the system will find another cluster somewhere on the disk and associate it with the file. Now the program will begin using the sectors within this new cluster for additional writes. Whenever a cluster is exhausted, the system will automatically provide another (provided there still is some room on the disk). Clusters in a file do not necessarily have to be physically contiguous. The system will try to put all the clusters for a file together in a linear string, but sometimes this is not possible. In any case, this whole mechanism is transparent to the user. He doesn't know the difference.

How many clusters are there on a disk? It seems that there should be 256, as suggested by the capacity of a standard CP/M disk. However, the operating system and disk directory have taken up some of this space. Because of this, there are only 241 clusters of free file space. CP/M numbers clusters on the disk from 1 to 241. The first space that is associated with allocated clusters is logical sector 17 on track 2. This sector belongs to cluster 1. The clusters are numbered in ascending order going around the tracks at the periphery of the disk and working in toward the center. Figure 8-9 shows which clusters are associated with which tracks. Incidentally, if you happen to total up the number of sectors on the disk in the cold start loader, the operating system, the

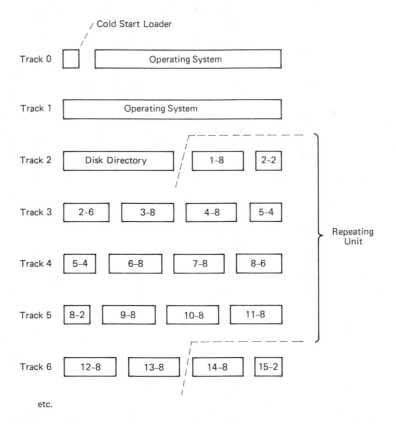

Figure 8-9: The Physical Placement of Disk Clusters. This map shows what clusters are associated with specific tracks on the disk. Each box denotes a cluster. There is a pair of numbers within each box. The first number is the cluster number, and the second number shows how many of the cluster's eight sectors are present at this location.

directory, and the 241 clusters, you will see that six sectors appear to be missing. That is because the last six on the disk are not used. Add them in and you'll get the correct number—2002 on the whole disk.

The allocation of clusters is kept track of in several places. The first place is in the File Control Block for each file. Within the File Control Block there are 16 bytes that are used to record the numbers of all the clusters associated with that particular extent of the file. This field is called the Disk Allocation Map (DM). When the system gives a file another cluster, it immediately marks that down in the File Control Block both in memory and in the disk directory.

There is a data structure in memory that the system uses to make judgments about what clusters to give to what file. It is called the Allocation Vector. It is 241 bytes long, and each byte refers to a cluster. The bits within each byte refer to the sectors associated with that cluster. The bit is 1 if the sector has been used in a file and is 0 if it is free. Figure 8-10 shows a sample allocation vector. This snapshot of the Allocation Vector shows that the low numbered clusters are all in use. Clusters 100, 103, and 104 are completely free. Clusters 102 and 105 are partially used up. In cluster 105, for example, three sectors have been written and the other five are available for use. The clusters toward the end of this numbered list are all free.

Every time a sector is written as part of a file, the appropriate bit will be set in the Allocation Vector. When deleting files, the appropriate clusters are cleared in the Allo-

Byte number	Corresponding cluster	Contents (bit map)
1	1	1111 1111
2	2	1111 1111
.	.	.
.	.	.
.	.	.
100	100	0000 0000
101	101	1111 1111
102	102	1111 1110
103	103	0000 0000
104	104	0000 0000
105	105	1110 0000
106	106	0000 0000
.	.	.
.	.	.
.	.	.
240	240	0000 0000
241	241	0000 0000

Figure 8-10:   The Allocation Vector. These 241 bytes are a condensed and easy to use representation of all the system's information about what clusters are free and what clusters are in use. It is equivalent to a free list. The Allocation Vector can also pin point those sectors within a particular cluster that have been used and those that have not.

cation Vector. The Allocation Vector is set up as part of system initialization. This data structure is a convenient and economical way of monitoring the status of the pool of free sectors and the pool of committed sectors as they exist on the disk.

Perhaps an example now will serve to make the idea of cluster allocation more concrete. We will consider a disk with several files of various sizes and a large pool of uncommitted clusters. This pool of uncommitted clusters will be called the Free List. We will follow through what happens to these files during a typical user session at the computer.

At the start of the session the various directories might show this pattern of space allocation:

Files	Associated clusters
File 1	1, 2, 3
File 2	4, 5, 6, 7, 8, 9
File 3	10, 11
File 4	12, 13, 14
Free List	15, 16, 17, . . . , 240, 241

Let us suppose that File 1 needs to expand. It will have to get another cluster from the system. After receiving a new cluster, that file and the Free List would look as follows. All other files would be unchanged in terms of their cluster ownership.

Files	Associated clusters
File 1	1, 2, 3, 15
Free List	16, 17, . . . , 240, 241

Cluster 15 has been removed from the Free List and given to File 1.

Later on during this session the user might delete File 3. Then the file structure would look like this:

Files	Associated clusters
File 1	1, 2, 3, 15
File 2	4, 5, 6, 7, 8, 9
File 4	12, 13, 14
Free List	16, 17, . . . , 240, 241, 10, 11

Note that, since the Free List is really maintained in the memory resident disk Allocation Vector, the list has no particular order. The list is implicit in the Allocation Vector data structure.

If File 2 now were to expand, it would get another cluster from the Free List. It could be one of the clusters that had belonged previously to File 3. The only file changes are shown below.

Files	Associated clusters
File 2	4, 5, 6, 7, 8, 9, 10
Free List	16, 17, . . . , 240, 241, 11

This example suggests an important question. When a file needs to expand, and there is a pool of free clusters, how does the operating system decide which cluster to give it? Cluster allocation strategies can be very complicated. In general, what new cluster to associate with a file depends on the physical placement on the disk of the other clusters already used by the file. The object is to minimize the movement of the disk read/write head during normal operations. This suggests that you want to give the file a cluster that is physically close to the ones it already has. In addition, if the file will be read sequentially, the cluster should be physically close and such that sequential reads will be able to proceed smoothly and quickly. For instance, say we are dealing with a file that owns these clusters:

$$4, 5, 6, 7$$

The file is going to expand. Clusters 3 and 8 are free. If the file was going to be accessed randomly, it wouldn't matter which cluster it got. If you were going to access it sequentially, then cluster 8 would be the better choice. In any case, somewhere deep within any operating system, there is a routine that makes this kind of policy decision. It can be simple or complex, depending on how much effort was expended to optimize the use of the disk system. CP/M uses a few simple heuristic rules to decide which clusters should be allocated.

8.5.4   Physical and Logical Disk Sectors

All clusters and all disk sectors to which we have referred so far in this section are logical entities. They are numbered in a way that is convenient to the internal use of the operating system. A disk controller, on the other hand, is usually a dumb piece of hardware. It understands only very simple things such as what track the read/write head is to move to, and what physical sector within that track is of interest. Evidently there is an additional level of mapping between the way the operating system refers to sectors and the way the controller does. Fortunately the mapping is a very simple transformation. All that is involved here is the way the 26 sectors are numbered around any particular track on the disk. If the sectors are numbered consecutively around the circumference of the track, starting at the index hole, the numbers then represent physical sector addresses on that track. A different numbering is used for the logical sectors. Each consecutive logical sector on a CP/M disk is separated from its predecessor by 5 or 6 intervening physical sectors. Figure 8-11 shows how to translate between the physical and logical numbering.

There is a very good reason for numbering sectors according to the logical scheme: A common type of program that uses files is one that reads or writes a sector, then does some computation, then reads or writes the next sector, etc. in exact linear order all the way through the file. The logical numbering was put in, in order to minimize the disk positioning time to access these sectors. If logically adjacent sectors in a file occurred

Logical Sector Addresses are on the Outside Ring

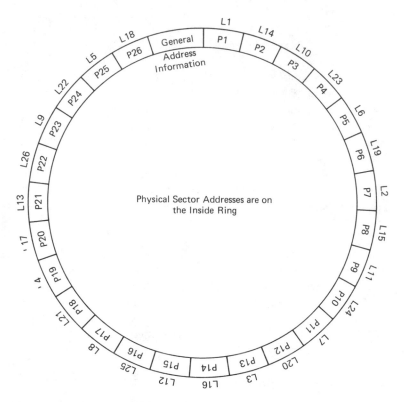

Figure 8-11:   Physical and Logical Addressing of Disk Sectors. There are two useful ways to number the 26 sectors along any disk track. Consecutive numbering yields physical sector addresses. Logical addresses are used by most operating systems. There is space between successive logical sectors to give some time for computation should this be necessary during the processing of a file.

one after another along the circumference of a track, there might not be time to do any computation between the accessing of one record and the next record. This might mean the disk would have to make one complete revolution before the next sector could be accessed. The logical numbering is a compromise. It requires about one quarter of a disk revolution between accessing one logical record and the next. This means about 40 milliseconds worth of computation can go on between the two accesses.

There is no corresponding mapping between a logical cluster and a physical cluster. The cluster is just a unit of allocation that owns eight logical sectors. There is also no mapping of track addresses. They are all physical. The only mapping that occurs is on the level of disk sectors.

8.5.5 Accessing Records Specified Within Files

As the reader can see, there is a lot of internal juggling from one way of describing the disk to another in CP/M. Most of this is hidden from the user. The problem for the operating system is always to take some high level call using some sort of file specification that is convenient to the user, and automatically map that down to a track and sector address to pass to the disk controller. The controller knows nothing about layers of mapping. It just knows the physical disk addresses to which the read/write head can be moved.

Let's take an example and go through all the steps of the mapping. Suppose we have been working with a file and we wish to add another record on the end of it. There is an operating system routine in the BDOS section of CP/M, which will write a record anywhere in a file. Let's assume we have set up the proper parameters and made a call to this routine. The BDOS routines will be described in more detail in a later section. The File Control Block might look as shown in Figure 8-12. For this example, the fields that are relevant are the Record Count Field, the Disk Allocation Map Field, and the Next Record Field.

The BDOS routine needs to identify what sector to use for the write. It can always

The File Control Block looks like this:

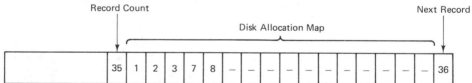

The relevant part of the allocation Vector looks like this:

Byte number	Contents
1	1111 1111
2	1111 1111
3	1111 1111
4	1111 1111
5	1111 1111
6	1111 1100
7	1111 1111
8	1110 0000

Figure 8-12:   Adding a New Record to the End of a File. This figure shows the two data structures that the system will consult during the course of adding a record at the end of a file. In the example, the first four clusters associated with the file have been entirely used up. Three records in the fifth cluster have been written. Space for five more is available.

do this using the contents of the Next Record Field and the Disk Allocation Map. The Disk Allocation Map shows what clusters are already owned by the file. And the Next Record Field contains the number of the record that will be written relative to the other records in the file. So, how do we find what sector to use for writing? Going back to the example, if we wish to write record number 36 in this file, we know that the preceding records will completely take up the first four clusters associated with the file, and part of the fifth cluster—three logical sectors in the fifth cluster. This is because one cluster is equivalent to eight sectors. Record 36 will use the fourth logical sector in the fifth cluster owned by the file.

We can formalize this argument in the following way. Suppose we are given a file and told to write a particular record in the file. It doesn't matter if the record is at the end of the file or somewhere in its interior. The same mechanism applies. We have to take the record number and transform that into a cluster number and one of the eight logical sectors associated with every cluster. The number of the sector within whatever cluster is being referred to is

$$\text{Sector Within the Cluster} = ((\text{Record Number} - 1) \bmod 8) + 1$$

To find the actual cluster number, we just have to look into one of the 16 single byte fields in the Disk Allocation Map of the File Control Block. Each byte corresponds to a cluster associated with the file. Which field to look in can be computed as follows. We are assuming the fields are numbered from 1 through 16 starting at the left.

$$\text{Field} = ((\text{Record Number} - \text{Sector Within the Cluster})/8) + 1$$

The BDOS does this sort of computation. However, it is easier for us to see what is going on by looking at the Allocation Vector in memory. We are trying to write a new record on the end of the file. The Disk Allocation Map shows that the last cluster owned by the file is cluster 8. Looking at cluster 8 in the Allocation Vector, we can see that three bits are set. This means the first three sectors belonging to this cluster have been used, and five more are available before the cluster is all used up. It is easy to identify the fourth logical sector in cluster 8 as the place where the new writing should occur. Now the only remaining problem is to find the physical sector to which this logical one corresponds.

The CP/M documentation doesn't state how this is done, but it is clear what type of algorithm must be applied. The algorithm must accept the cluster number and the number of the sector within that particular cluster, and a track number and a physical sector number on that track must be returned. There are so many different numberings that things may become confusing, but if we use the proper terminology, the algorithm can be expressed simply.

CN	= Cluster Number (1–241)
SC	= Number of a Sector Within a Cluster (1–8)
ALSN	= Absolute Logical Sector Number (1–2002)
	This is the number the sector would have if we numbered consecutively from the start of the disk.
TN	= Physical Track Number (0–76)

LSN   = Logical Sector Number Within a Particular Track (1–26)

PSN   = Physical Sector Number Within a Particular Track (1–26)

RN   = Record Number Within a File (1–128)

You may be wondering why tracks are numbered from 0 and sectors are numbered from 1. This happens to be one peculiarity of the IBM 3740 data storage standard.

Here is the algorithm for converting a logical specification of where a record is into a physical specification. The algorithm has three steps:

1. The first step is to find the Absolute Logical Sector Number. Remember, this is the number the sector would have if sectors were counted one by one from the beginning of the disk. The improbable term at the end of the expression for the Absolute Logical Sector Number takes account of the strange position CP/M 1.4 assigns for the first cluster—that is, it is at logical sector 17 on track 2.

$$ALSN = (CN - 1)*8 + SC + 68$$

2. The track can be found by subtracting increments of 26 from the Absolute Logical Sector Number, because there are 26 sectors per track. The remainder from this operation will be the Logical Sector Number (sector numbered from one within a specific track).

$$LSN = ALSN \bmod 26$$

$$TN = (ALSN - LSN)/26$$

3. The track number is a physical address. There is still a mapping between logical and physical sectors within a track to contend with. This last translation can be done by looking up the LSN in the table that is implied by Figure 8-11, and reading out the PSN.

If this algorithm is used, the designation of a particular record within a file can be completely translated to a physical track and sector which is the addressing form used by the disk controller. There are several reasons for this cumbersome arithmetic. We are laying files down on a mechanical device in which the size of some storage parameters —for instance, 26 sectors per track—have no relation to a superimposed file structure. We are tied to numbering standards, some of which begin at zero and some of which begin at one. Finally, the amount of space reserved on the disk for the operating system is not a multiple of the allocation unit in which space is given to files. These considerations should make the users happy that they can make simple references to a logical file system, and that they don't need to go through the above manipulations in their own programs.

One last feature we need to examine in order to understand low level disk operations is the machinery for sequential files and random access files. Essentially this comes for free after all the above work has been done. Actually, there is only a trivial difference between accessing a file sequentially and randomly. In each case, the Next Record Field in the FCB will be set to the number of the record to access. When this has been done, the whole translation procedure we described earlier can be used to produce the physical address of the proper disk sector. Whether you have been using the file randomly or sequentially up to now is a matter of history. It affects the current access not at all.

The trivial difference arises around who sets up the Next Record Field. If the file is being used randomly, the user program must set this field in the FCB before calling any BDOS routine that will access the record. If the file is being used sequentially, the Next Record Field just needs to be initialized at the beginning and then left alone. Every time the user program makes an access under the control of the FCB, the Next Record Field is automatically incremented by the system. This makes it easy to go from one record to the next with no work.

8.6 MACHINE INDEPENDENT INPUT/OUTPUT (THE BDOS ROUTINES)

The primary function of the BDOS section of CP/M is file management, and there is a set of subroutines that can be invoked to do everything that is necessary in this regard. It is also possible to do console and list I/O through the BDOS package. BDOS remains constant from one system to the next. It does not depend at all on specific hardware in the way that BIOS does. Figure 8-13 shows the complete set of all the BDOS calls that can be made in CP/M 1.4.

All the functions of BDOS can be invoked in the single uniform manner we have discussed before. A function number and possibly an address pointer will be set into registers, and then a call will be made to the BDOS entry point. For certain low level I/O functions, such as console and list I/O, BDOS merely provides a uniform calling mechanism. The code for these routines resides in the BIOS module. So BDOS handles these functions by forming an internal call to the proper BIOS subroutine. The file management primitives in BDOS can be quite involved. In the section on file concepts, we discussed in a global way the internals of what the system does to handle files. In this section we would like to present some details of what happens in connection with six of the most important BDOS routines.

BDOS file manipulation begins with a call to the subroutine that creates a file. To use this function, you set up an FCB in memory that contains just the file name and type. You pass the BDOS Create File routine the address of this FCB as a parameter. The BDOS routine creates a corresponding FCB on the disk directory. It returns an error code if there is no directory space. No clusters are allocated at this time. The NR field in the FCB remains set to zero.

When you open a file, your program must give another BDOS routine the address of an FCB that contains the name of the file. The BDOS routine will copy all the information from the disk FCB into the memory FCB. It produces an error code if the file is not there on the disk directory. Copying a file descriptor from disk to memory, then, is what it means to open a file in CP/M.

In order to close a file, your program must give a BDOS routine the address of the FCB associated with the file. The routine will copy all information from that FCB to the image of the FCB that is maintained in the disk directory. If multiple extents of the file

Function Number	Subroutine	Information Passed In	Information Returned1
Initialization			
0	* System Reset		
Console and List I/O			
1	* Read Console		ASCII character
2	* Write Console	ASCII character	
3	* Read Reader		ASCII character
4	* Write Punch	ASCII character	
5	* Write List	ASCII character	
6	(not used)		
7	Interrogate I/O Status		I/O Status Byte
8	Alter I/O Status	I/O Status Byte	
9	Print Console Buffer	Buffer Address	
10	Read Console Buffer	Buffer Address	
11	* Check Console Status		Ready Flag
File Management I/O Subroutines			
12	* Lift Disk Head		
13	* Reset Disk System		
14	* Select Disk	Disk Number	
15	Open File	FCB Address	Completion Code
16	Close File	FCB Address	Completion Code
17	Search First	FCB Address	Completion Code
18	Search Next	FCB Address	Completion Code
19	Delete File	FCB Address	Completion Code
20	Read Record	FCB Address	Completion Code
21	Write Record	FCB Address	Completion Code
22	Create File	FCB Address	Completion Code
23	Rename File	FCB Address	Completion Code
24	Interrogate Login		Login Vector
25	Interrogate Disk		I.D. of Disk
26	* Set DMA Address	DMA Address	
27	Interrogate Allocation		Address of Alloc. vector

Figure 8-13:   I/O Function Calls That Can Be Made Through BDOS. The subroutine names that are prefaced with an asterisk are parts of the BIOS package that can be called from BDOS. To set up a call to any of the routines shown here, place the function number in register C, and the data or the address of the data in the DE register pair. If results are returned, and they are one byte, they will be returned in register A. For two byte results, register B will contain a high order part; register A will contain the low order part.

are open, they must be closed separately. As always, there will be an error code if the system can't do it.

Deleting a file gives disk space back to the system. All extents on the disk directory belonging to the file will be marked as free. All clusters associated with the file will be cleared in the Allocation Vector. This has the same effect as returning clusters to a free list.

The Read Record Function can be used for both random and sequential reading. Here is how it must be set up. In the FCB in memory, the NR field must be set to the number of the record you want to access (1–128). The system computes which cluster this record must belong to using the clusters in the DM field, and what sector within the cluster. The system looks at the Allocation Vector to see whether that sector contains data. If so, it reads it. If not, it gives an error message. After reading, the NR field is incremented. When the last record in an extent has been read, the system closes the FCB for this extent and attempts to open the next extent. This may cause problems if you want to go back and read some earlier records. In that case, your program will have to reopen the original extent.

The last routine we will discuss is the Write Record Function. This function can be used for both random and sequential writes. The NR field must be set to the number of the record you want to write. For a random write, the user program will do this. For sequential writes, after the first usage, the system will do this automatically. If the record being written is the first record (1) or the last record (128) of an extent, then some special things happen.

Consider first the normal case where

$$1 < NR < 128$$

The system decides whether you are writing over an already written record or just extending the file with a new record. It does this by comparing the NR field to the record count (RC). If you are writing over, it identifies the cluster to be used and the sector within that cluster. It calls a mapping module to get the real address and then does the write. The NR field increments. The RC field does not increment.

If you are extending the file by one more record, then the system determines whether there is any space left in the last cluster being used. If so, the next sector in that cluster is used and the Allocation Vector is changed accordingly. If not, the system disk allocation routine is called to get another cluster. The first sector of that cluster is used for the write, and the memory FCB and the Allocation Vector are altered to reflect the sector just written. NR and RC are both incremented.

Now let's consider the end effects. If NR = 1, this is a new file and nothing has been allocated yet. So the system calls the system disk allocation routine, to get a cluster. The first sector of the cluster is used for the write. The new cluster is recorded in the memory FCB. The sector that was written is recorded in the Allocation Vector. And NR and RC are incremented.

What if the system is writing the last record in the extent? In this case, NR will have been set to 128 in preparation for the write. The last sector in the last cluster associated with the extent will be used up. The Allocation Vector will be changed to reflect the sector just written. The RC field will be incremented so that it too contains 128. Now the system will close the FCB extent and write it back onto the disk. Then it will automatically create a new entry in the disk directory for a further extent to the file, and it will write this new FCB into memory over the old one. The RC field in the new extent will be set to zero, and the NR field will be set to one.

8.7 THE CONSOLE COMMAND PROCESSOR (CCP)

The Console Command processor forms the CP/M user interface. Communication with the system is done via command lines. When you type a command line at the terminal, the Console Command Processor is the software that receives the command, decides what you want to do, and takes appropriate action. Most of the time, you will use the command line to tell the system the name of a program you want to run. File names or parameters, separated by blanks, can also be on the command line. The normal operation of the CCP is to treat the first field it sees on the command line as a program name. It will find the program, loading it from disk if necessary, and then start it up. The CCP also has a few other special functions which we will discuss later.

Some programs have to be loaded from the disk, and some are built-in (that is, they reside permanently in memory as part of the system). Since these five programs are always in memory, they can be set into execution by the Console Command Processor very rapidly.

ERA:	erase a file
DIR:	show contents of a disk directory
REN:	change the name of a file
SAVE:	write the contents of a memory buffer to disk
TYPE:	list a program from the disk on the console

When you specify any other program to the Console Command Processor, it will attempt to find the program on the disk, load it into the Transient Program Area in memory, and run it. Programs loaded in this way will appear, for all intents and purposes, just like the built-in commands except that they take several seconds longer to begin running. By using this mechanism, a designer could add commands of his own to effectively make a customized operating system. There are a number of relatively large programs, which are included as part of the CP/M system, that get loaded in this way. We have seen them before. They are called loadable command processors. They include such things as

EDIT:	the CP/M Line Editor
PIP:	Peripheral Interchange Program
DDT:	Dynamic Debugging Tool
ASM:	the CP/M 8080 Assembler
SYSGEN:	the CP/M System Generation Program

Logically, the Console Command Processor is divided into four parts: the input module, the command parser/interpreter, the program loader, and the built-in commands. It is clear, when you consider these functions, that the Console Command Processor is just a more evolved version of the ROM monitor class of software that we discussed earlier.

The input module is much the same as the input module described for the ROM monitor. This type of software was outlined in Figure 3-4. The input routine uses BIOS primitives to take in data, character by character, and store it in a line buffer. As the data is being brought in, the input module watches for two types of special characters. The carriage return is one. This character marks the end of a command line. When it is detected, control and the line buffer are given to the command parser. The other type of special character signals editing or some other special handling that is to be done as the data is arriving from the keyboard. Except for the rubout function, these special handling commands are all implemented using the CNTL key. There are control characters which allow deleting the last character typed, deleting the whole line, retyping the line to reflect editing, moving the cursor to the start of the next line if it is a very long line, copying the command lines on a printer as well as to the screen, etc.

The command parser/interpreter gets control after a command line has been built up in the input buffer. The first thing this module does is to isolate the command part of the line from the parameter parts. The parameters are then placed in a special parameter area. Actually, the parameters are treated as if they are file names, because most of the time they will be. The way the system deals with file names is very sensible. A file name passed in on a command line must indicate that a file of that name is going to be opened by the program that is about to run. Therefore the CCP does some initial work to establish a File Control Block on behalf of this program. If there is just one file name, the CCP installs this in the proper position in the system default File Control Block located at 005CH in the base page. To use this file, the program specified in the command line just has to open it.

If there are two file names, the second one will be written into the right half of the system default File Control Block. It cannot be used in this position, but it is a simple matter for the user program, when it gets control, to move the file name and file type to some other buffer in the Transient Program Area and establish a second File Control Block.

The parser/interpreter module does one other smart thing with the command line. All of the line beyond the program name is copied into the system I/O buffer beginning at 80H. Since the system extracts all parameters and places them in a known location, it is possible to invoke a user program from the command line and pass it virtually any kind of parametric information. This user program will just have to be written expecting to find its parameters in the System I/O buffer at 0080H. This flexible structure for passing parameters provides another dimension along which CP/M can be customized.

After the parameters have all been stored away, the command is interpreted. There is really very little work to be done here. If it is a built-in command, control is transferred to one of the five built-in command routines. Otherwise the program loader is given control.

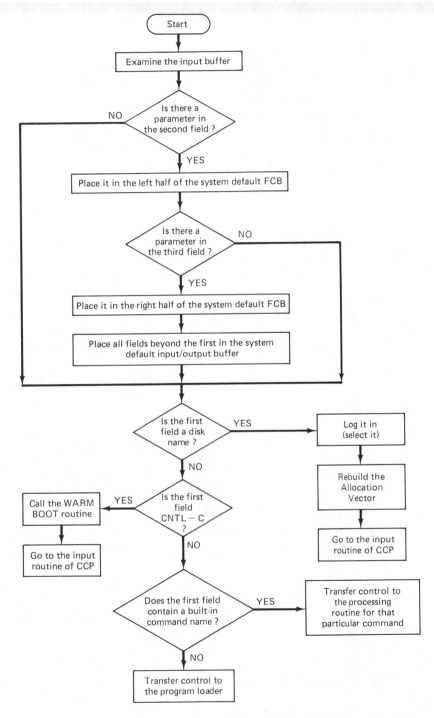

Figure 8-14: Simplified Logical Flow in the Parser/Interpreter Section of the Console Command Processor. This part of the Console Command Processor determines what the user wants and dispatches functions to satisfy whatever command has been given. The command will generally be the name of a program to execute.

A simplified logical flow for the parser/interpreter module is shown in Figure 8-14. The figure describes the principal actions and decisions that are made by the CCP during this stage of processing. However, it does not try to accurately model the internal organization of these functions.

How does program loading work? The program loader module examines the directory of the logged-in disk. It will be looking for a file with the same name as the program name part of the command line, and with a file type of COM. If it finds it, the file is loaded into memory starting at the system standard location of 100H. And then the program represented by the file is given control. If a file with the proper name is not found, an error message will be written, and control will be passed back to the start of the Console Command Processor.

There are several conceivable forms in which executable programs could be maintained on the disk. A reasonable way would be to use variable length blocks each prefaced by a byte count and a load address and terminated by several bytes for error checking. We discussed a loader for a similar kind of program representation in Chapter 5, so we won't repeat it here. Strangely enough, CP/M uses this sort of format for the output of its assemblers and compilers (it is called HEX format); but an even simpler format is

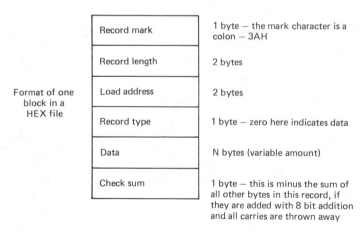

Figure 8-15: File Formats Used in CP/M for Processed Programs. (A) A HEX format file is the normal output of assemblers or compilers in a CP/M system. It consists of a number of variable length text blocks, the structures of which are indicated above, followed by an end of text character, CNTL Z. Each data byte in a HEX file is encoded as two ASCII characters. For example, the one byte 8080 HALT instruction is 01110110B (76H). In the HEX file, this instruction would be represented by two bytes: the ASCII code for 7, which is 00110111B, followed by the ASCII code for 6, which is 0110110B. (B) A COM file is in the easiest possible format for a loader. It is simply a string of characters that is to be loaded into memory starting at the system standard load point, 0100H. The COM file contains the characters on the disk exactly as they would appear in memory. If there are areas of embedded blanks in the load module, each blank is recorded as a character like any other. This is an inefficient load format.

used for programs ready to load. See Figure 8-15 for a diagram of these file layouts. For this purpose CP/M uses an exact image of the code as it will appear in memory. This is what is kept in a file with the file type of COM.

The loader for a file like this is very easy to write, but keeping programs in this form on the disk is inefficient. There is no way to identify areas of embedded blanks to the loader. For instance, the worst kind of program would be one that has some code at the beginning of the Transient Program Area and perhaps a data structure at the other end, and nothing in between. In this case, the system will maintain a COM file that consists of every byte in the TPA, one after another, even though most of them are not used.

Let's consider what the program loader is like. After it identifies the proper COM file in the directory, it will read the file sector by sector and install these sectors into memory, one after another, starting at the system standard loading address, 0100H. After the program is loaded, the CCP transfers control to address 100H to begin execution.

Now control is in the user program. It is pertinent to ask how the user program can give control back to the system when it has finished execution. A program can shunt control back into the Console Command Processor, if the last line of the program is

```
JMP  0000H
```

Why does this work? The system, as part of its own initialization, always puts a statement in the first 3 bytes of memory that will jump control to a BIOS routine called Warm Boot. Warm Boot reloads part of the system, reinitializes it, and jumps to the console Command Processor. Reloading the system takes a second or two, but to the user it appears that he has gone directly back into the Console Command Processor. This linkage is the principal way to traverse between user program control and system program control.

In addition to its main function of installing and executing programs, the CCP will also respond to a single alphabetic letter followed by a colon. This is interpreted by the system as the name of the disk drive that is to be currently used. CP/M can only interact with one disk drive at a time. When a new disk is logged in via this procedure, the CCP will call a BIOS routine to select the disk with the name given in the command. It will also call some code to rebuild the Allocation Vector. Whenever the system is turned on or whenever a disk drive is changed, the Allocation Vector must be rebuilt. The system can obtain all the information necessary to do this simply by scanning the Disk Allocation Map Fields for all the entries in the disk directory.

The other special situation to which the Console Command Processor will respond is if nothing but CNTL C appears on the command line. This is interpreted as a signal that the user wants the system to execute a Warm Boot. So a Warm Boot will be carried out, and then control will come back to the Console Command Processor in order to find out what to do next from the user. These operations are usually done because the user has changed the disk in the logged-in drive, and thus needs to get the system to rebuild the Allocation Vector.

The CP/M Console Command Processor is a relatively simple program with the main function of loading other programs and starting them into execution. There are many other useful tasks that can be given to a console command processor. We will look at a high end version of this kind of program when we study the UNIX operating system in Chapter 14.

8.8 SYSTEM LOADING AND INITIALIZATION

A number of nonobvious things have to be done to put CP/M in memory initially and bring it up to the point where the Console Command Processor will issue the user prompt. It is very instructive to look into these hidden interstices. Every system has them. They are frequently dismissed by academic systems programmers as too mundane to consider. On the other hand, certain industrial systems programmers would consider this to be the very blood and bones of systems programming. We will now discuss the procedure involved in activating a typical CP/M 1.4 operating system.

Unfortunately, some of the things that happen are dependent on the specific hardware configuration of the system, so the best we can do is talk about a typical system. Everything starts with the ROM monitor. Most systems will have one. It is usually located at the high end of memory. It should be the software that comes alive when the computer is reset or powered up. Since the reset location in 8080 type processors is location 0, some additional hardware outside of the processor itself must be used to set the monitor's starting address into the program counter.

After control gets into the monitor, we can give it a command that will begin the process of loading CP/M into memory. A standard that seems to be evolving in the microcomputer industry is for the monitor to contain a bootstrap disk loader. This is enough software to load one specific sector into program memory and transfer control to it. It is not just any sector; it is the 128 bytes that lie on the disk at track 0, sector 1.

So code in the very first disk sector will be loaded into memory, usually starting at location zero, and it will be placed into execution. This code is a more complicated loader called a Cold Start Loader. It will take the memory image of the complete operating system, which is on parts of disk tracks 0 and 1, and install it into the proper places in memory. The last thing the Cold Start Loader will do is to jump to an initialization routine (Cold Boot) which is part of BIOS. This routine will do its work and then transfer control to the Console Command Processor. The CCP, after some further initialization, outputs the system prompt to tell the user that everything is ready.

A typical Cold Start Loader is shown in Figure 8-16. Here is how it works. It makes use of the DMA apparatus for disk reads. The Cold Start Loader first sets the DMA address to the exact point in high memory at which the system should load, so that no space is wasted. Remember that typical CP/M systems take about 6.5 kilobytes worth of memory. Then it reads memory image code for the operating system off of the disk one sector at a time. Between each reading of a sector, the loader increments the address to be used by the DMA apparatus by 128 bytes so that the sectors are placed in memory immediately adjoining one another.

The Cold Start Loader will make use of BIOS type routines to read the sectors

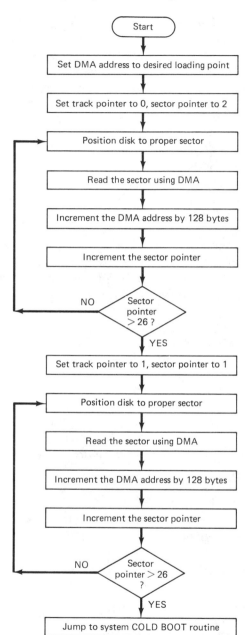

Figure 8-16: A Typical Cold Start Loader Routine. This routine can be loaded by the monitor into low memory. When it gets control, it reads by the monitor into low memory. When it gets control, it reads the disk and installs CP/M into high memory using the memory image on tracks 0 and 1.

which contain the operating system. However, these routines must be part of the loader, because BIOS would not be in the memory at this time.

For ease of programming, this Cold Start loader tries to load all of track 1 into memory even though the operating system usually ends a number of sectors (perhaps 5) before the end of the track. Remember that it is not possible to say exactly how long CP/M is because BIOS sections written by different people differ in length. However, there is an upper limit on its size because it is constrained by having to fit in track 0 and track 1. Loading all of track 1, even if the operating system doesn't require all of it, won't harm anything. If the initial load point is properly adjusted, the loader will try to load the superfluous sectors at the end of the disk over the ROM monitor which is in high memory. There is no harm in this, since ROM cannot be written into.

There are two initialization routines included in BIOS. The Cold Boot initialization routine is the one that receives control directly from the Cold Start Loader just after the entire system has been loaded into memory for the first time. For many systems, this would be the appropriate time to interrogate the user about a password, or display a sign-on message, or set values into the IOBYTE to establish the correspondence between physical and logical I/O devices. What happens in this part of Cold Boot is determined by whoever wrote the BIOS for this particular copy of CP/M. It is one of the most visible points where CP/M can be customized.

After sign-on protocols are taken care of, the Cold Boot routine initializes the system jumps and I/O summary information in the first eight bytes in memory, it sets up a default address for the DMA apparatus, and then it transfers control to the beginning of the Console Command Processor. The Console Command Processor will build the Allocation Vector for the system and display the system ready prompt. Now everything is ready for the user. These are all the things that happen when you boot up a typical microcomputer system running CP/M 1.4.

The other initialization routine is called Warm Boot. Using this routine provides a way to reinitialize the system if your computer was already up and running and one of the following situations occur:

1. The CPU is reset, causing a jump to location 0000H.
2. Your program finishes and you want to go back to the CCP to enter another command line. In this case, you can always terminate your program with a jump to location zero.
3. You physically change the disk in the drive that is logged in. To apprise the system of this, you must type CNTL C. This will cause a Warm Boot to take place.

The Warm Boot module uses the sector reading routine in BIOS to reload memory with a fresh copy of all the high memory parts of CP/M—that is, the CCP, BDOS, and BIOS. Of course if your program has wiped out crucial parts of BIOS, there is no way to recover except with a cold start. After Warm Boot reloads the system, it does exactly the same base page initialization as Cold Boot and it transfers control to the same entry in the Console Command Processor. The only operational difference between Warm Boot and Cold Boot is that the first routine reloads the entire system. Cold Boot doesn't have to do this because the Cold Start Loader has already loaded everything. However, Cold Boot elicits sign-on information from the user. The rest of their actions are just the same.

8.9 FEATURES OF MORE POWERFUL SINGLE USER DISK OPERATING SYSTEMS

We complete our discussion by pointing in the direction that CP/M and other similar systems are evolving. Think of the material we have just presented as a useful functional core. The things we mention now are the ways these ideas have been extended in later versions of CP/M and in similar systems from other manufacturers.

1. A menu-driven user interface has superceded the command line interface on some of the newer systems. Menus are user-friendly. In addition to being able to order the machine to do some function, you can always see what functions are available.

2. New versions of small operating systems have more device independence. Usually, another level of mapping is added between the logical structure of the file management and the underlying hardware. This has made it possible for the system to use many kinds of magnetic media (different disks and even tapes) and yet still refer to its files in a standard way. File reference is common for all hardware because it is abstracted from it.

3. The original CP/M's file size characteristics were restrictive. Newer systems usually have much longer files, all controlled by a single larger file control block. These systems also have more flexible ways of defining records so that the record size is not wedded to the disk sector size. Sometimes it can even be variable within the same file. Systems with this kind of flexibility always require bigger directories.

4. More complex access methods have been implemented, in particular, indexed random access files. One of the fields in a record is designated as an index field. Later, the record can be retrieved by giving the system a value of this index variable to retrieve on, rather than a record number.

5. Most systems now incorporate EXEC file processors. An EXEC file is a special kind of file that consists of a sequence of commands just as if the user had typed them from the keyboard. The system can be put in a mode so that it looks to the EXEC file for commands rather than the keyboard. This is useful for making single commands out of certain sequences of operations that have to be done often. For instance, in the program production cycle, a user might frequently assemble a program, when wait for output, then link it, and wait for that to finish, and then start the program executing. An EXEC file could chain this whole process together and make it into one entity that requires the user only to put it in motion.

6. Boot-up configuration programs are now common in small systems. These systems are set up to always load and execute a program with a special name when they are powered up. This is the boot-up configuration program. Its function is to initialize the system and configure it for a particular use. This is especially good for the users

of turn-key software. These users generally purchase a computer for one use only—word processing, accounting, business planning, etc. When they turn the machine on, they want the system to come alive as a specialized processor with everything properly configured and ready to go. The boot-up program can do this. In addition, it will shield naive users from any contact with the operating system. Frequently, they'd rather not know that it's there.

7. Many operating systems have a built-in overlay processor. This is special software machinery to allow a program longer than the machine's memory to be run. The program must be separable into conveniently sized modules. When one module is finished executing, and the natural course of the program makes it ready for another module which is not in memory, the overlay processor will find that module and load it so that execution can proceed automatically.

8. A number of small systems are appearing that utilize bank switching for the part of the operating system that is supposed to be resident in memory. This is another strategy to keep more of the computer's address space free for user programs. The user can program as if the part of memory that is set aside for the operating system is very small. What happens is that any time a call is made into the operating system, the system will manipulate the memory so that a large operating system area in ROM becomes accessible and some of the normal user memory is switched out of the system. The operating system routine will execute, and then restore the memory to its original state so the user program can proceed. We'll look more closely at bank switching in Chapter 13.

9. Using interrupts is not necessary with a single user disk operating system. However, newer systems are using interrupts in a minimal way to make certain kinds of timing information available to the control program. One important use is to permit time and date stamping for all files so that back-up files can be maintained in an orderly way. Another use is to implement a background printing capability. Frequently, it is desirable for a system to be able to work with a main program most of the time, but devote some fraction of its time to simultaneously putting out some data on a printer. This requires the involvement of the interrupt system. These kinds of operations are covered in detail in Chapter 13.

The next big development in operating systems will be software that allows a single CPU to be shared among multiple users and/or multiple independent tasks. We will look at this kind of operation after we examine the types of program production software that can flourish in the environment of a single user disk based operating system.

STUDY QUESTIONS AND EXERCISES

1. Write a character output routine (for a printer) that would be suitable for use in a CP/M BIOS. Assume that two printers can be accessed via this routine. They each have separate three port

interfaces consisting of a status port, a control port, and a data output port. The first thing the routine will have to do is look at the IOBYTE to select the proper printer.

2. If we wished to integrate a simple communications line driver into a CP/M system, what would the easiest way be to do this? Hint: an attachment point has been left in BIOS and the IOBYTE structure for this kind of thing. How could this primitive be used to transfer a file from one computer to another?

3. Give an example of a system wherein it might be useful to have logical sectors be in the same order as physical sectors. Give an example of a system where it is useful to have space on the disk between adjacent sectors.

4. This question asks about possible changes in the way CP/M records the usage of files. How would the Disk Directory, the File Control Block structure, and the Allocation Vector have to be changed for standard CP/M 1.4 disks if we wanted to do the following things (separately)?

    (a) Have a maximum of 128 files.

    (b) Have each FCB describe 32K worth of file.

    (c) Allocate space to files in units of 2K bytes rather than 1K bytes.

5. A power failure on a running CP/M system will erase whatever was in the memory but will probably not hurt the disks. Assume that a user program has opened a file and is doing (or has done) various record manipulations. What would be the consequences for the file of a power failure at the following moments?

    (a) The file has just been closed.

    (b) Records have been read, nothing has been written, but the file is still open.

    (c) The file has been extended with new records added at the end. It is still open.

    (d) The file has not been extended, but some internal records have been updated (changed).

    (e) The file is in the process of being closed.

6. This question focuses on the algorithm discussed in Section 8.5.5. Would it be possible to do the translation from a particular sector in a given cluster to the physical track and sector number via a table look-up? If yes, how big would the table be? What would it look like?

7. CP/M receives instructions from the user through single command lines. Menu driven systems are more user-friendly than command lines. Describe a way that the CP/M system could be altered (remember that it is very customizeable) so that when the user brings the system up there will be a single main menu. The menu will inquire whether the user wants to do assembly, editing, or file manipulations; and upon response, it will dump the user into the CP/M assembler, the CP/M line editor, or into the Peripheral Interchange Program. Of course, a real system would have a more extensive menu, or a hierarchy of menus.

8. Suppose you wish to integrate an elapsed time clock into a CP/M system. There will be some memory location(s) that keep a running count of clock ticks. The clock will tick every second. A program running under CP/M should be able to read the counter location(s) at any time to determine how much time has passed since the program last inspected this location. Don't worry about initialization. The interrupt system will be used with sufficient external hardware such that every time the clock ticks, a RST 2 instruction is forced into the instruction stream. This causes a trap to location 0010H. Outline the software that would be needed to handle this elapsed time clock.

9. For the short program shown in Figure 4-1, show byte for byte what the HEX format file would look like if this program had been processed by the CP/M assembler. Now show byte for byte what the corresponding COM file would look like.

9

Text Editors

9.1 INTRODUCTION: A ROUTE TO RAPID PROGRAM PRODUCTION

The editor is the piece of software with which the user spends most of his time interacting when he is in the process of developing a program. The editor is the software which makes it possible to compose the lines of text which constitute a program. It is also the tool with which that program can be modified. From a slightly more formal perspective, any program that you can write can be viewed as a string of characters built out of lines of text which are in a particular order and which are separated from one another by delimiting characters. An editor is a program that can compose a string like this, or that can modify any existing string of text characters.

If the editor on a given system is well designed, it will make a great contribution to the system appearing to be friendly to the user. A good editor can also dramatically affect programmer productivity.

Editors are to be found in two common varieties: the line editor and the screen editor. The line editor is an older and more rudimentary type. Line editors have the characteristic that the system numbers every line of text as it is created and identifies text by these line numbers when it is modified. The only way that a user can identify a site for modification is by giving the number of the line as part of an editing command. This works adequately, but it can be a little cumbersome for long pieces of editing. Still, a good line editor is a very useful tool.

Screen editors offer a more modern way to do basic editing. The screen editor will have special keys on the keyboard such that the user can display text on the screen and then move a cursor around via the special keys to indicate where changes are going to be made. Someone can easily edit twice as fast using a screen editor as compared to a line editor. From the point of view of learning about editing, however, screen editors are not the place to start. The way they are designed is much more tightly bound to the type of hardware being used in a particular machine than is the case with a line editor. They are also somewhat more complex to program.

In this chapter we will study in detail the mechanisms through which typical line editors operate. Our approach will be to isolate a core of functions which constitute a basic sort of editor, describe this in detail, and then approach more complicated editors by adding layers of extensions and additions onto the simple model. We will do this in three steps. The first step will be the design of a simple editor with a minimal set of commands that can compose relatively short files of text for programs. At the next stage we will add a few more functions and relax the restriction on short files. At the last stage we will take a brief look at screen editors.

The line editor we are going to examine will work with either a video terminal or a printing terminal. The screen editor can only be implemented on a good quality video terminal.

Our starting point in this discussion is a line editor with a very Spartan user interface. The user gives initial instructions to the editor in the format of single letter command names followed by parameters. The parameters are always a line number or a range of line numbers. For this program, the idea was to find a minimum set of commands that would still represent a useful piece of editing software. We have identified five such commands:

- Edit (or Create and Edit) a Text File
- Display (List) a Selected Part of the File
- Insert Line(s) into the File
- Delete Line(s) from the File
- Save Text After Editing is Finished

In the initial stages of our discussion, we are purposefully including no commands by which the user can move within a line and make changes there. We will include this function at a later stage. If the user wants to edit inside a line, he must delete the old version of the line and write a complete new version in its place.

Here are some overall perspectives on how the line editor (both versions) will work. From the outside, it will appear that the system automatically numbers the lines of text with integer numbers in the sequence 1, 2, 3, ... At the end of any insertion or deletion operation, the lines of text in the file will be automatically renumbered. This is how it will appear to the user. Internally it is not necessary for the system to maintain line numbers. It keeps track of the current line number by keeping a running line count and modifying this count every time it moves past a line of text for any reason.

In our simplest editor, the whole file will be kept in memory during editing. It is quite easy to program something like this. At the next higher level, part of the file will be in memory and part will be on disk. This type of system is harder to program. The part of the file that is in memory will be called the editing window. Any part of the file that is being modified must be inside the editing window. So there will be commands that essentially move the window around and commands that make modifications or additions or deletions relative to the text that is in the window.

Editors would be considerably simpler if it could be guaranteed that users would always work forward through the file being edited. Instead, we typically find users jumping back and forth throughout the file to various editing sites in an unplanned way. For instance, we might find a typical user doing some work around line 200, then going forward and editing some text around line 350, and then backing up to do some work at line 70. Back-up introduces significant problems because it is necessary to maintain all the data, in all parts of the file, continually in a state of readiness to be edited. This can certainly be dealt with, but the back-up problem is one of the things that make good editors complex.

We will make extensive use of linked lists, for various aspects of these designs, because they are very convenient to use for insertions and deletions, and for allocating and returning resources. There will be many examples of this later on. In all the designs discussed here, the different units of the text will be chained together on a doubly linked list. This means that no matter how we rearrange the text, it will always be possible to read forward through the file, in order, starting from any position, and to read backwards through the file starting from any position. It is necessary for the editor to have this capability because there is no way to know in advance where the user will want to move the site of editing.

At the beginning of any work, we will take what has become a standard precaution in real editors. Whenever a file is opened for editing, we will always automatically make a copy of it. This is a safety measure. In case our editing pass destroys the file, we can then always recover by using the copy.

With these general comments behind us, we are now in position to move ahead with the design of a simple editor. The first step, as always in a top-down design, will be to make sure we understand just how we want the editor to appear to the user.

9.2   THE USER INTERFACE FOR A TYPICAL DESIGN

In this section we must specify the set of basic commands to which the editor will respond and describe exactly what they will do. There are five basic commands to request various services from the editor. The editor will make a characteristic mark on the screen, i.e., a prompt, to indicate when it is time for the user to enter a command. For instance, when the editor program is initially set in motion, it will write the following text to the screen:

```
EDITOR
*
```

The asterisk is the prompt character. As we explain the various commands in the following section, we will put in boldface anything typed in by the user. Everything else that you see will be prompting material supplied by the editor.

Here are the various commands we are going to set up:

1. We need a command to get started and establish a file to work on. This command will be able to handle two circumstances: when the file is being created for the first time, or when the file was created previously and is now being set up to do more work. This function will be activated by the single letter command E, which stands for Edit Text. The dialog between the user and the system will be different in the two cases. Here is a sample dialog for the first case.

```
EDITOR
*E
What is the file name?
EXAMPLE.TXT
This will be a new file - go ahead.
1._
```

We are assuming that CP/M-type file naming conventions will be used. That is, the name of a file can be up to eight alphanumeric characters long and should be followed by a three alphanumeric character file extension. The extension labels the type of file.

After a file name has been established, the system gives a prompt and outputs a line number for the first line and then waits for the user to input some text. The text must be terminated by a Carriage Return. That is how the system tells that the user has finished one line and is ready to begin the next. Each time the editor detects a Carriage Return, it will move the cursor to the next line and output the next number in sequence at the left hand margin. The user continues to enter lines in this fashion.

How does one stop when done? The process can be completed by terminating the last line with two Carriage Returns instead of one. This is equivalent to giving null input for a new line. After this, the editor will maintain the file that was just created ready for further editing, and it will issue the edit prompt to find out what it should do next.

If you have just started up the system, and you wish to edit a file that already exists, then the Edit Text Command can be used as in the following dialog:

```
EDITOR
*E
What is the file name?
EXAMPLE.TXT
The first line is:
1    PROGRAM - GRAPHICS PACKAGE
Proceed with editing commands.
*
```

In the simple version of the line editor, where all files are short, this command will also load the entire file into memory.

You can see that starting this operation involves quite a few prompts from the editor. It doesn't have to be done this way, but it makes the system easier to use. The editor displays the first line in the file that has been requested as a check for the user. The way file systems seem to be used is that many files will have similar names. This feature is just to save some time that might be wasted working with the wrong file. The dialog ends with the editor prompt, because the user must now specify with further commands exactly what she wants to do.

2. Frequently, before any specific editing is done, the user will want to inspect certain parts of the file on the screen. He can do this at any time with the command L, which stands for List Text. The syntax of the command is L followed by at least one space and then a line number, or two line numbers separated by a hyphen to indicate a range. The command that will display line 100 is

```
*L  100
```

The following form will cause eleven lines of text to be displayed on the screen, starting with line 10 and ending with line 20.

```
*L  10-20
```

3. The line insertion function inserts lines *after* a specified target line. It can be accessed through the single letter command identifier I. The argument of the command is the number of the line that immediately precedes where the new text should go. When the editor learns where you want to insert, it will prompt you for input. It will produce prompting line numbers with three digits after a decimal point to specify the position of an in-coming line in the surrounding test. Up to 999 lines can be inserted through a single application of the Insert After Command.

Let's consider some examples. Suppose you wish to insert three lines between line 20 and 21. Here is a dialog that would have that effect:

```
*I  20
20.001      X = Y + Z
20.002      R = SIN(X)
20.003      PRINT R
20.004
*
```

Each inserted line must end with a Carriage Return character. If you terminate the last line with two Carriage Returns, it will signal the system that inserting is finished. As part of finishing up, the editor will renumber the lines that have been inserted so that the whole file is logically numbered with consecutive integers starting with the number one.

Inserting at the beginning or at the end of the file could conceivably cause difficulties. The system numbers all lines starting from the number one. Since our command is Insert After, we are going to need something special to put a line on the front of the file. The following dialog, in which line zero is mentioned, will be interpreted by the system as a request to put something at the beginning of the file:

```
*I  0
.001__
```

The system prepares to take in a group of lines for the front of the file and gives the first one the temporary number .001 to indicate its place in the surrounding text. Of course, after the insertion everything will be renumbered.

There is a different problem with inserting at the end of the file. Frequently, you don't know the number of the statement at the end and you don't want to take the time to find out with displays. Our editor provides some special help in this situation. All that is necessary is to use a line number that is clearly beyond the end of the file. Let's say there are 700 lines and you want to put some text at the end. Here is what the dialog would look like:

```
*I  10000
LAST LINE IN FILE IS 700.
700.001 __
```

The system tells you that you have gone too far, and then prompts for a new line immediately after the real last line.

4. Deleting text is the other big editing operation to consider in a first pass over an editor. The command is called D for Delete Text. Its syntax is just the same as for the List Command, that is, either a single line or a range of lines can be targeted for removal. This command removes line 2000:

```
*D  2000
```

This command removes the eleven lines that lie between line 10 and line 20, including the end points:

```
*D  10-20
```

After the targeted text lines have been ejected, the system automatically renumbers the remaining text.

5. At the completion of editing, prior to shutting down, the user must give the editor the command

```
*S
```

It stands for Save Text. This will cause any text in memory buffers to be transferred to the disk version of the file, and it will close the file. Finally, the command will cause the system to exit the editor, and pass control to whatever supervisor program or operating system environment the editor has been designed to work with.

9.3 EDITING WITH SMALL FILES AND LARGE MEMORY BUFFERS

It is easy to conceptualize and design an editor if there is enough buffer memory to completely hold the entirety of any file you might be working with. In this section we will discuss the design of an editor of this sort. It will form a baseline against which we can measure the added function and the added complexity that go with more complicated editors.

We will use the same user interface for this variant and for the next shell of complexity which will involve editing long files. Differences will be contained entirely in the internal mechanisms.

The process of text creation is quite simple. An input routine will be in control of the machine as the user enters each line of text. This routine can be very similar to the input routine used on the ROM monitor. Its function will be to fill an input buffer with a single line of text and implement certain editing functions that are easy and useful as part of line entry; for instance, the backspace function. The ROM monitor's input routine can be reviewed in Section 3.4.

Since all editing will be done in memory, it is obvious that the format in which text is kept in memory will be important and will have far-reaching consequences. This is what we have to focus on now. As soon as an input line is composed, it will be handed off to a buffer manager. This module will put the lines of text into the memory buffer so that they come right after each other with no gaps. We can imagine that the lines have been numbered starting from the integer one and using consecutive integers. It won't be necessary actually to keep line numbers with the text in the buffer. The system just needs to count each new line so that there always is a current line number.

When this buffer manager installs a line in memory, it will add four bytes on the front of the line. These bytes will be for a link to the line immediately before and a link to the line immediately after. That is, the whole memory buffer will be one huge linked list. There will be forward and backward links so that it will be possible to trace the text in order from any line to the beginning or the end of the file. Each link field contains the address in the memory buffer of the preceeding or following line. Linked lists are very useful in editing operations, because they allow insertions, deletions, and changes in order, all with a minimum movement of data. Frequently, only the links have to be adjusted.

There are three edit commands that require positioning in the text buffer before any work can be done. They are the commands that take line numbers as arguments. In each case, positioning means locating where the relevant line is in the memory buffer. Positioning is easy to program because we have the linked list and because the system will always keep track of the current line number. For instance, let's say we have just created a 200 line program. At the end of text entry, the current line pointer will be pointing to line 200. If a command is given that requires the system to position to line 100, it will be easy to get there. The backward link in line 200 gives the position of line 199. The backward link in line 199 gives the position of line 198. All that has to be done is follow the links until the current line pointer is pointing to line 100.

Link following can be done very quickly even over large parts of a file as long as the file is completely in memory. This is because on the order of 100,000 computer operations can be done within the $\frac{1}{4}$ of a second or so that can pass before the user will even perceive the slightest time lag. Slow text handling begins when we have to incorporate disk accesses into the editing loop between the human and computer.

When we are inserting lines into preexisting text, the good qualities of linked lists really stand out. For instance, if we wanted to insert two lines in order after line 100 in our program, an elegant solution would be to put the new lines immediately after the end of the last text line in the buffer. They would be out of order, but this can be accounted for by adjusting the links connecting between the insertion region and the new lines. Physical sequentiality of data is not needed with a linked list. The chain of links defines the sequence of the data items no matter where they are.

The elegance of linked lists is always appealing and is indispensible in larger editors. However, we should point out that in a small editor, there is another way to handle insertions. That is, you can just move the whole file down in memory by whatever amount is necessary to give you space after the insertion point. Now this could conceivably take many computer cycles, but since we are editing at human speed, they won't be missed if files are of modest length. However, we're going to stick with linked lists because we'll need them for all sorts of things on more complicated editors and on other kinds of systems software.

Figure 9-1 shows how our editor would insert two new lines in a BASIC language subroutine using the linked list method. We are assuming an insertion point which is somewhere in the middle of the text file.

The linked list also facilitates deleting lines from the file being edited. Let's imagine that several lines are to be deleted. How would this be done? The editor first positions to the line just before the deletion region and records its position for future use. Then it follows links forward until it finds the line just after the deletion region. We will call these the before and after lines. Next the forward link from the before line will be adjusted to point to the after line. And the backward link from the after line will be directed back to the before line. All the lines in between will just disappear from the system.

This is a simple way to delete lines. Its only disadvantage is that it is wasteful of memory. That is, the space occupied by the deleted lines is bridged over by the linked list and has been lost to the system. A better editor would have some mechanism for keeping track of the places where deletions occurred so that the space could be reused. Finally, we should point out that, for editors that will work only on short files, it is better to do deletions by block moves because there is no garbage collection problem. That is, you do deletions by simply moving up all the text beyond the deletion point so it becomes contiguous with the text that lies before where you are deleting.

Even though all editing will take place within the memory buffer, there are of course some disk files associated with this simple editor. There are commands in the user interface that will load the memory version of a file onto disk, and move the disk version into memory. We need to discuss the format in which the text is maintained when it is on the disk. A simple and adequate way to view the disk file is as a long character string. To lay the file down on disk, the editor simply reads through the file character by character, in the order defined by the forward links, and passes these characters to a disk manager module. The link fields are not passed, just the actual text. Every time the manager accumulates a buffer of the basic size that the disk accepts, a new record will be written to the disk file. It is possible, with this scheme, that the last record will not be entirely filled. This is no problem. The disk sectors have no relation to line boundaries at all.

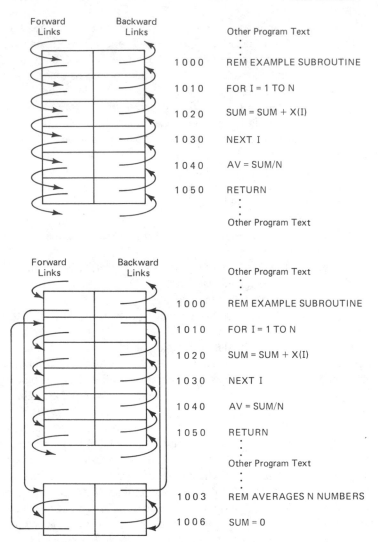

Figure 9-1: Inserting Lines into a Text File. By using linked lists, text can be logically inserted into the middle of a text file without opening up physical space at that location. The actual text is placed at the end of the file, but links associated with each line are manipulated so that the desired sequence is maintained. **(Top)** The text editor's internal representation *before* the lines are inserted. **(Bottom)** The text editor's internal representation *after* two lines are inserted.

The boundaries between lines are defined by Carriage Return characters. The end of the file should also be demarcated by some special character.

To load memory with a file prior to editing, we can do the opposite operation. That is, a module reads sectors from the disk into a buffer. As each sector comes in, another module works through it in order and detects line boundaries. As each line is found, it will be laid down in memory with four bytes reserved at the front of the line for links. The links will also be filled in at this time. This is no problem, because when text is brought in from the disk, everything is in the correct physical order. A useful side effect of writing an edited file out to disk and then loading it back into memory is that all embedded spaces caused by deletions will have been removed by the reloading process.

Another kind of file manipulation we need to focus on, even in a simple editor like this, is the automatic back-up facility. This is so easy to implement that it is probably appropriate to discuss it now. The idea of automatic back-up is that two versions of any file are always maintained (unless the user actively interferes with this process). There will be one version that contains the results of the most recent editing and another version that is the file in the form it had immediately before the most recent editing.

We can get an idea of what would be involved by examining some of the commands in the user interface which have to manipulate things in support of the automatic back-up. For purposes of example, let's say the most recent version of some file is called FILE.TXT and the version that was produced immediately before is called FILE.BAK. The commands we need to consider are Edit Text and Save Text.

When Edit Text is creating a file for the first time, back-up is not an issue, because no previous version of the file exists. When there is an existing file, the back-up strategy that leads to the simplest programming is the following. When editing begins, we discard the old back-up version. We make a copy of the current version of the file and name this as a new back-up. Now there are two identical versions of the file, both of which are current. The one that is named BAK is closed and left untouched throughout the editing session. It therefore freezes the state of the file before editing begins. The version of the file that is named TXT can be altered as required. At the end of editing it is the newest version of the file. For all the editors to be discussed, we will take this strategy to be the first work that the Edit Text Command performs.

The Save Text Command is responsible for transferring all text out of the memory into the disk representation of the most recent version of the file, and then closing the file. The BAK version has been closed since the beginning of editing. After Save Text, the TXT version is also closed, and editing on these files is finished.

This schematic description of data management strategies and command implementations completes our discussion of a simple editor. On this level such an editor is easy to program, very fast, and quite useful for modest sized programs. Now we will add another layer of features to this baseline model in our attempt to bootstrap up to more complicated editors.

9.4 AN EDITOR THAT CAN PROCESS FILES LONGER THAN THE MEMORY BUFFER

In this section we will extend our simple editor in two ways. These design changes will make it possible to handle files of any length (subject, of course, to disk size) and to do editing with a single line of text. The commands in the user interface will stay just the same, except that we add a new command that permits editing within a line. This feature is not related to longer files. It is just a command that is easily modularized so that we could postpone considering it in order to keep our first version of the editor relatively simple.

Longer files introduce significant complications in the design of an editor. The problems all stem from the fact that part of the active file (the file being edited) is going to be in memory and part is going to be on the disk. The totality of the file is too big to have it all in memory; so text in the area of where editing is being done will be in memory, plus as much other text as there is room for. Furthermore, since we can assume no set pattern in the way the editor is used, parts of the file may move back and forth between disk and memory a number of times before the file is completely edited. Our problems will be in the area of managing the traffic back and forth between memory and disk, finding an acceptable format in which to maintain the data, and managing resource allocation when a buffer that is completely filled with text has a need to accept some more.

We will approach these problems by blurring the distinction between disk memory and random access computer memory. A different kind of internal data representation from that used for the in-memory line editor is appropriate for the editing tasks at hand now. Here is what we will do. At any time the file being edited will be represented by a linked list of what we will call data segments. A data segment contains a fixed amount of text, perhaps equivalent to 5 or 10 program lines. A certain number of these segments will be on the disk and a certain number will be in memory. In addition to data, each of these segments contains a forward and backward link so that a path can be traced through them. This is especially important because no line numbers will be explicitly represented in the data. In addition to the forward and backward links there will be a few short fields in each segment that give summary information about its usage. A crucial point is that the data segment in memory and on disk will have exactly the same format, so there will be minimum difficulty moving segments between the two media when needed. Generally this will just be a matter of shifting the information and adjusting the links.

For purposes of example, we need to be more specific about the format of the data segments. Let's make several assumptions: The size of the data segment will be the same as the size of a sector on the disk. Let's imagine we're using a disk just like the standard IBM 3740 format eight inch floppy discussed previously, except that double density recording techniques have been used. This means that each sector contains 256 bytes instead of 128. Every sector on such a disk is identified by a unique number between 1 and 2002 if we count from track 0, sector 1. The essence of our strategy is that segments can be switched easily between disk and memory. The editor will have a segment buffer area in memory where the segments will be when they are being worked on. Let's assume that there is room for 100 segments in this buffer and that they will be numbered as an extension of the sectors on the disk. This numbering scheme is very important. When a segment is on disk, it will have a number between 1 and 2002. When a segment is in memory, it will have a number between 2003 and 2102. Its number tells everything there is to know about where a segment is located.

The file being edited will have the form of a doubly linked list of segments some of which are on the disk and some of which are in memory. If there is a lot of editing, the same segment may be shifted back and forth between disk and memory a number of times. Let us dedicate the first two bytes in the segment as a forward link. It will contain the number of the next segment in the file. Because our numbering system is flexible,

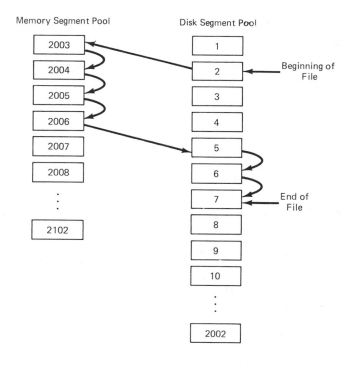

In-Use Memory Segments	Free Memory Segments	In-Use Disk Segments	Free Disk Segments
2003	2007	0002	0001
2004	2008	0005	0003
2005	.	0006	0004
2006	.	0007	0008
	.		0009
	2102		0010
			.
			.
			.
			2001
			2002

Figure 9-2: Segment Accounting for a Typical File. There is a pool of segments available to the editor for its use; some will be on disk and some in memory. Every segment that can be used by the editor will appear on one of four accounting lists. As editing proceeds, the contents of the lists will be continually changing. A file is simply a collection of filled data segments which are given an order via a linked list.

this segment may either be in memory or on the disk. The second two bytes will be a backward link, specifying the number of the data segment which contains the part of the file immediately previous to the current position. The next two bytes are reserved for various status indicators which we won't specify now. After that come 250 bytes for data.

Think of there being a pool of free segment slots available for the use of the editor when a file is created; initially there will be 100 in memory and a large number on the disk. As the file gets built, the slots in memory are taken up. Eventually, some of the file will be on disk as well as in memory.

Some simple data structures will be needed to manage all this segment traffic. Every segment in the whole pool, whether it is being used or not, will appear on one of a group of four accounting lists. There will be a list of In-use Memory Segments and a list of Free Memory Segments. There will be a list of In-use Disk Segments and a list of Free Disk Segments. Any time a segment is swapped, an entry will need to be changed on each of the four lists. An example will make this clear.

Figure 9-2 shows the complete pool of segments, the four accounting lists, and a small file which happens at this time to be partially in memory and partially on disk.

The basic operations that can effect movement of data between the memory buffer and the disk are positioning to a particular line for display, or any other purpose, and inserting and deleting lines. Let us now turn our attention to the implications of these operations.

9.4.1 Positioning to a Specific Text Line

When you are using a line editor, editing always proceeds in two steps: positioning to a specific line, and then making changes in the vicinity to which the positioning has been done. In our editor, positioning is done automatically as part of the commands that need it, but logically it is separate. We begin by looking at the positioning problem.

Figure 9-3 shows a convenient way to think about positioning in the file prior to editing. The squares represent all the data segments in the file. The light colored squares are on disk; the dark ones are in memory. We can think of the memory segments as an editing window giving access into the file. In order for work to be done at any particular line number, that line must be in the window. So the first part of any editing will be to position the editing window so the desired line is in it. This is done by swapping appropriate segments between memory and disk. We will talk more about the details of managing this swapping later.

Let's assume that the Edit Text Command has been given in anticipation of work on a text file that has already been created and filled with some text. Next we give a command that involves positioning to a particular line. Here is how that can be done. We are starting from the beginning of the file and nothing is in the memory buffer yet. All that is necessary is to scan through the active file, reading each line and counting them. Remember that no explicit line numbers are maintained in the disk files. That is why the lines must be counted. Segments from the file will be transferred one by one into the memory buffer. No matter where the data is, the proper order in the file will be continuously maintained by the links which connect the segments. Eventually we will

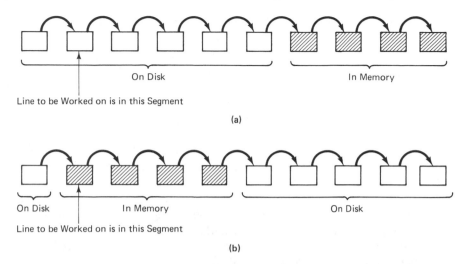

Figure 9-3:   The Memory Buffer As an Editing Window. The portion of the file that is in memory is called the editing window. Before a line can be edited, the window must be positioned so the line falls within it. The window can be moved back and forth through the file by swapping segments between memory buffer and disk.

load the segment which contains the requested line. If we are positioning deep into a long file, the buffer will become full. Then it will be necessary to begin moving the earlier segments out of the memory buffer and writing them back onto the disk.

Backing up from the current line position to find a new line to edit on is potentially a source of trouble. Let's assume we have done some as yet unspecified work, somewhere in the memory buffer, and now a command has been received that involves back-up and editing on a line near the start of the file. What should the system do? Here is a scheme that will work. The current line position is in one of the segments in the editing window. We must now follow the backward links from one segment to another. If we are still in the editing window when we reach the target line, everything can proceed easily. But let's assume the line is in a segment that lies beyond the window.

Now there must be some swapping of segments with the disk part of the active file. The most forward segment in the memory buffer (i.e., the one closest to the end of the file) will be shifted to disk and the forward and backward links adjusted so that the continuity of the file is maintained. The segment on disk that is immediately before the first segment in memory can now be put into the slot in the memory buffer that was just vacated. It is put there and the links are adjusted so the continuity of the file is maintained. This process can be continued as we work toward the beginning of the file. Segments toward the end are moved to the disk portion of the file to make room in the memory buffer for segments that were on the disk in the earlier portions of the file. Eventually, we will get the segment into the memory buffer which contains the line to be worked on and then positioning stops and editing work can begin. Managing the movements of data between memory and disk is a big task, and we will be more specific about it in the next section.

9.4.2 Swapping Data Between Memory and Disk

In this section we consider some of the subsidiary routines necessary to implement the editing operations smoothly when swapping is a necessity.

Remember that the essential feature of our editor is that there is no difference between a segment on the disk and in memory. And all the segments are linked on a doubly linked list so that the whole file can be read just by following the links.

There are many times when it will be necessary to take a segment that is part of the file and happens to be in memory, and move it to the disk part of the file, and vice versa. We are going to specify a piece of software here that will do that. We will call it the Swapper. It is really a utility routine for use of the editor. The calling sequence for the Swapper will have two arguments. The first one indicates whether movement is to be from disk to memory or memory to disk. The second argument gives the number of the segment that is to be swapped. Remember that all of our segments have unique numbers. The Swapper maintains the order of the file. It just makes one less segment in memory and one more on disk, or vice versa.

Here is an example of how it would work. Let's say we need to move a segment from memory to disk. Before changing anything, the Swapper would make a copy of the links in the region where the change was to be made which define the order of the file. Next it would get a free disk segment from the Free List for Disk Segments and it would record that the segment was now unavailable by marking it down on the In Use List for Disk Segments. Then it would copy the data in the memory segment that was being swapped into the disk segment. Then it would return the memory segment that was used to the Free List for Memory Segments and remove it from the In Use List for Memory Segments. Finally it would adjust the links on the new version of the file so that if you were reading through it, the order of the text would be just the same as before the swapping.

The Swapper will know how to move a specific segment between memory and disk. But sometimes things are more complicated than this. Frequently, a decision has to be made about what segment to swap. Making this decision and then calling the Swapper as required will be the function of a higher level piece of software called the Segment Manager.

The Segment Manager will need to be able to initiate swapping on behalf of a number of the other higher level routines. It will be callable in several different ways because there are many different cases in which some type of swapping is required. For example, consider what happens in this situation. Let's say we are positioning toward the beginning of the file through the memory buffer as part of some command, and we need to keep going beyond the text that is now there. The middle of the file is in the editing window, and the beginning and end are on the disk. There are no more free memory segments. The Segment Manager would be called with parameters that identify this situation. It would determine that the proper thing to do would be to swap out the segment at the bottom of the memory buffer. This would free up a memory segment. Then the manager would call for another swap going from disk to memory. This would bring in the next segment of text that lies along the path that must be traversed to get to

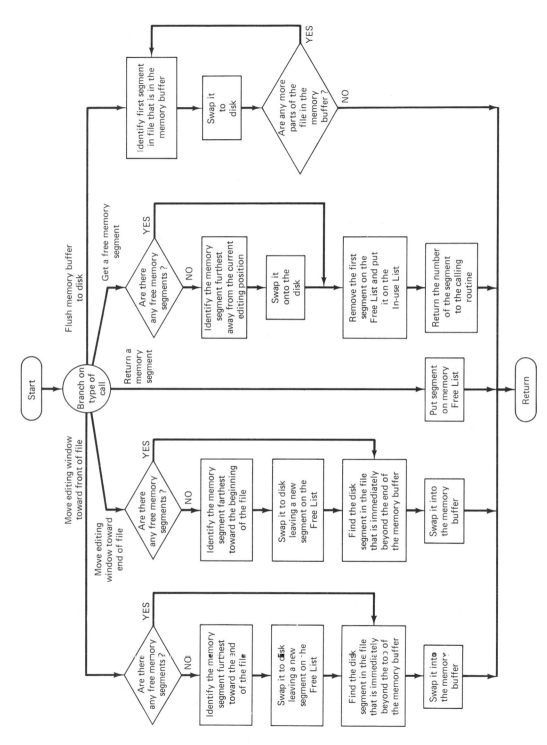

Figure 9-4: The Segment Manager. The Segment Manager manages all changes in the status of segments. It can be called to obtain or return a memory segment, to move the editing window, or to transfer all the memory parts of a text file onto the disk.

185

the positioning target. If the line being searched for was not in this text, this sequence would be repeated until the line was found.

Here's another use of the Segment Manager. In a later section, we will look at the deletion operation. If a long sequence of text is being deleted, it is likely that certain of the memory data segments will get entirely cleared out and can be returned to the system for reuse. There will be a way of calling the Segment Manager that will allow it to return a segment that has been freed up by putting it back on the Free List for Memory Segments.

In a later section we will look at the insertion operation. To insert requires one or more free memory segments. If there aren't any, the insert module will have to call the Segment Manager and ask it to provide one. The Segment Manager then needs to decide which memory segment to kick out of the buffer. When it makes this decision, it is easy to implement—just call the Swapper.

The Segment Manager will also have some work to do on behalf of the Edit Text module when text is being created initially. Every time Edit Text needs a memory data segment to work with, it will just make a call to the Segment Manager. The Manager will return the number of a memory segment that can be used for new text. It will either get it directly off the Free List or create a new segment by swapping an appropriate one to the disk.

Finally, at the end of editing, the Save Text module will be able to call on the Segment Manager to take all the parts of the file that are in memory and swap them to the disk. The manager will do this by identifying the first segment of the file in the memory buffer and then just calling the Swapper and reading the links to find the next memory segment and swapping that, etc., until all segments are moved to the disk.

Figure 9-4 outlines the operation of the Segment Manager. Let's summarize its capabilities one more time. The Segment Manager should always be called if some other routine needs to manipulate a segment. The Segment Manager can move the editing window by one segment toward the beginning or toward the end of the file. It can get a free memory segment. This may involve making a decision about ejecting some inactive segment from memory and putting it back on disk. It can return a memory segment to be reused if its data has been deleted. Lastly, it will have a call that will allow all the parts of the file that are in memory to be moved over to the disk in proper order. The movement of any particular segment between memory and disk, in either direction, is handled by calling the Swapper.

9.4.3 Deleting Lines

Now that we have considered the general movement of data during an editing session and the supporting temporary movements of data between disk and memory, it is time to focus on the editing operations themselves. We will now discuss deleting and inserting numbered lines. Making changes within a line will be saved for later.

We start with deleting, which is easiest to do. A delete operation is begun by positioning to the line where the delete is to take place. This means the line will be somewhere within the editing window, and the active file will look like the second case illustrated in Figure 9-3.

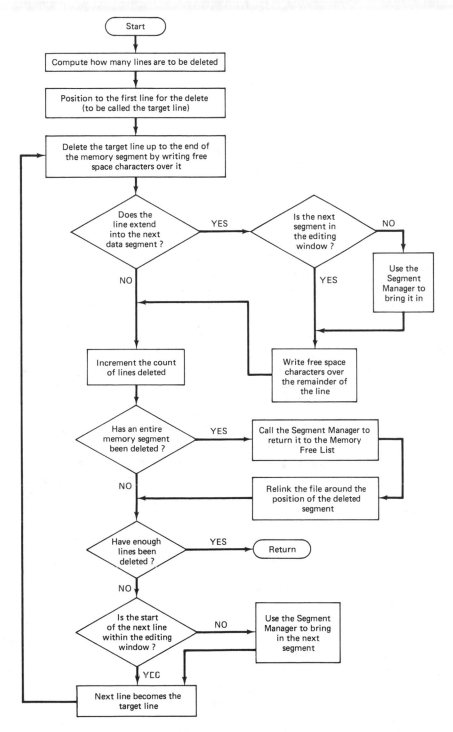

Figure 9-5: The Delete Lines Routine. This routine can delete a line(s) by overwriting with free space characters at the place in the file where the line(s) occur. For long deletes, it will also return memory segments if they become free and it will reposition the editing window if the delete runs off the end of the memory buffer.

The way we are going to delete is to write over unwanted lines with one of the unusual ASCII characters which we will call the free space character. We proceed forward through the memory buffer, deleting lines one by one and counting them so we know when to stop.

If we happen to cross the boundary between one segment and the next, there is no problem—just keep deleting and counting lines. If the delete is completed in the next segment just beyond where it started, then everything is finished. No text is moved around. No links are changed. All that happened was that a sequence of free space characters was written into these two segments.

If we happen to delete all the text in a memory segment, then some additional work must be done. The affected segment, which is uniquely numbered, must be returned to the Free List for Memory Segments. The Segment Manager can do this. The links of the segments before and after this one must be joined together (by the Delete Routine) to branch around it, and then deleting continues.

Next, it is possible that we may come to a major operational junction. Different things happen if the deleting is complete within the memory buffer, or if the locus of action comes to the end of the editing window and needs to go further. Here is how we will handle this. This is another problem for the Segment Manager. However, the work it has to do is really just the same as what it had to do when it moved the editing window by one segment during the course of positioning to a particular line. So the Delete Routine has to make a call to the Segment Manager that says move the editing window toward the end of the file by one segment. To do this, the Segment Manager will swap out the segment in the memory buffer that's furthest toward the beginning of the file. Then it will bring in a new segment from the disk. And then the delete operation will proceed as if nothing had happened, that is, as if the end of the editing window had not been reached. Figure 9-5 outlines the operation of the Delete Routine. Actually, if many segments have been deleted and the end of the memory buffer is reached, the Segment Manager won't have to swap anything out of the memory. There will already be free memory slots. It will just bring the next disk segment in the file into the editing window so the deleting can continue.

9.4.4 Inserting New Lines

The main problems with insertion are how to get space for the new text and how to incorporate that space into the existing file at the proper positon. Our strategy will be to get a free memory segment, link it into the file immediately after the segment that contains the insertion point, move the text after the insertion point down into the new segment to free up some space, and then put the new text into the free space.

To be more specific, these are the steps we must take. First we must get a free memory segment. This can sometimes be obtained from the Free List for Memory Segments, or, if none are free, then one of the memory segments currently in use must be swapped to the disk output file to free up some space. In any case, this is business for the Segment Manager. The manager will be called and will return the number of a memory segment that can be used. After we get the new segment, we fill it completely with free space characters. This can be any character we choose to denote free space. We also link the new segment into the file immediately after the segment containing the insert point.

Our objective now will be to distribute the text in the original segment between the original segment and the new segment so that 250 bytes of free space open up immediately after the insertion point. We can do this by moving all the text after the insert point into the new segment and establishing it so that it occupies exactly the same

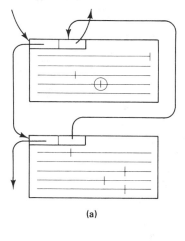

The Memory Segments in the Region of Insertion Before Creating Insert Space. Forward and backward links are shown. The lines in the memory segments represent lines of text. The vertical bars represent the carriage return characters that occur at the ends of lines. The point where the insertion is to occur has been circled.

(a)

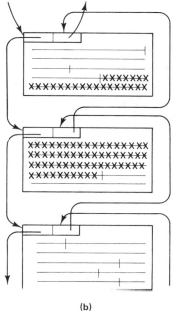

The Memory Segments in the Region of Insertion After Space has been Opened Up. A new segment has been obtained and linked into the file. The x's indicate 250 free space characters. Any of this can be used for the insertion.

(b)

Figure 9-6:   Obtaining Free Memory Space for a Text Insertion. As part of the insertion procedure, a free memory segment is obtained and linked into the list which represents the text file. Text immediately beyond the insert point is pushed to the end of this new segment to open up usable space.

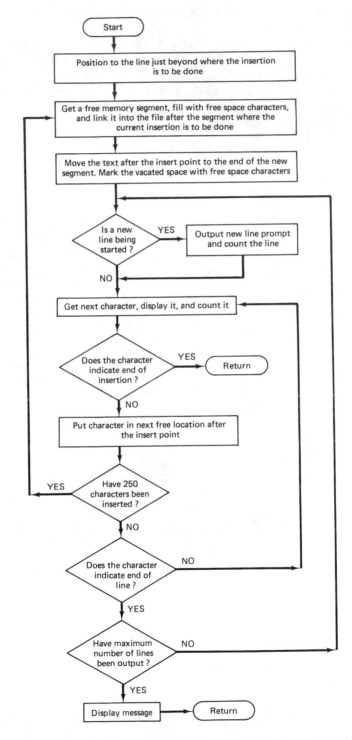

Figure 9-7: The Insert Lines Routine. The insert routine does its work by linking a free memory segment into the file at the point of insertion to provide 250 bytes of free space to write on. The procedure is repeated as necessary for long insertions.

relative locations in the new segment as it did in the original one. We also take all locations in the original segment beyond the insert point and fill them with free space characters. Now space has been created for up to a maximum of a 250 character insertion and the space is in the right position relative to the rest of the file. Figure 9-6 shows all the manipulations we have made up to this point to prepare for the insertion.

Now the user will be prompted to begin typing the insertion and it will be a simple matter to put the characters sequentially into the free space we have created. If there is enough room to fit the new lines in, they are inserted and that is all. The segments are already correctly linked, so there is nothing more to do. Of course, the insertion will probably have left some unused space in the region of the editing. There is nothing that can be done about this until some kind of compaction operation is done later.

If the insertion involves more than 250 bytes, all the opened space will have been used and in that case the Segment Manager will have to be called again to get another free memory segment in which there will be another 250 bytes of usable space. This can continue indefinitely.

Note that at the end of every few insert or delete operations, we may want to have a memory compaction routine run which will move characters around from one segment to another in the memory buffer with the object of squeezing out unused memory locations and adding memory segments to the free list. This routine probably will not compact the whole memory. It will do as much work as can be done in a quarter second or so (100,000 machine instructions) so that the human user will not experience any annoying degradation in the speed of the editor.

Figure 9-7 shows how the Insert Routine operates.

9.4.5   Making Changes Within a Line

The user interface that was defined for a simple editor had no commands that would allow changes to be made within a line. In this section we will specify an addition to the user interface so that our extended editor will have this capability, and we will discuss the internal workings of such a mechanism.

The new command will be called Change Line (C). Its argument will be the number of the line to change. After the user types this command the system will generate a prompt and then echo the line that is to be changed onto the screen. A sample dialog is

```
*C  17
LINE EDITING KEYS ARE ACTIVE
LINE 17 PRESENTLY IS:
100  SUN = SUM + I

—
```

Some special keys will be associated with the editing operation. We will explain their use a little later. Note that in the preceding example the number 100 is text information that was explicitly typed in by the user just like the rest of the line.

There are really just three kinds of editing a user might want to do within a text line: delete some characters, insert some characters, or type over some characters. There are many ways that this can be done. It would be nice to be able to see the whole line displayed on the screen and to be able to go back and forth in that line, via appropriate keys, and make changes. Furthermore, it would be desirable to have the line display be modified immediately to show the effect of any editing changes. Unfortunately this cannot be done if you are using a printing terminal or a simple video terminal that lacks an internal memory that can be extensively manipulated by the CPU. Such terminals can only do things like receive a character, print it at the cursor position, and move the cursor to the right by one space. For the time being, we are going to stick with a simple editor running on simple hardware. With simple video terminals, it is either difficult or impossible to do things such as backing up and writing over other characters. To do that, you need the hardware assistance of a terminal with an internal memory that is capable of being manipulated by the computer. We will discuss this type of editing in Section 9.6.

It is still possible to have convenient line editing even if your terminal doesn't have an easily accessible memory. Now we will describe the characteristics such a system might have. First, we are going to assume that the keyboard has some special keys that can be used by the editor. Four keys are required, and we call them:

- The Transmit Character Key
- The Delete Character Key
- The Insertion Mode Key
- The Type-Over Mode Key

Even if these keys are not physically on the keyboard, they can always be there in effect. This is because the editor can be written to interpret two key sequences involving the Control key as if these sequences came from dedicated keyboard locations. For example, the editor could be written to interpret the Control T sequence as meaning Transmit Character, the Control D sequence as meaning Delete Character, etc.

Now we need a few more details of the user interface. Here is the general pattern the within-line editing might take in a hypothetical system. Every time the user presses the Transmit Character key, a character from the line being edited will appear on the screen. The user can move through the line, up to any point of interest, by pressing that key repeatedly. If he keeps the key down, it will repeat automatically. When he arrives at the place to edit, the other special editing keys can be used to signal the editor as to what kind of work is required. After the line is altered, the user must continue to use the Transmit Character key to pass over the rest of the characters in the line. When all the characters have been transmitted, the user must hit Carriage Return to signal the end of editing on that particular line. What it means to transmit a character will be described later.

When any line is being edited, it will be convenient to build up a revised copy of the line in a temporary storage buffer in memory which we will call the New Line Buffer. What the special editing keys do can be best understood by thinking about the associated operations in this buffer. The Transmit Character key moves characters one by one into the buffer, in order, from the line being edited. The Delete Character key will discard the last character in the New Line Buffer each time it is pressed.

The Insertion and Type-Over keys toggle between two modes of changing text. There is a pointer that we can define that helps to implement the remaining within-line operations. The Line Position Pointer is associated with the original text line. It will be used to point to the next character to be transmitted in the line being edited. If we are working in the Insert Mode during line editing, any normal text characters that are typed will be appended on the end of the New Line Buffer and the Line Position Pointer will not be changed. If we are in the Type-Over mode, each character that is typed goes on the end of the New Line Buffer and the Line Position Pointer in the original version of the line moves over one position. This effectively discards the character that was there. All editing within the line finishes with the Carriage Return Character, or with a number of invocations of Transmit Character, followed by a Carriage Return.

A feature that is implicit in this scheme is that the end of any line can be intentionally snipped off if the user transmits characters from the beginning of the line and then hits Carriage Return before the rest of the characters have been transmitted. Carriage Return freezes what will be in the edited version of the line.

Figure 9-8 shows an example of editing within one particular line in a program written in BASIC.

Here are the details of implementing the Change Line Command. The editing will

The line to be edited is

100 SUN = SUM + I

We want the line to become

100 SUM = SUM*2 + I

The following is the interchange with the editor that will make the changes described above. The first line that follows shows everything the user types. The second line shows what appears on the screen as he does it. Note that ⑦ stands for the Transmit Character key, ⑩ stands for the Delete Character key, and ⑧ stands for the Carriage Return key. We are assuming that the editor has been put in the insert mode before doing this work.

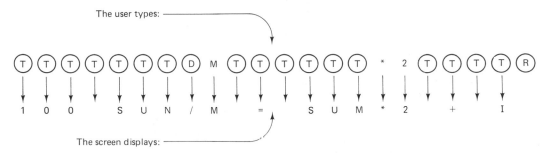

Figure 9-8 An Example of Within-Line Editing. Special function keys are used in conjunction with the Change Line Command to direct the changes within the line. These changes may be insertions, deletions, or type-overs. This example shows what is involved in making some alterations within one line from a program written in the BASIC language.

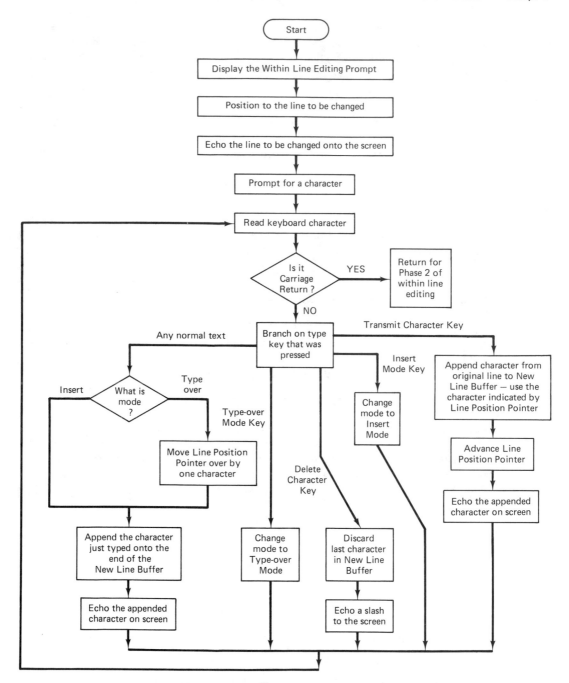

Figure 9-9: The Change Line Routine, Phase 1. The first part of within-line editing consists of composing a new version of the line being edited in the New Line Buffer.

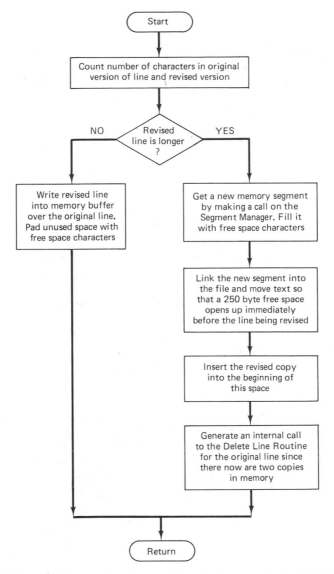

Figure 9-10: The Change Line Routine. Phase 2. The second part of within-line editing consists of putting the changed line into the proper position with respect to the surrounding text.

consist of two phases. In the first phase a revised copy of the line being edited will be produced in the New Line Buffer dedicated to this purpose. This will be done in the way we have already described. In the second phase, this revised copy will be inserted into the surrounding text in almost the same manner as if the Insert Line Command were being used.

If you recall, the Insert Line Command is one of the five basic commands that can be given directly from the keyboard by the user. However, there are some differences from the original Insert Line Command. If the revised line is shorter than the original, it will be convenient to let the new line overwrite the old one. The unused space will be padded with free space characters. If the revised line is longer than the original, then the Segment Manager will be called to open up another 250 bytes of space. The revised line will be written over the old line and will extend into the new space as needed. Since this procedure could involve the creation of much wasted space, we may want to have the Memory Compaction Routine run after every few instances of changing a line just as it ran after inserting or deleting whole lines. Figure 9-9 shows the details of how a changed version of the line being edited is built up in the New Line Buffer. Figure 9-10 shows how the new version of the line is inserted into the surrounding text.

9.5 ADVANCED FEATURES

There are two other capabilities that editors at the present level of complexity usually have: the global search and replacement feature and the text rearrangement feature. These things are very useful, so we wish to explain how they work. However, they are not at the core level of an editor's function, so we will not go into the same amount of detail as for the previous discussion.

The idea of searching as used in an editor is like this. In its simplest form, the user will specify a text string that he is interested in which is located somewhere in the text being edited. For example, suppose the user is looking for a statement that begins with the text "ALPHA". In an assembly language program this string could be a statement label. The search function in the editor will begin scanning through the whole file, as if it were one long character string, until it finds an occurrence of the pattern "ALPHA". Then the scanning will stop, the line containing the searched for string will be displayed on the screen, and the system will go into command mode to get instructions from the user. The user wanted to find the string. Presumably he now wants to do something with it.

In a global search, there is usually some way of restarting the scan through the file so that any other occurrences of the searched for pattern will be found, one by one.

The search function is sometimes incorporated as part of a search and replace operation. For instance, to begin this operation, the user might give "ALPHA/BETA" as the argument of the command. This would mean to search through the file until an occurrence of the string "ALPHA" is found, and then replace it with the string "BETA". There will also be some kind of parameter in the command so that you can tell the editor to do this at just the first place where "ALPHA" is found, or at all places where it is found.

Internally, the search and replace command will be quite complex. It will involve some kind of driver module that will administer alternating calls to a scan module and to some kind of line editing module that will do the actual replacement. The line editing module will be on the same level of complexity as the Change Line Command which was discussed in the last section. It is easy to see how things could get complex. If the replacement item is longer than the thing being replaced, all the same problems of getting space will arise that we have seen before.

The other advanced feature we want to discuss is text rearrangement. This is the electronic analogy of a cut and paste operation where you can rearrange a printed page by cutting it up and pasting it together in a different order. The rearrangement command is usually implemented in three parts: you must somehow identify the text to be moved, then you must identify a target location, then you must tell the machine to move the marked text.

It is easy to imagine an extension of the user interface that would allow doing these things. First there would be a Mark Line Command which would consist of a command identifier followed by the beginning and ending line numbers of the text to be moved. This is sufficient to identify the text to the editor. A rearrangement would be completed when the user issued a Move Text Command. This would consist of a command identifier followed by a line number that specifies the line after which the moved text would be transferred.

Internally the rearrangement sequence might look as follows. The Mark Line Command would simply input the line numbers marking the region. The Move Text Command would do the real work. It would need to scan through the file until the beginning of the region to be moved was found. Next, a free memory data segment would be obtained. The text to be moved would be put into the free memory data segment. Then the file would be repositioned so the target location for the move was in the editing window. The new memory segment would have to be inserted there. If a large amount of text was being moved, this procedure would have to be done a number of times until all the text was transferred. When the transfer was complete, the editor would have to position to the original marked text and delete it.

A closely related command to rearrangement is the Copy Text Command. Everything is the same except that at the end of the operation the marked text with which we started is not deleted.

The reader can see that text rearrangement is complicated. However, the complication is entirely made up of sequences of simpler operations which we have studied before. These are things like positioning the file, moving data between the memory and the disk part of the file, and inserting and deleting.

9.6 SCREEN EDITORS: THE LAST LAYER OF COMPLEXITY

We have been building a complicated editor by adding on functions in layers. First we considered an editor which could do all its work in the memory buffer, because we said we would only submit short files to it. At the next level we looked at a significantly more complex editor which could keep part of a file being edited in a memory window and part on the disk. File size with this kind of editor is limited only by the size of the disk. The last layer of complexity we want to look at is screen editing.

A screen editor displays information about the file being edited in a different way than what we have studied so far. It also receives commands from the user in a different way. We are going to give only a very high level account of screen editing for several reasons:

1. The internal mechanisms of a screen editor depend very much on the type of video interface or terminal that is being used. The display hardware has a much heavier impact on the programming of this kind of a system than it has on a line editor.

2. A screen editor will typically receive its commands from the user via special keys on the keyboard rather than by a typed in command line. This means that if we were to discuss a screen editor in detail, we would need to make a totally new user interface.

3. Finally, screen editors are complicated. It is our goal in this book to explore systems software only up to the level where we could see how to implement most of the function but not get lost in unnecessary refinements.

Let's look at the essential features of a screen editor. The screen becomes a viewing window into the text file. Instead of displaying single lines, the screen will be filled with everything that is in the file in the vicinity of where work is being done. A standard amount of text in many systems is 24 lines of text each of which can be up to 80 characters long. Newer systems are more dense and can display perhaps twice as many lines. Do not confuse the idea of a viewing window with the idea of an editing window upon which our line editor depended.

All editing takes place by the user positioning a cursor on the screen to indicate to the system where editing is to take place. The cursor can be positioned by keys that move it up, down, left, and right. There are usually also scroll keys that will cause the text in the viewing window to appear to move up or down. The scroll keys actually position the viewing window within the text file. The user can position the cursor into a part of the text where he wants to work much more quickly and conveniently using these types of controls than he can by specifying line numbers to a line editor.

With a screen editor most editing operations, after a file has been established, are done by using specialized keys that have been put on the keyboard specifically for the use of the editor. This is what we were referring to when we said the user interface would be quite different. We have already mentioned the cursor control and scrolling keys for positioning within the text. The other principal editing functions are inserting and deleting. There will be special keys for these as well. For instance, to delete a character, it is usually possible to do something like this—position the cursor over the character and then press a delete character key. That character will disappear and the line will move over by one space. To insert, it is typical to enter an insert mode via another special key.

When you are in the insert mode, any text that is typed will appear immediately after the cursor and the surrounding text will move over to adjust for it. Using special keys is quicker and more convenient than using command lines.

The human factors impact of being able to position visually and use special keys to select function is quite spectacular. It means that a given piece of editing can be done perhaps twice as fast with a screen editor as with a line editor.

An essential hardware feature that characterizes most screen editors is within the display system where there is an area of random access memory which corresponds to what is seen on the screen; and there will be some mechanism whereby this screen

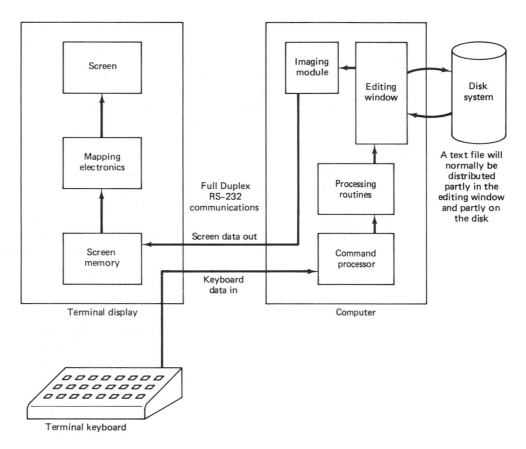

Figure 9-11:   A Screen Editing System. This is a schematic representation of the major components in a typical small computer screen editing system. This particular system utilizes a separate terminal which has an internal screen memory that can be easily altered by commands from the computer.

memory can be easily altered by the CPU. This may be via a large repertoire of command codes; or it may be because the display is memory-mapped. Each memory cell in this special memory corresponds to a particular character position on the screen.

The editor software can cause a character to appear at a particular place on the screen simply by writing the ASCII code for that character into the corresponding position in the screen memory. All the editor ever needs to be concerned with is what is in this screen memory. There will be a separate hardware subsystem which has the function of taking whatever is in the screen memory and making a picture that corresponds to it on the screen. It is typical to paint a new picture on the screen about 30 times a second, every second. The hardware will do this regardless of whether anything has been changed in the screen memory or not.

It would be possible to write a screen editor that didn't depend on a screen memory, but no one does it. It would make the system too slow. To see this, consider what would be required if you were going to insert a new line into a screen filled with text. With a "glass Teletype" terminal, for every character of the insertion you would have to send a long string of commands to redraw the entire screen. However, if there were an accessible screen memory, all that would be necessary would be some kind of block move in the memory to open up new space and move the text over. This can be done very quickly.

We can complete our very schematic discussion of screen editors by using a block diagram to indicate some overall features of a typical system. Please refer to Figure 9-11. The internal representation of the text file will probably be very similar to what we described for a line editor. That is, it will probably be a linked list of memory and disk data segments in which part of the file is on disk and part is within an editing window in memory. All the editing operations reduce to manipulating these segments. In fact you can think of the screen editing functions as just providing a new, very effective, but complicated interface through which these basic operations will be accessed.

We have shown three program modules within the computer. The command processor part of the editor determines what is wanted in response to editing keys pressed by the user. It then dispatches processing routines to manipulate the text file appropriately. The imaging module is something new. Its responsibility is to make sure that the screen memory is changed to reflect any changes that have occurred in the editing window. Thus it watches changes that occur in the editing window and formulates corresponding strings of commands and data to send to the screen memory. We have shown the communication to the terminal taking place over a standard two way (full-duplex) serial interface. The display electronics has an invariant task to perform. It must continually map what is in the screen memory into a corresponding picture on the screen.

STUDY QUESTIONS AND EXERCISES

1. Imagine an editor with the following very simple construction. All commands for editing are given through three keys. The Position key causes control to move forward through the file line

by line from the current position (at a fixed rate) and displays the lines on the terminal. If you press it again, the text will move in the opposite direction. The function continues as long as you keep the key pressed down. The Delete key will delete one line for each key press from wherever the cursor is now. It repeats if you hold it down. The Insert key allows one line to be inserted in front of wherever the cursor is now. Would this be an easy editor to learn to use? Would it be agreeable to use? In what ways would its implementation differ from the line editors we have discussed?

2. This question refers to our version of a line editor that can edit files that are longer than the memory buffer. Figure 9-2 shows the layout of a file as it might exist at some point during editing. Assume an IBM 3740 eight inch single density disk is being used. Each sector can hold 128 bytes. Assume when something is removed from a list, it comes off the top, and when it is added to a list, it goes on the bottom.

   (a) What is the approximate length of this file if it is laid out as shown in the figure?

   (b) Describe what changes will occur in the accounting lists if a relatively short new line is inserted between two lines which originally lie in segment 2005.

   (c) Draw the links as they would be in the memory segment pool after the insertion.

   (d) Describe what changes will occur in the accounting lists if the editing window is moved toward the end of the file by one segment. Hint: the size of the window doesn't need to stay constant.

   (e) Describe what changes will occur in the accounting lists if we exercise the Change Line function on a line that exists wholly in segment 2003, and the result of the editing is to shorten the line.

3. This question refers to an unsophisticated line editor which deals with short files in memory. We discussed two ways in which text could be maintained: having each line be a node on a doubly linked list, or having the whole file be one huge character string which is moved apart or closed up for insertions and deletions. Contrast these two data representations for ease of implementing the editor, speed of operation, and efficiency in memory usage.

4. Write a block move subroutine in 8080 assembler language that could be used to open up space for insertions with an in-memory editor. The address of the first byte to move can be assumed to be in the BC register pair. The number of bytes to move will be in the DE pair, and the address of the target point will be in the HL pair.

5. Assume an in-memory editor keeps its text in the memory buffer as a long character string. The lines are in order and are separated only by Carriage Return characters. No links or line numbers are maintained. Text lies in the buffer between locations 1000H and 8000H. The last 2000H characters are to be moved 100H bytes further toward the high end of memory to make room for an insertion. Compute how long this move would take using your program of Question 4. Assume the average execution time for an 8080 instruction is 2.5 microseconds.

6. Could we handle the problem of a file larger than memory for a line editor by doing all editing on short files and then having some kind of linking operation as the last step that would meld them into a big file? Would there be any disadvantage to doing it this way?

7. Why does a segment have to be in the editing window in order for it to be altered? Can you think of any alternative mechanism whereby this is not necessary?

8. Could you have an editor where the memory window was fragmented and not continuous? That is, if you wanted to work on a particular segment, you could bring it into memory basically anywhere and you would only have to free up enough segments to make room for it. In this scheme, it would not be necessary to move the whole editing window. Perhaps segments would

be swapped out of memory on a least recently used basis rather than on the basis that they are at one end or the other end of memory. What would be the implications of this strategy?

9. If we were moving text from the front of a long file to the end with the cut and paste text rearrangement command, it could be very clumsy if both regions were not in the editing window. The window would keep having to be moved back and forth. It would be very slow. Suggest a way to deal with this problem.

10

Description and Analysis
of High Level
Computer Languages

10.1 INTRODUCTION TO LANGUAGE SYSTEMS

Most computer programs written today are expressed in some kind of higher level computer language. Each program line in a high level language typically accomplishes a lot of work—the more the better. Assembler programming is only used in modern computing environments for special situations—for code that must be very fast, or that must make very efficient use of memory, or that must operate in close connection with the hardware. But, for most algorithmic computations and for standard repetitive data processing applications, and even for some control applications, debugged programs can be developed so much faster with higher level languages that this is the method of choice.

Two types of higher level language systems are in use today: interpreters and compilers. There are many examples of both sorts implemented on small computers, so it is appropriate that we now turn to discussing these language systems. If you were using an applications program to play a game, or to do some mathematical computation, or to do some business work, it would not be possible for you to tell whether the underlying language in which the program was expressed was interpreted or compiled. The results could appear exactly the same; but there would be large differences in the way the program was produced and in how it was handled at the time of execution.

One can view compilation as a simple extension of the basic ideas of assembly. It is a translational process from a language that humans can handle relatively well into one that they can't—machine language. However, the language being translated now is at a higher level. It prescribes work to be done in a more general and abstracted way than just allowing mnemonic specification of a machine instruction. Frequently, one compiled statement in a higher level language will produce the equivalent of 5 to 10 machine instructions.

Interpretation, however, is something quite different. It is not in any way an extension of assembly. In fact, it is not a translation operation at all. What an interpreter does is directly execute the operations that are implied by each program statement to produce whatever results the program was constructed to produce. The aim of the interpreter is to go from higher level language to computational results in a single step; there are no intermediate translations.

In the next few chapters we will explore how to build simple interpreters and compilers. However, there is some groundwork that must be done first. This chapter deals with the topic of how we can clearly, concisely, and usefully describe a high level language. It also deals with a related topic, parsing. Parsing refers to techniques for verifying that programs are grammatically correct and associated techniques by which a correct program statement can be decomposed into the underlying syntactic and semantic elements that make up the statement. This decomposition is an aid to further processing.

What are syntax and semantics? The syntax of a programming language describes the form and structure of programs written in the language. It is grammar. Implicitly, it defines the set of legal programs that can be written using the language. It also defines the constituent parts of a program, for example, constants, variables, expressions, and statements. The semantics of a programming language pertains to the meaning of programs written in the language, that is, what algorithm a program represents. This meaning is usually defined in terms of the constituent parts, which are fixed by the syntax.

Natural language provides good illustrations of syntax and semantics. Here is a sentence for which the syntax is correct and the semantics are meaningful.

Computers use data.

The syntax is correct because the noun-verb-noun form is proper in English. Here is a sentence in which the syntax is correct, but the semantics are all wrong.

Computers drink beer.

A clear way to describe a language is desirable for a number of reasons beyond the obvious that you will have a hard time learning it if it is not described properly. There are certain formal ways of describing a computer language from which it is much easier to build efficient interpreters and compilers than it is working from ad hoc informal definitions. More formal definitions are also useful for theoreticians who investigate the efficiency of a language for certain tasks, and the classes of algorithms that can be programmed in it.

Formal mathematics-like definitions find their largest use in describing the syntax of a language. It is much harder to describe language semantics formally, and we will not attempt it here. The three principal means in use today for describing language syntax are all closely related, and we will show how to use all of them in this chapter. They are the syntax chart method, the Backus-Naur formalism, and context free grammars.

In order to facilitate this study of language systems, we will also define a special simple language and use it as the uniform media for programs being interpreted or compiled. This language will be called TINY BASIC. We'll also show how TINY BASIC can be defined using all the formal methods.

The plan for this chapter, then, is as follows. First we will give an informal, narrative description of TINY BASIC. Then we will define it formally in three different ways. Then we will shift to the topic of parsing. It turns out that both our interpreter and compiler will be able to parse TINY BASIC in almost the same way. In preparation for doing this and because parsing can be closely related to formal language definition, we will work with it in this chapter rather than later on. There are many parsing techniques, and some are very complicated. However, the structure of TINY BASIC is such that a simple and widely useful technique can be used—parsing by means of finite state machines. We will develop two finite state machines, one to do syntactical analysis on TINY BASIC, and another that will act as a subprocessor to the syntax machine and will pick out the basic lexical elements in a program statement. Finally we will conclude the chapter by making a bridge between these methods and the more general methods used by advanced parsers.

Before we proceed, it is appropriate to say a few things in introduction of the BASIC language, because it is ubiquitous in the microcomputer world, and because we will do many things with it. The language was created at Dartmouth in 1966 by John Kemeny and a number of his associates. In its original form, it was something like a simplified FORTRAN that was set up to teach students programming. It also had the characteristics of being interactive, easy to learn, and susceptible to efficient use on a time shared computer.

Around 1975, BASIC began to appear on microcomputers. Most people in a position to use the original microprocessors viewed them as logical extensions of control electronics. They could be programmed in machine language or assembler language. There were no higher level languages because originally no one used microprocessors for general purpose computing elements. But, after they were around for a few years, a number of people realized that these complicated little chips were really computers, and that they could operate with the type of software found on bigger machines. Several stripped down high level languages were quickly produced. In particular, The People's Computer Company of Santa Clara, California, designed a compact verison of the BASIC language which they called TINY BASIC. This group and their friends went on to produce other languages for microcomputers such as TINY Pascal and TINY C.

Interpreters for some form of BASIC are furnished in a ROM as the primary language for all of today's popular microcomputers. The original BASIC mutated and adapted to a number of different niches. Today there are versions in sizes ranging from two kilobytes for control applications to a forty kilobyte version with complicated data structures, graphics, file handling, and accessible interrupt handlers.

All of today's systems are interactive and a program can be prepared on them very quickly. BASIC tends to be a very user friendly language. You can be doing simple programming on the machine after a half hour of instruction. It can be argued that the microcomputer revolution might never have gotten started if there were no user friendly languages like BASIC ready to be put on the new machines. For many people, if they had to start with a language like Pascal, they wouldn't have started at all.

Our dialect of the language has built upon the original microcomputer tradition.

We are also calling our interpreter TINY BASIC. This is not to steal the name but rather because, in the generic sense, this name suggests a compact, easy to learn, easy to implement, little language. Our language has a family resemblance to all other BASICs. However, its syntax was selected principally to illustrate factors that arise in the design of languages, rather than to meet any of the other goals that BASIC has traditionally served.

10.2 *DEFINING A LANGUAGE INFORMALLY—TINY BASIC*

The oldest way to define a language, and still the most useful for learning to use it, is the narrative description. In a narrative description, the overall structure is described as are the types of data allowed and the format of expressions, and then the working of each statement is explained. The advantage of this kind of description is that it parallels the way humans normally learn about things. The disadvantages are that it is sometimes hard to use it to resolve intricate questions of syntax and usage, such as an experienced user always finds in his work. Frequently the only recourse is to try out various examples until the matter is resolved. This kind of description is also not as helpful as it could be in writing language processors. Furthermore, an informal description blurs and mixes together two aspects of description that probably should be kept separate, namely, the syntax and the semantics.

We will give an informal definition of the TINY BASIC language. We will first outline how data can be represented in the language and what facilities exist for combining data in varying types of expressions, and then we'll describe the syntax of a modest but powerful set of program statements with which programs can be constructed.

Our version of TINY BASIC prescribes variables which are integers and can fit within a sixteen bit word. This means that the largest positive number allowed will be 32,767, and the largest negative number will be $-32,768$. The user specifies numbers as decimal integers. Standard two's complement form will be used internally. The names of variables can be any letter of the alphabet, or any letter of the alphabet followed by one decimal digit, that is, a number between 0 and 9. This means only $26*11 = 286$ different names are allowed in this version of BASIC. The fact that there are so few possible variable names will make certain parts of the language very easy to program.

All variables are global. That is, they can be used anywhere in the program or in any subroutine and have the same meaning. There is no provision to have local variables within a procedure that are not known outside the procedure.

Normal algebraic expressions are allowed with the operators being plus, minus, unary minus, multiply, and divide. The operators must be written out. This is a little different from algebraic notation where two numbers next to each other imply multiplication. If there is ever any ambiguity about what operations to do first, the system will do the operation with highest precedence. The precedence of multiplication and division is highest. Next comes the unary minus. The lowest precedence is held by addition and subtraction. Parentheses can be used in the normal way to change the order in which parts of an expression will be evaluated.

The results of expression evaluation are 16 bit numbers. Since TINY BASIC will be quite a bit easier to implement if no data ever become larger than 16 bits, we make a further restriction on algebraic expressions. Expressions must be such that the intermediate results needed to evaluate an expression (running sums, stack elements, etc.) never require storage in a number larger than 16 bits.

Simple Boolean expressions are allowed in the language. A Boolean expression is something that takes a value of true or false. This construct will have two variables as operands (or a variable and a number, or two numbers). Between the operands may be one of three relational operators. The operators are greater than, less than, and equals.

Every line in a program written in this language must be prefaced by a statement number. The main reason for statement numbers is to give the built-in editor that is usually associated with interpretative versions of BASIC a way to refer to various lines in the program. Labels are not used to identify the targets of branches because the statement numbers are already there and can serve the same purpose. Normally a program is executed in numerical order on the statement numbers. But this order can be altered by a conditional or unconditional branch or a subroutine call.

Blanks are not important to TINY BASIC, but they may be put in at reasonable places to enhance program readability. All statements must end with a Carriage Return character, and this is the only thing that the language uses to differentiate one statement from the next.

We describe the statements next. There are thirteen different statement types in the TINY BASIC language.

(a) The *Assignment statement* has a variable name on the left of an equals sign and an algebraic expression on the right side. A single variable or a constant can also be on the right side of the statement. An example is

```
10    X =  (A + B)  + 3
```

(b) The *Loop Begin statement* specifies a variable name for a loop counter, a beginning value for the variable, and an ending value for the variable. Here is how a typical loop is set up. A loop is demarcated by a Loop Begin statement, followed by some code, and at the bottom of the loop comes a Loop End statement. Control will cycle around the loop, and after each time through it, the loop counter is incremented. When the counter reaches the end value, the loop will be executed one more time, and control will pass to the first statement beyond the loop. On the last traversal, the loop counter is not incremented. The keyword which identifies the beginning of a loop is FOR. The syntax is shown in the following examples:

```
17    FOR  I = 1  TO  10
65    FOR  J = 1  TO  N
```

The ending value of the loop counter can be a number or a simple variable. The beginning value must be one.

(c) Every loop has a beginning and an ending point. The *Loop End statement* is identified by the keyword NEXT. All that is in the Loop End statement is this keyword and the name of the loop counter variable associated with the loop. Here is an example of how a loop using the loop counter J would be terminated:

```
100    NEXT  J
```

Loops can be nested to an arbitrary depth, but nested loops must be completely nested. They cannot interpenetrate at the End statements. You cannot jump into or out of a loop. That is, there is only one entrance and one exit. This is a little different from many versions of BASIC.

(d) The *Unloop statement* can be used to get out of a loop if for some reason you wish to cut short the normal pattern of loop traversal. Its effect will be to transfer control immediately to the first statement beyond the end of the loop. The loop counter variable remains at whatever value it had when the Unloop statement was encountered. The syntax of the statement is the keyword followed by the name of the loop counter variable that would be encountered soonest if the code were traversed sequentially past the Unloop statement. If you wish to exit from nested loops, you must do it with multiple uses of the Unloop statement starting with the innermost loop. Each use of the statement breaks control out of just one loop. Here is an example of the syntax for a loop in which the loop counter variable is K:

```
10    UNLOOP  K
```

Normally, well structured programs let loops run to their conclusion. That is, they don't use the Unloop statement. We only include it here because many versions of BASIC allow you to jump out of loops with the GOTO statement. We don't wish to give the GOTO statement this property because it turns out to be hard to implement. This type of use for GOTO is also the ultimate in unstructured programming and can lead to quite a few problems in debugging.

(e) The *Conditional Branch statement* is identified by the keyword IF. The next field is a Boolean expression which can be evaluated to true or false. The Boolean expression must have the form of two operands joined by a relational operator, with the whole expression surrounded by parentheses. A valid operand is an integer constant or a simple variable. After the expression there is a clause which specifies what statement number control will go to if the expression is true. If the expression is false, the next statement in sequence is executed. Here is an example of the syntax we are specifying:

```
40   IF  (A > B)   THEN  150
```

(f) The *Unconditional Branch statement* has the identifying keyword GOTO and specifies a statement number to which control will be transferred unconditionally. It is like a jump statement in assembler language. It has the form

```
25    GOTO   200
```

(g) The *Subroutine Call statement* uses the keyword GOSUB and specifies a line number which is interpreted as the first line in a subroutine. The effect of this statement is to set up the indicated line number as the next statement to execute. The statement also sets up a return mechanism that will be used after the subroutine is finished.

        30   GOSUB   2000

(h) The *Return statement* consists of this keyword and nothing else. Here is a peculiar fact about BASIC subroutines. Nothing distinguishes the start of a subroutine except that it is referred to from somewhere else in the program by a GOSUB statement. However, the last statement in a subroutine will always be the Return statement. The syntax is simply:

        47   RETURN

Subroutine calls can be nested to arbitrary depth. The returning mechanism will be the same as the most common method used at the machine level in microprocessors. That is, a stack will be used to receive the return address upon a subroutine call and to give it back when the routine is finished. Actually, since the program is executing in a higher level language, what will go on the stack will be something equivalent to the statement number at which to resume execution when the subroutine finishes.

(i) The *Input statement* allows variables to be taken into the program from the keyboard. This statement can have one, two, or three arguments. The arguments are the names of variables which will receive values. When an Input statement is executed, the program will print a specific prompt on the terminal screen indicating that it is waiting for the user to type in a value. The system may do this several times depending on how many arguments are given with the statement. For example, the following statement would allow the user to enter values from the keyboard for the three named variables during the program's execution:

        400   READ   A, Y, Z4

(j) The *Output statement* is the inverse of the Input statement. It may have from one to three arguments. When the statement is encountered, the values of the argument variables will be printed out on one line of the terminal screen. For example, an Output statement that will print out two values is

        310   PRINT   R, S

(k) The *Title statement* is used to produce descriptive comments on the screen as part of the program output. Remember that the Output statement itself has no capacity to output text, only variables. The layout of this statement will be the keyword, followed by a single dash, followed by the text to be output. Any text between the dash and the carriage return at the end of the line will be output on the screen at the current position of the cursor. The cursor will move to the next line after the text is output. Vertical spaces can be left in the output by successive use of the Title statement with no text. Here is an example:

```
30   TITLE-START OF PROGRAM
```

(l) The *Comment statement* is used for inserting descriptive material within the program text. It appears like any other statement within the program and begins with a statement number. When the program is being executed, all Comment statements are skipped. They are there only to help the programmer document the program. A Comment statement begins with the keyword REM which stands for remark, and then continues with any comment. An example is

```
32   REM     SUBROUTINE ALPHA STARTS HERE
```

(m) The *End statement* marks the logical end of a program. The action of the End statement is to halt the execution of the program. Every proper program must have at least one End statement. An example of its form is:

```
500   END
```

Note that being the last statement to be executed does not mean being the statement with the highest statement number. Subroutines are frequently placed at the end of a BASIC program with very high statement numbers.

```
10    REM     PROGRAM PRODUCES THE SUM
20    REM       AND PRODUCT OF A SERIES
30    TITLE-DEMONSTRATION PROGRAM
40    GOSUB 100
50    GOSUB 200
60    TITLE-SUM AND PRODUCT
70    PRINT S,P
80    END
100   REM     SUM OF A SERIES
110   S = 0
120   FOR  I = 1 TO 10
130   S = S + I
140   NEXT  I
150   RETURN
200   REM     PRODUCT OF A SERIES
210   P = 1
220   FOR  J = 1 TO 10
230   P = P * J
240   NEXT  J
250   RETURN
```

Figure 10-1: An Example Program in TINY BASIC. This program finds the sum and product of the integers from 1 to 10 and prints out the results.

Let's consider an example to see how this collection of programming statements can do useful work. In Figure 10-1, we show a program written in TINY BASIC which will find the sum and the product of a series of integer numbers. This program finds the sum of integers from 1 to 10 and the product of integers from 1 to 10 and prints out the results. The low numbered statements are a driver section in which two subroutines are called that fill S and P respectively with the values being computed. Then a Title statement prints a label on the screen to explain the answers. The final line on the screen will be the sum and product put there by an Output statement.

10.3 *DEFINING A LANGUAGE FORMALLY: TINY BASIC*

The first method of formal definition that we will consider, and the one that people seem to have the least difficulty with, is the method of syntax charts (sometimes called railroad diagrams). Figure 10-2 shows the set of these charts for TINY BASIC. The entities shown on the charts are the names of various syntactic components of the language. Some of the components are at a very high level and require considerable further description in order to acquire a meaning. "Statement" is like this. Other components are at a low level, mean only what you see, and require no further description. The equals sign is like this. The components requiring no further description are called terminal components. They have rounded shapes on a syntax chart. Those which require further description are called nonterminal components. They have rectangular shapes on a syntax chart. The highest level chart is the one for "Program." As you can see, there is not much detail here. Most of the components require subsidiary charts to explain what they mean, and this process may continue down for four or five levels until we arrive at components which are terminal and require no further elaboration.

The syntax charts implicitly contain a procedure whereby all the legal programs allowed by TINY BASIC could be generated. The idea is to start in the highest level diagram and follow the arrows until you come to the end of that diagram. However, there's a catch; any time you come to a nonterminal component you must make a switch to the diagram for that component and traverse to the end of it by some path. Of course, if nonterminal components are found here, they must be treated the same way. A complete program is said to be generated if you move through to the end of the highest level chart in accordance with the above rules, and touch only terminal symbols. These symbols are output in the order in which they are encountered, and they form the program. *If a program written by a user could have been generated in this way, then its syntax is correct*.

Occasionally certain facts about the syntax of a language will not be directly representable on the charts. A subsidiary note recording restrictions on how a particular part of the chart is to be used will be required. For instance, TINY BASIC allows no positive numbers larger than 32,767; but this doesn't show up in the charts where a constant is defined. A full definition requires both the syntax and this caveat.

Notice that when using the syntax charts it is easier to generate a correct program (syntactically correct) than it is to tell if an existing program conforms to the rules of the

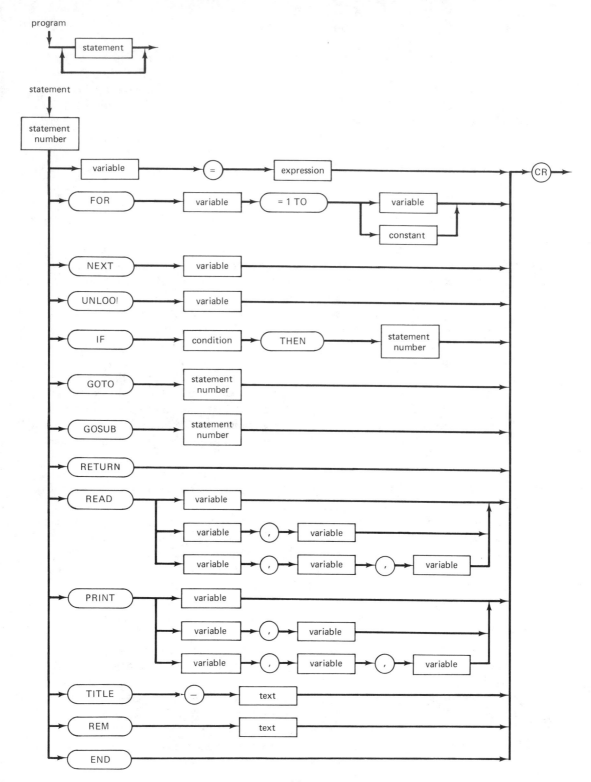

(a)

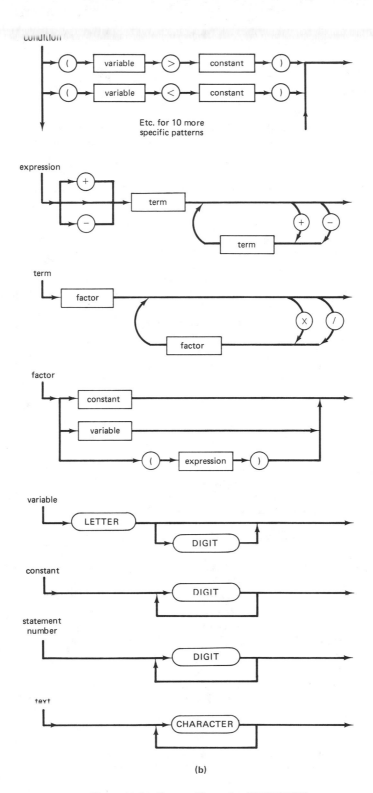

(b)

Figure 10-2: Syntax Charts for TINY BASIC.

language. There are no *easy* ways to tell if an existing program is correct, and all the formal definitions suffer from this deficiency. There are hard ways to tell if an existing program is correct, and parsers make use of them.

The next type of formal definition we want to look at is the Backus-Naur form. Figure 10-3 shows TINY BASIC cast in this mold. Once again the process of definition of a program starts at a high level and works down to definitions at a low level. The process of refining definitions can lead to all possible legal programs in the language just as following through the paths on the syntax charts can. A Backus-Naur form looks like some sort of an equation. The way it should be read is that the entity on the left can be defined in terms of simpler entities on the right of the equation. These may in turn be defined with even simpler entities through their own defining equations, until the process stops with terminal components that cannot be defined or refined further.

⟨program⟩ : : = ⟨statement⟩ {⟨statement⟩}
⟨statement⟩ : : = ⟨statnum⟩⟨variable⟩=⟨expression⟩CR
    |⟨statnum⟩<u>FOR</u>⟨variable⟩=1TO\⟨ variable⟩|⟨constant⟩\CR
    |⟨statnum⟩<u>NEXT</u>⟨variable⟩C̅R̅
    |⟨statnum⟩<u>UNLOOP</u>⟨variable⟩CR
    |⟨statnum⟩<u>GOTO</u>⟨statnum⟩CR
    |⟨statnum⟩<u>GOSUB</u>⟨statnum⟩CR
    |⟨statnum⟩<u>RETURN</u>CR
    |⟨statnum⟩<u>IF</u>⟨condition⟩<u>THEN</u>⟨statnum⟩CR
    |⟨statnum⟩<u>READ</u>\⟨variable⟩|⟨variable⟩,⟨variable⟩
       |⟨variable⟩,⟨variable⟩,⟨variable⟩\CR
    |⟨statnum⟩<u>PRINT</u>\⟨variable⟩|⟨variable⟩,⟨variable⟩
       |⟨variable⟩,⟨variable⟩,⟨variable⟩\CR
    |⟨statnum⟩<u>TITLE</u>-⟨text⟩CR
    |⟨statnum⟩<u>REM</u>⟨text⟩CR
    |⟨statnum⟩<u>END</u>CR

⟨condition⟩   : : = (\⟨variable⟩|⟨constant⟩\\)|⟨|=\\⟨variable⟩|⟨constant⟩\)
⟨expression⟩   : : = [+|−]⟨term⟩{\+|−\⟨term⟩}
⟨term⟩   : : = ⟨factor⟩{*|/\⟨factor⟩}
⟨factor⟩   : : = ⟨constant⟩|⟨variable⟩|(⟨expression⟩)
⟨variable⟩   : : = ⟨letter⟩[⟨digit⟩]
⟨constant⟩   : : = ⟨digit⟩{⟨digit⟩}   Note: the size limits of 16 bit words apply.
⟨text⟩   : : = ⟨character⟩{⟨character⟩}
⟨statnum⟩   : : = ⟨constant⟩
⟨character⟩   : : = ⟨letter⟩|⟨digit⟩
⟨letter⟩   : : = A|B| . . . . . |Z
⟨digit⟩   : : = 0|1| . . . . . |9

Figure 10-3   The Backus-Naur Definition for TINY BASIC. BNF provides a concise way to indicate all the possible syntactic variations in a computer language.

The Backus-Naur formalism is a system for describing language. To do this easily, it is necessary to use some symbols that are not in the language as part of the description. These special purpose symbols are called metasymbols, and together they form a meta-language. The meanings of the commonly used metasymbols are as follows:

⟨ ⟩ These symbols delineate a nonterminal entity which must be defined further.

: : =   This is the definition operator. It means the entity on the left can be defined or can be rewritten as one of the patterns indicated on the right.

| This symbol denotes alternatives. One of them must be chosen.

\ \ Occasionally, in a complicated definition, it is necessary to delineate the boundaries of a group of alternatives that are at the same logical level. We are using these symbols for that purpose. Note that this particular usage is not standard BNF.

_____   The underline denotes reserved words of the language being defined.

[   ] Brackets indicate part of a definition that can either be used or be left out. It is for indicating optional elements.

{   } Braces denote something which can be repeated zero, one, or more times as part of a definition.

Backus-Naur definitions frequently contain an implied recursion, as do the syntax diagrams. This is to be expected. If a language has a recursive character, its definition must mirror that character. We will see more of this a little later when we look at the highest program components of Pascal. The definition of TINY BASIC is not recursive except in one respect—the way expressions are defined. Consider the following four definition lines:

$$⟨\text{expression}⟩ : : = [+|-]⟨\text{term}⟩\{\backslash +|-\backslash ⟨\text{term}⟩\}$$

$$⟨\text{term}⟩ : : = ⟨\text{factor}⟩\{\backslash *|/\backslash ⟨\text{factor}⟩\}$$

$$⟨\text{factor}⟩ : : = ⟨\text{constant}⟩|⟨\text{variable}⟩|(⟨\text{expression}⟩)$$

$$⟨\text{variable}⟩ : : = ⟨\text{letter}⟩[⟨\text{digit}⟩]$$

Expressions are built from terms, which are built from factors, which may be built from expressions.

A program structure in a language described by a Backus-Naur form can be proved to be syntactically correct by starting with the highest level definition and then deriving the structure through repeated applications of the definition rules. For instance, Figure 10-4 shows two different records of the defining process for an example of an expression that is permitted in TINY BASIC:

```
3*A  +  8  -  (A/C)
```

In the first representation we see repeated applications of the defining rules until the desired expression is finally produced. The high level definition that is being worked with at each step is underlined.

$$\langle expression \rangle \quad :: = \quad [+|-]\langle term \rangle \{\setminus + | - \setminus \langle term \rangle \}$$
$$\langle expression \rangle \quad :: = \quad \underline{\langle term \rangle} + \langle term \rangle - \langle term \rangle$$
$$\langle expression \rangle \quad :: = \quad \underline{\langle factor \rangle}*\langle factor \rangle + \langle term \rangle - \langle term \rangle$$
$$\langle expression \rangle \quad :: = \quad 3*\underline{\langle factor \rangle} + \langle term \rangle - \langle term \rangle$$
$$\langle expression \rangle \quad :: = \quad 3*A + \underline{\langle term \rangle} - \langle term \rangle$$
$$\langle expression \rangle \quad :: = \quad 3*A + \underline{\langle factor \rangle} - \langle term \rangle$$
$$\langle expression \rangle \quad :: = \quad 3*A + 8 - \underline{\langle term \rangle}$$
$$\langle expression \rangle \quad :: = \quad 3*A + 8 - \underline{\langle factor \rangle}$$
$$\langle expression \rangle \quad :: = \quad 3*A + 8 - (\underline{\langle expression \rangle})$$
$$\langle expression \rangle \quad :: = \quad 3*A + 8 - (\underline{\langle term \rangle})$$
$$\langle expression \rangle \quad :: = \quad 3*A + 8 - (\underline{\langle factor \rangle}/\langle factor \rangle)$$
$$\langle expression \rangle \quad :: = \quad 3*A + 8 - (A/\underline{\langle factor \rangle})$$
$$\langle expression \rangle \quad :: = \quad 3*A + 8 - (A/C)$$

Figure 10-4A: Deriving an Expression Through Repeated Applications of Backus-Naur Definitions. A program fragment can be proved to be syntactically correct by deriving it from Backus-Naur definitions. In this case we use the part of the TINY BASIC definition that deals with expressions and show that the expression

$$3*A + 8 - (A/C)$$

is in correct form.

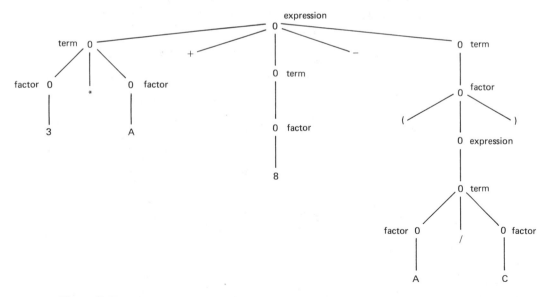

Figure 10-4B: The Corresponding Parse Tree for This Derivation. A parse tree is another representation of the order in which elaborating definitions have been applied.

The second representation is a tree. A tree that arises in the context of proving a program fragment to be correct is usually called a parse tree. It is a representation of the sequence of transformations done on the original terse high level definition to arrive ultimately at a more elaborate definition that is built up from terminal characters. Each circle is both a node in the tree and a representation of a program fragment. The children of any node represent the results of applying an elaborating definition to that particular program fragment.

One interesting feature of these parse trees is that the final derived program or program fragment can be read out in proper order simply by moving from left to right and listing the symbols attached to the terminal nodes of the tree. This is equivalent to moving through the tree in the manner of a depth first search and listing all the terminal nodes in the order in which they are encountered.

Some of the obvious low-level rewriting steps have not been shown in Figure 10-4 in order to keep the size of the example manageable. However, for a consistent application of the BNF, they should be shown. For instance, in one part of the derivation, we have rewritten ⟨factor⟩ as 3. The complete sequence is ⟨factor⟩ rewritten as ⟨constant⟩ which is rewritten as ⟨digit⟩ which is rewritten as 3.

The third formal method that we wish to consider is the method of context free grammars. The data structures used in this method are more suitable for direct inclusion into a parsing program than are the structures of BNF. A context free grammar consists of the same set of terminal elements we have examined before (these are characteristic of the language being defined), plus a set of nonterminals chosen for convenience, plus a set of productions. The productions are very similar to the BNF language definition rules.

The productions again take the form of rewrite rules. The entity on the left of one of these rules can be rewritten as the grouping of things on the right side of the rule. As in all the other formal systems there is a hierarchy of rules. There is one particular rewrite rule at which all work must begin. The entity on the left side of this rule is called the Sentence Symbol. The rules that are used early in a derivation will correspond to high level program constructs. Those at the end will be quite close to terminal symbols.

The idea of context free grammars came from the work of linguists who were trying to find rules that would describe the structure of natural speech. It is appropriate, then, that we take an example from this context. Figure 10-5B shows some productions from a grammar that describes natural language. The right facing arrow means "can be rewritten as." The vertical bar indicates that alternatives should be selected. In this particular grammar, nonterminal symbols are enclosed by arrows facing opposite ways. Terminal symbols are not enclosed. Figure 10-5A shows all the symbols to be used in this example.

To verify that a sentence is grammatically correct, it is only necessary to start with the Sentence Symbol and apply the rewrite rules until arriving at the target sentence. Figure 10-5C shows how this can be done.

A context free grammar for TINY BASIC is shown in Figure 10-6. We will use it in a later section. We need to warn the reader of a notational difficulty that exists here and in many grammars of this sort. The terminals of the grammar are keywords, capital

A. The Alphabet of the Grammar.

Terminals	*Nonterminals*
a, the	np (noun phrase)
robot, Robbie, block, pyramid, table	vp (verb phrase)
grabs, lifts, picks-up, puts-down	pp (prepositional phrase)
moves, drops	
on, behind, from, near	det (determiner)
big, green, old	adj (adjective)
slowly	adv (adverb)
	verb
	noun

B. The Productions of the Grammar.

⟨sentence⟩→⟨np⟩⟨vp⟩|⟨np⟩⟨vp⟩⟨np⟩|⟨sentence⟩⟨pp⟩
⟨np⟩   →⟨noun⟩|⟨det⟩⟨noun⟩|⟨det⟩⟨adj⟩⟨noun⟩
⟨pp⟩   →⟨prep⟩⟨np⟩
⟨vp⟩   →⟨verb⟩|⟨verb⟩⟨adv⟩

C. Proving a Sentence to be Grammatical.

The sentence to be verified (or parsed) is:
Robbie lifts the block from the big table.
⟨<u>sentence</u>⟩
⟨<u>sentence</u>⟩⟨pp⟩
⟨<u>np</u>⟩⟨vp⟩⟨np⟩⟨pp⟩
⟨noun⟩⟨<u>vp</u>⟩⟨np⟩⟨pp⟩
⟨noun⟩⟨verb⟩⟨<u>np</u>⟩⟨pp⟩
⟨noun⟩⟨verb⟩⟨det⟩⟨noun⟩⟨<u>pp</u>⟩
⟨noun⟩⟨verb⟩⟨det⟩⟨noun⟩⟨prep⟩⟨<u>np</u>⟩
⟨noun⟩⟨ verb⟩⟨det⟩⟨noun⟩⟨prep⟩⟨det⟩⟨adj⟩⟨noun⟩
Robbie lifts the block from the big table

Figure 10-5:   A Simple Context Free Grammar. A context-free grammar is a set of rewrite rules which allow syntactically correct strings of various sorts to be generated. This particular grammar generates a restricted universe of sentences from natural English language. Remember, these sentences are syntactically correct, but not necessarily meaningful.

letters, digits, and certain operators and punctuation symbols. When we intend a capital letter to be used as a terminal, it is enclosed in single quotes, because some capital letters are serving double duty as nonterminals. These should perhaps have been indicated by a different set of symbols. However, too many symbols tend to make the grammar look unreadable. Normally, the way the grammar is used will clarify ambiguities.

A.   The Alphabet of the Grammar.

Terminals that are abbreviations for other things

f	(stands for FOR)	s	(stands for " = 1TO")
i	(stands for IF)	t	(stands for THEN)
n	(stands for NEXT)	u	(stands for UNLOOP)
j	(stands for GOTO)	g	(stands for GOSUB)
b	(stands for RETURN)	r	(stands for READ)
p	(stands for PRINT)	c	(stands for REM)
h	(stands for TITLE-)	e	(stands for END)
ˆ	(stands for Carriage Return)		

Terminals that are Complete in Themselves
'A' through 'Z'
0 through 9
+ − * / > < = ( ) ,

Nonterminals

P	(denotes program)		
X	(denotes text list)	R	(denotes read list)
W	(denotes write list)	S	(denotes statement)
E	(denotes expression)	$\mathfrak{I}$	(denotes term list)
T	(denotes term)	$\mathfrak{F}$	(denotes factor list)
F	(denotes factor)	C	(denotes constant)
U	(denotes unsigned constant)	O	(denotes condition)
N	(denotes a digit)	L	(denotes a letter)
I	(denotes an identifier)		

B.   The Productions of the Grammar.

P → USˆ P|USˆ   (P is the sentence symbol.)
X → LX |L
R → I|I,I|I,I
W → I|I,I|I,I
S → I = E|fIsI|fIsU|nI|uI|i(O)tU|jU|gU|b|rR|pW|hX|cX|e
E → T$\mathfrak{I}$| − T$\mathfrak{I}$|T| − T
$\mathfrak{I}$ → +T| − T| + T$\mathfrak{I}$| − T$\mathfrak{I}$
T → F$\mathfrak{F}$|F
$\mathfrak{F}$ → *F$\mathfrak{F}$|/F$\mathfrak{F}$|*F|/F
F → U|I|(E)
C → U| − U
U → N|NU
I → L|LN
O → I)C|C)I|I⟨C|C⟨I|I)I|I⟨I|I = I|I = C |C = I|C)C|C⟨C|C = C
N → 0 | . . . . | 9
L → 'A' | . . . . | 'Z'

Figure 10-6:   A Context Free Grammar for TINY BASIC.

10.4 *PROGRAM ANALYSIS AND PARSING BY FINITE STATE MACHINES*

Language processing software needs to perform analysis on incoming program text for two basic reasons. The first reason is in order to error check the program. The type of error checking that is the easiest to do automatically is checking for syntax errors, i.e., for whether the program statements observe the precise form required by the language definition. Frequently, a data base created from a formal language definition will be at the heart of this process. The other reason for analysis is to render the program into some intermediate form that makes clear and relatively easy the further steps that have to be taken to do the computation indicated by the program (in the case of an interpreter) or to generate code that will do the computation when it is executed (in the case of a compiler).

It is traditional in language processors to attack both these objectives in a phase of the work that is known as parsing. The parsing phase is used to check syntax and to abstract and conveniently package the information in program lines so that its further processing can be done efficiently.

Parsing, in general, is a very complicated subject. As you might expect, the more complicated the language, the more complicated the parsing will be. One language feature that makes parsing difficult is compound statements. A compound statement is one in which there is a top level program statement, but clauses in that statement contain places where other fully formed statements can be inserted. Deeply nested IF-THEN-ELSE statements are notorious for this kind of thing. For instance, suppose the language allows this construct:

```
IF (CONDITION)   THEN   STATEMENT  1
                 ELSE   STATEMENT  2
```

It doesn't look too bad here, but the potential for nesting is infinite, as in

```
IF (COND1) THEN IF (COND2) THEN IF (COND3) THEN CALL ALPHA

                                           ELSE CALL OMEGA

                           ELSE CALL OMICRON

           ELSE IF (COND4) THEN IF (COND5) THEN CALL ALPHA

                                          ELSE CALL BETA

                           ELSE IF (COND6) THEN CALL GAMMA

                                           ELSE CALL HELP
```

Indenting the program helps some, but the programmer can still quickly lose sight of what this sort of construction means, and so can the parser unless elegant, advanced techniques are used.

Another thing that makes for a complicated parser is a recursive rather than a hierarchical structure to the way a language is defined. We can call this factor recursively controlled nesting of program elements. Pascal has this character. It is illustrated by Figure 10-7, where we see railroad charts for some of the higher level constructs in a subset of Pascal.

Notice that on the highest level, the main element in a program is the construct called a BLOCK. Inside a BLOCK comes a construct called DECLARATIONS. But

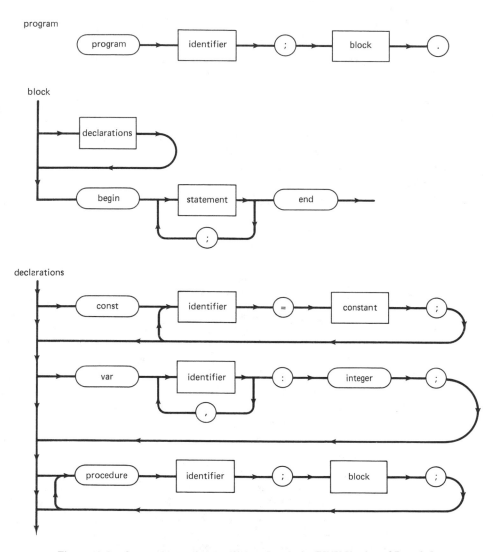

Figure 10-7:   Syntax Charts for the Highest Level of a TINY Version of Pascal. In its definition, Pascal is a thoroughly recursive language. The same constructs can appear simultaneously at both a high and a low level in the hierarchy of the definition.

inside DECLARATIONS we see a subsidiary slot for another BLOCK. This can go on and on.

Pascal is an elegant language. It has a consistent, concise, recursive language definition. One feature that follows from this is that the language needs very few keywords. Control does not reside in atomic entities represented by keywords as much as it resides in the overall structure of the program. Tightly coded recursive algorithms can be set up to parse Pascal, but they are not particularly easy to understand. These topics are properly taught in a class on compiler theory.

Our example language, BASIC, on the other hand, is very easy to parse. It has a sequential, hierarchical flavor rather than a recursive one. The overall unit is the program. Within the program are smaller elements called statements. Within the statements are clearly defined atomic units such as keywords, variables, and expressions. The structure of BASIC is such that it can be completely parsed using a simple technique based upon finite state machines.

Before we explain how we are going to parse our example language, we need some introduction to finite state machines. A soda vending machine or an elevator are real life examples of devices that have been designed as finite state machines. The elements of a finite state machine are a set of states the system can be in; a set of rules that explain under what circumstances the system changes from one state to another; a set of inputs that the machine can accept and that will drive it between states; and a set of outputs that the machine will produce. Frequently these outputs are actions that the machine takes as it makes particular transitions or subroutines that are to be called when transitions are made.

An example of a finite state machine that will have some familiarity to people involved with computers is the serial adder. This is a very simple machine that can add two binary numbers together. It does it one column at a time starting from the right just as a human being would. Of course, when any two columns are being added together, the carry generated from the immediately previous addition must be incorporated. You know about serial adders because you do exactly what the machine would do when you add two binary numbers. Figure 10-8A shows the adder. We can imagine that the numbers at the X and Y inputs are simultaneously inserted into the machine, one bit position at a time, and for every bit movement into the input side, one bit appears at the output. The output bits concatenated together are the result of the addition. Each step in the addition process produces a carry bit which is fed back to enter into the next addition step.

It is not important to discuss the circuitry that is inside the adder. For this discussion we only need to know its input/output characteristics. They can be summarized in the truth table shown in Figure 10-8B. The machine follows two different addition tables depending on whether a carry from the last operation is present or not. For this reason, we say the machine has two states.

Figure 10-8C shows the customary balloon diagram for a finite state machine. The balloons represent the states. The directed arrows show state transitions. Notice that there are two numbers above each transition. The number on the left shows what input will cause this particular transition to happen. The number on the right is the output that is

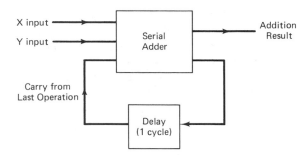

A.   Overall Block Diagram

State	X Input	Y Input	C Input	Output	C Output
S0	0	0	0	0	0
S0	0	1	0	1	0
S0	1	0	0	1	0
S0	1	1	0	0	1
S1	0	0	1	1	0
S1	0	1	1	0	1
S1	1	0	1	0	1
S1	1	1	1	1	1

State S0 means no carry from before. State S1 means there is a
carry from the previous cycle.

B.   Truth Table for Adder Functions

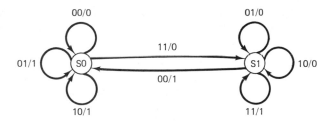

C.   Transition Diagram

Figure 10-8.   The Serial Adder as a Finite State Machine. (A) Overall Block Diagram.
(B) Truth Table for Adder Functions. (C) Transition Diagram. The serial adder is a simple
example of a deterministic finite state machine. It has two states (corresponding to the
value of the last carry) and four transitions that can be made from each state.

produced in the course of making the transition. In general, this last number can be any action that it is convenient to have the machine do while it makes the transition. We must remember that the finite state machine is a control structure but the only reason it would ever be set up is so that these actions could be done in an appropriate sequence.

Now let's examine how we plan to use finite state machines for parsing. It is customary to break parsing up into two steps: lexical analysis and syntactic analysis. The business of lexical analysis is to identify the tokens in the program input. A token is an atomic element of some sort. It is a single logical entity, but frequently it will be composed of a number of characters. For example, keywords are tokens, operators are tokens, and numbers are tokens. Beyond this, other things can be chosen as tokens if it is convenient.

The lexical analyzer is often written as a subroutine that is callable from the syntactic analyzer whenever the syntax unit needs another token to inspect. Each time the lexical analyzer is called, it furnishes the next token in the input string.

Frequently, returning a token means returning several fields of information about the atomic entity that has been discovered. Our tokenizer will return a type field, a value field, and a count field. The type field will contain a code of 1–6 to indicate a keyword, a variable, a fixed number, an operator, a text string (as in a Remark or Title statement), or a punctuation mark. The value field is used for several purposes. If the token is a keyword, then the value field has a code to indicate which keyword. In TINY BASIC, there are 14 keywords. If the token is an operator, the value field will have a code to indicate which one. The possibilities are

$$[+, -, *, /, (,), >, <, =].$$

If the token is a punctuation mark, the value field will indicate whether it is a comma or a carriage return. On the other hand, if the token is a variable or a text string, the value field will point to where the entity begins in the text buffer and the count field will indicate how many characters compose it. The other token types don't need to use the count field.

Figure 10-9 shows a finite state machine for lexical analysis. The lexical machine has an indicator called the character pointer which will be adjusted so that it always points to the next character from the program to be taken in for analysis. The first time the lexical machine is entered at state L1, the indicator will be pointing to the first character in the program. In subsequent uses, whenever the lexical machine is entered, the character pointer will always be pointing to the first character beyond the end of the last token that has been identified. The notations above the arrows in the lexical machine call for the input of a character and indicate what character is necessary to force the transition that is shown. When there are two notations associated with an arrow, the second indicates an action to be taken as the transition is executed. In several places, the action is to back up the character pointer in the input stream by one or two places, because the finite state machine was following out the implications of a lead which turned out to be false.

The states with double circles are called accepting states. To arrive at one of these states means that a token of some sort has been identified. Presumably, then, the routine that is driving the lexical finite state machine will package the token in the way we have specified and pass it on up to whatever other routine asked for the token. We have not

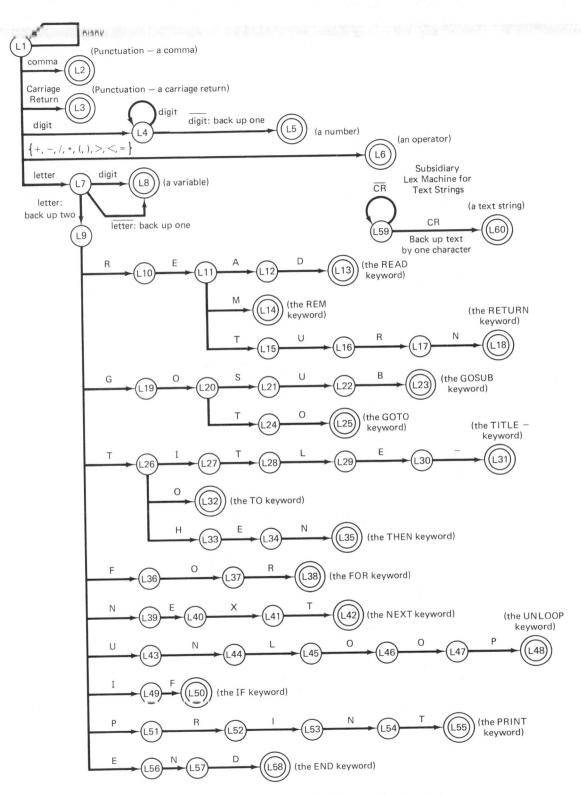

Figure 10-9: Lexical Analyzer for TINY BASIC.

specified many of the actions to be taken in conjunction with state transitions. Most of them will be for the purpose of packaging or preparing to package the tokens as they are being discovered.

Several exception conditions of the lexical machine need to be explained. In general, whenever the machine is in a particular state and a character appears that does not correspond to a known transition, that character represents an error. Every state must have an error exit, which we have not shown. The various states in a finite state machine represent detailed information on a recognition process that is under way. Because of this, it is usually possible to associate quite descriptive error messages with the various error paths out of the states.

Figure 10-9 shows a subsidiary lexical machine associated with states L59 and L60. What is this for? There is a potential problem in recognizing the text strings after TITLE and REM keywords. What if those strings contain other keywords of the language embedded in them? If the main lexical machine starts analyzing such a text string from state L1, it could make a faulty recognition. The solution is simple. After entering the accepting states for TITLE or REM, the machine will reset and start its further work at state L59. After any other accepting state, the machine will reset and start its further work at state L1. This will take care of it.

Figure 10-10 shows the finite state machine for syntactical analysis. Every transition involves calling the lexical analyzer to get another token. The transitions are labeled with the particular tokens that will drive a given transition.

Getting to an accepting state in the syntactic machine means that a particular kind of program statement has been identified, analyzed, and found to be correct syntactically. An important part of the syntax analyzer is to change the form of the statement into some intermediate form that is suitable for further processing. We have not shown the actions that accompany these transitions, but their goal will be to build this intermediate form.

An intermediate form data structure that turns out to be very convenient to a language processor working on BASIC is a table of descriptors that is produced for each statement. This table separates and highlights information in the statement that is necessary for further processing. It also casts everything in a fixed length form so that any routine dealing with this table doesn't have to scan back and forth to find the bounding points of various entities. Scanning is very time consuming.

This structure is suitable for use in both an interpreter and a compiler although the tables will need to be in slightly different formats. The tabular result of parsing a single statement in TINY BASIC can be seen by looking ahead to Figures 11-6 and 12-3, in the chapters on interpreters and compilers.

The following is the kind of information that we have found useful to keep in a parse table. The statement number is useful, converted to a 16 bit binary representation. Obviously the most important information is the statement type, that is, whether we are working on an assignment, an IF Statement, a RETURN, or some other. Finally, it is useful to do a small amount of analysis at parsing time on the various fields in a statement which can contain varying information. Obviously, the keywords and place holders never vary. But, for each of the variable fields, we will want to know what kind of entity occupies the field. That is, is it a number, a variable, a Boolean expression, an algebraic

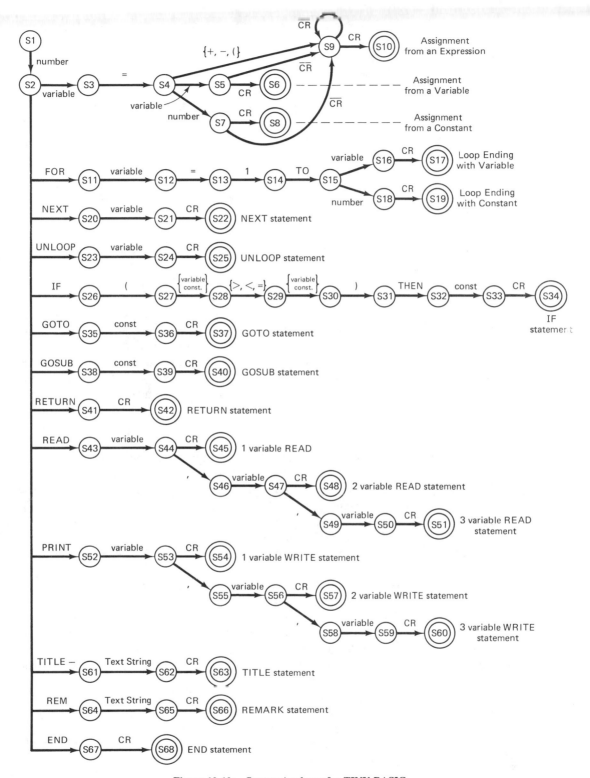

Figure 10-10: Syntax Analyzer for TINY BASIC.

expression, or text from a REMARK or TITLE Statement? In addition to this, we will find it convenient to record where the field starts in the text buffer and how many characters long it is.

All this material can be developed in the course of traversing the syntax analyzing finite state machine. The language processors will then use this information to carry on finer grained analysis after the parsing stage.

10.5 MORE ADVANCED PARSING TECHNIQUES

Most modern compilers for complex languages parse their input with the aid of a data base which represents the syntactical rules of the language. This is called syntax-directed compilation. The essential principle is to derive the syntax of the whole program, or perhaps each line, from the syntax rules, and thus determine whether the grammatical form is correct.

We have seen that a parse tree evolves naturally as part of a syntax derivation and that it represents the order in which rules have been used in the derivation. For many language processors, this tree is an important by-product of parsing.

For compilers in particular, the parse tree is closely associated with code generation. Frequently a compiler will produce its output code in two stages. First, low level code will be generated in a form that is almost, but not quite, equivalent to assembler code. Frequently this can be generated directly from the parse tree. The intermediate code is then subjected to an optimization process, to make it short and efficient. And finally, the intermediate code is converted to the ultimate target form.

There are two strategies by which syntax parsing is done: top-down and bottom-up. What are these strategies? Let's say a line in some program is being parsed. The top-down method begins with the highest level production in the context free grammar. The Sentence Symbol is rewritten, and then various parts of the resulting sentence are elaborated according to the productions of the grammar until finally this procedure recreates the line being parsed or determines that this is impossible because of a syntax error. Figure 10-11 shows an example of top-down parsing to verify the syntax of a statement in TINY BASIC.

Bottom-up parsing begins with the entity being parsed rather than with the Sentence Symbol. Then the line being parsed is gradually reduced back to the Sentence Symbol by successive applications of the productions (worked in reverse), so that complex low level structures are transformed into simpler high level structures. Figure 10-11 can also be read as an example of this type of parsing. To see the program parsed bottom-up, just start with the last line and apply all the transformations in reverse to work back to the Sentence Symbol.

In the examples this all looks very simple. The difficulty with all these methods is in knowing how to pick a sequence of productions to use to advance you toward your goal, and to know when to stop if you have come to a dead end because of an error. There are a number of algorithms which can direct these parsing processes efficiently, but they are beyond the scope of this book.

A. A Sample Program in TINY BASIC.

```
10   FOR  K  =  1   TO   10
20   X  =  X  +  K
30   NEXT   K
40   END
```

B. The Same Program Expressed as a String in the Symbols of the Grammar.

UflsU^ UI=I+I^UnI^Ue^

C. Showing that the syntax of the program is correct.

P → US^P
  → UflsU^P
  → UflsU^US^P
  → UflsU^UI=E^P
  → UflsU^UI=T?^P
  → UflsU^UI=T+T^P
  → UflsU^UI=F+T^P
  → UflsU^UI=F+F^P
  → UflsU^UI=I+F^P
  → UflsU^UI=I+I^P
  → UflsU^UI=I+I^US^P
  → UflsU^UI=I+I^UnI^P
  → UflsU^UI=I+I^UnI^US^
  → UflsU^UI=I+I^UnI^Ue^

Figure 10-11: Parsing A TINY BASIC Program Using Context Free Grammar Productions. Top-down and bottom-up parsing can both be done using context free grammar productions. To do top-down parsing, start with the Sentence Symbol and progressively elaborate as in part C until arriving at a string identical to the whole program. Bottom-up parsing starts with a string identical to the program and works backwards through reductions to get to the Sentence Symbol.

STUDY QUESTIONS AND EXERCISES

1. Show what changes there would be in the definition of the TINY BASIC READ statement if it could take any number of variables, rather than only up to three. Show the impact of this change in each of our formal language definitions.

2. Suggest a way the three formal definitions could be changed to make it clear that the largest constant in TINY BASIC can have only 5 digits and cannot be larger in magnitude than 32,767 if the number is positive or 32,768 if it is negative.

3. Show the BNF validation and the parse tree for the following statement in TINY BASIC:

```
10  X  =  ((J  +  K)  /  3)  −  C
```

4. Using the natural language grammar of Figure 10-5, determine whether the following sentences are legal according to this grammar.

    Slow robots move blocks.
    The new robot lifts the table.

The new robot lifts table.
Robbie lifts the pyramid from the green block
   near the table.
Behind the table the robot lifts the block.
The robot lifts the block behind the table.

5. How would the productions of the natural language grammar have to be altered to permit the use of the pronoun "he" in sentences that otherwise could be built from the words composing the grammar?

6. Would it be possible to design a useful computer language that was entirely hierarchical in its definition, i.e., had no recursive elements at all? Could our definition of BASIC be changed to make it that way?

7. Produce the balloon diagram for an elevator that is controlled the way a finite state machine is. It can visit three floors. The top floor has a down button, the bottom floor has an up button, and the middle floor has both.

8. Consider this statement in TINY BASIC:

```
10   IF (X > Y) THEN 500
```

List the tokens the lexical analyzer would find if it was run across this text.

9. Suppose the example program listed in Figure 10-11 was being parsed by the Syntax Analyzer finite state machine. List the states the analyzer would pass through in doing this analysis. Assume it resets and starts again at each new statement.

10. Show that the syntax of the following program is correct using bottom-up parsing and the context free grammar for TINY BASIC:

```
10   READ  I
20   IF (I > 10) THEN 50
30   X = (A + B)/C
40   GOTO 60
50   X = (A - B)/C
60   END
```

11. Show that the syntax of the following program is correct using top-down parsing and the context free grammar for TINY BASIC.

```
10   REM  EXAMPLE
20   READ  X,Y
30   Z = (X*Y) - 30
40   PRINT  Z
50   END
```

11

Interpreters: Tiny Basic

11.1 INTRODUCTION TO INTERPRETIVE SYSTEMS AND A TYPICAL DESIGN

This chapter contains our study of interpreters. We will look into all the aspects of building an interpreter for TINY BASIC and use this as a test-bed for exploring the characteristics of interpretive software.

Remember that an interpreter is a complex program that directly executes the statements of a high level language, just as if those statements were part of the instruction set of an underlying machine. This may seem an odd idea, but seeing an actual implementation of the idea usually makes everything clear.

A program in a high level langauge is a notation for an algorithmic transformation that is to be carried out on some set of variables. An interpreter will do this transformation and present the required answers. There is no intermediate translation as with a compiler which takes a program stated in a high level language and produces an equivalent program stated in a lower level language. With an interpreter, the program goes in one side and answers come out the other. We are now going to study what happens in between.

Interpreters appeared as part of the standard software repertoire very early—shortly after assemblers, and before compilers. The earliest perhaps was John Mauchly's SHORT-CODE interpreter for algebraic formulas, which appeared in 1949.

It may seem puzzling that interpreters developed before compilers, since the idea of compilation is just a straight-forward extension of the idea of assembly, whereas software interpreters go off in another direction. The reason for this early development is as follows. One of the first classes of systems programs, after the assembler, was packages of systems subroutines that could be appended to assembly programs and called to accomplish specific purposes. The main use of the early computers was for scientific computation, and this required a number of specialized subroutine packages. These early computers had some difficulty in dealing with scientific problems because they had no floating point numbers. The obvious solution was to set up subroutines that would simulate what a better machine would do if it had floating point instructions in its instruction set. If you try to write such a package, you will see that it naturally develops into an interpretive style of execution. This is where the idea of interpreters came from.

Even though the idea of a software interpreter was an early one, widely used interpretive language systems did not appear until the mid 1960's. How can we explain this? Part of it was accidental. The early FORTRAN compiler systems were so efficient that they diverted thought away from interpreters. Another reason is probably that, since early computers were rather slow, it was always a design goal to get the fastest possible program execution; and compiled programs are faster than interpreted programs. With the different sorts of computer architectures that are available today, speed is not the problem it once was.

From the mid 1960's until the present, interpreters have been an important part of language processor technology. Some of the more familiar programming languages today are generally cast in a compiled form; examples are FORTRAN and PL/1. Others are typically found in association with an interpreter; examples are LISP and APL. In addition, several common languages, most notably BASIC and Pascal, have been set up in both interpreted and compiled versions. There is usually nothing in the language itself that requires one or the other of these processing strategies. Each type of processing has its own advantages and disadvantages. We will make a detailed comparison at the end of the chapter on compilers.

We start our investigation of language systems with interpreters rather than compilers. An interpreter is not necessarily a less complex item than a compiler, but it is probably easier to implement a simple interpreter than a correspondingly simple compiler. Also, interpreters are usually found combined with editors into single integrated systems. Since we have just discussed editors in Chapter 9, now is the natural time to continue with interpreters.

The interactive nature of an interpretive system for the BASIC language requires that an editor/loader be part of the package. If you watch someone developing a program using a system like this, you will see something like the following. The user begins in the "EDIT" mode. He types in a rough version of the program at his terminal. He executes the program by entering the "RUN" mode after he has typed in the program text. The program appears to execute immediately and to produce results, or perhaps an error message will appear. Usually, the first version of the program is not correct. After deciding what changes need to be made, the user can reenter the "EDIT" mode and change lines in his program, or add or delete other lines. When he has the program the way he wants it, he can run it again and it will execute immediately. The user can continue in this manner, switching between editing and execution until he is satisfied that he has a correct program. One very nice feature about typical interpreters with built-in editors is the speed with which programs of moderate length can be developed.

Editors and interpreters are a natural operational unit. On the other hand, what an editor does and what an interpreter does are quite different things. We will pick up our discussion of interpretation at the point where the program has already been entered into memory by some sort of editing process.

It may be helpful to look back frequently at Chapter 10, in which TINY BASIC is described, while reading this chapter. In particular, we will have occasion to refer back to certain features of the language definition, to an example program that we will want to continue here, and to certain details of parsing technology.

There are several other preparations to be made before getting into the interpreter itself. The first one is to describe the form in which a program will exist in memory after it is turned over to the interpreter by the associated editing system.

In some interpreters, the internal form of a program is just exactly the string of ASCII characters that the user typed in from the keyboard. However, the more usual case is for the internal form to be a compressed and more machine readable form of the original program. Frequently this mini-translation operation will be done by the editor as the code is being placed in memory. In other systems, there is a so-called precompile phase in which another piece of software makes a pass over the initial code to transform it into some more congenial form before it is interpreted.

Converting arithmetic expressions to Reverse Polish Notation (RPN) is one of the most important preprocessing operations on the raw program text. Another crucial item of preparation for us will be to explain several algorithms associated with the RPN form that are used in virtually all language systems.

With these preparations in place, we will then give an overview of the processing in our interpreter. We will discuss the ubiquitous operations of statement parsing and symbol table management. And then we will discuss the routines that do the actual work of interpreting TINY BASIC.

11.2 EDITING AND THE INTERNAL FORM OF THE PROGRAM

As we have mentioned, a typical interpreter for a language like BASIC comes equipped with a built-in editor that can initially install a program in memory and that can be used to make modifications if the program needs to be changed. This built-in quick change ability is very important for the rapid development of programs. In addition, the editor will typically develop and maintain certain tables that are useful to the interpreter. These tables are built as the code is installed in memory. They must be modified any time editing is done on an already installed program. We are not going to do any more description of editor programs here, but we need to describe carefully the output that such an editor produces, because our interpreter will manipulate that output.

Let us assume the editor uses two buffers. One is a line buffer that receives a raw program line as it is typed from the keyboard. Any transformations that must be done on this line to get it into internal form will be done in this buffer. The other place where the program text resides will be a large text buffer which contains the program statements in internal form and in the order in which they were typed in. So, when a statement is typed in, a modest amount of preprocessing will be done on it in the line buffer, and then it will be transferred to the text buffer.

What kind of processing would it be reasonable to have the editor do in order to get the program in internal form? The reason for having an internal form is to save memory and to do any transformations on the code that we can discover which will allow it to be interpreted (executed) faster. By keeping this goal in mind, we can discover what is necessary. One possible transformation would be to convert all keywords of the language to single byte ASCII codes using some of the more obscure ASCII codes so that these will not conflict with the representations for letters, digits, and the few other characters used by the language. For instance, all of these keywords can be significantly shortened because they can be coded in one byte each:

FOR	GOSUB
TO	RETURN
NEXT	READ
UNLOOP	PRINT
IF	TITLE
THEN	REM
GOTO	END

This conversion is done to shorten the length of the program in the form in which it will ultimately appear in memory. The execution speed of a program is inversely proportional to the length of the internal form which must be interpreted.

Another thing that will be done to the raw text in the line buffer is that all blanks will be squeezed out. They add readability to the text but lend nothing to program execution, nor are they necessary as delimiters for parsing.

Statements in TINY BASIC that have the possibility of a branch all include the number of a new statement to branch to. Examples are

```
GOSUB   1000
GOTO    200
IF (A>B) THEN 1500
```

In the original text these line numbers are expressed as strings of ASCII digits. A space saving will almost always result by converting these fields into simple two byte binary numbers. Any other numbers in the program that are expressed in ASCII will also be converted to this two byte binary format.

Preprocessing algebraic expressions offers another saving. The kind of algebraic expressions we allow in TINY BASIC are the ordinary parenthesized forms you would expect in normal algebra, but with all the operators written out. A routine to evaluate an expression in this form is quite clumsy, so we will have the editor transform any algebraic expression into a better form. This is called Reverse Polish Notation. The RPN form is more compact than a normal algebraic expression because it has no parentheses. An example expression written with normal algebraic notation is:

(A*D) − (B*C)

The same expression rendered into the RPN form is much shorter:

AD*BC* −

In the next section we will discuss algorithms for making this conversion and the implications of specifying computational recipes in this fashion.

After all these changes have been made, a program line will be in internal form. It will have become considerably shorter than it was on input. Now it can be stored into the text buffer and is ready for the interpreter.

The editor for the system we are about to describe will need to build a table as it places the compacted code into the text buffer. This table is the Statement Descriptor Table (SDT). Each line in the table is a statement descriptor; that is, it describes one line of the source program. This table is central to all processing that goes on in the interpreter and the associated editor. Each statement descriptor consists of three fields: the statement number, a pointer to the first character of the statement in the text buffer, and a link to the next statement descriptor. The descriptors are kept as a linked list. This will be very useful for editing. By following the list, you will encounter descriptors for all the statements arranged in numerical order by statement number. The fact that the statement number of each statement is contained in the descriptor for that statement means it is not necessary to keep these numbers in the text buffer. They can be stripped off. This allows a further compression of the program text when it is stored in internal form.

The most important table in the whole interpreter from the standpoint of control is the Statement Descriptor Table. It expresses the order of the program. We will now give an example to clarify its usage and to explore the sense in which the table is a linked list. Figure 11-1A shows the text buffer as it might appear for the example program that was given in Figure 10-1. Note that the buffer is *not* shown in internal form, because you would have difficulty reading it. But for the example, it won't matter. Let us suppose, just for the purposes of this illustration, that raw text will be kept in the buffer exactly as it is typed in. The Statement Descriptor Table describes the text in this buffer. It shows at what byte, numbered relative to the start of the buffer, the various program statements begin. The last field in the Statement Descriptor Table is a link field. It gives the table line which contains the descriptor of the next statement in numerical order in the program.

The Descriptor Table is really a directory to the text buffer. It allows software to do two crucial things: find the code associated with a statement without having to scan the raw text, and follow the statements of the program in sequential order. This is done by using the link field in the table.

As soon as any editing is done to the program, the text buffer will get out of order, but the SDT will still describe the real order of the program. For instance, let us assume

The Text Buffer

```
10. REM. . PROGRAM. PRODUCES. THE. SUM ˆ 20. REM.
. . AND. PRODUCT. OF. A. SERIES ˆ 30. TITLE-DEMON
STRATION. PROGRAM ˆ 40. GOSUB. 100 ˆ 50. GOSUB. 2
00 ˆ 60. TITLE-SUM. AND. PRODUCT ˆ 70. PRINT. S, P
ˆ 80. END ˆ
```

```
        etc.
```

The Statement Descriptor Table

Descriptor Number	Statement Number	Offset in Text Buffer	Link Field: this is the Descriptor Number for the Next Program Statement in Sequence
0	10	0	1
1	20	33	2
2	30	66	3
3	40	97	4
4	50	110	5
5	60	123	6
6	70	148	7
7	80	161	8
(descriptors for other statements)			
19	250	345	—

Figure 11-1A: Editor Tables and Buffers After Creation of a Program. This figure shows the tables that would result if the editor installed the program of Figure 10-1 into memory. The Text Buffer is one long character string. There are no lines in it other than those defined by Carriage Returns. We have used "." to represent a blank, and " ˆ " to represent the Carriage Return character. The Statement Descriptor Table is a directory into the Text Buffer.

we wanted to insert a new line in the original program between lines 30 and 40. Say some initialization was required and we wanted to insert the line

```
25     X = 0
```

This line adds nothing to the logic of the program. It is being used here just to provide an example of editing.

To get this new line into the program, the user would put the program in editor mode and just type the line. Figure 11-1B shows the changes this would cause in the tables we are examining. Note that because we use a linked list to describe the program statements, the new statement can go out of order at the end of the text buffer. The descriptor for the program line numbered 25 can also go out of order at the end of the Statement Descriptor Table. This is most important. The only thing we have to do to keep track of things is change two links in the Descriptor Table.

This software will have the same kind of garbage collection problems associated with deleting lines that any editor has. The statement descriptors are fixed length entities

The Text Buffer

10. REM. . PROGRAM. PRODUCES. THE. SUM ^ 20. REM.
. . AND. PRODUCT. OF. A. SERIES ^ 30. TITLE-DEMON
STRATION. PROGRAM ^ 40. GOSUB. 100 ^ 50. GOSUB. 2
00 ^ 60. TITLE-SUM. AND. PRODUCT ^ 70. PRINT. S, P
^ 80. END ^

etc.

25. X. = . 0 ^   Note: The new line will be placed in
                        the buffer immediately beyond the
                        position of any text that is
                        already there.

The Statement Descriptor Table

Descriptor Number	Statement Number	Offset in Text Buffer	Link Field: this is the Descriptor Number for the Next Program Statement in Sequence
0	10	0	1
1	20	33	20
2	30	66	3
3	40	97	4
4	50	110	5
5	60	123	6
6	70	148	7
7	80	161	8
(descriptors for other statements)			
19	250	345	—
20	25	356	2

Figure 11-1B: Editor Tables and Buffers After Creation of a Program and One Line of Editing. This figure shows the changes in the editor's tables for the sample program when one more line is added to the program. All text and descriptors go at the end of existing tables. This makes editing fast. Changes in program order are reflected in changes in links in the Statement Descriptor Table.

so they can be returned to some kind of free list when they are no longer needed. However, with the text buffer, things are different. Unusable holes will inevitably appear in the text after there has been much deleting. Interpreters usually do not make any provision for dealing with this other than a remedy that always exists. If you store the program back on disk and then reload it, all the holes will be squeezed out.

11.3   PROCEDURES FOR USING REVERSE POLISH NOTATION

Before proceeding with the high level processes of the interpreter, we need a brief discussion of RPN. The editor will transform expressions to RPN as part of setting up the internal form of a program. RPN notation is just a different way of specifying how a computation, which is a sequence of arithmetic operations, should be done. The answer will be the same whether the computation is specified in RPN or normal algebraic form. The reason we bother with all this is that RPN expressions are much easier for a computer to deal with than the forms that humans are used to. RPN expressions are shorter, and they can be evaluated moving left to right through the expression without any backing up.

It is relatively difficult to program the evaluation of a normal parenthesized algebraic expression because the evaluation cannot be done left to right. The algorithm must scan the text to find the innermost unevaluated parenthesized part of the expression; and then it must scan further to apply precedence rules within any such unit in the course of reducing it to a single value. RPN makes all this scanning unnecessary.

To proceed, then, it is necessary to consider two things: how to transform an expression into RPN, and how to evaluate such an expression (do the arithmetic it calls for).

First we will state and demonstrate the so-called Bauer-Samelson algorithm for converting a normal algebraic expression to its RPN form. The Bauer-Samelson algorithm makes use of the precedence of arithmetic operations. In the absence of parentheses, precedence determines what operations should be done first in order for an expression to be correctly evaluated. The higher the precedence, the earlier the operation is done in the evaluation. As mentioned earlier for the operators supported by TINY BASIC, the precedence of multiplication and division is highest. Next comes the unary minus. The lowest precedence is held by addition and subtraction.

Normally arithmetic operators are binary. They stand between two operands and specify a recipe by which the operands should be combined to produce a single result. The unary minus is an exception. It is a minus sign with only one operand, and the recipe it specifies is that the sign of the operand should be changed. An example of an expression that begins with a unary minus sign is

```
(-A + B) / C
```

The RPN conversion algorithm that we will examine needs two data structures. It operates with a stack and with an output string. The expression to be converted will be scanned from left to right, and the characters encountered will either be put on the end of the output string or will be put on or taken off the stack. The output string that is built by this process is the expression in RPN form. Here are the rules for the conversion:

1. In scanning the expression from left to right, when a number or a variable is encountered, put it on the end of the output string.
2. If a left parenthesis is encountered, put it on the stack.
3. If an operator is encountered, there are two cases:

   If the incoming operator has a higher precedence than whatever operator is on the top of the stack, then push the new operator onto the stack. Note that any operator can be put on the stack over a left parenthesis.

Otherwise, remove operators from the stack in order and put them on the end of the output string until the incoming operator has a higher precedence than what is left on the top of the stack. Then push the new operator onto the stack.

4. When a right parenthesis is discovered in scanning the input, unstack operators, one by one, and put them on the end of the output string until a left parenthesis comes off the stack. Then discard both parentheses and continue.

5. After the input expression is completely scanned, unstack all the remaining operators, one by one, and put them on the end of the output string.

Sometimes parentheses are considered to be operators just like addition, subtraction, multiplication, and division. The foregoing rules contain an implied statement of the precedence of parentheses. A left parenthesis, before it is on the stack, has the highest precedence possible. When it is on the stack, it has the lowest precedence possible. The right parenthesis is not assigned a precedence, since it never appears on the stack.

This algorithm can best be understood by an example. Figure 11-2A shows all the steps in the conversion of an algebraic expression to RPN form. Figure 11-2B shows a similar conversion for an expression which contains a unary minus. We have written the two minus signs in a different way to accentuate that two different kinds of operations are being called for. In the example, the tilde mark represents a unary minus. An editor

Example: (A + B)/C converts to AB + C/

Step	Contents of Stack	Contents of Output String
1	(	
2	(	A
3	+ (	A
4	+ (	AB
5		AB +
6	/	AB +
7	/	AB + C
8		AB + C/

Figure 11-2A: Conversion of an Expression to RPN Form. This example illustrates the Bauer-Samelson algorithm for converting a parenthesized algebraic expression into Reverse Polish form. In all places where we have represented stacks, the leftmost element is also the top element on the stack at any given time.

Example: (-A-B)/C can be written as (˜A-B)/C
(˜A-B)/C converts to A˜B-C/

Step	Contents of Stack	Contents of Output String
1	(	
2	˜(	
3	˜(	A
4	-(	A˜
5	-(	A˜B
6		A˜B-
7	/	A˜B-
8	/	A˜B-C
9		A˜B-C/

Figure 11-2B: Expression Conversion with the Unary Minus. This is an example of the Bauer-Samelson conversion on an expression which contains a unary minus. The unary minus has a precedence intermediate between that for multiplication and division and that for addition and subtraction.

that was changing an algebraic expression to RPN to create the internal form of some program would code the two kinds of minus signs differently so they could be differentiated. In a normal algebraic expression, it is easy to tell whether we are dealing with a unary minus or not. If the minus sign has a number or a variable to its immediate left, it is a binary minus. If it has anything else, it is a unary minus.

The other problem associated with expressions is how to do the arithmetic implied by an RPN form. We will state a simple algorithm for doing this and give an example. Once again the algorithm will depend upon the use of a stack. We will refer to the RPN expression as consisting of tokens. In this context, a token is either an operator or a variable name or a number. The evaluation program must be constructed to scan through the RPN expression token by token (left to right) and apply the following rules. Figure 11-3 is an example of the process. The following is a statement of the algorithm.

1. If the current token is a number or a variable, then put its value on the stack and move the scan to the next token.

2. If the current token is an operator, it will be either a unary or a binary operator.

If it is a unary operator, then pull the top value off the stack, apply the operator, and put the result back on the stack. Then move on to the next token.

If it is a binary operator, then pull the top two values off the stack, apply the operator, and put the result (a single value) back on the stack. Then move on to the next token. We need to specify the order in which the binary operator will be applied. The order should be

(2nd element on stack) operator (top element on stack)

3. When the end of the expression is reached, the result will be on the top of the stack.

Scan Position in Expression	Stack Contents	
	Symbolic	*Actual*
A̲B + C/	(A)	(3)
AB̲ + C/	(B)(A)	(2)(3)
AB +̲ C/	(B + A)	(5)
AB + C̲/	(C)(B + A)	(5)(5)
AB + C/̲	((B + A)/(C))	(1)

Figure 11-3: Interpretive Evaluation of an RPN Expression. (A + B)/C has been converted to RPN form and is undergoing evaluation. The RPN form is AB + C/. The values of the variables are

$$A = 3$$
$$B = 2$$
$$C = 5$$

The result of the computation should be one. Parentheses around an item mean it occupies one stack location. The underscore character indicates the scan position at any given time.

11.4 OVERVIEW OF THE INTERPRETER

We are now in a position to examine how the interpreter does its work. Let us imagine that the code for a program has been introduced into memory and that it has been transformed into an efficient internal format. This could have been done by the editor as each line was typed, or by a separate precompile phase. The only table that has been built at this point is the Statement Descriptor Table, which gives the location in the text buffer of the start of all program lines. This table along with the text buffer is a complete representation of the original program. That is, the original program could be reconstituted, if necessary, from these two data structures.

The interpreter will control its activities in the following way. It will be convenient to define a software register, called the Instruction Pointer (IP), which will always contain the number of the statement descriptor of the statement to execute next. The whole interpretive mechanism will work using statement descriptors rather than the text itself. The descriptors reflect the inherent order in the program whereas, because of editing, the program text may not be in this order. The use of an Instruction Pointer is a software analogy to the hardware program counter register that all computers maintain to control statement execution at the machine level.

When the interpreter is set into motion to execute a program, the first thing it will do is set the Instruction Pointer to the descriptor of the very first statement. This descriptor will be at the head of the linked list. Then, using the descriptor, the corresponding program statement will be identified in the text buffer. It will be parsed to find out what the statement is asking to be done. Then a subsidiary processing routine will be given control to do whatever computation has been specified. Finally, the number of the descriptor for the next statement to execute will be determined (and placed in the IP) and the whole process will start again. The driver routine for the interpreter is just a loop that finds a line, parses it, processes it, and starts over again until it runs out of lines.

It is not difficult to determine the next line to process. There are only two possibilities: either it is the next line in sequence, or a branch must be made to some other line that is specified in one of the fields of the current line. If the current program line doesn't call for a branch of some sort, then the next higher program line in numerical order should be executed next. The number of the descriptor for this line will be in the link field of the descriptor for the current line, and it becomes the new value of the Instruction Pointer.

This can be seen clearly by looking at the example program shown in Figure 10-1 and at the corresponding descriptor layout shown in Figure 11-1A. Suppose the system is about to execute the statement

    60   TITLE-SUM AND PRODUCT

It will have identified descriptor number 5 as the one associated with this line. The link field of descriptor 5 identifies descriptor 6 as the one detailing the next statement to work

on. This is correct because descriptor 6 is associated with the statement that follows in
the numerical order:

```
70   PRINT S,P
```

Things are more difficult for branches. If the current program line calls for a branch,
then the statement number of the next statement will be included as part of the text of
the current statement. However, what the interpreter needs is the descriptor for the next
statement. Where to find this descriptor will definitely not be available explicitly in the
descriptor for the current line. As an example, suppose the interpreter is working on the
line

```
40   GOSUB 100
```

Descriptor number 3 is associated with this line. It points to descriptor number 4 as the
next program statement in numerical order. However, the statement that should be done
next is the one at line number 100. What descriptor is associated with this line? The
interpreter has no easy way of knowing. So, in this case, the Descriptor Table will have
to be searched to find the descriptor associated with line 100. After it is found, the number
of this descriptor (8) will become the next value of the Instruction Pointer.

The preceding paragraphs are a logical description and an example of how to find
the next line to process. The operational details are a little different. They involve the
use of a convenient table built and used by the parser and the processing routines. We
will describe details of how to fetch the next instruction in a later section.

There are two other high level processes in the interpreter besides control. They
are parsing and statement processing. Examining the text of a statement in the line buffer
and deciding what it means is called parsing. This is always a relatively complicated
process even in simple interpreters or compilers. We will discuss it in the next section.
After a statement has been parsed, it must be processed. The approach we will take is
to dispatch a special purpose processing routine for each type of statement that is allowed
in the language. Thus, there are thirteen of these routines. We have now discussed all
the activities in the interpreter that occur at the top level. Figure 11-4 shows a flowchart
which formalizes this discussion.

Before we go into more detail, it would be useful to show a map of typical memory
usage for an interpreter of the sort we are discussing. The normal thing would be to have
the text buffer at one end of memory and the interpreter and its associated tables at the
other end. Both the tables and the text buffer need to expand as more lines are added.
If we let these regions grow towards each other from opposite ends of the memory, the
unused space will be kept in the center of the address space. This scheme will guarantee
that no space is wasted and unusable. The biggest program the system can handle is
bounded by the situation in which the text and the table regions extend until they are
touching and there is no more free space.

It is also normal practice to have part of the address space occupied by RAM
memory and part by ROM. Any fixed software, if it is heavily used, would be an excellent

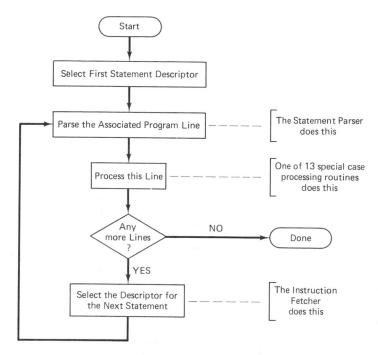

Figure 11-4:   Top Level Control Flow in the Interpreter. The top level driver routine for the interpreter is just a loop that finds a line, parses it, processes it, and then starts over again until it runs out of program lines. At that point the program has been completely executed.

candidate to occupy the ROM portion of the address space. The interpreter itself is frequently found in this position. Figure 11-5 illustrates the kind of memory map we have assumed.

11.5 STATEMENT PARSING

The top level flow chart of Figure 11-4 shows that the first step in executing any program line is to parse the line. What we want the parser to do is extract all the information that is given in a program line and put it in some convenient form for further processing. In particular, we would like the parser to produce some kind of fixed length descriptive table for all program statements. The fields in this table will be filled in describing what the statement is, where the operands are, etc. The fact that all fields in the table are of fixed length will make any further processing that must be done much more convenient. This data structure is frequently called a parse table, but, since we are going to use it in an extended version for multiple purposes beyond parsing, we will call it the Execution Summary Table (EST).

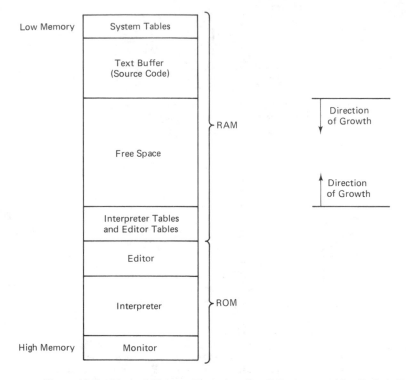

Figure 11-5: Typical Memory Usage in a Small Computer with a Built-in Interpreter. Interpreters are frequently laid out so that the text buffer is at one end of memory and the code of the interpreter itself and associated tables are at the other end. Free space is in the middle. This arrangement ensures that the system will have maximal use of memory.

In any interpreter, every time a new program statement is encountered, it must be parsed. With our interpreter, this means that the Execution Summary Table must be built for every line. Interpreters are very inefficient in executing code that involves a great deal of looping because the loop statements must be parsed every time they are passed over, even if the loop is traversed many, many times.

What type of information belongs in the Execution Summary Table? We want to use the table to record any salient information about the current program statement while it is being interpreted. Most of that information will be discovered during the parsing phase. Some will be developed later when the statement is processed. The following things are the information we need for the TINY BASIC interpreter.

1. A code for the type of statement that is being interpreted. Remember that there are thirteen statement types in this language. They are numbered in the order in which they were described in Section 10.2.

2. We need the operands in the statement in the form of a pointer to where each operand can be found in the text buffer and its length. Length is simply the number of characters the operand takes up in the program text (after it has been cast in the internal form). It will be convenient to list the operands in the order in which they appear in the statement. Here is a point that must be emphasized. We will consider an operand to be any field in a statement which can be filled with variable information. Thus, whole expressions are regarded as single operands.

3. Along with each operand there should be a code for the type of operand, that is, is it a number (1), a variable (2), a Boolean expression (3), an algebraic expression (4), or text to be used for a title or a comment (5).

4. We also need the number of the next statement descriptor. This is the link field from the current line in the Statement Descriptor Table. It is very important to have this information in the Execution Summary Table. It will provide a convenient route to the next statement to execute if the program is to proceed sequentially. Of course, this field will be useless if it turns out that a branch is to be made.

5. After the processing of any statement is finished, there is a module (the Instruction Fetcher) which must find the next statement. To aid this module in its work, there should be a field in the Execution Summary Table where we can indicate S (sequential) or B (branch) as the source of the next statement. This information is different from most of the other items we discussed because it cannot always be filled in at parsing time. In some cases (IF statements), the decision must be delayed until the statement is processed.

6. The last item of information will also be filled in at statement processing time. If the statement is processed and found to require a branch, the statement number for this branch will be taken from the text buffer and left in this location so that the Instruction Fetcher can use it.

This may be a little hard to see when stated abstractly. Figure 11-6 shows an example of the Execution Summary Table that is the result of parsing a Conditional Branch Statement.

Now we have stated what information we need, but how will we get it? How will the parser work? A large technology in computer science has built up around how to parse general types of program statements. If you have a big language with a great deal of flexibility, like PL/1 or Ada, a great deal of effort must be spent on parsing and sophisticated methods must be used. Our language, on the other hand, is so simple that it will be easy to parse. Furthermore, because parsing takes so much time in interpretive languages, the syntax of such a language will frequently be set up in subtle ways that make the language a little harder to use, but very simple to parse. TINY BASIC has this character.

TINY BASIC has a hierarchial, nonrecursive character that makes it suited for parsing with a deterministic finite state machine. This type of operation was described in the last chapter. Let's imagine then that the heart of the parser will be a finite state

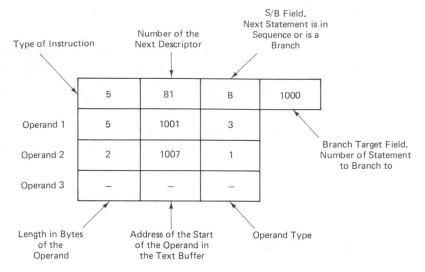

Figure 11-6: **The Execution Summary Table.** This table is the result of parsing one line in a TINY BASIC program. The particular statement that resulted in the table is

        50   IF   (A > B)   THEN   1000

To understand the table, assume that this statement is associated with descriptor number 80 in the Statement Descriptor Table. Its compressed text begins at location 1000 in the text buffer. Remember that with text compression, line numbers are discarded and keywords are coded for by single bytes.

machine syntactic analyzer quite like the one described in Chapter 10. The syntactic finite state machine will be given tokens on demand by a lower level lexical machine. The lexical machine will also be similar to the one described in Chapter 10. However, some differences arise because this machine must operate on the program text after it has been transformed into compressed internal form.

Diagramming the syntactic machine is already quite complicated, and some things have not been shown on the diagram. Remember that a FSM can be easily set up so that a specific action (usually a subroutine call) will be taken as one part of what happens during the transition from one state to another. It is these actions that will be responsible for pulling out the various elements in program statements and for inserting them into the Execution Summary Table in the format we have described.

We need an example of the action routines that accompany syntactic transitions. Look again at Figure 10-10 for the following discussion. Let's assume that the statement being parsed is

    50   IF   (A > B)   THEN   1000

The reader should also refer to Figure 11-6, which shows the Execution Summary Table, many fields of which will be filled in during this parsing.

The syntactic machine starts in a state equivalent to State S2, since statement numbers are not kept in the compressed text used by the interpreter. If the "IF" token is recognized, this will drive the machine to State S26. The associated action routine will enter the type of statement that has been discovered into the Execution Summary Table. If the proper text is available to drive the machine through to State S31, this will mean that a first operand has been discovered. An action routine, as part of this sequence, will have to record the type, length, and location of the operand. Further transitions drive through to State S33. An action routine then will record the type, length, and location of the second operand. The final token will be a Carriage Return, and it drives the syntactic machine to an accepting state, S34, which completes the recognition of this program line.

Somewhere along this sequence, perhaps as part of the last transition, there must be an action routine that puts the number of the next descriptor into the Execution Summary Table. This information is not accessible in the compressed program text; rather, it is stored in the Statement Descriptor Table.

Remember that the parser, as we have set it up, doesn't do much analysis on operands that it detects. That is work for routines further along in the processing. All it does is indicate the length of the operand (number of characters), where it is, and what type it is. Remember also that we are regarding any variable field in a statement, that is, any field between two place holders, as an operand. The keywords are place holders; a Carriage Return is a place holder; etc. The various statements in the language take between one and three operands. This is why there is space for up to three operands in the Execution Summary Table. The reader should be aware that if the TINY BASIC READ and PRINT statements allowed an unspecified number of variables (rather than up to three), parsing information into a table of fixed format would become impossible, because we wouldn't know how long to make the table. This is one example of where the language has been constrained to make parsing easier.

11.6 FETCHING THE NEXT INSTRUCTION

The reader will note that we have shown a module in the high level flowchart of the interpreter which is invoked at the end of the processing for every statement and which will determine the next statement to work on. This module is the Instruction Fetcher. The output that the Fetcher must produce is the number of the descriptor for the next statement to execute, and this is put into the Instruction Pointer.

Most statements in most programs are executed in sequential order. In this case, the Fetcher should be very fast. In fact, all it has to do is inspect the S/B field in the Execution Summary Table in the expectation of finding S there. If S is in this field, then the descriptor for the next statement is already prepared and is part of the Summary Table. The only other thing the Fetcher needs to do is put the descriptor number into the Instruction Pointer.

However, if the current processing routine has discovered that the next statement will be a branch, then there is a lot of work to do. The Summary Table will have been prepared for this situation in the following way. The S/B field will contain a B, and the branch target field will contain the statement number of the statement to branch to. At this point, the system doesn't know where the text for this statement is, so, before execution can proceed, the descriptor that is associated with the branch target must be found. In general this may be a time consuming process because the Statement Descriptor Table must be searched in order to find the proper descriptor. Parsing in loops and searching for branch targets are the two things that, more than any others, make interpreters slow.

How will the Statement Descriptor Table be searched to find the descriptor associated with a particular statement number? If the table is a linked list with the nodes scattered all around as a result of editing, then about the only thing that can be done is to scan through the list, following links, and looking for the target descriptor. But we can do better than this. A great improvement in search speed can be gotten as follows. Whenever the system is placed in execute mode, it should rebuild the Statement Descriptor Table so that even though the descriptors are linked they also lie one after another in correct numerical order. If the list is ordered in this way, the statement number fields can be subjected to a binary search whenever it is necessary to find the descriptor associated with a particular statement number. This will make the processing for statements involving branches significantly faster.

11.7 MAINTAINING THE SYMBOL TABLE

Every interpreter, assembler, or language translator will have a symbol table of some kind, and this one is no exception. As the interpreter executes various program lines, it will manipulate entries in the Symbol Table. Before we can continue, we will have to discuss this important data structure.

The TINY BASIC language is an integer BASIC, and it was specified that each integer variable should be kept in two bytes of storage. There are only 286 possible variable names allowed in this TINY BASIC, so the size of the Symbol Table should be 286 * 2 = 572 bytes. Figure 11-7 shows the layout of the table.

We can now indicate an unusual and powerful advantage that this organization provides. We are only allowing 286 variable names. Space is being explicitly reserved in the Symbol Table for each of these variables, whether it appears in the program or not. Because of this we never have to go through any manipulations to allocate space for a new variable when it is discovered in the program, and we can count on the Symbol Table being a fixed length. Fixed length is a sacred word in systems programming.

In addition, because of the way we choose to name variables, symbol table access will be lightning quick. The table never has to be searched for the value of a symbol. Instead the address at which the value resides can be calculated quickly from the name of the symbol. This is a very simple example of a table accessed by hashing. Hashing means you compute the location associated with a symbol rather than search for it.

The reader should closely examine the pattern of variable names in the Symbol Table before trying to understand the hashing mechanism. A variable name will be one or two ASCII coded characters. The corresponding address can be determined by a

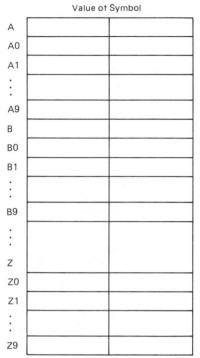

Value of Symbol

Each Cell on this Diagram Represents One Byte.

Figure 11-7: The Symbol Table. Storage for the values of symbols is very simple in TINY BASIC. Since so few variable names are allowed (only 286), the system maintains storage for every symbol whether it is used or not. Accessing the value of a symbol given its name can be done quickly by hashing.

transformation of the name. We will do this as follows. The location of a variable in the table can be determined by adding together three numbers. We will compute a letter offset to the start of the block of locations where all the names beginning with a certain letter are found. Then we will compute a digit offset to the address within any block where a name ending with a certain digit can be found. The total address computation requires adding these numbers to the location at which the table starts.

Here are the formulas for the two offsets that must be computed. The blocks of names all of which begin with a certain letter start at offsets of 0, 22, 44, 66, etc. into the Symbol Table. So the letter offset is given by

$$\text{Letter Offset} = (\text{ASCII code for letter} - 65) * 22$$

The number being subtracted is the ASCII code
for the letter A.

Within a block of names, the single character name starts at offset 0, and the names terminating in digits start at 2, 4, 6, etc.

$$\text{Digit Offset} = 0,$$

if it is a single character name.

Digit Offset = ((ASCII code for digit − 48)*2) + 2,
    if it is not a single character name.

The number being subtracted is the ASCII code for the digit zero.

These formulas, then, show how to find the address of a variable in the Symbol Table given its name. The transformation involves computing and adding together three separate items, but it is faster than searching. Again, the algorithm is

Variable
Address = Table Start + Letter Offset + Digit Offset

11.8 PROCESSING ROUTINES FOR INDIVIDUAL PROGRAM STATEMENTS

After any given statement is parsed, the top level driver of the interpreter will dispatch a routine to deal with that specific type of instruction. For instance, there will be a routine to handle assignment statements, a routine to handle conditional branches, and a routine to handle subroutine calls. This section will describe how each of these routines can manage to execute the operations called for in whatever program line is current. This is the actual process of interpretation, and we are now at the very heart of this kind of software. You may be surprised to see how simple it is.

1. Processing for Assignment Statements

There are only three forms that an assignment statement can take. On the right hand side of the statement there can be a number, a single variable, or an expression. This routine must detect which situation applies and take appropriate action. For example, the simplest kind of assignment would be something like

```
10   X = 7
```

The only processing necessary to interpret this statement is to take the value 7 and put it directly in the Symbol Table at the location associated with X. A slightly more complicated assignment would be

```
12   X = Y
```

The processing appropriate to this statement is to enter the Symbol Table and find the value of Y. This value would then be copied into the table at the position associated with X. Expressions complicate things only a little bit:

```
13   X = A + B
```

In this case, the expression would be detected and a routine dispatched to evaluate it. This routine would return a value that would be computed by pulling the values that reside at location A and at location B out of the Symbol Table and adding them together. The result from evaluating the expression would then be stored back in the Symbol Table at the location associated with X. The evaluation routine is essentially the second RPN algorithm that was discussed in Section 11.3.

2, 3, 4. Processing for Loops

The next statements we discussed in defining the TINY BASIC language were the loop control statements. Loop control is the most complicated issue in an interpreter like this. We will put off discussing it until after the simple statements.

5. Processing for Conditional Branches

This statement depends upon the evaluation of a Boolean expression, such as

    (A > B)

So there will be a subroutine which has the express purpose of evaluating expressions of this sort and returning a result which will be either true or false. If the result is true, then the branch must be taken; otherwise, it should not be taken.

Nothing more needs to be done if the Boolean expression is false because the parser will have already set up the Execution Summary Table for the normal case which will be sequential execution. If the expression is true, then the line number to be branched to must be fetched out of the program text in the text buffer, converted to a two byte binary number, and stored in the Branch Target Field in the Summary Table. The S/B Field also needs to be set to B for branch.

Recall that most of the Execution Summary Table was set up during parsing. But there were cases when some of the fields would not be known until execution. This is one of those cases.

6. Processing for Unconditional Branches

The text of the Unconditional Branch Statement uses the keyword GOTO followed by the line number that is the branch target. What we have to do here is prepare the way for the Instruction Fetcher to get the next statement. Therefore, the line number to be branched to must be fetched out of the text buffer, converted to a two byte binary number, and stored in the Branch Target Field in the Summary Table. Also the S/B Field in the Summary Table needs to be set to B to indicate a branch for the next statement.

7. Processing for the Subroutine Call Statement

The routing to subroutines in this interpreter is very much like the machine level subroutine calls on most microprocessors. The interpreter needs a return stack, and it may be any stack that is handy, either in hardware or in software. We will just refer to it as the Subroutine Return Stack.

The processing routine for subroutines has to do two things. The first thing is to place the number of the descriptor for the next statement in sequence onto the Subroutine Return Stack. This number of this descriptor can be found in the Execution Summary Table. It defines the statement that will be executed immediately after the subroutine finishes. The other thing is to prepare for a branch in the same way as in ordinary branch statements. That is, set the S/B Field in the Summary Table to B and get the statement number to be branched to out of the text buffer, convert it, and put it in the Branch Target Field of the Summary Table. The Instruction Fetcher will then select the start of the subroutine as the next statement to be executed.

8. Processing for the Return Statement

The Subroutine Call and the Return statement work as a pair to control routing to subroutines. When the Return statement is encountered, all that must be done is to pop the Subroutine Return Stack to get the descriptor number for the next statement to execute. Put this in the Next Descriptor Field of the Summary Table and set the S/B field to S for sequential execution.

This is a devious strategy. It should be realized that the statement that will be executed next is definitely not executed in sequence. The RETURN statement essentially causes a jump back to some prior site of execution. However, the most economical way to do that jump is to trick the Instruction Fetcher and set up so that it thinks it is getting the next statement in numerical order. Subroutine calls can be nested to an arbitrary level controlled only by the size of the stack used for returning.

9. Processing for the Input Statement

This routine is dispatched to prompt for and receive up to three values from the keyboard. The routine will generate prompts on the screen for however many numbers need to be input. As the numbers are brought in, they will be entered into the Symbol Table at the locations corresponding to the variables named in the Input statement. These variables names are pointed to by the operand fields in the Execution Summary Table.

We are intentionally vague about the details of the Input statement. This is because there are usually routines included as part of the operating system which can be used in a simple manner to get a value from the keyboard. The interpreter will undoubtedly make use of these routines. The details depend very specifically on what operating system is available. Routines for input were considered previously in the sections of this book on monitors and simple operating systems.

10. Processing for the Output Statement

This routine is quite similar to the Input statement. The operand fields will be inspected to determine how many variables are being output. These items will be printed to the screen one by one. The data to output are obtained by looking up the variable names in the Symbol Table. Again, this processing will use operating system routines.

11. Processing for the Title Statement

This statement is included to make generated output readable. The processing routine will simply locate the text in the text buffer (it is already in ASCII) and pass it to any convenient operating system routine that is available to write one line of text on the screen.

12. Processing for the Comment Statement

This statement requires no processing. It is totally ignored.

13. Processing for the End Statement

When this statement is discovered, the interpreter will go back to some higher level of control where the user can either call for more editing, or restart execution, or return to the monitor or operating system. The specific processing required of this statement is to set a flag indicating that the last executable line in the program has been read. This allows the top level driver routine of the interpreter to detect the end condition and take appropriate action.

11.9   CONTROLLING THE PROCESSING OF LOOPS

The processing of loops is a little more complicated than what must be done on behalf of the other statements in this language, for several reasons. The number of loops that may be active at any time is variable; they may be nested to various levels; and they do not always terminate in a standard manner. That is, the UNLOOP statement can be used at any time to cause an exit from the loop triggered by a statement anywhere in its interior.

Several data structures will be required to deal with this amount of programmatic complexity. The first one is called a Loop Control Table. One of these tables will become associated with every loop when the loop becomes active. It maintains information necessary for the control of this particular loop. Four pieces of information are kept in the table. They are: the descriptor numbers of the first statement inside the loop and the first statement after the end of the loop, the address in the Symbol Table of the variable used for the loop counter, and the ending value of the loop counter. If the loop is traversed many times, the loop counter will have to be incremented many times. We record the address rather than the name of this variable so that the address doesn't have to be hashed from the name with every pass through the loop.

The Loop Control Table is a dynamic entity. It is built when a loop comes into existence, and it disappears when the loop is finished. These tables are reusable. There will be a pool of Loop Control Tables any of which may be in use at a given time. The others will be free. Each table will be identified by its number. They are numbered beginning with the number one. There will be a dedicated area in memory where 10 or 20 such tables reside. The exact number to be included in the system is an implementation decision. It corresponds to the maximum number of loops the system will allow to be active at one time. The allocation of Loop Control Tables can be accomplished conveniently by using a linked list. We will discuss the details later. For now the reader should just imagine that, somehow, the system will provide one of these control tables whenever a loop comes into existence. Figure 11-8 shows the format of the control table data structure.

Another important data structure needed to implement loops will be called the Loop Return Stack. The purpose of this stack is to make a connection between the first and

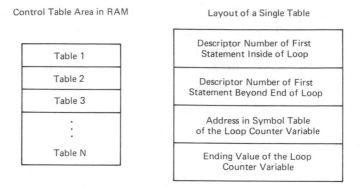

Figure 11-8: **Loop Control Tables.** Every loop that becomes active will have an 8 byte Loop Control Table associated with it. This table contains steering information for the interpreter at various stages in the loop's lifetime. Tables are returned to the system for reuse when a loop terminates. The number of tables corresponds to the maximum number of loops that can be active at one time.

last statements in a loop. When the interpreter is working at the end of a loop, it has to have some way of knowing how to get back to the beginning again. The NEXT statement at the end of the loop doesn't tell how to get back, so we must find out some other way. The basic idea is to have every FOR statement put something identifying itself onto the stack when a loop starts. The NEXT statement at the end of the loop can then inspect the stack to decide the location of the FOR statement at the top of the loop so that control can be routed back to the start. Of course, a stack is ideal for accommodating nested loops.

It turns out that the most useful identifier to put on the stack is the number of the control table that is associated with each loop. After all, these tables are supposed to contain all the necessary information about any loop. What the stack process buys is an easy connection between the statement on either end of a loop and the controlling table.

The only other data structure we need to examine supports the mechanism which implements the allocating and deallocating of Loop Control Tables. We will look into this after we specify what the three loop processing routines must do:

1. Processing at the Loop Begin Statement:
    (a) A control table must be allocated for the loop.
    (b) The fields in the control table must be filled in.
    (c) The number of the control table must be pushed onto the Loop Return Stack.
    (d) The loop counter variable must be initialized to its starting value in the Symbol Table. This will always be one.

Note: A given FOR statement is only executed once. The associated NEXT statement will return control to the first statement in sequence following the FOR statement. There is no need to go through the FOR statement again.

2. Processing at the Loop End Statement:

   (a) Inspect the top element on the Loop Return Stack to access the control table associated with the loop. However, don't change the contents of the stack at this time, i.e., don't pop it.

   (b) The action to be specified here may appear unnecessary, but it is required as set-up for an UNLOOP statement which might appear anywhere in the body of this loop. In the Loop Control Table, check the field which records the descriptor number of the first statement beyond the end of the loop. If this field has not been filled in, do so now. This will be easy because the current statement being interpreted is the one at the end of the loop.

   (c) Do the end test. Check if the loop counter variable is equal to its ending value.

      1. If it hasn't hit the ending value, increment the loop counter variable and prepare control to go back to the first statement inside the loop. This can be done by filling the descriptor number for that statement into the Execution Summary Table in the Next Descriptor Field and indicating that the next instruction is to be done in sequence. The Instruction Fetcher will take it from there. The next instruction really won't be done in sequence, but, since we know the descriptor number, it is a quick way to get where we want to go.

      2. If the ending value has been reached, some bookkeeping must be done to terminate the loop. Pop the stack to erase any record of the use of the present Loop Control Table. Clear the fields in the table and deallocate it (give it back to the pool of free tables).
      Note: In the absence of any action to start a branch, the next instruction to execute will always be done in sequence; so, at this point, control will fall through the NEXT statement to the part of the program that follows.

3. Processing at the Unloop Statement

   The basic idea of this statement is to deallocate the Loop Control Table and set up a transfer of control to the first statement beyond the end of the loop. The following is what must be done:

   (a) Pop the stack to find the current Loop Control Table and to remove its association with the present loop.

   (b) Set up a transfer of control to the first statement beyond the end of the loop. The descriptor for this statement may or may not be in the Loop Control Table. Usually it will be there. But, if the UNLOOP statement was encountered before the first time the end of the loop was reached, it will not be there. In this case processing will have to follow links in the Statement Descriptor Table to find where the end of the loop is.

   (c) The last thing to be done for an UNLOOP is to clear and deallocate the current Loop Control Table.

Before we conclude our discussion of loops, we would like to fill in a little more detail on the process of allocating and deallocating Loop Control Tables. As we mentioned previously, each Loop Control Table is eight bytes long. There will be a section of memory dedicated to these tables. How much space is in this area determines the maximum number of tables and thus the maximum number of loops that can be active at one time. In addition to the tables themselves, each table will be represented by a node in a linked list. Each node needs to contain just two pieces of information: something to identify a particular Loop Control Table and a pointer to the next node in the list.

The nodes will be linked up in various ways that correspond to the dynamics of the program at any time. Any node will be in one or the other of two lists—a free list or an in-use list. There will be a pointer to the start of the Free List and a pointer to the start of the In-Use List.

We have been identifying each table by its number. This is the first field in the node. We will assume that a simple formula can be incorporated into the program that will relate the number of a control table to its starting address within the area set aside for these tables.

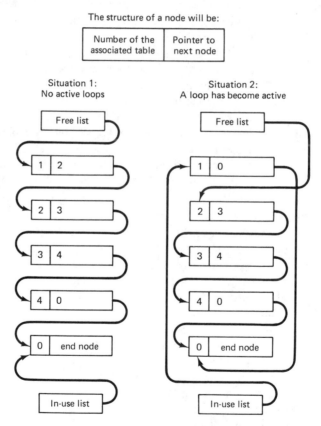

Figure 11-9:   **The Loop Control Table Allocation Lists.** Loop Control Tables are used and returned dynamically according to how many loops are active. There is a fixed pool of tables. Each table is recorded on one or the other of two lists—the In-Use List or the Free List, as the situation dictates.

Figure 11-9 shows an example of the linked list structure before and after the first loop begins to be interpreted in the source program. Before the loop was encountered, all the nodes were threaded together on the Free List. This means none of the Loop Control Tables are in use. When the first loop is encountered in the source code, the interpreter will provide a control table for it. In our example, Table No. 1 has been allocated to this loop. This decision is reflected in a relinking of the linked list nodes. Now the Free List starts with node 2, and the In-Use List, which was empty before, now contains the node associated with Table No. 1. Any pattern of allocation or deallocation of control tables can be easily recorded by manipulating the links of these nodes to rethread the lists in which they participate.

11.10   THE BASIC LANGUAGE IN PERSPECTIVE

This completes our discussion of the details of a TINY BASIC interpreter. The number of functions in the language were kept to a minimum so that, hopefully, one could keep all the details of the interpreter in mind at once. Now we can relax this restriction and try to imagine a more capable BASIC. How could we increment the interpreter for better performance? Would BASIC then be a good language? The language is obviously still evolving; where is it going? How does it stack up against the highly structured languages like Pascal? These are the kinds of questions we want to deal with in this concluding section of the interpreter chapter.

First, let's consider certain obvious and necessary improvements that could be made without a great deal of trouble. We will try to list these things in order of implementation difficulty starting with the simplest first, but you should consider the ordering to be quite approximate.

1. Arrays

Subscripted arrays of variables instead of simple single valued variables are very useful and easy to add. They usually require a dimension statement at the start of the program to alert the interpreter so that it can compute how much space to set aside in the Symbol Table. With this done, we can simply regard a subscripted variable as a different way of naming a variable. Some simple computations are required by the interpreter to find where a particular element is stored in the space set aside for a particular array.

2. Floating Point Numbers and Larger Integer Numbers

Another useful feature would be for the interpreter to recognize floating point numbers as well as integers. This change really doesn't have too much effect on the interpreter's overall structure. Variables would have to be named in some consistent way so that integers and floating point numbers could be distinguished. Floating point numbers would require a few extra bytes in the Symbol Table to store each value. Some modules would have to be added to the system in obvious places to do floating point arithmetic and to convert between numbers in ASCII string form and in floating point form. It would be easy and useful to expand integer arithmetic to longer numbers. For many applications, 16 bits aren't enough.

3. *String Handling Functions*

BASIC is traditionally quite strong in string handling ability, and we have not included this capability in TINY BASIC. We would need to have a new type of variable—a string variable that would contain text. There would also need to be a set of four or five built-in functions for string handling. The basic work would be done in an extension of the assignment statement. A string on the right side of the statement would be manipulated in some way by a string function and then assigned to a new string variable on the left side.

4. *Built-in Functions for Scientific Computation*

Most forms of BASIC have a collection of functions that extend the language's capability for mathematical programming. These are things like random number generators, trigonometric functions, and various logarithmic forms.

5. *Better Ways to Name Variables*

It would be very helpful to have character strings of arbitrary length be used for naming variables. If we did this, another way of managing the Symbol Table would have to be used. It would no longer be possible to preallocate storage space for all possible variables because there would be so many. A typical implementation strategy would be to maintain the Symbol Table in alphabetic order so that a search would be involved in retrieving the value given the name. A better strategy would be to implement a hashing algorithm so that the characters in the name itself could be combined in such a way as to compute the location where the variable would be stored. In an interpreter, of course, it is important to be able to get at variable values quickly.

6. *Error Checking*

Good error checking is a feature that most comprehensive BASICs have and that complements their use as good interactive languages. It is usually quite a burden to make really useful error checking. The checking has to be done in many places, and it takes a lot of code to do it.

7. *Better I/O Capability*

A great deal of work could be expended in giving the system better I/O capability—allowing the input and output statements to deal with lists containing an arbitrary number of variables; allowing output statements to print comments as part of the same output lines in which values are output. One more important extension would be to give the system the capability of defining and manipulating disk files from inside the language. This would involve making calls to an underlying operating system.

Most good BASICs have the features described above, and the whole interpreter is a program that is 10K to 15K bytes long. There are several other features that are important and probably will become common in newer versions of the language:

1. *Structured Programming Control Constructs*

Devotees of structured programming like to see programs written in terms of a few simple control constructs and nothing else. The ones most frequently mentioned are:

- The CASE statement
- The IF-THEN-ELSE statement
- The DO WHILE or REPEAT UNTIL statements

All of these things are very easy to add to the traditional repertoire of BASIC control constructs.

2. *Linkable Code*

It is desirable to be able to develop large programs in separate modules that can be tested separately and then integrated together with little trouble. BASIC traditionally has been weak in this regard because it was hard to plan for the line number usage among modules and because all the variable names were global, leading to unwanted side effects. Designers tended to handle linking by writing software to renumber the lines in various modules. The problem of global variables was ignored entirely, but better solutions are on the way.

3. *Local Variables*

It is desirable to have the capability for making some variables local to subroutines. This can be a very complicated matter depending upon how it is done, but benefits can be derived if we simply allow the language to pass variables to a subroutine in two separate ways: through variables that are global to the entire system or through argument lists. Local variables make for better modularity. They eliminate many of the problems that are encountered in trying to link code written by a number of different people. If the local variables are dynamically allocated storage space as part of the procedure of entering the subroutine and if they are somehow associated with a particular invocation of that subroutine, then it becomes possible for the language to be recursive—that is, a subroutine can call itself.

How good a language is BASIC? The merits of languages are the subject of death-grip debates and religious wars in computer science.

Its detractors say BASIC is a bad language for several reasons:

1. Since it is so easy to plunge in and develop a program quickly, people develop masses of poorly thought out code that don't work very well.

2. It is hard to make reliable large programs in BASIC because it is rather unstructured; modules don't interface well together.

Supporters of BASIC tend to reply:

1. How can rapid program development be a defect? That people don't think things out carefully is a defect of the people, not of the language.

2. The language, in many of the forms in which it exists today, is unstructured, but that can be remedied by some fairly easy extensions to the language while keeping its interactive, user friendly nature.

3. Some very good computing environments are now being developed around BASIC which will lead to convenient production of big programs. In particular, it is becoming common for people to work with two versions of the same language. When the code is initially being developed and many errors are to be found, then an interpretive BASIC is used because programs can be tested and changed quickly. When the program is correct, then a compiler for the very same language is used to produce an efficient machine coded version that runs perhaps five times as fast

as the interpreted BASIC. The interpreter-compiler unit is a natural for good program development. This is not a common feature in the way most other languages are used.

Clearly, in its present form, BASIC is very good for some things—like short programs that need to be developed quickly. It is not as suitable for other assignments such as large complex programs involving complicated data structures. However, we should now be thinking of the language in forms to which it could be extended easily. The language is evolving toward these forms (which show a great deal of promise) and will continue to improve.

STUDY QUESTIONS AND EXERCISES

1. What is the length of the text of the sample program shown in Figure 10-1? How long would it be when compressed to the internal form for an interpreter that was discussed in this chapter?

2. Show how the Execution Summary Table would be filled out immediately after parsing for each of the following program statements. In each case, assume that the statement being parsed is associated with statement descriptor No. 50 and that its text begins in the text buffer at location 1000. Remember that the text is compressed.

       10   X = (A + B) + 3

       40   IF (A > B) THEN 150

       400   READ A, Y, Z4

       25   GOTO 200

       47   RETURN

3. Consider the Symbol Table of Figure 11.7. Let's assume that in addition to the value of the symbol two more bytes are used on each line in the table to record the name of the symbol. Analyze the speed with which accesses can be made by searching for a symbol position in this table vs. the hashed access discussed in the book. Hint: the best way to do this is to write some code for the two methods.

4. Suppose that the Symbol Table for our interpreter is organized a little differently. The new order is A, B, . . . , Z, A0, A1, . . . , A9, B0, B1, . . . , B9, . . . , Z0, Z1, . . . , Z9. Develop a hashing algorithm that will transform the name of a variable into its address.

5. Suggest an organization and access strategy for the Symbol Table in our interpreter if we relax the restriction on how variables are named. Now names can be any alphanumeric string (starting with a letter) that is up to 8 characters long.

6. Write an 8080 subroutine to evaluate Boolean expressions. Assume that the possible Boolean expressions and the storage of symbols are as described for TINY BASIC. The Boolean expression exists as a string with blanks squeezed out and single parentheses at each end.

Assume that the entire expression is in ASCII. The HL pair contains a pointer to the first character in the string (left parenthesis). The result of the computation should appear in the accumulator: 1 for true, and 0 for false. You will need some help in changing various parts of the string to actual values before evaluations can be performed. Assume that you have the use of a routine called HASH, which takes the name of a variable in the BC pair and returns its value in the DE pair. Assume also that you have a routine CONV to convert numbers from ASCII to two byte binary form. To use this routine, the B register should contain the numbers of digits in the ASCII number. The DE pair should point to the first digit. The converted value is returned in the HL pair.

7. Flowchart a routine that could interpret (find the value of) an arithmetic expression in normal algebraic form with parentheses, i.e., not in RPN form.

8. Can the same stack be used for the Loop Return Stack and the Subroutine Return Stack? Show how to implement a stack in software that is completely independent of the 8080's hardware stack. You will need a subroutine to push a 16 bit value onto this stack and another one to pop values off.

9. Suppose a loop starts and immediately unloops. Show an example of some BASIC code wherein this could happen. Outline the processing that will occur to get out of the loop. What is the next statement? How will the system find it? Be explicit.

10. Imagine a different representation of the program an interpreter will work on than the one we have described. The raw text is kept in a text buffer in a compressed form as has been discussed. But, when a new line is to be inserted in the text, its proper position is found relative to the other statements, and all the text after that position is moved to create a place for the new line. The Statement Descriptor Table is somewhat simpler than before. It is not a linked list. Each line in the table contains the statement number of the statement and the offset of the statement in the text buffer. This table is sorted in numerical order by statement number. When a new statement is added to the text, its descriptor must be inserted in the descriptor table in the proper sorted position, not at the end. What effects would this organization have on editing speed, garbage collection, and the speed of program execution?

11. In order for the editor to display arithmetic expressions that have been converted to internal form for the interpreter, it will have to convert them back from RPN to normal algebraic notation. Design an algorithm that will do this.

12. What changes would be necessary in the present structure of TINY BASIC in order to incorporate an additional looping control statement of the DO-WHILE variety?

12

Compilers: Tiny Basic

12.1 *INTRODUCTION TO COMPILATION AND A TYPICAL DESIGN*

Compilation is a translation process. The compiler takes a program written in a higher level language and converts it into an equivalent program written in a lower level language. A lower level language is one in which the statements are more easily understood by a machine and less easily understood by people. There are two common types of compilers which can be classified by the languages into which they render programs submitted to them. Sometimes the output of a compiler is machine code, ready to be executed by the target computer or, at least, ready to be executed after it is relocated and linked. Other compilers simply transform the high level language programs submitted to them into equivalent programs in assembler language. With software like this, to get a runnable program, the source code must first be processed by the compiler and then by an assembler. The final output is machine code.

The second type of compiler can be viewed almost as a preprocessor for an assembler. It is easy to write a program like this. Because we are looking for the simplest examples of major systems software types on small computers, this is the type of compiler we will study. The language for which we will study compilation is going to be TINY BASIC. Examining compilation and interpretation on the same language should facilitate comparisons between the two major types of language systems.

Compilers that go the whole distance from higher level language code to relocatable machine code are generally a more complicated type of software than interpreters. That is the reason for the positioning of this chapter near the end of the book. However, because of the structure of TINY BASIC, and because of our decision to offload part of the compilation process onto a macroassembler, implementing the compiler example given in this chapter would probably be a simpler task than coding the interpreter of Chapter 11.

Traditionally compilation has been viewed as five processes that cooperate and occur more or less in sequence. The first process is *lexical analysis*. A lexical analyzer takes in a stream of raw program text and outputs text in a form more useable by the stages to follow. For instance, it might recode keywords into a shorter form, squeeze out blanks, and convert numerical constants from their ASCII representation into binary numbers. Of course, these shorter forms are called tokens and this process is sometimes referred to as tokenizing the input. The next stage is *parsing*. The parser extracts all the information in a program line and usually builds a table or some other data structure that describes that line. The table will contain the information in a fixed format. The parse table may have information such as what operation is being called for, what the operands are, where they are, and how long they are. The parsing phase is also the most convenient time to do error checking on the syntax of the program. Lexical analysis and parsing were discussed in some detail in Chapter 10. Next comes an *optimization phase*. The optimizer normally works on the tables put out by the parser. Its job is to eliminate certain possible redundancies and make sure that efficient code can be generated. The next stage in traditional compilers is called *code generation*. Here the parse table and any other global tables the system may have are used to generate a string of assembler statements or machine language statements that are equivalent to the current higher level language statement being translated. The last stage is optional. It is called *compilation assembly*. The purpose is to take the raw machine code from stage four, reformat it, and build any necessary tables so that the output code will be in exactly the same form as if it were relocatable code produced by an assembler. This is especially necessary for big machines that have complicated linking/loaders. It would not make sense to have code that is ready for linking and loading be produced in two formats, one from the compiler and one from the assembler.

Because of the extreme simplicity of the TINY BASIC language, we will be able to bypass or combine many of the traditional compiler stages. For instance, lexical analysis and parsing will be combined into one process. This process produces as output a parse table that is almost the same as the one used by the TINY BASIC interpreter. We will omit optimization entirely because this complex topic is more suited to advanced courses. Most of the work of our compiler will be in code generation. The final stage, which is compilation assembly, will be unnecessary because this compiler is designed to output code that must be passed through an assembler later on. Since it must undergo this additional processing, the final output will be produced in the same standard form as any other assembled code.

The easiest way to do code generation is to keep tables of template code for each program statement in the higher level language. The template code for a statement is a sequence of assembler language statements whose execution would have the same effect as the higher level language program line. This kind of code is called a template because it is only partially configured. The names of certain variables and certain constants must be filled into the template code to complete its configuring. A natural way to do this kind of operation is to use a macroprocessor. Thus, most program statements will be changed by the compiler into macro calls. When these macros are expanded and have certain parameters substituted, an assembly language version of the original program will have been produced. This process is at the heart of our strategy for producing a compiled program.

Now we are in a position to focus on the operation of the compiler at the top level. This compiler will require two passes over the source code. The first pass will be to generate a table that indicates all statements which are the targets of branches of all sorts. We will see why this is necessary presently. For instance, let us consider the following program fragment:

```
10   IF   (A > B)    THEN   50
20   GOSUB   200
30   GOTO   80
```

Program lines 50, 200, and 80 are all targets of branches. The statements in this example illustrate the three types of branches that are possible in TINY BASIC. There are no others.

The second pass of the compiler will be to convert each program line in the higher level language into a macro call with appropriate parameters for substitution. Occasionally, a small amount of straight assembler code will be output instead of a macro call. It will also be necessary on this second pass to insert a special macro call before every line that is the target of a branch. Here is why we do this. A program branch in a higher level language like BASIC is essentially a jump to a particular line number. However, when you do a branch in assembler language, it must be a branch to some label. The special macro, called the Branch Point Macro, will supply a suitable label everywhere there is code that must be branched to from somewhere else.

Consider what the output of this compiler will look like. It will be a file consisting of a number of things. At the front of the file will appear a set of standard macro definitions most of which correspond to particular program statements. Next will come a string of macro calls interspersed with some assembler code that represents the translated program. At the end of the file, there will be attached a data declaration in assembler language, which will represent the Symbol Table for the compiler. There will also be at least three library routines, written in assembler language, which will be used to implement 16 bit subtraction, multiplication, and division. TINY BASIC requires these operations, but they are not part of the instruction set of many microprocessors. Of course, whatever hardware capability a microprocessor has should be fully utilized in the fundamental routines for arithmetic. Finally, there will be an appended utility routine which collects in one place all the logic needed to evaluate the type of Boolean expressions that occur in TINY BASIC "IF" statements.

The composite file, which we have just described, is the complete output of the compiler. It is in a form that can be used as input to a macroassembler which will complete the transformation of a program into machine code. The complete processing cycle we have in mind requires two pieces of software, a compiler and a macroassembler, and it requires, in all, five passes over the code. The compiler requires two passes. What happens

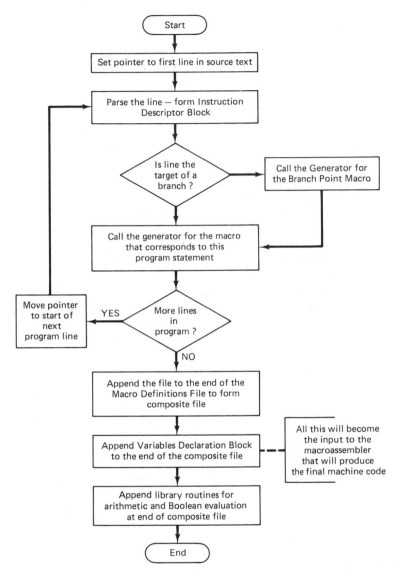

Figure 12-1: Top Level Operation of the Compiler. This compiler works by transforming most program lines into tailored macro calls. Assembler code for arithmetic expressions will be output where appropriate among the macro calls. The output of the compiler must be further processed by a macroassembler before relocatable machine code can be produced.

on the principal compiler pass is shown in Figure 12-1. The macroassembler requires three passes. One is for macro expansion and the other two are for standard assembler operations.

Before going on to more details, we need to say a few words about the compiler's Symbol Table. It doesn't really become a symbol table until the code is assembled. What we want to do is lay out some memory space for all the possible named variables that could occur in a TINY BASIC program. Recall that only 286 variable names are allowed. The philosophy we will implement is exactly the same as for the interpreter. That is, we will reserve two bytes for each variable, whether it is used or not, because there aren't very many allowed variables, and this will permit us to avoid complicated allocation schemes. The way to do this is to append some data storage declarations on the end of the compiler output. These will ensure that adequate space is reserved for the variables when the compiler output is assembled. We will call this collection of declarations the Variables Declaration Block. Its layout is shown in Figure 12-2.

Notice that the variable names we have used in the compiler output are different from those used in the interpreter: every name has a "%" appended onto it. This is necessary because certain variable names as used by the interpreter would have special meaning to an 8080 assembler. To the assembler, "A" means the register A rather than a variable with this name. An easy way to prevent any difficulties with reserved words for the assembler is simply to change the name of every variable from the way it exists in the source program to a closely related form in the assembly language version. And an easy way to effect this change is to append some character on the name for the assembler version. This is what we have done.

In this introduction we have given an overview of the general strategies to be used by our simple compiler, its pass structure, and its use of the Symbol Table. The main processing that occurs is that lines are parsed and then corresponding tailored macro calls

```
A%    DS    2
A0%   DS    2
A1%   DS    2
 .
 .
 .
A9%   DS    2
B%    DS    2
B0%   DS    2
B1%   DS    2
 .
 .
 .
B9%   DS    2
 .
 .
 .
Z8%   DS    2
Z9%   DS    2
```

Figure 12-2:   The Variables Declaration Block. When these declarations are assembled, they will become a de facto symbol table for a compiled and assembled program in TINY BASIC. Two bytes of RAM space are reserved for each possible variable, even if the program doesn't use it. Notice that every variable as it occurs in the source program has been consistently altered into the form that will be used in the assembler code version of the program. This is because certain names allowed in TINY BASIC are reserved words in 8080 assembler.

are output. Thus our next business will be to discuss parsing, and then the area in which the bulk of the work occurs—code generation. Not all code is generated as macro calls. Straight sequences of assembler code that are tailored to evaluate arithmetic expressions will be output wherever those expressions are encountered. We will need to devote some attention to how we can employ the basic Reverse Polish Notation algorithms to this purpose. Next, to tie all these ideas together, we will present a detailed example that shows all the steps of compilation applied to a representative program. Finally, as a general conclusion to our discussion of simple language systems, we make a comparison of the strengths and weaknesses of interpreters and compilers.

12.2 PARSING STATEMENT LINES

The compiler does its work by making two sequential passes over the code. There are parsing operations during each pass, but they are very simple on the first pass. The code must initially be parsed to determine statement numbers that are the targets of branches. This can be done by inspecting the whole program source file, character by character, to find certain keywords. Whenever any of the following keywords are found:

```
THEN
GOSUB
GOTO
```

then the number that immediately follows is a statement number that is the target of a branch. The compiler must collect these line numbers and make a sorted table out of them that is available for use during the second pass. In the second pass each program line will be parsed in a more complete manner and then translated into equivalent macros and assembler code. The compiler does all the work that has to be done for the current line before going on to the next one.

We have not yet stated in what form the text of the source program will be kept in order for this work to be done. Actually, since the compiling algorithms work line by line, the text could either be kept as an unprocessed ASCII file in a large memory buffer or, be brought in in small chunks as necessary from the disk. Either procedure would be suitable. The form of the text can be just as it was created by the editor when the programmer typed in the program. It does not need to be preprocessed or compressed in any way. Recall that several manipulations are performed on the source text in interpretive systems. There is no need to do this here, because the source text will not be required and will no longer be in memory at the time the compiled program is executed.

The object of parsing is to pull all the important elements out of a program line and put them in an easily used form (fixed length descriptors). The parser for the compiler will operate internally in almost the same manner as the parser for the interpreter. The output, too, will be almost the same. In each case, ASCII source text is the input, and the output is a table of descriptors. The compiler, however, doesn't need all the information extracted in interpretive parsing. The descriptor table will be smaller, and one field will have a different meaning. We will call the output of the parser the Instruction Descriptor Block. Figures 12-3 and 12-4 show what it looks like.

The parsing method will be to analyze statements via the syntactic finite state machine which was discussed in Chapter 10 and which is shown in Figure 10-10. The action routines associated with state transitions in this machine will be somewhat different than those used by the interpreter. The action routines will be specialized to fill in the various fields of the Instruction Descriptor Block as this information becomes available.

The Instruction Descriptor Block of Figure 12-3 has been drawn with some strange symbols in some of the fields. What are they for? The symbols are the names of dummy parameters that will be used in macro definitions. They are shown here just as a reminder. Essentially, they also name the fields in the IDB.

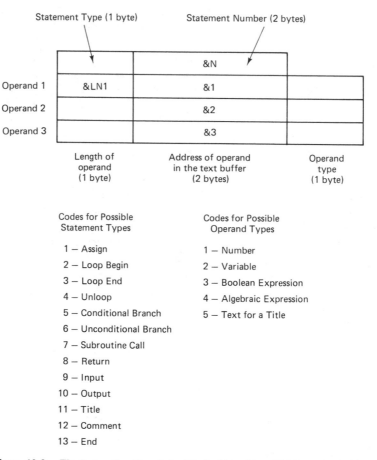

Figure 12-3: **The Instruction Descriptor Block.** This table, which is produced during the parsing phase for each program statement, contains all relevant information about that statement. Parsing has abstracted the information and cast it into a convenient form for subsequent code generation.

Assume that the statement being parsed is

    100..IF.(Z > 10).THEN.500^

This particular text starts at location 2000H in the memory buffer. Marks have been included in the text to show where the blanks and the Carriage Return occur. Remember that the system regards as an operand any field that can hold variable information. The IDB looks as follows:

	Statement Type	Statement Number	
	5	100	
Operand 1	6	2008H	3
Operand 2	3	2014H	1
Operand 3	—	—	—
	Length of Operand	Address of Operand in the Text Buffer	Operand Type

Figure 12-4:   An Example of the Instruction Descriptor Block Filled in for One Particular Statement. This table tells the code generator exactly what to expect from this statement. It is a statement of type 5, conditional branch, with a statement number 100. The first operand must be a Boolean expression. It is in the memory buffer at 2008H and extends for six characters. The second operand is the statement number for the branch. It is in the buffer at location 2014H and is three characters long.

We want to name certain fields in the IDB simply because the contents of these fields will be parameters, or closely associated with parameters, that are used to configure macros we are interested in for code generation. For instance, whenever &LN1 is used in a macro definition, it will refer to the field in the IDB that specifies the length in bytes of operand 1. Our macro calls will all be set up so that this number is substituted into the expanded macro at all the positions where &LN1 appears. Similarly the statement number, from the IDB, will be substituted into macros whereever &N appears. Whenever &1, &2, or &3 are used, something associated with the 1st, 2nd, or 3rd operands in the statement will be substituted into the expanded macros. These names have a wider usage than the other ones because different code generators use them in slightly different ways.

12.3   THE CODE GENERATOR FOR BRANCH POINTS

We now turn to a consideration of the other main body of work this compiler has to do, which is code generation. When work begins on the compilation of a new program line, the first thing that must be done (after parsing) is to note whether this line is the target of a branch from somewhere else in the program. A sorted list of these places was developed during Pass One of compilation. If it is a branch target, the line will require special handling. An appropriate label will have to be inserted in the sequence of macro calls to allow reference at this point from remote locations. It is the function of the Branch Point Macro to insert that label.

Let's examine a little more closely why the compiler needs this labeling procedure. We need to look at the translation activities that will go on at the statement which initiates a branch and at the statement that is the target of the branch. There will be a common way of using labels in the system that all modules can count on.

These are the kinds of things that happen where the branch is initiated. Let's say there is a statement in the BASIC program that says:

```
GOTO  1000
```

Ultimately, what we will want to produce as the assembler language equivalent of this statement is something like

```
JMP  S1000
```

The compiler, then, must arrange to put the S1000 label at the beginning of the assembler translation of whatever code happened to lie at line 1000 in the original program. In the assembler code, whenever it is necessary to make a label out of a line number, some alphabetic character must be appended on the front because straight numeric labels are not allowed by most assemblers.

Now let's look at what we need to have happen when the compiler reaches line 1000 in the source code. Whatever that line happens to be is going to be translated. But since some other part of the program is going to try to jump to this location, the compiler needs to make sure there is a target label to jump to. This means it has to output something like the following statement before it translates the code:

```
S1000  EQU  $
```

This establishes for the assembler the address that it should associate with the label.

The operational details of putting in the label at the right place are quite simple. The compiler simply needs to output a particular macro call before it begins further translation. This macro call has the statement number as a parameter. It will look like

```
BPT  1000
```

We showed earlier the single line of assembler code that must ultimately be produced when this macro is expanded. The macro definition that makes this possible is

```
1              MACRO
2              BPT  &N
3       S&N    EQU  $
4              MACEND
```

The &N indicates that when a call to this macro is generated, the parameter given in the call should be taken from the contents of the &N field in the current Instruction Descriptor Block.

As we go deeper into the compiler, we will see that the only times it is necessary to label statements in the assembler output are when the statements are the targets of branches, or when they demarcate the boundaries of loops. For loop labels, we will again create labels out of relevant numbers, but we will preface them by different character strings: LSTR for the start of a loop, and LEND for the end of a loop.

12.4   CODE GENERATION FOR SIMPLE PROGRAM STATEMENTS

We are now going to go through a process of discovering what the compiler should do for its code generation. It will be sufficient to follow the same procedure for each of the thirteen different statement types in TINY BASIC. Knowing the intent of the statement, we will write down a fragment of good assembler code that clearly accomplishes what is asked for in the higher level language statement. Then we will design a macro call and a macro definition which could produce this code, with proper parameters, wherever we need it.

12.4.1   Code Generation for the Assignment Statement

We remind the reader that three kinds of assignment statements are permitted in the TINY BASIC language. All of them have a variable name on the left hand side of an equals sign. On the right hand side, there may be a numeric constant, the name of a variable, or an algebraic expression. The code generator for assignment statements will detect which of these three situations corresponds to the statement being translated and a specific macro call will be generated. Three different macros will be available corresponding to the different types of assignment statement.

Before we fill in any more details, we need an example. Let's say we wish to generate code for the statement

```
10  X = 12
```

The type of assembly code we want to be generated ultimately will be of the form

```
LXI  H,12
SHLD X%
```

Remember that in the assembler version of the program which we are producing, all names have been altered from their original form so they end in the percent sign. This code, when it is executed, will load the HL register pair with the number 12 and then will store the contents of the HL register pair into the symbolic location called X%. This is one of the locations in the Symbol Table. Space was reserved for X% in the data structure that we called the Variables Declaration Block.

These manipulations clearly accomplish an assignment. Now the problem is to see what kind of macro we need to have the compiler generate to output the assembler code we have just described. The macro definition will look something like

```
1    MACRO
2    ASGN1      &1, &2
3    LXI        H, &2
4    SHLD       &1%
5    MACEND
```

The work of the compiler will be to recognize the type of assignment statement and to abstract the proper parameters from the Instruction Descriptor Block so that a configured macro call can be made. Then the output of the compiler for this particular assignment statement is

```
ASGN1    X, 12
```

Later on, when this macro is expanded, the assembler code we have described will be produced.

```
CASE 1.    1    MACRO                    Typical Call:
           2    ASGNI     &1,&2            X = 12
           3    LXI       H,&2          This generates:
           4    SHLD      &1%              ASGN1   X,12
           5    MACEND


CASE 2.    1    MACRO                    Typical Call:
           2    ASGN2     &1,&2            X = Y
           3    LHLD      &2%           This generates:
           4    SHLD      &1%              ASGN2   X,Y
           5    MACEND


CASE 3.    1    MACRO                    Typical Call:
           2    ASGN3     &1               R = (X+Y)*2
           3    POP       H             This generates:
           4    SHLD      &1%              Machine code for the
           5    MACEND                     expression followed
                                           by: ASGN3   R
```

Figure 12-5: Macro Definitions for the Assignment Statement. Assignment statements put values in the Symbol Table at the time that the compiled program is executed. There are three sorts depending on what is on the right hand side of the equals sign: a number, a variable, or an expression. The compiler will output a call to one of the three macros shown when it translates assignments. If the statement involves an expression, some assembler code that computes a value for the expression will be output as well.

There will be two other macro calls available to the code generator if the assignment statement is of the sort where one variable is assigned to another or where an expression is assigned to another variable. The definitions for these macro calls are shown in Figure 12-5. A high level flowchart for the Code Generator for Assignment Statements is shown in Figure 12-6.

Notice that the situation is a little more complex when the assignment involves an expression. Since expressions are so variable in format, in this case, the compiler will call a module named the Algebraic Expression Generator as part of code generation. This module will output assembler code to compute an expression. After this, the system will always output a macro call to the macro ASGN3, which will generate code to store the result of expression evaluation in the proper place in the Symbol Table. We will examine the Algebraic Expression Code Generator in more detail later. All we need to know about it now is that it can output tailored sequences of assembler code sufficient to evaluate any expression. And the result of its work is left in a standard place—the top element (16 bits) on the stack.

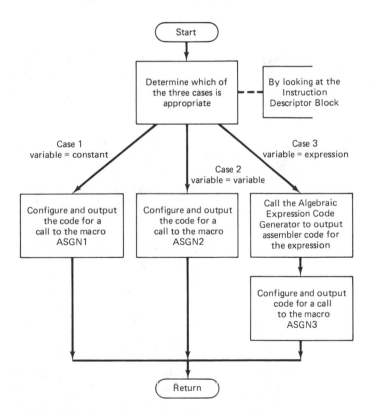

Figure 12-6:   The Code Generator for Assignment Statements. This code generator is called whenever the compiler encounters an assignment statement. The generator will analyze the type of the assignment statement and output a call to an appropriate macro.

12.4.2   Code Generation for the Conditional Branch

Our simple language can accept twelve different types of Boolean expressions in the IF statement. Only nine of these are useful, but the other ones are nonetheless allowed because we want to keep the language definition simple. The task of the code generator will be to detect which variation occurs in a given statement and then call a corresponding macro. The names of these macros will be

IF1   through   IF12

The reason we can have twelve different types of clauses is that the language definition allows three operators:

$$>, <, =$$

and the various permutations of constants and variables as the operands of these operators generate twelve possibilities. These are displayed in Figure 12-7. An example of a case that doesn't make sense would be

```
100   IF (3 > 2) THEN 500
```

It doesn't make sense because 3 is always greater than 2 so that the effect of the statement could be accomplished more easily with a simple jump statement.

In order to get an idea of what the macros will be like, consider a particular program

Case	Operator	On Left of the Operator	On Right of the Operator
1	>	constant	variable
2	<	constant	variable
3	=	constant	variable
4	>	variable	constant
5	<	variable	constant
6	=	variable	constant
7	>	variable	variable
8	<	variable	variable
9	=	variable	variable
10	>	constant	constant
11	<	constant	constant
12	=	constant	constant

Figure 12-7.   Possible Formats for Boolean Expression Clauses in the IF Statement. The IF statement incorporates a simple Boolean expression that evaluates to true or false. This is how the system decides whether a branch is to be taken or not. There are only twelve allowable formats for these expressions.

statement and the assembler code that would represent a desirable translation. Let us examine the translation of the following line:

    100   IF (Z > 10) THEN 500

This is an example of case 4 in Figure 12-7. What is this code asking for? It says, compare Z with 10 and if it is greater than 10, then branch to the point in the code that is equivalent to the statement at line 500. If Z is not greater than 10, then continue executing in normal sequence. A fragment of assembler code that seems to do what we have just discussed is

```
LXI     D, -10
DCX     D
LHLD    Z%
DAD     D
JC      S500
```

In the code fragment, we establish the minus ten in a register pair (DE) because in general the operand might be a sixteen bit number. We then decrement this register pair so the it contains -11. Then we load the HL pair with the contents of Z%. Then we add the HL and DE registers. If a carry is generated, it will mean that Z was indeed greater than 10, and therefore we generate a jump on carry to the label S500. This is a label that will be inserted into the code, via the Branch Point macro, to identify the area that corresponds to line 500. Otherwise we just continue to execute the next code in sequence.

Some further thought, however, will reveal that this code gives the wrong answer under certain circumstances—for instance, if Z happens to be a negative number. Obviously we have encountered some difficulties in evaluating the Boolean expression. We need a better algorithm. One that looks promising is

> To see whether (ALPHA > BETA) is true or not, subtract BETA from ALPHA. If the result is greater than zero, then the expression is true.

We are going to modify this algorithm in one respect that makes for less testing in the code:

> To see whether (ALPHA > BETA) is true or not, subtract (BETA + 1) from ALPHA. If the result is nonnegative, then the expression is true.

Indeed, from the basic laws of arithmetic, this test has to give the correct answer. However, problems arise in trying to carry out the test using 16 bit two's complement arithmetic. If the computation of ALPHA $-$ (BETA + 1) gives a number which is not representable in 16 bits, then the test will fail. This can happen in many ways. For example, let ALPHA be 32,767 and BETA be -2. When we subtract (BETA + 1) from ALPHA, the result is a negative number, which would suggest that 32,767 is not greater than -2. The trick is obviously to detect when ALPHA $-$ (BETA + 1) is going to produce an unrepresentable number.

However, good tricks are hard to come by in evaluating these expressions, and by doing some extra work with multiple precision arithmetic, proper results can be easily obtained. Here is the essence of an approach that will always work. Represent both ALPHA and BETA as 24 bit numbers. This can be done by adding another byte in the most significant position. The byte will be all zeros if the number being extended is positive, and all ones if it is negative. Then increment BETA by 1. Then simply subtract BETA from ALPHA using the instruction for 8 bit multiple precision subtraction that is part of the 8080's instruction set. It was put there for this kind of circumstance. If the result of the subtraction is nonnegative, then ALPHA is indeed greater than BETA. Actually the numerical result of this operation is not needed to evaluate the Boolean expression. All that is required is the sign of the result; so some shortcuts can be taken with the multiple precision arithmetic.

A sequence of assembler code that will adequately translate the original instruction we were working on is

```
; CODE TRANSLATES "IF (Z > 10) THEN 500"
; BRANCHES IF LEFT VARIABLE GREATER THAN RIGHT CONSTANT
; START BY FORMING BETA IN EXTENDED PRECISION
CASE4:    MVI    B, 0        ; ASSUME BETA POSITIVE
          LXI    D, 10       ; GET BETA
          MOV    A, D        ; TEST IF POSITIVE
          ANA    A
          JP     GAMMA1      ; IF YES, GO ON
          MVI    B, -1       ; IF NO, CHANGE HIGH BYTE
; NEXT FORM BETA + 1 IN EXTENDED PRECISION
GAMMA1:   INR    E           ; FORM BETA + 1
          MOV    A, D        ; DO IT 8 BITS AT A TIME
          ACI    0           ; USE ADD WITH CARRY
          MOV    D, A
          MOV    A, B
          ACI    0
          MOV    B, A
; NEXT FORM ALPHA IN EXTENDED PRECISION
GAMMA2:   MVI    C, 0        ; ASSUME ALPHA POSITIVE
          LHLD   Z%          ; GET ALPHA
          MOV    A, H        ; TEST IF POSITIVE
          ANA    A
          JP     GAMMA3      ; IF YES, GO ON
          MVI    C, -1       ; IF NO, CHANGE HIGH BYTE
; FINALLY SUBTRACT BETA + 1 FROM ALPHA
GAMMA3:   MOV    A, L        ; SUBTRACT LOW ORDER BYTE
          SUB    E           ; DON'T KEEP ANSWER
          MOV    A, H        ; SUBTRACT MID ORDER BYTE
          SBB    D           ; DON'T KEEP ANSWER
          MOV    A, C        ; SUBTRACT HIGH ORDER BYTE
          SBB    B           ; ONLY SIGN IS IMPORTANT
          JP     S500        ; IF NON-NEGATIVE, TAKE THE BRANCH
```

How does this code work? The number ALPHA (Z) is held in the HL pair with its sign bit extended through the C register. The number BETA (10) is held in the DE pair with its sign bit extended through the B register. (BETA + 1) is formed by three 8 bit addition operations that are linked by the carry bit. Finally the subtraction is performed by three 8 bit subtract operations linked by the carry bit. Only the sign of the final result matters for deciding whether the branch should be taken or not.

It is easy to make a macro out of this code that can handle all possible variations of a Case 4 type of Boolean expression occurring in a Conditional Branch statement. However, we will not write it out because that macro would be just like this code except for parameters inserted in three places.

There will be twelve macro definitions like this in all, corresponding to the twelve different types of Boolean clauses that are allowed in Conditional Branch statements. If we wish to generate in-line code, it will be the job of the code generator for IF statements to look at the Boolean clause, decide which case it is, and then output a configured macro that corresponds to the current program statement. In the example we have been looking at, the macro call that would be output is

```
IF4   Z,10,500
```

The code generator can determine which of the twelve macros to use and which parameters to use by inspecting the Instruction Descriptor Block and the text in the text buffer. Frequently the contents of fields identified in the Instruction Descriptor Block can be transferred directly into the macro call as it is being configured. However, in this case, the code generator has more work to do than usual, because the IDB only contains a pointer to the whole Boolean expression. The code generator will have to pull out for itself the elements of the expression that are to the left and right of the operator.

Because the 8080 instruction set is clumsy for Boolean expressions of the type we need, and because it takes so much code to translate a conditional branch, compiler builders would probably take a different approach in this instance than a macro for in-line code. That is, a single large subroutine might be written that could evaluate any Boolean expression. It would presumably use a minimal amount of extended precision arithmetic where necessary for testing numbers against each other. This routine could then be appended onto all compiled programs. Essentially it would become part of a run-time package. With such a subroutine in the system, the translation of a conditional branch would simply amount to code that set up parameters for the subroutine, called the subroutine, then branched or not depending on a completion code that would be returned at execution time.

We will assume that this approach has been taken in our compiler. However, some code generation macros will still be necessary. Let's follow a little further to see what the macros look like. Assume that any compiled code will contain an appended utility routine for the evaluation of Boolean expressions. This routine is called BOLEVL. It must be passed the case number (1-12) of the expression in register B. It must be passed the value of the operand to the left of the relational operator in register DE and the value of the operand to the right in register HL.

Given the availability of this utility routine, a desirable translation of our original conditional branch instruction would be

```
MVI     B, 4        ; ESTABLISH CASE NUMBER
LHLD    Z%          ; GET LEFT OPERAND
XCHG
LXI     H, 10       ; GET RIGHT OPERAND
CALL    BOLEVL      ; CALL THE EVALUATOR
ANA     A           ; SET FLAGS BY RETURNED CODE
JP      S500        ; POSITIVE CODE MEANS JUMP
```

The corresponding macro definition would have the form

```
 1      MACRO
 2      IF4         &L, &R, &2
 3      MVI         B, 4
 4      LHLD        &L%
 5      XCHG
 6      LXI         H, &R
 7      CALL        BOLEVL
 8      ANA         A
 9      JP          S&2
10      MACEND
```

The macro call itself would once again be

```
IF4  Z, 10, 500
```

12.4.3 Code Generation for Unconditional Branches

This routine will configure a macro to provide for jumps in control; for example,

```
100  GOTO  1000
```

will result in the following macro appearing in the code:

```
JUMP  1000
```

This macro will expand according to

```
1  MACRO
2  JUMP &1
3  JMP S&1
4  MACEND
```

Remember that we took great pains to ensure that there would be a label, S1000, at the appropriate place in the code to jump to. We did this by making a table of jump targets and inserting a call to the Branch Point Macro as every target line was processed.

12.4.4 Code Generation for Subroutine Calls

This generator is very similar to the routine for the GOTO statement. Consider this example in TINY BASIC:

```
100  GOSUB  200
```

The code generator would output a macro call which would be

```
SUBR   200
```

The corresponding macro definition is

```
1      MACRO
2      SUBR      &1
3      CALL      S&1
4      MACEND
```

Notice that this involves a machine language subroutine call. The machine language call statement will take care of the return address automatically. Our branch point procedures ensure that a label, S200, will exist in the code at the appropriate place.

12.4.5 Code Generation for the Return Statement

This generator simply needs to insert the machine language return statement in the output stream at the place corresponding to the RETURN statement in TINY BASIC. No macro call is necessary.

12.4.6 Code Generation for the Input Statement

In designing the compiler, we can arrange to have the input process make use of whatever operating system routines or monitor routines are associated with the system. For instance, CP/M 1.4 has two routines for simple input from the keyboard. One brings in a single character. The other brings in a complete line. Let us assume there is a routine called INP which, when called, will prompt for input from the screen and leave the input in the HL register pair. Also, we will assume that INP is written to expect an ASCII string that is equivalent to a sixteen bit number. Thus, for a BASIC statement such as

```
100  READ  X,Y,Z
```

the following assembler code should ultimately be generated:

```
CALL    INP
SHLD    X%
CALL    INP
SHLD    Y%
CALL    INP
SHLD    Z%
```

Remember that the Input statement can involve up to three operands. The compiler can cause appropriate code to be set up by generating one, two, or three calls to the same basic macro depending on whether there are one, two, or three operands in the Input statement. Of course, in the case of inputting more than one value, the macro calls would be configured with different parameters in each case. The basic macro definition we need is as follows:

```
1       MACRO
2          INPUT    &V
3          CALL     INP
4          SHLD     &V%
5       MACEND
```

Of course, the code generator will know how many operands there are because it can inspect the Instruction Descriptor Block which is the output of parsing.

For the example that we gave earlier in this section, the output the code generator should produce is three macro calls that look like this:

```
INPUT   X
INPUT   Y
INPUT   Z
```

12.4.7 Code Generation for the Output Statement

Let us assume that there is an operating system routine called OUTP which takes a value from the HL register pair and puts it out on the screen. Once again, this code generator will have to determine how many operands are being output; and it will generate one, two or three calls to the same basic macro. There will be different parameters in the calls reflecting the variable names of the output data. As an example, let us suppose code is being generated for the statement

```
300  PRINT  R,S
```

The generator would produce the following two macro calls as the output of compilation:

```
OUTPUT    R
OUTPUT    S
```

These calls would ultimately be expanded according to the macro definition that follows, giving us what we need:

```
1    MACRO
2    OUTPUT    &V
3    LHLD      &V%
4    CALL      OUTP
5    MACEND
```

As far as code generation is concerned, the output process is in every way the inverse of the input process.

12.4.8 Code Generation for the Title Statement

The architecture of this routine will depend heavily upon what operating system or monitor routines are going to be available to do text output in the integrated system of which our compiler will be a part. For instance, the CP/M operating system has a routine as part of its BDOS package which allows you to output whole lines of text to the screen all at once rather than character by character.

To show what code generation would be like for the TITLE statement, we will assume we have a typical operating system input/output package and we will show how it would be set up. Let us assume our operating system has a collection of input/output routines that can be accessed by putting parameters in some of the registers and executing a subroutine call to the beginning of the package. Specifically, to use the package, let's assume we need to place a function number in register C. If the desired operation is outputting a line of text, let's assume the following set-up is necessary: register C should be given the number 12, register B should have the length of the line of text, and the HL register pair should contain the address in some text buffer where the text begins. After the registers are set up in this way, the actual outputting can be done by giving the operating system control through

```
CALL  IOSYS
```

The code for a TITLE statement will look different in several respects from most of the other macros we have produced, so you will need to follow this example carefully. Let's say the line of text we want to output is as follows:

SUM AND PRODUCT EXAMPLE

A fragment of assembler code that could handle this titling assignment by using the operating system routine we mentioned above is

```
MVI    C, 12
MVI    B, 23
LXI    H, $ + 9
CALL   IOSYS
```

```
JMP       $ + 23 + 3
DB        'SUM AND PRODUCT EXAMPLE'
```

The first two lines in the fragment set up the function number for the I/O package and establish how long the output string is. The third line establishes the address of the string for the output routine. Notice that since we have to keep the string around somewhere until execution time, we might as well keep it as part of the code of the translated instruction. The operand $ + 9 is an expression which computes the address of where the string is kept. In this case, the string lies nine bytes beyond the instruction that is referencing it. All the setup has now been taken care of, so we can make a call to the I/O package. The final executable code associated with this statement is a jump beyond the text string to where the code for the next program statement will begin. Once again, an expression is used to compute the address for the jump, and it is computed as an offset from the present address.

The reader may not be familiar with a "$" used in assembler expressions. This is shorthand for the value of the assembler's location counter at the particular instruction being translated. Actually it is the value at the first byte of the instruction. Recall that as the assembler does its work, it keeps a location counter that specifies where the statement being translated will lie in memory. It is useful to let programmers access this value. This is what the "$" represents. Normally the "$" will be used as part of an expression to refer to some other line at an offset from the current line. Indeed that is what we use the symbol for here.

Now we simply need to make a macro, and then we can handle the TITLE statement as we would any other statement. The macro definition is

```
1       MACRO
2       TITLE     &LN1, &STRG
3       MVI       C, 12
4       MVI       B, &LN1
5       LXI       H, $ + 9
6       CALL      IOSYS
7       JMP       $ + &LN1 + 3
8       DB        '&STRG'
        MACEND
```

The dummy parameter &LN1 refers to the field in the Instruction Descriptor Block which contains the length of the first operand. With TITLE statements, there is only one operand, and its length is the length of the string to output. Since parsing will have already determined this number, we will have the code generator for TITLE statements take it out of the IDB and pass it right into the TITLE macro through a parameter. The actual string to be output will also be passed into the macro as a parameter. The dummy parameter that holds place for this information we are calling &STRG, for string. Quite a few characters may be passed through this parameter if it is a long string. Although this may seem unusual, it is certainly all right to do this. The construction of the macroprocessor puts no particular restriction on the length of parametric information.

Now, to complete this discussion, we have only to show what a typical macro call will look like. The call that our original example would generate will look like this:

```
TITLE   23, SUM AND PRODUCT EXAMPLE
```

Incidentally, there is no reason why the name of a macro, in this case TITLE, should not be the same as a reserved word in BASIC. This is perfectly all right because it is convenient to do so, and because the names are used in different stages of the compilation process.

12.4.9 Code Generation for the Comment Statement

Generally, no one ever inspects the code coming from a compiler since it is produced reliably and automatically. Any questions are resolved by looking at the version of the program that is stated in high level language. Thus, comments are not needed in the compiler output. This means the Code Generator for Comments can be some sort of dummy routine that does no work.

12.4.10 Code Generation for the End Statement

The End statement in a TINY BASIC program will be the last statement in the program that is executed. Remember, this does not mean it must be at the end of the program text. Frequently, it will be internal to the text. The language even allows multiple End statements in the same program.

After the End statement, the user program is no longer controlling the computer. Therefore control must be returned to the monitor or to the operating system to find out what to do next.

Each End statement can be translated as a single line of assembler code that causes a jump to the entry point of the operating system which is supervising the program. For instance, if our program were executing in a CP/M environment, then a reasonable translation would be:

```
JMP   0000H
```

Since only one line of code is required, it is probably better to output it directly rather than involve a macro.

12.5 CODE GENERATION FOR LOOPS

Looping in the compiler results in a complicated code structure just as it did in the interpreter. Whatever is done on behalf of the FOR statement must be closely coordinated with the NEXT statement, because they are part of a single logical entity.

Let's examine some assembly code that could conceivably result from the compilation of a FOR/NEXT loop to see the type of features that would be needed in the code generator. Two variants of a loop coded to be an example are shown in Figures 12-8A and 12-8B. Two different ways of doing the loop arise because our language is allowed to specify the ending value of the loop counter as either a variable or a constant. The beginning value of the loop counter is always the same. All loops start with the counter equal to one.

Here is how the examples work. The loop counter is initialized. Then the loop begins. The counter value is tested immediately to see if it has exceeded the ending value. If not, the body of the loop is executed. Then the loop counter is incremented, and control branches back to the top of the loop. When the loop counter goes past the ending value, the end test catches it. Control is passed to the end of the loop. The counter's value is adjusted for end effects and then control moves on to code for the next statement.

There are some points that need further explanation. Both examples do the end test in the same way. Here is the basis of that test. We use a manipulation with the one's complement of the loop counter's ending value for the end test. Please recall several facts. The one's complement of a number is that number with all its bits inverted. If a number and its one's complement are added, the result will be a binary number with ones in all bit positions. Thus, when the loop counter has become equal to the ending value, adding the loop counter and the previously prepared one's complement of the ending value gives a result with a one in every bit position. If the loop counter has become one unit greater than the ending value, when we add it to the previously prepared one's complement, the sum will overflow and a carry will be generated.

We look for this carry. When it occurs, it means the loop counter has just passed its ending value. Before leaving the loop, it is necessary to decrement the counter variable by one unit. Why? The language definition for TINY BASIC requires that the loop counter be equal to the ending value after the loop is finished, not one unit greater.

In the second example, the one's complement of the ending value of the loop counter is formed in a way that is not obvious. First we form the two's complement by subtracting the number from zero using a 16 bit subtract routine; then we decrement the result. Decrementing a two's complement changes it into a one's complement.

Configuring this assembler code won't be difficult. Once again we can use a macroprocessor in the normal manner to insert the name of the loop counter and its terminating value. The only problem is the labels in the machine code. It is unacceptable to generate LSTR as a label over and over every time we have a loop. Instead, we need to be able to generate LSTR1 and then LSTR2, LSTR3, etc. The same requirement exists for LEND labels. The labels associated with any particular loop must be unique. Here is how we can accommodate this requirement in the compiler's design. We must arrange to have the compiler keep a running count of the number of loops it encounters as it sequentially processes the source code. We will arrange to have the loop number concatenated onto any labels in the loop so that they will become unique. If the compiler keeps count, this can be done as a normal parameter substitution operation by the macroprocessor.

The code generator for the NEXT statement needs to have access to the loop number. It needs this number in order to construct a proper label at the end of the loop, and in

```
TINY BASIC                    8080    ASSEMBLER
FOR I = 1 TO 10               LXI     H, 1        ; INITIALIZE LOOP COUNTER.
                  LSTR:       SHLD    I%          ; STORE ITS CURRENT VALUE.
                              LXI     D, -10      ; ADD LOOP COUNTER TO THE
                              DCX     D           ; 1'S COMPLEMENT OF ITS ENDING
                              DAD     D           ; VALUE. CARRY SETS WHEN
                              JC      LEND        ; COUNTER PASSES ENDING VALUE.
Body of Loop                  Body of Loop
NEXT I                        LHLD    I%          ; INCREMENT LOOP COUNTER.
                              INX     H
                              JMP     LSTR        ; GO BACK FOR NEXT PASS.
                  LEND:       LHLD    I%          ; MAKE SURE LOOP COUNTER
                              DCX     H           ; CONTAINS PROPER END VALUE
                              SHLD    I%          ; WHEN ALL DONE.
```

Figure 12-8A: A Typical Loop With a Constant for the Ending Value of the Loop Counter.

```
TINY BASIC                    8080    ASSEMBLER
FOR I = 1 TO N                LXI     H, 1        ; INITIALIZE LOOP COUNTER.
                  LSTR:       SHLD    I%          ; STORE ITS CURRENT VALUE.
                              LHLD    N%          ; FORM 2'S COMP. OF THE
                              XCHG                ; END VALUE BY SUBTRACTING
                              LXI     H, 0        ; FROM ZERO. THEN ADJUST
                              CALL    SUBT        ; SO THE COMP. IS A
                              DCX     H           ; 1'S COMPLEMENT.
                              XCHG                ; ADD LOOP COUNTER TO THE
                              LHLD    I%          ; 1'S COMP. OF ITS ENDING
                              DAD     D           ; VALUE. CARRY SETS WHEN
                              JC      LEND        ; COUNTER PASSES ENDING VALUE.
Body of Loop                  Body of Loop
NEXT I                        LHLD    I%          ; INCREMENT LOOP COUNTER.
                              INX     H
                              JMP     LSTR        ; GO BACK FOR NEXT PASS.
                  LEND:       LHLD    I%          ; MAKE SURE LOOP COUNTER
                              DCX     H           ; CONTAINS PROPER END VALUE
                              SHLD    I%          ; WHEN ALL DONE.
```

Figure 12-8B: A Typical Loop with a Variable for the Ending Value of the Loop Counter. In our TINY BASIC, there are two variations in the way a loop may appear. The ending value of the loop counter may be specified as either a constant or a variable. The beginning value is always one. These examples show assembler code for the two variants of a particular loop.

order to generate a jump back to the unique label at the start of the loop. The best way to provide this is for the FOR generator to put its loop number on a stack, and the NEXT generator to take a loop number off the stack. This scheme can accommodate infinite nesting of loops. We will call this stack the Loop Return Stack.

We have seen that there are several bookkeeping tasks associated with the code for loops in TINY BASIC. The tasks are: initialize the loop counter, perform an end test for each passage through the loop, and increment the loop counter for each passage through the loop. It is necessary to consider where these tasks should be performed: at the top of the loop or at the bottom. In general, everything except the initialization can be implemented either way.

Here is why we chose to code the examples as they are shown. First of all, initialization has to be done at the top of the loop because it makes no sense to go through an uninitialized loop. The loop counter might be used in the computations inside the loop so it must always have an appropriate value. We chose to do the end test at the top of the loop because the whole translation mechanism is easier if we do. Why is this? When a FOR statement is being translated, the ending value of the loop counter is right there available to be used in configuring code. If we attempted to do an end test at the bottom of the loop, the ending value would have to be passed to the code generator for the NEXT statement somehow, probably on another stack. Remember that the ending value of the loop counter is a parameter in the BASIC statement that begins a loop, but it does not appear in the statement that terminates a loop.

We chose to increment the loop counter at the end of the loop for the following reason. If it is done first thing at the beginning, then it will mess up the initialization procedure. That is, the loop will have to be initialized to zero rather than one in order for the loop counter to have the correct value the first time through the loop. This makes the code less clear and it results in a longer construct that's harder to generate with a macro.

Let us now state all the things that the code generator for the FOR statement must do:

1. Get the loop number from the counter that the compiler increments every time it sees a loop. We will call this &L.
2. Put the loop number on a dedicated stack for subsequent use by the NEXT statement that goes with the loop.
3. Configure a macro call for the FOR statement such that the loop number will be used as part of appropriate labels.

The things that the code generator for the NEXT statement must do are the following:

1. Remove a loop number from the Loop Return Stack.
2. Configure a macro call for the NEXT statement such that the loop number will be used as part of appropriate labels.

The macro definition that will be used in association with the top of the loop is shown in Figure 12-9. Notice that what we have done here is use the conditional assembly feature of our macroassembler to reduce the number of macro definitions that need to be maintained. We can think of the loop which has a constant for its ending value as a Type One Loop and a loop that has a variable for its ending value as a Type Two Loop. The code generator for the FOR statement must determine which kind of loop is being specified and then pass the number one or two as a parameter to the macro shown in Figure 12-9.

```
 1                      MACRO
 2                      FOR        &C, &1, &2, &L
 3                      LXI        H, 1
 4          LSTR&L:     SHLD       &1%
 5                      CONMB      (&C = 2) , 9
 6                      LXI        D, –&2
 7                      DCX        D
 8                      CONMB      (&C = 1) , 16
 9                      LHLD       &2%
10                      XCHG
11                      LXI        H, 0
12                      CALL       SUBT
13                      DCX        H
14                      XCHG
15                      LHLD       &1%
16                      DAD        D
17                      JC         LEND&L
18                      MACEND
```

Figure 12-9:   Macro Definition Used for Loop Beginnings. Loops are one of the most complicated constructs a simple compiler has to deal with. Variations in the way a loop can start can be accommodated in one macro definition by using conditional assembly. The code at the beginning and ending of a loop are related through a set of commonly understood, unique labels that are passed on a special stack.

We are using &C as the dummy parameter associated with the loop type indicator. Depending on which value is passed in, the macro will be expanded in one or the other way, whichever is appropriate.

Let us see what the macro call would look like. The following is what the code generator would output if it were working on a loop of the type shown in Figure 12-8B, and if this were the third loop that had been discovered in translating the program:

```
FOR   2, I, N, 3
```

Now we need to consider how code is generated at the other end of the loop. Both kinds of loops terminate in the same way. Figure 12-10 shows what the macro definition looks like. We have taken this macro in a straightforward manner from the code in the examples. Only two parameters need to be passed into the macro: the name of the loop counter variable and the number of the loop for which an ending is being generated. The code generator for NEXT gets this number off the Loop Return Stack. If the third loop is being processed as in our example, the macro call will be

```
NEXT   I, 3
```

We still have the problem of unlooping to contend with, but it can be handled simply. When an UNLOOP statement is encountered in the body of a loop, all that needs

```
1                         MACRO
2                         NEXT         &1 , &L
3                         LHLD         &1%
4                         INX          H
5                         JMP          LSTR&L
6            LEND&L:      LHLD         &1%
7                         DCX          H
8                         SHLD         &1%
9                         MACEND
```

Figure 12-10:   Macro Definition Used for Loop Endings.

to be done is to generate code that will cause a branch to the first statement beyond the end of the loop. There is a label near where we need to jump. It is LEND with the number of the loop concatenated on the end. In fact, if we always cause a jump to the address seven bytes beyond this label, control will arrive at the code for the next statement. The seven bytes is to get past the adjustment in the loop counter that is done for a normal loop termination.

This strategy for exiting loops means that the code generator for UNLOOP statements will have to get a loop number off the Loop Return Stack. It will have to inspect (but not remove) the top element of the Loop Return Stack (since one loop is being exited). Then it will use this to form the name of the label in the jump statement. The state of the stack cannot be changed at this time because the code generator for the NEXT statement at the end of the loop will also need the information contained on the stack.

There will be just one line of assembler code ultimately generated for each UNLOOP statement. There was a much greater amount of work to be done on behalf of this statement in the interpreter. This was because a reusable resource of the interpretive system—a control table—had to be deallocated and returned. No such table is necessary in compiled code. In fact, the UNLOOP statement itself isn't necessary. We included this statement in the language because of the difficulties caused by jumping out of loops in an interpretive system. There are no such difficulties with compiled code. Even a GOTO taken out of the middle of a loop will produce compiled code that will run successfully. However, it was our desire to show an interpreter and a compiler for exactly the same language, so we must implement the UNLOOP statement in the compiled version.

The macro definition for this statement would be as follows. Remember that the code generator will furnish the number of the loop being exited.

```
1      MACRO
2      UNLOOP     &L
3      JMP        LEND&L  +  7
4      MACEND
```

If the source program called for a jump out of the third loop to be encountered, the number three would be on the Loop Return Stack; and the macro call generated by the compiler would be

```
UNLOOP   3
```

12.6 *CODE GENERATION FOR ALGEBRAIC EXPRESSIONS*

The types of algorithms used by this compiler to generate code for algebraic expressions are very similar to the algorithms used by the interpreter to handle expressions. We ask the reader to review those algorithms now. There are two steps in generating code to evaluate an algebraic expression. The first step is to convert the expression to Reverse Polish Notation. We do this using exactly the same algorithm that was described for the interpreter. In the second step, instead of evaluating the RPN string by our evaluation algorithm, we will output assembler code that will set up the evaluation in the way we have described, but postpone the actual evaluation until execution time. This idea may seem strange, but an example will serve to clarify it.

Recall that what you had to do in order to evaluate an RPN string was to move through the string from left to right. Any time an operand was encountered, it would be put on the stack. Any time an operator was encountered, the proper number of operands would be popped from the stack, the operator applied, and the result put back on the stack. After the string was exhausted, the result would be on the top of the stack. What we will do now is generate assembler code which will cause this same process to be carried out, but it will be carried out at execution time, not at compile time.

Let's look at an example. The expression that we will generate code for is on the right hand side of the following assignment statement:

        10 K = (X + Y)/2

The expression (but not the whole statement) converted to RPN looks like this:

        XY + 2 /

The assembler code which would be generated to reduce this expression to a single value (i.e., evaluate it) is shown in Figure 12-11.

The reader may be wondering about the fact that the expression is only one part of an assignment statement. What happens to the rest of it? The Code Generator for an Algebraic Expression would be called as a subroutine of the Generator for Assignment Statements. The Generator for Assignment Statements will append a macro call onto the end of the code that corresponds to the algebraic expression. This macro will assume that the result of evaluating the algebraic expression is to be found on the top of the stack. So it will prescribe code that will obtain that value and write it into the storage location associated with the variable (K%) that is being assigned a value.

For instance, the code that would be appended at the end of the code shown in Figure 12-11 would be

        POP   H
        SHLD K%

This code, taken together with the code produced for the expression, is the complete equivalent of the particular assignment statement shown in the example.

The expression being evaluated is (X + Y)/2.
In Reverse Polish Notation, it would be written as XY + 2/.

X generates:	LHLD	X%
	PUSH	H
Y generates:	LHLD	Y%
	PUSH	H
+ generates:	POP	D
	POP	H
	DAD	D
	PUSH	H
2 generates:	LXI	H,2
	PUSH	H
/ generates:	POP	D
	POP	H
	CALL	DIV
	PUSH	H

Figure 12-11:   An Example of Generation of Code from an RPN Expression. This shows the assembler code that would be output by the compiler to evaluate a simple algebraic expression. Evaluating an expression means reducing it to a single number.

Other expressions can all be handled in a similar way. Figure 12-12 shows a general routine which will take any expression written in RPN and generate code from it. In the design of this routine, we have assumed that multiplication and division will be done by calling two machine language routines. They find their operands in the DE and HL register pairs and leave their answers in the HL pair. In order to use the divide routine properly, a convention will have to be established for which operands are in which registers. For addition and multiplication, this doesn't matter. For division we will assume that the number in the HL register is divided by the number in the DE register and the quotient is left in the HL pair. If there is a remainder, it is discarded.

The 16 bit routines will need to be appended to the output the compiler produces. Most microprocessors, at least of the older sort, do not have provision for hardware implemented multiply and divide.

Actually, we are going to do subtraction as well by calling a subsidiary subtract routine, since the Intel 8080 has no sixteen bit subtract instruction. It is probably best to deploy the arguments for the subtract routine on analogy to the 8 bit subtract instruction. That is, the DE pair will be subtracted from the HL pair and the result will be left in the HL pair. This subtract routine will also be useful in processing a unary minus. In this case, we just want to change the sign of the top element on the stack, so we can pop it off, subtract it from zero, which changes the sign, and then push it back on the stack.

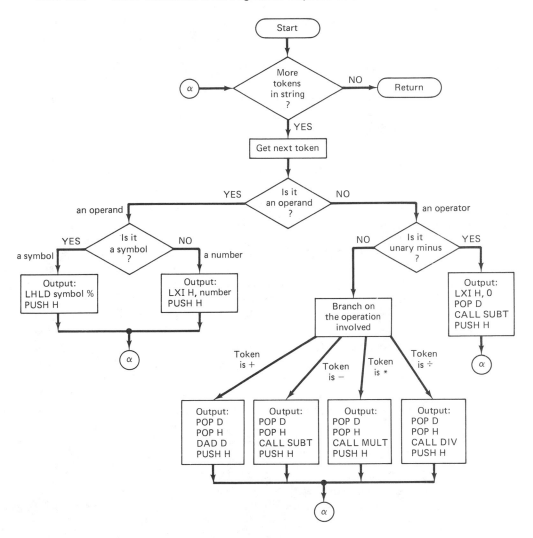

Figure 12-12:   The Algebraic Expression Code Generator. The routine translates any RPN string into a sequence of assembler language instructions which, when executed, will produce a value that is the same as the value of the RPN string.

Before concluding this section we must point out a serious but not obvious deficiency in our otherwise very simple way of handling arithmetic expressions. Expressions in TINY BASIC must be such that no intermediate results pursuant to evaluating an expression are larger than can be represented in a 16 bit number. This is part of the language definition. If an intermediate result is larger than this, our 16 bit arithmetic routines wouldn't be able to handle the number and it wouldn't be able to fit within one unit on the stack which is a 16 bit word. A computation like the following, then, is illegal:

```
Z = (3*32767 - 2*32767 - 16384)
```

In a more usable language from the standpoint of expressions, all arithmetic would have to be done to a greater precision than the number of bits in the largest number allowed in the language. For BASIC, with 16 bit integer variables, it probably means all arithmetic would be done with 32 bit routines and all transactions with the stack would be in terms of these larger data units.

12.7 A COMPLETE EXAMPLE OF A COMPILED PROGRAM

We now wish to show the results of compilation on an entire program. Figure 12-13 shows a short program written in TINY BASIC which computes the sum of all of the integers from 1 to 100. Figure 12-14 shows the primary output of the compiler which is a string of configured macro calls and assembler code. Figure 12-15 shows what the program would look like after it was expanded by a macroassembler.

It is interesting to notice the number of program lines it takes to express this program in high level language (TINY BASIC) vs. the number of lines for the equivalent program in assembler language (after macro expansion). Depending on how you count, there are about 4.5 assembler lines per program line in TINY BASIC. This is typical. Such a comparison normally depends both on the sophistication of the higher level language and on the strength of the instruction set of the computer.

TINY BASIC implemented on an advanced microprocessor or minicomputer would probably expand by a factor of 3 or 4 in going to assembler language, because the computer instruction set would be more powerful than the 8080. If we restrict our view to the 8080, each statement in a more complex language, like FORTRAN or PL/1, might expand to something like 8 lines of assembler code. Statements in these higher level languages do more than statements in BASIC.

Figure 12-15 does not show all of the output of the compiler. For instance, appended to the end of the macro file, there will be a Variables Declaration Block, and several library routines (depending on what computer is being used) such as sixteen bit routines

```
10      REM     SUM INTEGERS FROM 1 TO 100
20      S = 0
30      FOR  I = 1 TO 100
40      S = S + I
50      NEXT  I
60      PRINT  S
70      END
```

Figure 12-13:   The Sum of Integers Example Program Before Compilation. This is a simple baseline program in TINY BASIC. It involves a short loop with some arithmetic inside it. We will follow this example through the compilation process.

```
ASGN1      S, 0
FOR        1, I, 100, 1
LHLD       S%
PUSH       H
LHLD       I%
PUSH       H
POP        D
POP        H
DAD        D
PUSH       H
ASGN3      S
NEXT       I, 1
OUTPUT     S
```

Figure 12-14:   Partial Compiler Output for the Sum of Integers Example Program. This mixture of macro calls and assembler code is the directly relevant part of the output of the compiler working on our baseline program. The complete compiler output would also contain macro definitions, the Variables Declaration Block, and subroutines for 16 bit arithmetic.

8080 Assembler Version

```
         LXI     H, 0     ⎫
         SHLD    S%       ⎬  S = 0
                          ⎭

         LXI     H, 1     ⎫
         SHLD    I%       ⎪
LSTR1:   LHLD    I%       ⎪
         LXI     D, -100  ⎬  FOR I = 1 TO 100
         DCX     D        ⎪
         DAD     D        ⎪
         JC      LEND1    ⎭

         LHLD    S%       ⎫
         PUSH    H        ⎪
         LHLD    I%       ⎪
         PUSH    H        ⎬  the expression
         POP     D        ⎪  S + I
         POP     H        ⎪
         DAD     D        ⎪
         PUSH    H        ⎭

         POP     H        ⎫
         SHLD    S%       ⎬  S = S + I
                          ⎭

         LHLD    I%       ⎫
         INX     H        ⎪
         SHLD    I%       ⎬  NEXT I
         JMP     LSTR1    ⎪
LEND1:   EQU     $        ⎭

         LHLD    S%       ⎫
         CALL    OUTP     ⎬  PRINT S
```

Figure 12-15:   The Sum of Integers Example Program After Macro Expansion. This is the form the program would be in after the first processing in a macroassembler. One can clearly see here how much more economical it is to program in a higher level language. In this system, one statement in TINY BASIC is equivalent to about 4.5 assembler statements.

for subtraction, multiplication, and division, and the routine for the evaluation of Boolean expressions. The standard macro definitions of the language will be at the front of the file, before all macro calls. And finally, since compilers usually produce linkable output, an RORG (relocatable origin) statement will be inserted at the very beginning of the file and an END statement will be placed after all of the other output.

12.8 A COMPARISON OF INTERPRETERS AND COMPILERS

The principle difference between these two important classes of language processors is that interpreters directly execute algorithms while compilers translate algorithms into another language, usually on a lower level. In addition to this fundamental conceptual difference many other subsidiary differences arise when the language processor is implemented. We've looked at the same language implemented in two different ways so we should now be in a good position to appreciate further comparisons. The following points seem relevant:

1. The primary issues that must be dealt with in designing an interpreter are
   - Symbol Table Organization
   - Parsing
   - Evaluation of Algebraic Expressions
   - Processing Routines for Each Possible Statement Type

   Compiler construction deals with a parallel set of issues:
   - Symbol Table Organization
   - Parsing
   - Code Generation for Algebraic Expressions
   - Code Generation for Each Possible Statement Type

2. When a program processed by an interpreter is being interpreted (executed), the program exists in memory as an ASCII string of characters. The program may exist in exactly the same form in which it was typed in from the keyboard, or it may exist in a slightly modified and compressed form if the editor does some preprocessing on the program as it is installed in memory. Even with preprocessing, essentially the only form in which the program exists is raw text. A compiled program, on the other hand, exists in memory at execution time as machine code. It is ready to be executed by the CPU with no intermediation by any other software module.

3. At execution time, interpreted code needs a run time package called the intrepreter. That is, the program alone is not enough. Compiled code can run on its own. The CPU is just unleashed at the beginning of the program, and from there on executing the program is a matter for hardware.

4. At execution, interpreted code is generally much slower than compiled code. On the average an interpreted program will run an order of magnitude slower. The

reason for this is that with an interpreter, every line has to be parsed before it is executed. This becomes a particular burden in loops. If a loop will be done 1000 times, each statement inside the loop will be parsed 1000 times. With compiled code, each statement is parsed only once, and that is at compilation time, not at execution time.

5. An interpreter is generally easier to implement than a full-blown compiler which takes code all the way to machine language. This is one reason why the only software supplied when a newly designed computer enters the market place is frequently an interpreter for one of the common languages. Another reason is that low-end interpretive systems can run with cheap peripherals. A compiler system requires at least a disk to be able to prepare programs in a reasonable amount of time.

6. Programs in interpreted form require less storage space than the same program in compiled form. This is particularly evident on time sharing systems where each user is given only a small piece of memory. Quite respectable sized programs can still be run at each terminal if the system is interpretive. A system like this will generally be set up so that all the programs running concurrently will share the same run time package (which is the interpreter itself). Systems code that can be shared in this way is said to be reentrant.

7. The program code for interpretive programs generally has poor internal documentation (i.e., comment lines in the program) relative to what would be found in a program to be compiled. The reason for this is that with interpretive systems, all the program text is stored in raw form in memory, both comments and program statements. Programmers are reluctant to put in many comments because this will eat up space and make the program run slowly. In compiler systems, when the program is compiled, the comments are stripped off, so the output contains nothing but executable code.

8. A program to be interpreted is usually developed all at once, as a single big module, because there is usually no facility for linking together code to be interpreted. Compiled programs can be developed as separate modules and linked later.

9. Short programs can be developed and debugged much more rapidly on interpretive systems than with compilers. This is because interpreters are interactive. The ease with which you can go back and forth between editing and execution is such that problems can be identified and corrected quickly. On the other hand, when programs grow beyond a certain length, it becomes easier to develop the program on a compiler system. The modularity that you can enforce in longer programs, by developing them in modules and then linking them together, and the better internal commenting, explain why people find that long or complex programs can be developed best in compiler implementations.

It appears, in light of these comments, that the ideal programming system would have two components. One would be a fast interpretive language that is interactive, that is user friendly, that can be commented well, and that can be linked. There should also be an associated compiler that can take the exact code debugged on the interpreter and make fast, compact machine code out of it. Most programming systems do not have these properties, but some are just beginning to emerge that do, and they are beginning to emerge in the microcomputer world, where things change faster than in other segments of the computer industry.

STUDY QUESTIONS AND EXERCISES

1. Write down the assembler code that would be generated by the compiler in order to translate the statement that follows. Include the two lines of code that assign the result to K. That is, instead of writing the assignment macro, write down the code that it stands for. The statement to be translated is

    K = (X − (Y*2))/(Z + 3)

2. For the following program in TINY BASIC, show the output of the compiler and show what that output would look like after the compiler output was passed through the macroassembler.

    ```
    10    X = 0
    20    FOR  I  =  1 TO L
    30    FOR  J  =  1 TO M
    40    FOR  K  =  1 TO N
    50    X  =  X + K − I
    60    NEXT  K
    70    NEXT  J
    80    NEXT  I
    90    END
    ```

3. Write a single macro for the Assignment statement that encompasses all three cases of assignment by using conditional assembly.

4. Write a macro for loop beginnings that could be used if the syntax of loop statements were relaxed so that the beginning value of the loop counter could be any constant or variable instead of the constant "1." Assume that the loop will only be used to count in the upward direction.

5. How would the compiler design have to be altered so that the number of arguments in Input and Output statements would not be limited to three?

6. In our discussion of the IF statement, we showed that twelve different kinds of Boolean expressions were possible as the criteria for whether the branch indicated in the statement should be taken or not. A macro was written for Case 4. Write a similar macro for Case 6. Produce the macro in two forms—one that depends on in-line code, and one that uses the utility routine for Boolean expression evaluation.

7. Compare the way the TINY BASIC interpreter and the TINY BASIC compiler access their symbol tables. The interpreter uses hashing. What method does the compiler use?

8. Compiled code generally does not need any kind of a run time package, except the operating system. Can you think of a circumstance where a run time package would be desirable for

compiled code? Hint: if there is something every program uses, should it be appended to each program, or should the system somehow have only one copy?

9. Outline what would be necessary in order to add a Computed Jump statement to the TINY BASIC language. Here is an example of the syntax of this hypothetical statement:

```
COMJUMP  (10, 100, 70), I
```

If I is negative, the next statement to be executed is 10. If I is zero, the next statement is 100. If I is positive, the next statement is 70. Of course, any variable name can be used in place of I. Write a macro for the COMJUMP statement.

10. Make a list of the most important syntax and logic errors that should be checked for by the TINY BASIC compiler, and suggest the best place(s) to do this within the overall architecture that has been presented.

11. This question asks you to imagine a TINY BASIC compiler that takes TINY BASIC program text as input and produces relocatable machine code as output. Suggest an architecture for this compiler. How many passes would be required? What would happen on each pass? Hint, some operations can be coalesced or omitted so the number of passes will be less than the five required for a compiler that produces macroassembler output.

13

The Systems Environment: III

13.1 INTRODUCTION TO LARGER MICROCOMPUTER SYSTEMS

The next natural grouping of microcomputer systems overlaps the traditional territory of the minicomputer. These are systems with enough inherent computing power so that a number of users or tasks can share the CPU and the supporting peripheral devices. The lower ends of this range have clearly been taken over by the micros, and the rest of the range is about to go. From a systems programmer's point of view, the type of programming required will be very similar whether we are dealing with a mini or one of the upstart micros. The hardware is similar, except it has been integrated and compacted. The functions that must be served by a system at this level have not changed from traditional requirements, so we might expect to see a high degree of continuity in the systems programming. Indeed, it is there.

The type of systems software which is characteristic of this level of computing power is a simple multi-tasking operating system with interrupt driven input and output. The following is what multi-tasking means. There will be a number of programs in different parts of the computer's memory at the same time. Each one is called a task. The CPU's attention will move among the tasks spending a short period executing the code for one task and then switching to another. The total amount of execution time available is divided among the executing tasks. Because the switching is done very fast, from the outside, it will appear that the tasks are executing simultaneously. Actually there is a better word to describe this kind of task execution. It is not simultaneous, but concurrent execution.

One common use for this kind of computer is in instrumentation or in engineering applications. For instance, the computer might have the job of collecting, processing, and displaying data simultaneously, or it might be controlling a complex machine of some sort. The common characteristic of all these applications is that they are best serviced by constructing a program in which a number of loosely coupled tasks will appear to run simultaneously. Frequently, this area is called real time programming.

As an example, imagine an instrument that has the task of creating a picture of a patient's heart using an array of ultrasonic sensors that can bounce sound off internal body structures and receive echoes—in effect, a medical sonar. The task of the instrument is to create a television picture of the heart that moves in real time as the heart beats. The program to control this kind of an instrument would probably be set up with the work divided among a number of tasks that would run in the computer concurrently. The following is one way that this work might be done. Task 1 continually scans the heart with the ultrasonic ranger and fills raw data into a series of buffers. Task 2 does computations on the raw data to generate an instantaneous outline of the heart. And Task 3 takes the outline data and continuously updates a picture on the television screen. All of these things have to be done more or less simultaneously; otherwise, data and picture quality will be lost. It is the job of a multi-tasking operating system to coordinate tasks that must act as if they are executing at the same time.

Perhaps the most common use for a small multi-tasking operating system is in the small business computer. This kind of a machine will typically have several terminals geographically close to the CPU and a printer and disk subsystem that is shared by everyone at the installation. See Figure 13-1. A typical work pattern on this equipment might be the following. At one terminal, a typist might be composing a letter using a word processing program. At another terminal, someone might be preparing the bills for last month's sales. At a third terminal, a clerk might be using a computerized inventory system to record a shipment of parts that has just arrived.

There are some common characteristics shared by these business applications. Quite a bit of computer memory space is required for the programs. They do not require much computation time compared, say, to what would be needed for a task in engineering or scientific computation. And the speed at which these programs can execute is usually limited by the rates of various input/output processes. One limiting rate will be the speed at which the disk can be accessed. Another will be the time it takes the operator to type in commands from the keyboard. Since most of these tasks really do not require much computing power, they are eminently suited to sharing the resources of a single CPU.

How will the software picture change as we move into these larger microcomputer systems? The new software features that we will find will be in the areas of input/output programming and system control. The program production software—assemblers, editors, compilers, etc.—is essentially the same. In the second part of this chapter we discuss how to write I/O handlers that take advantage of the interrupt system. It has been our plan all along, when introducing a new systems environment, to introduce simultaneously the type of I/O programming that belongs in that environment. The more complex demands for system control made by multiple users and/or multiple tasks require a new kind of operating system. This is a big topic, and the details will be covered in the next chapter. However, we wish to spend a little more time here introducing the topic so that the reader will appreciate how interrupt driven input/output programming fits into an operating system environment.

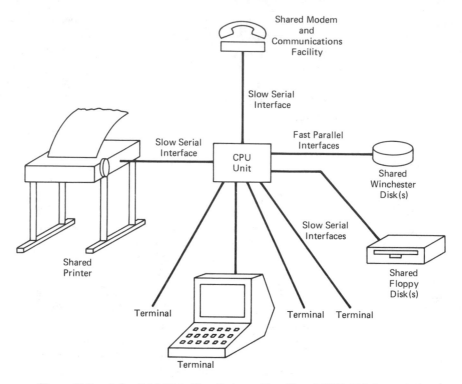

Figure 13-1:   A Small Multiple User System with a Shared CPU. This is a typical hardware configuration for a small business computer that would employ a multiple user operating system. The operating system would supervise the sharing of all the expensive peripheral equipment among all the users. The only equipment not shared would be terminals—one per user.

A multi-user system and a multi-tasking system are very closely related. The basic feature is that several programs share the CPU. If there is a terminal associated with each of the programs, then it is a multi-user system. If there is a terminal associated with only one of the programs and that terminal is used as the system I/O device, then we are dealing with a simple multi-tasking system. Combinations are also possible.

To develop the context for interrupt driven input and output programming, let's look at the memory map for a typical multi-user computer system, like the one in Figure 13-1. There are, of course, many variations in multi-user operating systems which we can't touch on now. But we certainly can construct an example which contains many features representative of this class of software, and that is what we are going to do. The memory map is shown in Figure 13-2. We are not at this time specifying any particular CPU.

Most of the memory space in this example system is taken up by three different programs which will share the CPU. As the CPU switches its attention among these programs, it is said to be time slicing. Each of the three programs controls a terminal through which a user interacts with the system.

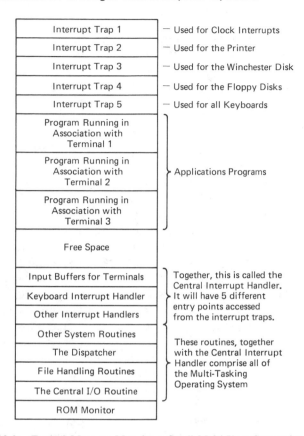

Interrupt Trap 1	— Used for Clock Interrupts
Interrupt Trap 2	— Used for the Printer
Interrupt Trap 3	— Used for the Winchester Disk
Interrupt Trap 4	— Used for the Floppy Disks
Interrupt Trap 5	— Used for all Keyboards
Program Running in Association with Terminal 1	
Program Running in Association with Terminal 2	Applications Programs
Program Running in Association with Terminal 3	
Free Space	
Input Buffers for Terminals	Together, this is called the Central Interrupt Handler. It will have 5 different entry points accessed from the interrupt traps.
Keyboard Interrupt Handler	
Other Interrupt Handlers	
Other System Routines	These routines, together with the Central Interrupt Handler comprise all of the Multi-Tasking Operating System
The Dispatcher	
File Handling Routines	
The Central I/O Routine	
ROM Monitor	

Figure 13-2: Typical Memory Map for a Small Multi-User Computing System. This figure shows three programs which are sharing the use of a single CPU. It also shows some of the operating system modules that will be necessary to manage such a system.

The lowest five locations in memory are taken up with interrupt traps. This organization implies that there may be up to five different interrupt sources in the system. When an interrupt arrives from any of these sources, the CPU will stop what it is doing and then go and execute the code that begins in the interrupt trap that is associated with the source of the signal. We will discuss this process in more detail later. The interrupt traps will usually contain jump instructions that move control to particular entry points in a part of the operating system called the Central Interrupt Handler. This module contains code to service the interrupt, that is, to take whatever action is appropriate given that some external device is calling for attention. After the interrupt is serviced, the original program will be placed back in execution at the place where it left off.

There will be another part of the operating system that is associated with I/O. It is the Central Input/Output Routine. This is a routine that is always in memory. It can be called by any program any time that program needs to do a piece of input or output. It is like the BDOS package in CP/M except that this code is reentrant and it works in cooperation with the interrupt system. The Central Input/Output Routine and the Central Interrupt Handler work together. The Central Input/Output Routine is used to begin an I/O process, and the Central Interrupt Handler oversees its intermediate stages and completes it.

Let's follow a typical scenario for the work that the CPU does in a system like this over a short time period. Perhaps it starts by executing in Program 1 for some predetermined interval, say, $1/10$ of a second. The end of this period will be marked by a clock interrupt. This will cause control to get into the operating system dispatching function via the interrupt handler for clock interrupts. The dispatcher and associated task switching routines will cause the system to stop work on Program 1 and start work on Program 2 for the predetermined period that the system uses as a time slice. There will be another clock interrupt. Program 2 will be suspended and work will start on Program 3, etc. We will discuss how to implement this kind of sequence in the next chapter.

If the running programs are doing input and output, it will be desirable to alter this even-handed division of CPU time so that no time is wasted in waiting for slow I/O devices. For instance, suppose that an interactive program comes to a point where it must get a response from the user via the terminal. A prompt will be issued that appears on the terminal screen, and then all the program can do is wait. It may take the user several seconds to respond to the prompt. In order that this time not be wasted, the program will interact with the I/O system in such a way that the program will be suspended, i.e., removed from the time slicing rotation, until the user finally makes a response. The system finds out that the user has made a response because a keyboard interrupt will come in when he finally presses a key. Using the keyboard interrupt handler (which is part of the Central Interrupt Handler), the system will collect the user's entire response. When this has been acquired, the system will reinstate the suspended program into the time slicing rotation, because now it has data and it can proceed efficiently with its work.

The fact that devices signal their status with interrupts allows the operating system to allocate its time to tasks that can use that time. This is why interrupt driven I/O and multi-tasking operating systems are found together. Programs no longer have to sit in unproductive waiting loops monitoring a status port to see when some I/O activity is finished. This makes for much more efficient use of the CPU, but it also makes for fairly complicated systems programs. We will explore interrupt driven I/O handlers in detail later in this chapter.

We have introduced the new software that occurs in this systems environment. There will also be substantial increases in hardware performance on these larger microsystems. We will catalog these capabilities here, and cover the details in the next section of this chapter. We speak now of multi-user systems because they are somewhat more demanding of the hardware than simple multi-tasking systems.

What increments in hardware performance will these systems have to work with? First of all, there will be more powerful microprocessors. Multi-user systems have been set up with the traditional 8-bit microprocessors, but, except for certain specialized applications, they have tended to be too slow. The newer 16 bit processors have enough horsepower to run multi-user applications efficiently.

A second factor is that more users generate a requirement for more disk storage capacity and faster access times so that the shared disk doesn't become a system bottleneck. A new kind of disk technology services these needs—the Winchester disk. More users also mean that there will be competition for the amount of memory the machine has available to hold its programs. We will consider various techniques that have been used to expand the amount of memory that the processor can access.

A final factor is that all these kinds of computers make heavy use of the interrupt system. Very frequently this requires use of supplemental hardware outside of the processor to sort out information having to do with where the interrupts come from, what priority they have, and what interrupt trap should be used in response to a particular interrupt. It is not surprising that this should be so. After all, an interrupt is just an on/off digital signal calling for attention in the world external to the CPU. A one bit signal line cannot carry much information by itself.

Consider all these things to be the hardware attributes of the last systems environment that we will study.

13.2 HARDWARE CHARACTERISTICS AND INTERFACING

13.2.1 More Capable Microprocessors

The 16 bit microprocessors were developed to fill some system niches for which the 8 bit machines lacked sufficient strength. These devices appeared on the market roughly 5 years after the first 8 bit microprocessors. They are much more complicated machines. For instance, a Motorola 68000 processor incorporates about 70,000 transistors on the chip, while an 8 bit processor like the Intel 8085 uses about 5000 transistors. These numbers are an illustration of the empirical law which says that the number of transistors on microprocessor chips has tended to double every year. The 16 bit processors that are presently in widest use are the following:

- Intel 8086
- Motorola 68000
- Zilog Z-8000
- Texas Instruments 99000
- National Semiconductor NS16032

The first 16 bit microprocessor was the Texas Instruments 9900. This machine was slow by present standards, but it had a very elegant and ingenious architecture.

In this section we want to discuss all the 16 bit microprocessors together and to try to quantify in what ways they are more powerful than the preceeding generation of 8 bit processors. The advantages appear to lie in three areas. The newer processors are faster. They have expanded address spaces. And they have better instruction sets.

How did the 16 bit processors get to be faster? This does not just mean that the clock rate on the processor was speeded up so more execution cycles occur in a given time. This certainly has happened. But the same type of improvements have been made in the 8 bit processors, so, speaking relatively, there has been no change. Many of the newer processors are pipelined, so that while one instruction is being executed, another is being fetched. This has definitely resulted in speed increases—perhaps on the order of a 20–30 percent improvement in performance over a nonpipelined architecture.

The main speed increases come from two other factors. The 16 bit buses are twice as wide so that a larger chunk of information can be manipulated at one time. It doesn't matter whether the information is an instruction, an address, or data. The same advantage applies. The other thing is that the 16 bit instructions do more than similar instructions on a smaller processor. We need an example of this. Let's compare an 8 bit and a 16 bit processor working on the same task. The task will be to move the information in a single word (16 bits) from one location in memory to another location. Let's also assume that all instructions take one clock cycle for set-up plus one additional clock cycle for every memory read or write that has to be done in connection with the instruction. Let's assume the two addresses are called ALPHA and BETA. A program in 8080 assembler language to do this task would be

```
LHLD   ALPHA
SHLD   BETA
```

The same program written in the instruction set of a typical 16 bit microprocessor would be something like

```
MOV   ALPHA, BETA
```

Obviously there is an immediate advantage in one instruction doing the work of two.

The other advantage comes from the wider bus. Fewer memory accesses are required. The 8080 type program requires 10 hypothetical clock cycles to do memory accesses to set up both the instructions and the data. It also requires 2 clock cycles to actually decode and execute the instructions. The total number of cycles is 12. The hypothetical 16 bit processor requires 5 clock cycles to move instructions and data and 1 cycle to set up to do the work. The total number of cycles is 6. Here we see time required to do a typical task dropping by a factor of two. The execution of other tasks will show a similar pattern.

Another advantage of the 16 bit microprocessors is that they have expanded address spaces, and here we need to look at both memory and registers. There usually are more registers, which makes programming easier. For instance, the Motorola 68000 has sixteen 32 bit general purpose registers. We can think of the registers as a special part of the address space.

All of the newer processors have more address lines coming off the CPU chip than the 8 bit processors had. In some machines this means there is a large and clear memory address space any location of which is equally usable. In other machines, those with the so-called segmented address spaces, the address space has been enlarged, but it is difficult to use all the addresses at once. These machines typically have a 64 kilobyte window that can be positioned anywhere within the machine's full address space. All of these locations are immediately accessible, but to access any other area of memory, an instruction has to be executed that will reposition the memory window. This is not as desirable as having a single large address space.

One other address space feature that has become common on the new machines is for there to be as many as four completely separate address spaces. For instance, there could be one space for user programs and one for systems programs. There could also be one space for user program data and one for systems program data. Enforcing this kind of separation decreases the chances of one program accidentally destroying other programs or the operating system in a multiprogramming environment.

A final common advantage that the newer processors have is better instruction sets. Not just richer, but better. The older instruction sets had just about all the necessary instructions, but some of them were difficult to use. Some of the instructions could only be used in particular ways that were hard to remember. A goal in the design of the newer instruction sets has been orthogonality—that is, every instruction should reference its operands in exactly the same ways through a uniform set of addressing modes.

The newer sets have tended to converge toward a small number of instructions, which can be easily remembered but can be used in many different contexts through many addressing modes.

The instruction sets of many of the newer processors are the result of analyses which were conducted to determine which instructions are used most frequently in typical programs. These instructions were given the shortest operation codes. The result is that programs written for these processors are very compact in the amount of memory used for program storage.

The 16 bit processors also have a few really new instructions that were not on the original 8 bit processors. For instance, it was predictable that users would want 16 bit multiplication and division instructions if they could get them. All the new processors have included this type of instruction. Other less obvious ones are the Test and Set instruction, which is useful only in a multi-tasking environment. There also are instructions for coordinating processors if they are going to be used in a system with multiple CPU's.

13.2.2 Winchester Disks

Small multi-terminal microcomputer based computer systems frequently have a hard disk storage device for their bulk memory. Cheap Winchester type disks are becoming very popular in this capacity. Conceptually there will not be much difference in what is required to set up a comptuer system using a floppy disk or a hard disk. The software looks much the same.

There are, however, extreme performance differences between the two types of disks owing to a different type of media used for recording and a different deployment of the read/write heads. The media used by a Winchester type disk is a platter of aluminum coated with magnetic material. Floppy disks of course can be removed from the disk drive. The platter on Winchester drives usually can not be removed. This will affect the pattern of how some installations do business.

Winchester disks have a considerably faster data transfer rate than floppies. This is because they rotate faster—typically ten times faster than a floppy disk. A Winchester disk can rotate faster because the read/write head floats above the media surface on a cushion of air. The head in a floppy disk actually is in contact with the disk surface when it is reading or writing. In a disk in which the head floats, contact with the media is disasterous. A particle of dust between the head and the media would have a similar effect. This is one reason why these type of disks are sealed and the air inside is continually filtered.

Winchester disks can also hold much more data than floppies. Since the unit is sealed, all mechanical parts can be made to operate at much more critical tolerances. This means the tracks can be closer together. The thermal properties of the media also affect tract density. On a floppy disk the track density is 48 tracks per inch. There is a severe problem with higher densities. The Mylar of the disk expands unevenly with increasing temperature, and so a thin data track can wander away from under a head. The aluminum disks used in the hard disk technology expand much more evenly with temperature. So track densities in the neighborhood of 500 per inch are possible. Typical data storage capacities for eight inch Winchester disks are in the 5, 10, or 20 megabyte range.

The controllers used with Winchester disks are very complicated and costly. They have to do much more than simple floppy disk controllers. The positioning problem is more acute, and, since data transfer rates are so high, much electronics must be devoted to keeping various noise sources from corrupting the data signal. These things are a problem for the interface between the controller and the disk drive. The interface between the computer and the controller, however, will be quite simple. Most controllers will contain built-in microprocessors so they will respond to even higher level commands than simple disk drives. The typical way to make a disk access using one of these systems would be for the computer to set up the DMA apparatus, and then make a request for a particular track and sector to the controller. The controller will handle positioning. It will access the data using DMA, and it will give the CPU an interrupt signal when it is finished.

The fact that a Winchester disk is not removable from the drive has some consequences for how the storage system is used. In particular, back-up is a problem. How is the user to protect himself against loss of critical data if the drive crashes? The remedy with floppy disks is to make frequent copies of all important information on back-up disks. This can not be done with a Winchester system short of maintaining a second costly drive that does nothing but back-up the first drive. An alternate solution is to build a fast tape drive directly into the Winchester unit. The disk can then be backed-up onto the tape, and the tape can be removed for archiving.

How can we sum up the capability of the Winchester disk? These devices can hold between 10 and 100 times as much data as a floppy, and they cost only 2 or 3 times as much for a complete disk subsystem. From the programmer's viewpoint, they are also just as easy to use as a floppy disk.

13.2.3 Expanding the Memory Address Space

Applications that are natural for multi-tasking operating systems generally demand more memory than can be easily attached to 8080 type microprocessors. A number of ways around this bottleneck have been devised. Let's now look at the problem of extending memory on a small system. If you are lucky, the processor has a large direct addressing range and you are not at present using all of that range. In this case more memory chips, with associated decoders, can quite simply be attached to the data and address buses. Modern 16 bit processors like the Zilog Z-8000 and the Motorola 68000 have direct addressing in the megabyte range. These processors have 23 and 24 address lines coming directly off the processor chip so that large amounts of memory can be handled easily.

Older processors such as the Intel 8080, the Zilog Z-80, or the Motorola 6800 only have 16 address lines coming off the processor chip. This means a maximum of 64K bytes of memory can be directly addressed. The most common way to expand the memory space with these processors is to use bank switching. This is a procedure whereby different sets of up to 64K worth of memory chips can be electronically switched into contact with the CPU. With bank switching, the processor can have as much memory as you want, but only 64K bytes of it will be active at any given time.

A simple way to implement bank switching is to attach as many memory chips to the buses as you want (with suitable drivers and receivers), but only deliver enable signals to a certain subset of the chips at any time. This can be done by writing a word into a

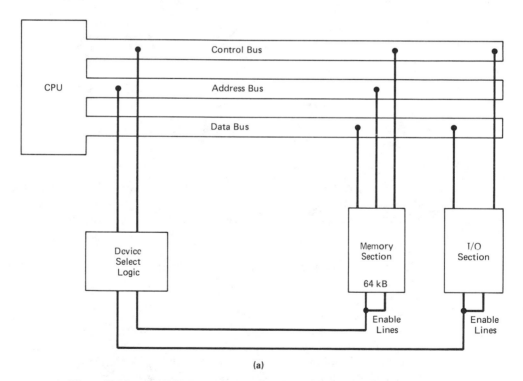

(a)

Figure 13-3A: An 8080 Type System Using Directly Addressed Memory. This is a simple computer system in which all the memory address signals are received directly from the CPU's address bus. The width of that bus determines the maximum size of system memory.

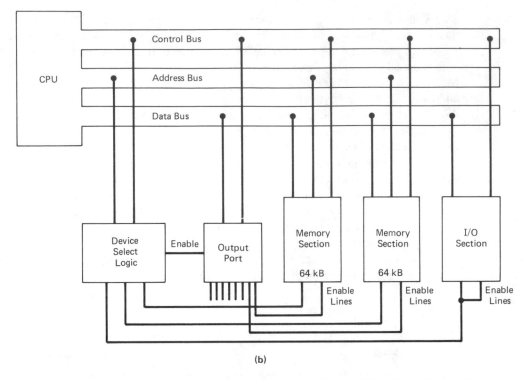

(b)

Figure 13-3B: An 8080 Type System Using Bank Switched Memory for Extended Addressing. This system has implemented a 128 kilobyte memory section attached to a processor that can only directly access 64 kilobytes worth of memory. By writing into the controlling output port, the processor can effectively switch one half or the other half of the memory into contact with the system at any given time.

port that will latch this data and use it in a simple logic network to steer enable signals to the correct chips. Figure 13-3A shows an 8080 type processor with 64K bytes of normal memory. Figure 13-3B shows the same processor set up so that one or the other bank of 64K capacity can be switched into use, depending on what word is written into the control port.

The 16 bit microprocessors with segmented memory address spaces have basically implemented a bank switched memory with all the controlling electronics residing inside the CPU chip.

Bank switched memories are a reasonable solution for setting up multi-tasking systems on microcomputers wherein the program belonging to each user is not longer than 64K bytes. If you require programs longer than 64K bytes, this kind of memory is really not a viable solution. It is too hard to write an application program if you are always conforming to the 64K limit or switching back and forth between two banks. It is not efficient to make a programmer watch these things. He should be able to program just as if he had as long an address space as is needed. And by far the best way to do this is to get a microcomputer with a large addressing range.

A third way to recover from addressing limitations on a processor with a small addressing space is to use some memory management hardware—typically a chip made for this purpose that will go with a particular processor. Coming into the chip are the address lines from the microprocessor. Coming out the other side is an expanded set of address lines that represent new addressing capacity. The memory section will be built to interface to the memory management chip rather than the processor itself. What the management chip does is map the processor's small address space into some part of a bigger address space defined by the number of output lines. This mapping can be changed at will by writing into a control register on the manager chip. For instance, let's say this mapping chip controls a 256K byte addressing space. It divides the basic address space of the eight bit processor into four blocks of 16K bytes, which we will call pages. It will allow you to make dynamic associations between each of the 16K pages in the micro-processor's address space and any 16K page in the larger space available to the memory manager. The larger address space contains sixteen of the 16K pages.

At some given time the address mappings might look like this:

- 1st page in processor space—1st page in manager space
- 2nd page in processor space—2nd page in manager space

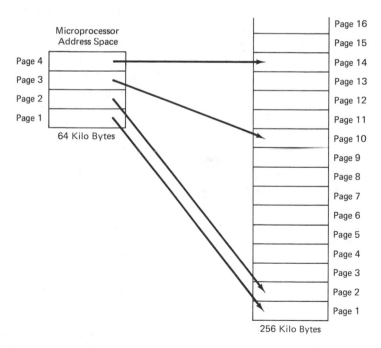

Figure 13-4: Expanding the System Address Space with a Memory Management Unit. A memory manager stands between the microprocessor's address bus and the address lines that contact the physical memory. It expands the number of address lines. The computer can still generate only 64K addresses, but they may be retargeted to land on memory cells at arbitrarily different places within the 256K physical memory.

- 3rd page in processor space—10th page in manager space
- 4th page in processor space—14th page in manager space

Figure 13-4 diagrams this process. The CPU will be able to adjust the mappings between the two spaces simply by writing information into the control registers of the memory manager chip.

This technique is cleaner than bank switching, where enable lines on all the memory chips must be maipulated. However, there is no way to get around the same inherent limitation as in bank switching, i.e., only one 64K part of the computer's address space can be active at one time. Therefore, for long programs, a memory managed system is almost as hard to program in as a bank switched one. The best solution is to use a processor with a larger address space because they are now commonly available.

13.2.4   Using the Interrupt System

Since the programming of interrupt handlers is a considerable part of practical systems programming, we want to use this subsection to review some general characteristics of the interrupt process. The next section will discuss the software of interrupt handlers in detail.

An interrupt is a signal that some device in the outside world requires the attention of the CPU. The interrupt is sensed by the CPU when a signal line coming onto the chip becomes active. The interrupt mechanism is provided in computers to allow them to respond very quickly to some important external situation. It is as if the CPU calls time-out, and stops the currently executing program, goes off for a short period to do an urgent chore, and then restarts the original program. There are many variations in the details of how interrupts can be handled, but certain features of the process are always the same. Regardless of how they are done, the system must always take the following actions:

1. Suspend the program that is currently executing in a manner so that it can be restarted later on with all data in good order and nothing scrambled.
2. Begin executing a program called an interrupt handler that has code in it designed to deal with incoming interrupts.
   (a) Determine which device in the outside world caused the interrupt.
   (b) Take appropriate action. Usually the action will be some minimal operation like transmitting a character to an interface or incrementing an event counter somewhere.
3. Restore the registers and data environment of the program that was executing before the interrupt, and then place that program back into execution.

The requirement to suspend the current program is handled automatically by hardware that is part of the CPU chip. The most common way to do this is for the current program counter to be placed on the stack. In some processors it is also automatic to place all the registers on the stack when an interrupt signal comes in.

Once we have suspended the program, how do we get into the interrupt handler? There are two basic ways. Sometimes there is a specific location in memory, usually on the base page, that is associated with an interrupt line. This is called an interrupt trap. Whenever the interrupt line becomes active, the CPU will save the environment of the currently executing program and then set the program counter to the address of the interrupt trap. This causes whatever code begins at the interrupt trap location to begin executing. Of course, the operating system will have initialized any interrupt traps in the system to contain appropriate code. Usually, all that will be there will be a jump instruction to the beginning address of an interrupt handler. The complete interrupt handler itself won't be on the base page. This part of memory frequently has special functions, and it is best left for the exclusive use of the operating system. Sometimes there will be several interrupt lines coming onto the CPU. If interrupt traps are used at all, each of these lines will have a separate trap location.

The other common way of getting into the interrupt handler is as follows. Some processors are set up to work with external hardware that can insert one instruction into the normal instruction stream. This is like inserting a single new card into a deck of cards at an arbitrary location. The hardware can do this any time it is activated, and it will do it at the exact instant of the interrupt signal. Since only one instruction can be injected into the CPU, usually it will be a special form of jump instruction that causes a jump to the start of the interrupt handler. The 8080 processor uses this method to find its way into the proper interrupt routine. The 8080 Restart instruction was included in its instruction set for this purpose. This instruction is really a subroutine call that is one byte long. It causes a jump to a specified location and also puts the value of the program counter (before the jump) on the stack. Of course, this stacking is necessary so that the original program can be restored later on.

After the environment of the machine is saved and control is transferred to the interrupt handler, there are no more automatic activities performed by the CPU for this particular interrupt. The CPU cannot distinguish interrupt handler code from any other code. The handler is just a program. Now it takes over, and it will do what needs to be done.

The first task of the interrupt handler is to find out what external device caused the interrupt. After all, this may not be apparent because a number of external devices may be connected to a common interrupt line. Again there are several ways to do this. Some of the larger microprocessors and most minicomputers have a number of interrupt lines coming onto the CPU. A typical number might be six lines. If there are many interrupt lines, every external device, or group of devices, can be connected to its own line. In this case, the CPU will know who caused the interrupt because the different lines direct control to different interrupt traps as part of the hardware interrupt process. The traps will usually be filled with jumps to different entry points in the interrupt handler so that it will know what line was active.

Microprocessors with only one or two interrupt lines can't use this method. They require more external hardware to help sort out the source of interrupts. There are special peripheral chips that have been designed with this purpose in mind. For an 8080 type processor, there is a Peripheral Interrupt Processor chip that accepts 8 separate interrupt lines. It transmits the information to the CPU about which line was active by injecting a different Restart intstruction into the 8080's instruction stream for each interrupt line. The location that is jumped to is different in each case, so the CPU can determine who caused the interrupt.

Another common solution to this problem is to have the interrupting device write a word identifying itself into an input port at the same time as it causes the interrupt. Control will get into a general interrupt handler by whatever method the CPU uses. The first thing the interrupt handler code will do is read the identification of the signaling device from the input port. Now the handler knows who did it. Figure 13-5 shows in block diagram form how the elements of this kind of system would be connected up.

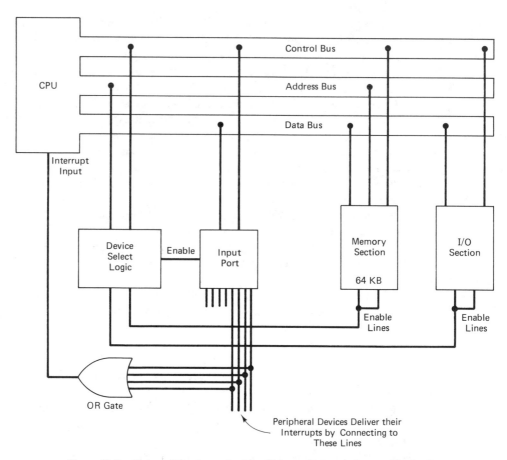

Figure 13-5:   External Hardware for Identifying an Interrupt Source. This hardware represents one way for a CPU with only one interrupt line to decide which of several system devices are causing an interrupt. The CPU can read the input port. The bit pattern in the port will identify which interrupt line(s) was active.

After the interrupt handler has determined where the interrupt came from, it must take some action to service the interrupt. There is no general way to say what this service will be. It depends on what the device is and why it is signaling. Of course, all of this information is known to the system designer when the system is being laid out. He will design or specify the appropriate interrupt handlers.

After the interrupt has been taken care of, there is nothing more to do except get the original machine environment back and restart the program that was interrupted. This is usually a matter of taking the original register contents off the stack and putting them back into the registers. The last statement in the interrupt handler will be a Return From Interrupt instruction. Control will get back into the original program using whatever technique has been provided with the CPU being used. The most common technique is for this instruction to pop the top element off the stack and use it for a new value of the program counter. Of course, we only can do this if we saved the program counter on the stack at the start of the interrupt process.

With very broad strokes, we have outlined the kinds of things that happen in small computers when interrupts come in. Now we want to turn to examining a specific way of organizing the interrupt system to manage the I/O activity in a simple multi-tasking operating system.

13.3 INTERRUPT DRIVEN INPUT/OUTPUT PROGRAMMING

When the CPU is time-shared between various tasks, as on a larger microcomputer system, it is desirable to have the CPU switch between the tasks in a way that will maximize the amount of work being done. Input/Output processes can represent an impediment to this goal. Disks and printers and other electromechanical apparatus can operate very slowly relative to CPU speeds. So, if a program is written so that it requests a certain amount of I/O to be done, and then waits for it to be carried out, millions of cycles of potentially useful CPU time can be wasted in the execution of waiting loops. Most single user operating systems have I/O of this sort.

A more desirable way to cycle the work load of a multi-tasking computer will be to in some way provide for the following type of operations. A program will start up its I/O operation, then it will suspend itself from execution, and the CPU will spend time working on behalf of other programs. Eventually a signal will come in from the outside world (the peripheral device) that the I/O which was requested is finished. This signal should be used to reactivate the program that was suspended so that it can proceed through its normal pattern of execution.

The essence of what we will try to do is prevent the CPU from wasting time in waiting loops. If it becomes clear that a program can do no more useful work until something happens in the outside world, then that program should be inhibited from execution and the CPU should be devoted to something else. The most common cause for a program having to stop is in order to wait for some I/O event it has initiated. The most common solution is to use an interrupt driven device handler that can suspend a program if its further execution is inefficient, and that can be triggered to do parts of an

I/O task upon signals from the outside world (interrupts). We will study the characteristics of such handlers in this section.

To set the scene for this discussion, imagine that we are using a computer system similar to that shown in Figure 13-1. There will be several terminals, a shared printer, and a shared disk subsystem. The operating system will be a standard multi-tasking system that can run a small number of tasks concurrently. The operating system proceeeds by cycling through the tasks and applying small time slices to each in succession. The operating system keeps track of tasks with at least three linked lists—one shows jobs that are ready to run, another shows jobs that, for one reason or another, have been blocked (other terms are inhibited or suspended), and the third indicates the task that is actually running at the present time.

We shall need some new data structures and types of operating system modules to administer this kind of arrangement. Let us first focus on what information needs to be recorded for each I/O device. The normal thing is to keep a device control block for each physical device that can generate any kind of I/O. There will be one for each terminal, one for the disk, and one for the printer. Figure 13-6 shows the kind of information to be recorded in the Device Control Block.

We need a Busy/Free flag because several of these devices (like the printer) can be used by only one task at a time. The Next Routine Field is used to route control to the proper code when the I/O device generates an interrupt. The next two fields name the device this block describes and the task that is (perhaps temporarily) using the device. Next we have the address of an I/O buffer. The I/O buffer can be any region of memory from which the operating system wishes to take characters or into which it wishes to load characters. We also need fields to give the length of the particular buffer to be used, a pointer to indicate the next free space in the buffer, and something to count characters if we are to do character by character I/O. Finally we may need to specify the number of characters to input or output. It is not necessary to use all of these fields for each type of I/O operation, but it is probably desirable to specify a control block that is uniform for all devices.

1. Busy/Free Flag
2. Name of Next Routine to Execute
3. System Identification of the Device Associated with This Control Block
4. System Identification of Any Task Using This Device
5. Address of an I/O Buffer
6. Length of the Buffer
7. Buffer Pointer
8. Buffer Counter
9. Number of Characters to Input or Output
10. Pointer to a Queue for Tasks Waiting to Use This Device

Figure 13-6: A Typical Device Control Block.   This set of data items is called a Device Control Block. The DCB collects in one place, all the information which the system needs to maintain in order to monitor and control the operation of any peripheral device. The system has one of these data structures for each device it can access.

In addition to these items in the Device Control Block, some devices will have a queue associated with them. All devices that must be shared between tasks will have their own queues. The queue will not be in the DCB, but the DCB will include a pointer to the queue's location. Here is what the queue is used for. If a device is busy working on behalf of one task and another task requests the device, then the requesting task will be blocked and its name will be put on the device queue. Later, when the device becomes free, the operating system will remove the name of the requesting task from the queue, give it control of the device, and unblock its execution.

There are, of course, many variations on the basic theme of how an interrupt driven I/O system should be organized. We are going to describe a kind of system that is very common in minicomputers. It allows for high I/O speeds with a minimum of supervisory overhead; and it results in rapid availability of I/O devices to the tasks that need them.

The operating system software that relates to I/O will be organized as follows. There will be a *Central I/O Routine* (CIO) and a *Central Interrupt Handler* (CIH), each of which does a piece of any I/O operation. The general pattern of operations will be like this. To set some I/O going, any task can call the CIO as a subroutine. The task has to pass the CIO information about what it wants done, so it passes in some parameters just as they would be passed in to any other subroutine. The CIO will, in general, start up the I/O and then cause the task that is currently executing to be suspended. Now the operating system gives control to some other task that is ready to execute.

Later, when the I/O started by the first task completes or needs some attention, the I/O device will generate an interrupt. The code in the Central Interrupt Handler will have to take it from there. In general what the CIH will do will be to output another character or detect the end of I/O and do some bookkeeping associated with that. It usually returns to whatever task was executing before. However, after the last interrupt associated with this I/O operation, the CIH will pass control back to the operating system rather than to the previously executing program so that the operating system can decide what task should run next.

So responsibility for the complete execution of an I/O process is divided between the Central I/O Routine in the operating system and certain modules in the Central Interrupt Handler. The various modules in these routines have standard names. The part of the CIO that starts up an I/O operation at a particular device is called the initiator for that device. The module in the CIH that will supply any further attention that an I/O device requires after it is started is called the continuator for that device. And the module in the CIH that does any bookkeeping at the end of an I/O operation is called the terminator for that device. Each device has one set of these three modules that are specialized to control its operations. Once again, all initiators reside in the Central I/O Routine. All continuators and terminators reside in the Central Interrupt Handler.

It is now time to look at an example. Figure 13-7 shows the duties for the initiator, continuator, and terminator modules for the printer. What kind of printer do we have? We are assuming a machine that takes one character at a time and generates an interrupt after each character. This interrupt indicates when the printer is ready for the next character. The initiator obtains control of the printer and feeds it the first character. After that, the task using the printer is going to be suspended because there is nothing more

INITIATOR
1. Mark the device as busy.
2. Output the first character.
3. Adjust any pointers and counts used to keep track of this output.
4. Do an end test.
   a. If there are more characters, set the Next Routine Field to continuator.
   b. If the last character has been output, set the Next Routine Field to terminator.

CONTINUATOR
1. Output the next character.
2. Adjust pointers and counts.
3. Do an end test and set the Next Routine Field as in item 4 of the initiator.

TERMINATOR
1. Mark the device as free.
2. Unblock the calling program.
3. Unblock the first program waiting on the queue for this device, if any are waiting; and remove it from the queue.

Figure 13-7: A Device Handler for a Shared Printer. This is a character at a time device handler that can output a buffer of text to the printer using the interrupt system. The printer associated with this handler generates an interrupt after each character it receives. The interrupt signals when the printer is ready for another character.

that can be done until the printer generates an interrupt. However, before the initiator finishes, it must set up things so that when the interrupt occurs, it will trigger the correct code in the interrupt handler. It can do this as follows. It writes the name of the code to be executed after the interrupt into the Next Routine Field in the printer's Device Control Block. What code is this? If only one character was to be output, so that the interrupt will actually signal the end of I/O, then the name of the next routine is the terminator code for the printer. If more characters are to be output, then the next routine is the continuator code for the printer. After the initiator finishes, control goes back to the operating system and some other task will execute for a while.

When an interrupt finally comes in from the printer, the CIH will route control to either the continuator or the terminator for the printer. They are embedded in the CIH code. If the continuator gets control, it will output another character, adjust any pointers or counters associated with keeping track of the I/O, and then it will set things up for the next interrupt. The way it does this is standard. It will write the name of the next code to execute into the Next Routine Field in the printer's Device Control Block. Then the CIH will return from the interrupt to whatever program had been executing.

If an interrupt causes the terminator code to get control, it means the I/O is finished.

On the preceding interrupt, the CIH had output the last character and recognized it as such by setting up the terminator. What does the terminator have to do? It has to free up the printer for use by other programs. And it has to reactivate (unblock) the program that initiated the printer I/O and also reactivate any other program that may be waiting to use the printer. The terminator does this by taking the name of a program to activate off the printer queue. If several programs are waiting, it will reactivate the one on the top of the queue. Reactivation and blocking are done by making calls to routines in other parts of the operating system that are specialized to this purpose. After the terminator has done its work, the Central Interrupt Handler, in which it is embedded, will pass control directly to the operating system dispatcher so it can decide what task should be running next.

The initiator, continuator, and terminator grouping is called a device handler. The initiator will always be in the Central Input/Output Routine in the operating system and the continuator and terminator in the Central Interrupt Handler. The general pattern of things these modules do is always the same. The differences that occur are generated by the condition that different devices will create different numbers of interrupts and that the interrupts will mean different things.

A device handler for input from a dedicated keyboard is shown in Figure 13-8. A keyboard is a character by character input device. The interrupt generated by a simple keyboard signals that a key has been pressed and that a character is waiting in the interface to be accepted by the CPU. The relationship, in time, of an interrupt to the associated character is different in printers and keyboards. To illustrate this, imagine that we are

INITIATOR
1.   Nothing needs to be done in this module. (Note: the Next Routine Field in the Device Control Block is permanently set to continuator.) The CIH takes care of everything at this stage.

CONTINUATOR
1.   Take in a character.
2.   Do an end test by examining the last character to see whether it is Carriage Return.
    (a)   If there are more characters to come, nothing else needs to be done now.
    (b)   If the input is finished, go directly to the terminator code.

TERMINATOR
1.   Unblock the calling program.

Figure 13-8:   A Device Handler for a Dedicated Keyboard. This is a character at a time device handler that can take in a single line of text from a keyboard using the interrupt system. We are assuming a keyboard that generates an interrupt whenever a key has been pressed; and we are assuming there is a character ready and waiting for the CPU to pick up.

going to transfer ten characters to each device. With the printer, some time after the tenth character has been sent out, the printer will cause an interrupt. The interrupt signals that the printer is ready for the next character even though we aren't going to send any more. With the keyboard, there will be an interrupt before the last character, and then no more interrupts.

This different pattern of interrupts results in differences in the initiator and continuator parts of the device handler for a keyboard. The terminator part is also different (simpler), but for other reasons. The initiator has nothing at all to do. However, you must remember that the initiator is embedded in the Central I/O Routine and the CIO does have some work to do. It will block the program calling for keyboard input, since no more useful computation can be done until a key is actually pressed.

The continuator code responds to an interrupt. It needs to do only two things: take in the next character, and decide if this is the last character that will be input. The usual way to do this is to examine the character and see whether it is a Carriage Return. We are assuming that all program lines in this system end with a Carriage Return. If there are going to be more characters, then there is nothing more for the continuator to do, so the CIH exits in its normal manner. That is, it returns to whatever program was executing. If the last character has been detected, then there will be no more interrupts coming. So control will be passed to the terminator for the keyboard. This module will execute immediately. It will request the operating system to unblock the program that started this keyboard I/O sequence. After the keyboard terminator code, the CIH will pass control back to the operating system dispatcher so that it may choose what task should run next.

The keyboard device handler is much simpler than the printer handler. Because of the pattern of interrupts generated by a keyboard, the initiator has nothing to do. Also because of the pattern of interrupts, the terminator is not interrupt triggered. It is called directly from the continuator code that responds to the last interrupt. This means that, for at least this particular device, the Next Routine Field in a keyboard Device Control Block can always be set to continuator. It will never be changed. We have one more potential simplification. A keyboard will not in general be shared between programs, so the Busy/Free Field in the control block loses its significance.

The device handler for a disk is different from the ones we have looked at so far primarily in that there will be only a few interrupts associated with a particular I/O operation. To give an example of the device handler, we need to assume a particular kind of disk and disk controller. So we will assume that the disk transfers information in units of 128 byte sectors, and the controller works through a direct memory access (DMA) mechanism. This controller is going to be a little more intelligent than the one we discussed in connection with CP/M. We will assume that the controller can be given a command to position to the proper track and sector and it will give an interrupt when it has done this. Then the DMA mechanism will be set up and started by the CPU, and the I/O transfer will proceed automatically. There will be another interrupt when it is finished. It is easy to set up the DMA. There will be several ports on the disk interface for configuring DMA. The program will have to shift down to the interface words that specify the address of a buffer where the data should go or from which it should be taken, a word that says whether the transfer will be input or output, and a word that starts the transfer. Because so much of a disk I/O operation is mediated by intelligent hardware, the device handler is very simple. It is shown in Figure 13-9.

The initiator continuator, terminator code for all devices are embedded in two larger pieces of code. They are the Central I/O Routine and the Central Interrupt Handler. All through this discussion we have been suggesting what these modules do. Figures 13-10 and 13-11 give explicit listings of their duties.

To tie everything together, we would like now to imagine a scenario in which several tasks in a multi-tasking system compete for the use of a printer on a first come, first served basis. For our example, let's say the computer has three users (tasks) and things are arranged as shown in Figure 13-2. The printer is being used to log the activities of the three tasks. Perhaps the tasks are doing phone answering or processing some sort of transactions. Occasionally each task sends a single line of status information to the printer to record its progress. The system is set up to allocate $^1/_{10}$ second time slices to each task unless a task gets blocked in performing I/O.

The pattern of activity in the system might be something like this. Task A gets a time slice and expends it on pure computation with no I/O. Task B gets a time slice. It starts computing and then comes to a point where it needs the printer. So, it calls the Central I/O Routine. This module sees that the printer is free, sets up the Device Control Block for the printer, and calls the printer's initiator code. This code marks the printer busy, outputs the first character, and sets the Next Routine Field to continuator. Then the CIO suspends Task B, before its time slice is finished, because no more useful work

INITIATOR

1. Mark the device as busy.
2. Set the Next Routine Field to continuator.
3. Initiate positioning by giving commands to the controller.
   (There will be an interrupt when the positioning is done.)

CONTINUATOR

1. Set up and give the command to start the I/O using DMA.
   (There will be an interrupt when the I/O is finished.)
2. Set the Next Routine Field to terminator.

TERMINATOR

1. Mark the device as free.
2. Unblock the calling program.
3. Unblock the first program waiting on the device queue, if
   any are waiting; and remove it from the queue.

Figure 13-9: A Device Handler for Disk Input or Output. This device handler will supervise bringing in or sending out an entire sector of data to the disk through a DMA apparatus. Only two interrupts are involved: one to signal correct positioning of the read/write head and one to signal completion of the data transfer. Notice that the disk, even though it is a more complicated device than a keyboard or a printer, requires a simpler device handler because it is a more intelligent device.

1. Inspect the Device Control Block to see whether this device is free:
   (a) If not, then block the program that wants to use the device. Put its name on the queue of programs waiting to use the device, and exit to the dispatcher in the operating system.
   (b) If the device is free, continue with the rest of these directions.
2. Set up the Device Control Block.
3. Start up the I/O by a subroutine call to the appropriate initiator code.
4. Block the process that is asking for the I/O so that the CPU can do some other useful work.
5. Exit to the dispatcher in the operating system so that another task may be selected to run.

Figure 13-10:   Duties of the Central I/O Routine. This routine is the central point through which all programs must pass when making a request for I/O service. The Central I/O Routine will begin the service if the requested device is free. If it's not free, the Central I/O Routine will suspend the requesting program until resources become available. This module performs one half of the I/O process. The other half is taken care of by the Central Interrupt Handler.

can be done until the I/O finishes. The CIO relinquishes control to the operating system's dispatcher.

The dispatcher next gives a time slice to Task C, which uses it for computation. Occasionally, an interrupt arrives from the printer. When this happens, the continuator code for the printer in the Central Interrupt Handler gets control. It outputs the next character and returns to Task C.

When Task C's time slice expires, Task A is given a time slice and uses it up for computation. Task A and C alternate, and each is interrupted by short periods in which the CIH furnishes another character to the printer on behalf of Task B. Task B gets no time slices because it is suspended.

Now task A is executing, and it arrives at a point where it needs the printer. It calls the CIO. The CIO determines that the printer is busy, so it suspends Task A and adds its name to the queue of tasks waiting for the printer. Now all time slices for a while are given to Task C because nothing else is ready.

At some point while Task C is executing, the CIH sends the last character to the printer and sets up for terminator code on the next interrupt. Task C continues to execute. The final interrupt comes in. Now many things happen. The printer is marked free. Task B is marked ready, and Task A, which was on the waiting queue, is also marked ready. Task C does not complete its time slice. Instead the CIH causes the current task to suspend and jumps directly to the dispatcher so another task can be selected.

Now three tasks are ready again. The next time slice will go to Task A. It will resume its attempt to acquire the printer. This time it will be successful, and the whole

1. Save the machine environment.
2. Determine which device is causing the interrupt.
   (There are many ways to do this which are system dependent.)
3. Look at the control block of the interrupting device:
   (a) If the device is not marked Busy, then the interrupt is a wild interrupt. Issue an error message and return.
   (b) Otherwise, continue with the rest of these directions.
4. Make a subroutine call to the address of the routine shown in the Next Routine Field of the Device Control Block. Execute this routine. It will be either a continuator or a terminator.
5. After this, there are two possible ways to exit:
   (a) If the I/O is not finished (continuator code has just run) then restore the machine environment and return to whatever program was just executing.
   (b) If the I/O is finished (terminator code has just run), do not restore the machine environment. Instead, make an operating system call to suspend the current task, and then jump directly to the operating system dispatcher so that it may decide what task should be run next. The operating system will tidy up the machine environment.

Figure 13-11:   Duties of the Central Interrupt Handler. This routine supervises and completes all I/O activities begun by the Central Input/Output Routine. The I/O devices signal the status of various phases of their jobs by interrupts. All the interrupts cause the Central Interrupt Handler to gain control for a short period. It will assess the situation and pass control down to subhandlers that are specialized for particular devices.

process just described will be repeated. The protocols of how the operating system suspends, resumes, and switches tasks are fairly involved. They will be given in Chapter 14.

The kind of interrupt system we have outlined is about as good as can be had for a classical single CPU system with interrupts. The same kind of activities always have to be done in any interrupt driven system, but they are sometimes packaged differently. For instance, big computer systems frequently have small satellite computers that are used to manage I/O. These I/O processors intercept all the intermediate interrupts associated with some I/O that they have been commanded to do. They will typically deliver just one interrupt to the main computer when their work is completed.

Another kind of packaging occurs in small systems in which most of the operating system is furnished by a vendor; but a certain small set of routines are to be written by the user in order to mate the operating system to his hardware. Of course, CP/M and its descendants provide an example of a system with this philosophy of limited customization. If there are interrupts in this kind of a system, the user has to write the handlers because this kind of code is very close to the hardware. However, the system concept is that the handlers are to be extremely simple (so they will be easy to write).

A common way to implement user written interrupt handlers is to have a separate simple handler for each device. Each handler does only two things: sets a software flag to indicate that an interrupt came in, and then exits to the dispatcher for selection of a new task. De facto, the flag system records which device caused the interrupt since there is one flag for each device. The operating system can inspect those flags. When the operating system is entered from an interrupt handler, the equivalent of continuator and terminator code in the operating system itself, rather than in the handlers, will take care of the interrupt.

There are, unfortunately, overhead penalties associated with this approach. Here is the crux of the problem. With this kind of set-up, if n interrupts come in while a task is trying to expend its time slice, the system will have to endure the overhead of reselecting that task to run n times, just to get through the time slice. So system efficiency is being traded off against ease of customization.

STUDY QUESTIONS AND EXERCISES

1. Four copies of the same program are running asynchronously in a multitasking environment with interrupt driven I/O. The programs act as independent entities, with no correlation in their timing. The time slice period is 1/10 second. Assume that task switching and suspension and resumption and interrupt handling take essentially zero time. Approximately every one second each program needs to output a single character to the single shared printer. The outputting program can do no further work until that character has been printed. It takes the printer 1/10 second to accept and print a character and be ready for the next one. Estimate the percentage of time the printer will be in use. Estimate the percentage of time (on the average) that each program will be suspended waiting for I/O. Make these same estimates if it takes the printer 1/100 of a second and if it takes 5/10 of a second to handle each character.

2. Suggest several benchmark programs that could be written in assembler and that could provide a basis for a good execution speed comparison between 8 and 16 bit processors. Benchmarks are small programs that are typical of the type of processing a computer will be used for. What characteristics should good benchmark programs have?

3. Consider this program fragment written in the assembly language of a hypothetical 16 bit microprocessor:

```
ADD    REG1, REG2, GAMMA
```

It means, add the content of register 1 to register 2 and store the result in a memory location called GAMMA. This instruction is four bytes long, of which two bytes specify the address GAMMA. The machine uses 16 bit addition, and registers are 16 bits wide. Assume the time to execute any instruction on this processor and on an 8080 type processor is 1 clock cycle plus 1 cycle for each memory access. How much faster can the work of this program fragment be done on a 16 bit processor than on an 8 bit machine?

4. Imagine that we are constructing an absolute assembler for the bank switched computer system shown in Figure 13-3B. We want the assembler to be able to assemble programs that are longer than 64 kilobytes. All programs will start in Bank 1. What problems will we run into? How should we change our basic two pass assembler to deal with them?

5. Describe the difficulties that might arise in the production of long compiled programs if they are to be used on a machine with a segmented address space such as is found with typical bank switched or memory managed computers. What will the compiler do with a program that is longer than the address window? Is the linking of modules more complicated in this environment? How might the linking be done?

6. Device handlers of the sort discussed in this book can be made simpler if the code in the Central Interrupt Handler always returns to the program that is currently executing rather than sometimes returns to the operating system. If handlers were constructed in this way, what performance penalties would the system pay?

7. Consider the simplified interrupt handlers, mentioned at the end of this chapter, for systems in which the bulk of the interrupt handler code is incorporated with the rest of the operating system. Basically all the interrupt handler has to do, other than the normal bookkeeping that all handlers do, is to set a flag that corresponds to the interrupting device and then exit to the operating system. This question asks you to write such a handler for an 8080 system. Assume there are four interrupt causing devices. They work through a peripheral interrupt controller which will insert the instructions Restart 1-4 (depending on which device interrupted) into the normal instruction stream. This will cause the characteristic one byte subroutine call to locations in low memory. The handler itself should begin at location F000H. It should be entered at four different points to preserve the information about what device interrupted. Upon entry, it should stack the 8080 registers. Then it should set one of the memory locations labelled FLAG1, FLAG2, FLAG3, or FLAG4 to one. And finally, it should branch into the operating system at a special entry point for interrupt handlers that is labeled OPSYS2. Write the code for this handler and specify how the low core restart locations should be initialized.

8. Imagine that an interrupt has triggered the handler mentioned in Question 7. The operating system has done its processing. The flag relating to the interrupting device has been reset by the operating system so more interrupts can come from the device in the future. Now it is time to return to the program that was executing before the interrupt came in. Write a code fragment that illustrates the things the operating system must do from this point to get back to the original program. Assume the stack is in the same state it was in when the handler transferred into the operating system.

9. A program is in the middle of its time slice with plenty of execution time before its end. An interrupt from Device A comes in, and the system starts to process it. While in this processing, an interrupt from Device B comes in and interrupts the processing for Device A. Can the initiator-continuator-terminator type interrupt system that we discussed handle this contingency? Outline a plausible sequence of modules that might get control in this kind of circumstance. Follow the sequence all the way from the first interrupt up to the restoration of the original program.

10. Assume you are asked to write the complete Central I/O Routine and Central Interrupt Handler for an 8080 based system. These routines will be part of a multi-tasking operating system. The system will always be used with three terminals and one printer. Make a detailed list of the additional hardware and software information you will have to be told in order to complete this assignment.

14

The Multi-Tasking Operating System

14.1 *INTRODUCTION: OPTIMIZING COMPUTER USAGE*

Multi-tasking operating systems are significantly more complicated than the single user operating systems we have already studied. The complications have to do with sharing out the system resources so that all tasks have what they need to run, coordinating tasks that are working together on different parts of a common activity, keeping tasks that should be separate from interfering with each other, and managing what is usually a much expanded file system.

These operating systems are also characterized by much greater variety than we have seen before. What kind of variety can we expect? Let's look at the common cases. First of all, there is *the real time environment*. Sixteen bit microcomputers are frequently used in complicated control applications such as managing a high speed machine tool, or managing the electronic countermeasures aboard an airplane, or controlling the flow of data coming into a switching point from many different communications lines. These kinds of applications call for a real time operating system. The keynote in this type of environment is speed. There will typically be a number of ongoing asynchronous processes, which receive information from the environment via interrupts, which analyze the situation in fractions of a second, and which take immediate action. The operating system code itself, in a real time system, will be small relative to the applications code. The main jobs for the operating system will be handling interrupts and administering the sharing of the CPU. Managing many terminals or maintaining fancy file structures won't be a consideration at all.

Another type of system that is in common use might be called *a multi-user execution*

324

environment. The multi-tasking capability is really put there to run many varied applications programs and because you want to be able to use multiple terminals and other slow I/O devices in connection with those applications. Business systems will be of this type. Efficient, high capacity, secure file systems will be important here. Business systems usually spend most of their time reading and manipulating disk records, rather than doing large amounts of computation.

A third type of system will be called a *multi-user development environment*. This type of system is used mainly to produce new programs. The environment needs to be optimized for the frequent running of complicated systems programs such as editors or compilers. These kinds of programs are computation intensive. It also needs features to make it easy for teams of programmers to cooperate efficiently on doing separate parts of a large project.

In this chapter we will look at various parts of three operating systems that correspond to the categories introduced earlier. For our example of a real time system, we will use VRTX, which is a real time operating system nucleus or kernel. It was written by a small company in California, Hunter and Ready. What is a kernel? Real time systems are usually memory resident because they have to be fast, and they are usually small, since they don't really have that much to do. A kernel is a piece of code that coalesces dispatching and a few other essential operating system features into one small module. Some real time kernels are only about 4K bytes long.

Our example of a multi-user execution environment will be MP/M-II from Digital Research. This system looks like a traditional minicomputer operating system that has been slimmed down for use on micros. It can be made to have some real time responses if needed, and it can also handle a fair number of terminals and a respectable file system. Typical implementations require 30K bytes for the memory resident system and floppy disks for attendant programs and data storage.

To call MP/M-II an execution environment does not mean programs cannot be developed there. The same software exists for program development under MP/M-II as there was in CP/M. It just means this environment is not optimized for program development. Program development cannot be its primary use because the system would be quite slow if it were running a number of simultaneous computation intensive tasks.

Here are some characteristics of the MP/M-II operating system:

- Multi-terminal support (up to 16 terminals).
- Multi-programming at each terminal.
- Interrupt driven I/O and task switching.
- Uses the file structure of CP/M 2.2.
- Each terminal can be made to look like an independent microcomputer running CP/M.
- Rich primitives in the operating system for task synchronization.
- System clock allows time scheduled execution of programs.
- Machine dependent part of the operating system is localized in one module.

- Programs must be completely memory resident and stay in memory for all the time that they are executing (no swapping).
- Maximum length of program code for any single program is less than 64 kilobytes.
- The operating system is written in the Intel systems programming language PL/M, with the consequence that this operating system can only execute on processors that run Intel instruction sets. It is essentially an operating system for 8 bit processors, although 16 bit extensions have been developed.

To summarize MP/M-II, think of it as being very much like CP/M with some crucial additions: a dispatcher run from a system clock, interrupt driven I/O, the ability of the operating system to switch various leaves of memory in and out (bank switching), and a few key primitives for synchronizing the tasks.

Our example of an operating system for the development environment will be UNIX. This system was developed at Bell Labs in 1969 and has evolved through four successive versions since then. Its original focus was to be a system that was very friendly to programmers and on which they could produce code efficiently. Later, as the system elaborated, it was used as a test bed for many advanced features in operating system design. At the beginning, this system used rather large PDP-11 minicomputers and it required the type of hardware facilities found in such an environment. However, Version 4 of UNIX has now been rewritten to execute in a more modest hardware environment. The Microsoft Company of Bellevue, Washington, now markets and supports the complete UNIX system, under the tradename of XENIX. It has been adapted to run with typical microcomputer equipment (Winchester disks), and any 16 bit processor from the group Intel 8086, Zilog Z-8000, or Motorola 68000. Even so, this system still occupies a place at the high end of the range of operating systems we want to examine. Typical implementations require perhaps 50K bytes for the memory resident part, and at least 5 megabytes of hard disk space for utilities and program swapping. Several other companies are now selling UNIX look-alike operating systems for sixteen bit microcomputers which mirror the external characteristics of the operating system more or less faithfully.

The following are some of the characteristics of a UNIX system:

- A fairly typical minicomputer operating system kernel that supports task switching, interrupts, multiple terminals, etc. The task synchronization primitives are weaker than what you would find in a real time system.
- A large memory address space supported by a memory manager that can dynamically reconfigure the association between physical and logical memory pages.
- A convenient file structure arranged in the form of an inverted tree. Any user's file can be identified as a particular path through this tree.
- A flexible and powerful user interface program (the Shell) which is actually an interpreter. It has its own language and it can be manipulated at the command level to do easily many complex system tasks that would require explicit programming efforts in other systems.

- The multi-programming environment is very fluid in UNIX with the operating system continually creating and destroying tasks that run asynchronously to execute the commands you have issued.

- UNIX is not a real time system because it makes very heavy use of the disk. There are several reasons for this. The type of file directory used is convenient, but it can require many accesses to find files. Also, it is integral to the system that many tasks are running concurrently and that tasks are swapped back and forth between memory and the disks frequently while they are executing. This takes time.

- Data from any program or device can easily be connected, without programming, to any other program or device through the use of intermediate disk files automatically created by the system. The connecting entities are known as pipes.

- Programs can be of whatever length is allowed by the address space of the underlying hardware.

- UNIX is written in the systems programming language C. It is not tied to any particular hardware. The target machine must of course support C, and it must support memory management and some rather hefty disks.

Because of the variety of objectives in these larger operating systems and because of their greater complexity, it's difficult to introduce multi-tasking operating systems properly. We have chosen to do it in the following way. We are not going to examine any particular system in great detail. Instead, the first thing we will do is examine some general features that all multi-tasking systems must have, like a dispatcher and some means to synchronize concurrent tasks. Then we will attempt to select and examine the most interesting features, in a systems programming sense, from our three baseline operating systems. In addition to describing features, we want to leave the reader with some fairly definite ideas about how they could be implemented.

We can give some more specifics of our plan for this chapter. All multi-user systems, of whatever type, have at their core some kind of task dispatching module. Some systems are little more than a dispatcher. This is where we will start.

Sometimes a multi-user system will be running n tasks where each task is associated with a separate user and they all are doing completely independent things. This is the easy case. However, it is also very common for an application or systems program to be organized as several tasks which work together. They will execute in parallel to accomplish a certain objective. In this case, there is a new burden on the operating system: how can we make it possible for the tasks to synchronize with one another and pass information back and forth when necessary? There are several common ways to do this, but the method chosen in MP/M-II strikes the author as being the most flexible and elegant, while also being easy to implement. We will study the general problem of task synchronization and the solution to this problem that has been incorporated in MP/M-II.

Next, we will examine VRTX, because it is a good example of a minimal system that has been well thought out and that has all the features needed for multi-tasking.

The final three topics are from UNIX. We have attempted to cover the aspects of

UNIX that are different from traditional small operating systems. The organization of the file system in a multi-user environment has a large impact on how easy it is for a team of people all working on the same project to cooperate. UNIX has a particularly flexible and comfortable file system which we will want to examine. Further, there is much to be gained in terms of elegance and programming ease if we let the operating system create and destroy system tasks on its own initiative as it goes about its work. This topic is the tree structured process hierarchies found in UNIX. Finally there is the matter of the UNIX Shell. This is an embedded command interpreter with which the user interacts rather than directly touching the operating system. It is probably this part of the system, more than any other, that lends UNIX its distinctive power, programmer friendliness, and programming style. It will be our last topic.

14.2 TASK DISPATCHERS AND SCHEDULERS

A dispatcher is at the very heart of all multi-tasking operating systems. It is the dispatcher's duty to decide which task should be allowed to run next, when the system reaches a change point. It also must administer a smooth transition between one task and another that is being started or restarted. The dispatcher can decide what task to run next in a very simple-minded fashion, or complex algorithms may be employed. If simple strategies are used for this decision, the code is usually called a dispatcher. When things get complex, it is called a scheduler. We will discuss some of the methods used a little later.

It has become customary to maintain all tasks in the system in one of three possible states: running, blocked (sometimes we say suspended), or ready to run. The operating system must manipulate these states and the associated tasks so that the whole system works smoothly and efficiently. We must deal with several important issues: How does the dispatcher tell what task to start up? How is the switch from one task to another made? How does control get in and out of the dispatcher?

Let's first examine the various policies used by dispatchers to determine what task should run next. The simplest scheduling policy is *round-robin scheduling*. To use this policy, a dispatcher will maintain a simple list of all the tasks in the system. There will be a pointer to the position of the current task in this list. Whenever the dispatcher gets control, it will scan through the list and select the next nonblocked task beyond the current task.

The data structure needed to maintain this kind of dispatching is a circular linked list. The items on the list are task descriptors. They are data entities that are several bytes long and contain the following information: the name of the task, a status field which says what state the task is in, and a link to the descriptor of the next task on the list. A complete task descriptor will require some other fields which are to be discussed later. This kind of structure is shown in Figure 14-1. When dispatching occurs, the operating system will follow the links around the list from the currently executing task until it finds another one to run. In Figure 14-1 we see that Task B is running. When dispatching occurs, the next task to run will be Task E. Tasks C and D will be passed over because they are blocked.

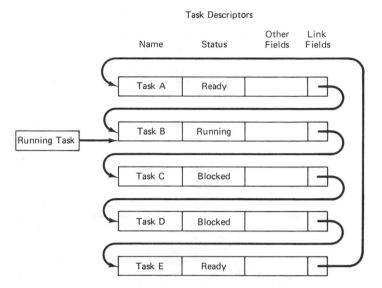

Figure 14-1:   A Data Structure for Round-Robin Task Dispatching. This structure
is called the Dispatch List. It is a circular linked list of task descriptors, and it is the
primary data structure needed to control round-robin task dispatching. Task B is running
now. Tasks C and D are blocked. The next task that will be dispatched is Task E.

Another scheduling policy is *priority scheduling*. In this variation, whenever the
dispatcher is entered, it will always find the highest priority ready task and run it. Lower
priority tasks are run only if all the higher priority tasks are temporarily blocked. There
are some cases in which this simple policy works well. In systems in which all tasks are
doing large amounts of I/O, every task will be blocked for significant periods of time
while slow peripheral devices digest or produce character strings. But, in systems where
many of the tasks do nothing but computation, a high priority task could preempt the
CPU for a long time. In these systems it is common to have the clock interrupt handler
temporarily increase the priority of low priority tasks every now and then. The priority
is increased just long enough for them to get a time slice for some reasonable fraction
of the time.

What are the data structures like for priority scheduling? They are very similar to
those used in the round-robin scheme. There will be a linked list of task descriptors as
before. But we must make a few changes. Consider the data structure shown in Figure
14-2. There must be an additional field for task priority, and the list is linked in order
of priority. It is no longer circular. The descriptor for the lowest priority task will be on
the end of the list. This descriptor will usually correspond to a dummy task. That is, it
doesn't do any work. The task itself will just be a waiting loop of some sort. The dummy
task never gets blocked. We need something like this because occasionally all the other
tasks will be temporarily blocked waiting for various things. The dispatcher must dispatch

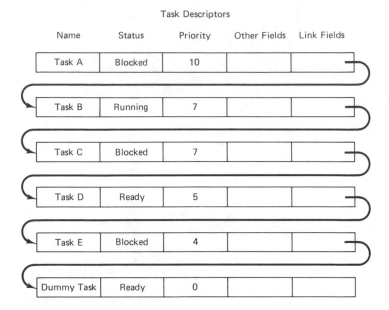

Task Descriptors

Name	Status	Priority	Other Fields	Link Fields
Task A	Blocked	10		
Task B	Running	7		
Task C	Blocked	7		
Task D	Ready	5		
Task E	Blocked	4		
Dummy Task	Ready	0		

Figure 14-2: A Data Structure for Priority Dispatching. Any time the dispatcher gets control, it will scan the dispatch list starting at the first entry looking for the first task that is ready. Since the Dispatch List is linked in order of priority, this will result in the highest priority ready task being selected. If no legitimate tasks are ready, the dummy task will be selected.

something. So it will start up the dummy task until some higher priority task becomes ready.

Sometimes people attempt to make the dummy task do useful work. It can obviously be used to keep track of the fraction of the time the CPU is lying idle. This is helpful for performance evaluation and tuning. Sometimes it is used to run noncritical tests on various other parts of the system.

The way a priority list is used differs from what we looked at before. Every time the dispatcher gets control, it will start at the top of the list and look for the first ready task. This will also be, de facto, the highest priority ready task. In the round-robin scheme, after a dispatch, the list would be searched starting not at the top, but at the descriptor of the currently executing task.

The most common dispatching policy for small multi-tasking computers is to use a combination of both methods we have looked at. This is *priority scheduling with round-robin scheduling within groups of tasks that have the same priority level*. This is a very flexible strategy. If all tasks are assigned the same priority, it becomes round-robin scheduling. If all tasks have different priorities, then it is a straight priority based scheme. If tasks occur in subgroups all of which have the same priority, then we get a combination of the two strategies.

Now we must turn our attention to the actual mechanism by which the operating system stops (blocks) one task and starts up another. This process is called a task switch. The first thing we need to be aware of is the Task Control Block. This is a table maintained by the system that collects all relevant information about a task into one place. Most multi-tasking systems have one of these for each task. Typical contents of this table are shown in Figure 14-3. The Task Control Block in some ways parallels the Device Control Block, introduced in the last chapter, which encapsulates all important information about a device.

Let's examine the task switch mechanism from a general viewpoint first. We will discuss implementation details later. The first thing the system has to do is save the environment of the currently executing task. To do this, it will store the program counter, the registers, the condition codes, and the stack pointer of the currently executing task into the Task Control Block. Taken together, these things are called the resume parameters, because they are what will be needed to start the task up again later.

The next thing the operating system will do is use the dispatcher to select some other task to run. We have already discussed how this can be done. To bring the new task into execution, the system needs to find its control block and then restore the task's environment (that is, make things the way they were when the task was last running). It can do this by taking information out of the control block to restore the registers, the condition codes, and the stack pointer. The last thing the system will do is set the program counter to its previous value. That completes the task switch. Now the new task will

1. Name of the task
2. State—blocked, ready, or running
3. Task Priority
4. Information on the owner of the task
5. Resource Usage: a statement of all the resources the task needs to execute successfully, such as a printer, a disk, and a communications line.
6. Allocated Resources: system resources that have been temporarily assigned to this task, such as a terminal or a particular printer.
7. Open Files: the names of files currently being used. They will have to be taken care of if this task is aborted.
8. Memory Bounds: the part of memory in which the task is loaded.
9. Stack Pointer: a starting value for the stack pointer.
10. Resume Parameters
    (a) Space to save a program counter value.
    (b) Space to save the condition codes.
    (c) Space to save the registers.
    (d) Space to save a stack pointer value.

Figure 14-3: Information in the Task Control Block. The Task Control Block is a data structure which serves the purpose of recording all important information about a task executing in the multi-tasking system.

take over and run until its time slice expires, or until it becomes blocked by virtue of doing an I/O process, or until some I/O process completes and the dispatcher gives the CPU to another task because it is of higher priority.

The last general issue we want to discuss is: How does control get into the dispatcher so it can do its work? There are several ways. Certain kinds of interrupts should be set up to invoke the dispatcher directly. For instance, all multi-tasking systems have a clock that generates clock interrupts at regular intervals related to the time slicing period. This clock is external circuitry that periodically delivers a pulse to one of the interrupt pins on the CPU. Frequently the 60 cycle/second pulse period of normal power lines is used to generate the clock interrupts. So, after every clock interrupt, or perhaps after every n clock interrupts, the clock interrupt handler will pass control to the dispatcher. When the clock handler passes control to the dispatcher, it means the time slice for the current task has run out. Note that the clock interrupt is inherently different from the I/O interrupts. There is no need or use for an initiator-continuator-terminator type of processing. Thus the clock handler will frequently be completely separate from the Central Interrupt Handler; or, if it is incorporated in the CIH, the incorporation will be pro forma and the clock handler will be treated as a special case.

The other common way for the dispatcher to be entered is from the I/O system. If a task requests to do I/O, by calling into the Central I/O routine, and if the I/O resource it needs is busy, then the task must be suspended and control transferred to the dispatcher to select something else to run. Another route to the dispatcher from the I/O system is via an I/O completion interrupt. The Central Interrupt handler will normally be set up to trigger a redispatch whenever an I/O process is finished. Something important might be waiting to run. We'll look at these paths in and out of the dispatcher in more detail with an example.

Since this discussion has been quite general so far, let's examine the construction of a realistic dispatcher a little more closely. This dispatcher will combine priority scheduling with round-robin scheduling within priority levels. It will use a task descriptor like that shown in Figure 14-2. This descriptor layout has an unspecified area left free for "Other Fields." One of the things that must go in this area is a pointer to the Task Control Block that is associated with the descriptor.

Let's specify that our dispatcher will execute within a system where the CPU is an Intel 8080. It is necesssary to say what the processor is because there are different methods that can be used to traverse between dispatcher and interrupt handlers and user code. What method is best depends in detail on what instructions have been provided in the CPU's instruction set.

We need to give attention to how we can achieve round-robin scheduling within a group of tasks that are all of the same priority. The following is a good way to do it. Remember that the dispatch list is linked in order of task priority. Whenever the dispatcher is entered, the first thing the software should do is check whether the current task (the one executing most recently) is a member of a group of tasks with the same priority. If it is a member, the dispatch list should be relinked so that the descriptor for the current task comes after the descriptors for all the other tasks within its group. This ensures that the other tasks in the group will be examined first the next time the list is scanned to find a task to dispatch. After this, the dispatcher can proceed with its normal pattern of scanning from the top of the list to identify the highest priority ready task.

So some relatively simple manipulations on a priority dispatch list will give us the kind of scheduling we need. To define our example further, we need to look carefully at all the steps involved in a task switch, and try to identify some primitive subroutines we can construct that would make the task switch clean and easy to understand.

The first thing the system must do is identify the precise time when the task switch will occur. It may be that our system is constructed so that every clock tick is an occasion for a task switch. Or, if the ticks are very fast, it may be that the clock interrupt handler will count and on every *nth* tick, the handler may request that the operating system do a task switch. The other way the system can learn that it is time for a switch is when it receives a specific call from some routine asking to suspend the current task and select another. The Central I/O Routine, for instance, will do this frequently.

The next thing the system must do is prepare for the switch. To do this, it will have to mark the current task as blocked and save resume parameters so that the current task can be started up again later. Of course, the proper place to save the resume parameters is in the Task Control Block of the current task. Here is our first primitive. It will be useful to have a subroutine that can do the work just outlined. This routine will be called SUSPEND. It should get the resume parameters from a standard place. The best place turns out to be the stack. SUSPEND will pull a complete set of register values followed by a Program Counter value off the stack and use them for storing in the current Task Control Block. It will also store the Stack Pointer after it has popped the other values. By the time SUSPEND has been called, one half of the task switch is done.

As we proceed through the switching sequence, it becomes obvious that the next thing to do is find out what task to run next. This is the territory of the dispatcher. And here we discover a second primitive. DISPATCH is a section of code that scans the Dispatch List, according to whatever policy we are using, and selects the next task to run.

The other half of the task switch consists of placing the new task in execution. Here we need another primitive subroutine which will be called ACTIVATE. The DIS-PATCH code jumps to ACTIVATE after deciding what task to run next. ACTIVATE marks the new task as Running. It removes register values and condition codes from the Task Control Block of the new task and establishes them in the CPU. It establishes a new Stack Pointer according to the saved value in the Task Control Block. The last thing it does is put the program counter value from the Task Control Block onto the stack. Then it ends the way any subroutine does—with a Return statement. This causes the machine Program Counter to be set according to the top element of the stack. Now control has passed into the user code for the new task and the switch is complete.

The reader should be sensitive to the fact that it is very important to know whether these primitive routines are subroutines or in-line code and to know how they are entered and exited. SUSPEND and ACTIVATE are normal subroutines; DISPATCH is not. SUSPEND is always used as a normal subroutine would be. DISPATCH and ACTIVATE are entered with jumps rather then calls. DISPATCH exits with a jump. ACTIVATE exits with a normal subroutine return. It is characteristic of operating system code that the procedure whereby connections are made between modules has to be very carefully thought out in order to get them to do what you want them to.

Of course, the way to find out the exact connection details of the primitive routines is to rethink and follow through the three critical occasions on which a task switch may occur: a clock interrupt, a request for task suspension, or an I/O completion interrupt.

Figure 14-4 shows a flowchart for a clock interrupt handler. We are assuming that this is a special handler distinct from the CIH system. The clock handler increments a count every time there is a clock interrupt. Any task can look at this count and use it as raw material for timed operations. Every *nth* tick, the clock handler will initiate operations to cause a task switch. It does this by calling SUSPEND to deactivate the current task and then by jumping to DISPATCH. The interrupt handler is never returned to if a task switch is being set up. But that is all right, because it is not a subroutine.

Recall that SUSPEND found the register values and program counter value to use as resume parameters on the top of the stack. SUSPEND was designed to get its input

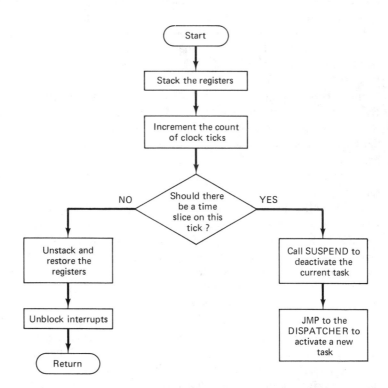

Figure 14-4: The Clock Interrupt Handler. This handler is distinct from all the other handlers in the system. Its primary function is to define the time slicing interval. The clock tick is the one interrupt source that is indispensable for a multi-tasking system. Of necessity there are two exits from the handler corresponding to whether the current tick ends a time slice or not.

this way because those things will automatically be on the stack if SUSPEND is called from inside an interrupt handler.

Another way a task switch can happen is when a task asks for its own suspension. This can always be taken care of by using the SUSPEND routine. The most common occasion for this kind of switch will be when the CIO Routine determines that a task can't continue because the I/O resources aren't available. Once again a call to SUSPEND and a jump to the dispatcher will be used. Constituting the resume parameters is a little tricky in this case. When this task is restarted later on, where do we want it to start up? It should start up immediately before the place where there is a test to see if the I/O device is free. So the Program Counter value that is pushed on the stack in preparation for SUSPEND will point to this location. Figure 14-5 shows how a task can be suspended in the course of an I/O call.

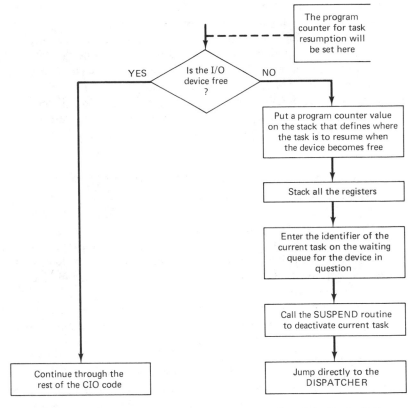

Figure 14-5:   How a Task Is Suspended if it Calls for I/O and the Device is Busy. This shows what happens in the Central I/O Routine when the current task has asked to do some I/O, but the CIO has determined that the requested device is busy. The task must then be blocked, and the dispatcher should choose a new task, since nothing more can be done here.

The last way into a task switch is via an I/O completion interrupt. Our interrupt system is set up to cause a redispatch at the end of any I/O process. This is obviously desirable because the interrupt might mean that some high priority task has finished I/O and should be started up again immediately. On the last interrupt associated with any I/O process, the terminator sets a flag so that the Central Interrupt Handler knows to initiate dispatching operations rather than to execute its normal return. The normal return is to go back to whatever program was currently executing.

What exactly does the CIH have to do in order to obtain a task switch? It will require almost the same sequence of events as for a clock interrupt. The correct Program Counter and register values are already on the stack. Therefore, the CIH can call SUSPEND to deactivate the present task. Now comes a crucial difference. Perhaps it is appropriate that the current task should continue running, since the chances are that it did not fully expend its time slice. Therefore, the CIH must mark the current task as Ready (SUSPEND just marked it as blocked). And finally a jump to DISPATCH will cause a new task to be selected and started up. It may turn out that the task that had been running is still the highest priority task. In this case, it will be reselected and started up.

This completes our more detailed look at integrating the dispatching function with the rest of the operating system. Instead of remembering the details of this example, it is more important to focus on what must be accomplished to have a good multi-tasking system. The methods of entries, and exits, and integration details are all very much bound up in what kind of CPU is being used on the system. On the other hand, you can expect to have this much complexity, perhaps packaged a little differently, with whatever computer you may be using. Multi-tasking always carries this kind of overhead.

14.3 CONTROLLING INTERACTION BETWEEN CONCURRENT TASKS: MP/M-II

Multi-tasking systems generally need to provide a means for tasks to interact in three related areas: communication, mutual exclusion, and synchronization. In this section, we will look at what these concepts mean. Then we will explore the traditional ways of dealing with them, and finally we will look at a very nice mechanism provided in MP/M-II to accomplish these interactions.

Communication simply means passing information. An electronic mail system whereby different users can send messages to each other is an example. Since each user will be represented in the system by a particular task, the more general case is that of tasks being able to send messages to each other.

Another kind of task interaction we need to look at is *mutual exclusion*. For an example, let's say a system has one disk which is used fairly heavily by a number of independent tasks. The disk must be used in the following way. There will be some protocol whereby a task can acquire temporary possession of the disk. Then the disk will be positioned to the correct track and sector. Then information will be transferred, and then possession of the disk will be relinquished so that some other task can use it. There must be some mutual exclusion mechanism so that while one task is executing this chain of events, some other task doesn't break in and interfere. It is easy to see that catastrophes could result if some other task was allowed to issue commands to the disk in the time between when it was positioned and when the commands for the transfer of information were issued.

Synchronization is something that is necessary when several asynchronous tasks have been set up to work together to accomplish a common goal. The traditional example of this is called a producer-consumer system. Many environments characterized by co-operating tasks can be analyzed according to this simple model.

Let's look at an example of a producer-consumer system. Several independent tasks produce buffers full of raw information. Perhaps they are doing data collection. Several other tasks "consume" these buffers, usually by processing the raw information and displaying it or passing it on to somewhere else. There is a fixed pool of buffers that are to be used by whatever task needs them. Empties are returned by the consumers for reuse by the producers. Synchronization becomes an issue if the rates of filling buffers with data and the rates of emptying them out are different. Even worse, the rates might vary unpredictably during the course of the problem.

Figure 14-6 diagrams the flow of buffers through a system in which there is a simple producer-consumer relationship with just one producer task and one consumer

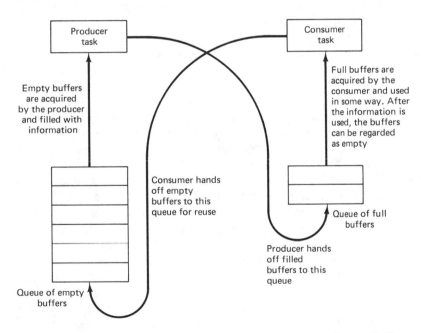

Figure 14-6:   The Flow of Buffers in a Producer-Consumer System. Buffers carry information in a one way flow from the producer to the consumer. The consumer returns them when finished. Synchronization problems can arise if buffers are either filled too rapidly or emptied too rapidly. The object is to maximize system throughput. This buffer flow must be visualized in the context of a multi-tasking operating system that also needs to work on other tasks unrelated to this producer-consumer subsystem.

task. When the consumer empties a buffer, it is returned to the producer so it can be filled again. At all times, each buffer is attached to one or the other of two possible queues: a queue of empties or a queue of buffers that are full.

Producer-consumer systems cannot be made to work efficiently by any simple dispatching rule such as "always give x time slices to the producers and then y time slices to the consumers." The allocation should vary depending on circumstances. For instance, if the producer tasks work very fast and the consumers work slowly, so that all the buffers become filled with raw data, then the best thing to do is to temporarily retire the producers from action and give all the CPU time to the consumers so they can catch up. If the consumers suddenly begin working extremely fast, then the reverse solution should be applied. Synchronization primitives in the operating system make it easy to do this kind of thing.

We need a more concrete example because this sounds quite abstract. In a large computer network, a message from computer A to computer B may be sent through a number of intermediate computers before it gets to its destination. Each time one of the intermediaries gets a message, it will store it temporarily, choose the best available route that will bring the message closer to its destination, and then send it on to the next computer. Eventually, the message will get to the destination.

Many different routings are possible. Each computer in the network runs a multi-tasking operating system, and each computer has among its tasks two that are always active: a handler for incoming messages (the producer task) and a handler for outgoing messages (the consumer). Arriving messages are placed in buffers from a fixed buffer pool and passed to the consumer task. The consumer determines the best way to continue each message's travel and returns the empty buffer for another message. Obviously the whole process has to be tuned to keep everything flowing smoothly.

So communication, mutual exclusion, and synchronization are intertask operations that somehow need to be made easy to work with. Operating system designers deal with the need for controlling task interactions by making relevant primitive routines available in the operating system. These routines can be called by individual tasks whenever they need to do something that might affect other tasks. Let's look at some of the traditional primitives that have been used frequently.

A very simple structure for intertask communication is the mailbox. The name is suggestive of its use. It is a data structure belonging to a particular task into which any other task can write information. There will be primitive routines in the operating system that allow tasks to create mailboxes, destroy mailboxes, read their own mailboxes, and write to other mailboxes. The message that goes into the mailbox is usually of some fixed length (frequently the size of a disk sector) that has been agreed upon by the tasks that will be using these messages. The message size can usually be specified when the mailbox is created. Another variable specified at creation time is the capacity of the mailbox—the number of messages it can hold.

Reading and writing the mailbox data structure is straight-forward except in one case. What should a task do if it tries to read from an empty mailbox or write a message to one that is full? Two possibilities are usually provided. Sometimes a status code is returned alerting the calling routine to the fact that it can't use the mailbox in the way it intended. The program can then decide what alternate action it would like to take. Another possibility is for the operating system to suspend a task that tries to use a mailbox when it is in an unusable state. When some other task changes the state of the mailbox, by reading or writing it, the first task will be reactivated by the operating system and it will try again.

The mailbox is really a very simple data structure. It is easy to imagine some extensions to this simple scheme, but they do not commonly occur in small computer operating systems. Two possibilities are to extend the capacity of a mailbox infinitely by making it a disk file, and to make it possible to select certain messages out of the box during a read rather than just taking whatever happened to arrive first.

Mailboxes take care of intertask communication. The traditional mechanism for setting up mutual exclusion and for implementing various kinds of task synchronization is the semaphore. The name suggests the signaling device that is used by the railroads. Railroad semaphores are used to control the access to a section of track when there might be more than one train attempting to get on the track at the same time. The semaphore works as follows. It is a flag that stands at the entrance to the protected block of track. No train will pass a semaphore that is down. If a train comes up to the protected block and the semaphore is up, it can enter the track. After it goes by the signal, the semaphore will be lowered to prevent any following trains from coming in. When the train leaves the protected block of track, there will be a mechanism whereby the semaphore at the entrance can be raised so that another train can now use the track.

The software implementation of this simple physical concept is used in much the same way. What does a logical semaphore do? In the simplest case, it serializes access to a block of code that is protected by the semaphore. It makes sure that no more than one task will use the code at a time. The protected block of code is called a critical region. There will be operating system primitives that allow any task to create a semaphore, or delete a semaphore. There will also be two routines that allow tasks to manipulate semaphores. The names in common usage for these routines are the Wait On Semaphore Routine, sometimes called the P Routine, and the Signal Semaphore Routine, which is sometimes called the V Routine.

Let's explore the analogy between physical and logical semaphores. When a train wants to enter a protected block, it inspects the semaphore. If the semaphore is up, the train goes past and causes the semaphore to be lowered. If the semaphore is already down, the train waits for it to be raised. What does the software do if a task wants to enter a block of code protected by a semaphore? The task tries to enter the block, and the first thing it encounters is a call to the Wait On Semaphore Routine. This will cause one of two possible things to happen. If the semaphore is up (set), then the Wait On Semaphore Routine will lower (reset) the semaphore and just return. The task then proceeds into the protected code and begins executing it. If the semaphore is already down (reset), then another path will be taken through the Wait On Semaphore Routine so that a call is made to the operating system to suspend the current task. This is analogous to the train waiting. If several tasks are trying to get into protected code that is in use, they will all be suspended.

Actions at the end of the block of protected code are also analogous to what the train does. When the train leaves the protected block, it arranges for the semaphore at the entrance to be raised. When a task finishes executing protected code, at the end of that code there will be a call to the Signal Semaphore Routine. What this does is raise (set) the semaphore and make an operating system call to reactivate the first task that tried to get into the protected code and was suspended because the code was in use. In the software implementation, there is a queue associated with each semaphore on which are recorded the names of any tasks that were suspended during a wait on the semaphore.

The semaphores we have discussed so far are usually called binary semaphores because they have just two states. There are more complicated semaphore entities which we will discuss in a little while.

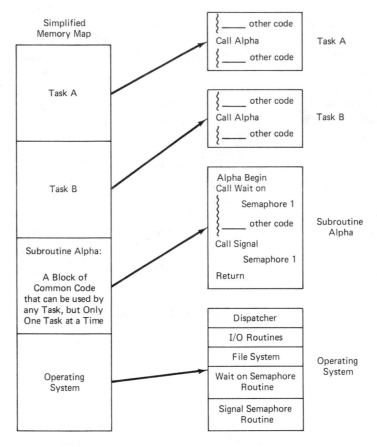

Figure 14-7: An Example of Using a Binary Semaphore. A multi-tasking system has two tasks which execute in time slices and which try at unpredictable times to access a subroutine that both of them need to use. Only one task should use this particular subroutine at a time. If one of the tasks tries to use it when the other is still using the shared code, the task attempting entry will be suspended. The system will reactivate it later after the first task is finished. A semaphore manages this process.

If you haven't used these types of operations before, it is usually a little difficult to see where all the code is and how the calls are made to the operating system. Figure 14-7 shows how the programs might be laid out when there are two asynchronous tasks that attempt to access a common piece of code (a subroutine) protected by a binary semaphore. Figure 14-8 shows what the semaphore manipulating primitives look like. Remember that these routines are reentrant. They are part of the operating system, and many different tasks could conceivably be trying to use them concurrently.

Let's run through a scenario wherein Tasks A and B of Figure 14-7 interact through a semaphore. At the time we pick up the action, the semaphore has already been created by one of the tasks, and let's say it is now raised (set). Task A is executing. The task comes to a point in its code where it will try to use the common subroutine ALPHA, which for some reason is protected by a semaphore. The way it gets into this code is by a simple subroutine call:

    CALL   ALPHA

Now control moves into ALPHA. At the beginning of this subroutine, there is a call to another subroutine, Wait On Semaphore. So control moves into this next subroutine, which is in the operating system. ALPHA is free, so the Wait Routine resets the semaphore and returns. Now control moves further into subroutine ALPHA and the computer begins to execute that code, whatever it may be.

Suddenly a clock interrupt comes into the system, signaling that the time slice for Task A has expired. The dispatcher suspends Task A and sets up Task B, which starts executing. Task B gets to a point in its code where it will try to use the subroutine ALPHA. Remember that Task A is not finished with the subroutine and was suspended somewhere inside it. Task B calls subroutine ALPHA. Control moves into ALPHA. The first code in ALPHA is a call to the WAIT Routine. Control moves into the WAIT Routine. There are two possible paths through this module. Since the semaphore is down (reset), the WAIT Routine makes a call to the operating system to suspend Task B. Notice where Task B was suspended. It was suspended inside the WAIT Routine just after the call to the operating system. However, the place where B should eventually wake up is right before the semaphore test; so, as part of the suspension process, the Program Counter value that is stored away will be set to this point.

The dispatcher is always the next module to get control after any call to the operating system to suspend the current task. Since no other tasks are ready, the dispatcher wakes up Task A, which continues executing where it left off—in the interior of subroutine ALPHA. Ultimately Task A finishes the code in the subroutine. It gets to the SIGNAL Routine. This raises (sets) the semaphore and requests the operating system to mark whatever is on the top of the semaphore queue, Task B in this case, as ready to continue. Task A then leaves subroutine ALPHA and continues to execute its own local code.

Eventually, the time slice for Task A runs out. The dispatcher restores Task B to execution. It begins executing where it was suspended—right inside the WAIT Routine at the semaphore test. It inspects the semaphore, lowers it, and returns from the WAIT Routine. Now Task B is using the protected code and any other routine that wants to get

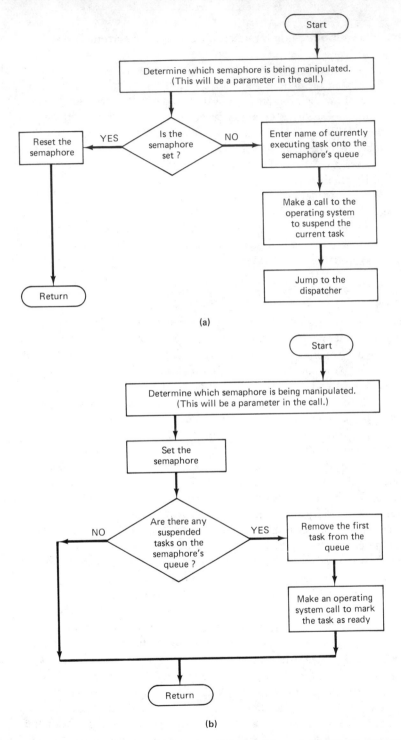

Figure 14-8: Primitive Routines for Manipulating a Semaphore. (A) The Wait on Semaphore Routine. (B) The Signal Semaphore Routine. The WAIT Routine is called by a task that is trying to get past a semaphore into some shared code. It acts as a gate. A call to the SIGNAL Routine should be the last instruction in the shared code. It resets things to allow other tasks to enter if any are waiting.

at that code will have to wait its turn and make calls to the semaphore primitives in the way we have illustrated.

There have been two traditional uses of semaphores. One use is to enforce mutual exclusion, that is, to make sure a piece of code was only used by one task at a time. With mutual exclusion, we speak of serializing access to a piece of code. This use is easy to appreciate. In fact the detailed example we just went through can be understood as a case of mutual exclusion. We could imagine that subroutine ALPHA was the part of an I/O system that dealt with a disk. Then it is easy to see why we would want to enforce a usage pattern so that only one task at a time would use the code. This is equivalent to saying one task at a time would use the disk.

Semaphores are also used for more complicated synchronization problems. A counting semaphore is an extension of the binary semaphore idea. There is a count associated with the semaphore. It is usually initialized to some positive number n. When a task wishes to pass the semaphore, it calls the WAIT Routine. The following pseudo-code shows what WAIT has to do:

```
Decrement COUNT by 1
If COUNT < 0
    Then Suspend Current Task and Jump
        to Dispatcher
    Else Continue
Return
```

There are several points to note about the correct use of this code. Whenever there is a task suspension, a resume point must be specified. In this case, a suspended task should wakeup at the RETURN statement at the very end of the WAIT Routine. All necessary testing and manipulation of COUNT has already been done. The other point to mention is that delicate code like this should be run to its natural exit points with no possibility of interruption. This means the interrupt system should be turned off during execution of WAIT (and SIGNAL).

When a task departing the critical region signals the semaphore, the SIGNAL Routine will do the following:

```
Increment COUNT by 1
If COUNT <- 0
    Then Remove the First Task on the
        Semaphore Queue and Mark it Ready
    Else Continue
Return
```

If a task has been reactivated by this code, the next time it gets a time slice it will return from WAIT and enter the critical region.

When a counting semaphore is initialized to one, it becomes a binary semaphore. The reader should notice that this implementation of a binary semaphore is different in several respects from the binary semaphore routines shown in Figure 14-8. The differences are in the resume point of suspended tasks and in a mechanism for keeping track of how many tasks are waiting on the queue. Figure 14-8 was intended to show an analogy with railroad signaling and did not specify how to tell what was on the queue. If we use the count to tell what is on the queue, a consequence is that the place where suspended tasks resume will be different. Both implementations will work, but the counting semaphore idea is extendable to more general situations.

Counting semaphores have a couple of important uses. This device can act as a gate to a shared piece of code such that n tasks at a time will be allowed to execute in the code concurrently. The binary semaphore would only let in one task at a time. To enforce this pattern of usage, it is just necessary to surround the code with Wait and Signal Calls and to initialize the semaphore count to n.

What is the other use? The most common way to achieve task synchronization in a producer-consumer relationship is through the use of counting semaphores. It works as follows. Remember that all buffers are connected to one or the other of two queues. Access to the Queue of Empties is controlled by one semaphore and access to the Queue of Fulls is controlled by another. If the system starts with all empties, then the Semaphore for Empties is initialized to n and the Semaphore for Fulls is initialized to zero. When a producer task tries to acquire an empty buffer it will go through a piece of code that causes it to wait on the Semaphore for Empties. Similarly, when trying to get a full buffer, the consumer must first wait on the Semaphore for Fulls. When the producer attaches a buffer to the Full Queue, it must signal the Semaphore for Fulls. When the consumer passes back an empty buffer, it must signal the Semaphore for Empties. Each routine manipulates both semaphores at certain times. The counting property of the semaphores keeps track of the number of available buffers and ensures that a task will not run if the buffers it needs for its work are not available.

Incidentally, at this point the reader may notice similarities between the semaphore operations we have been describing and the kinds of things that happen to tasks which use the Central I/O Routine structure discussed in Chapter 13. We are really seeing different aspects of the same process here. All multi-tasking operating systems provide some means for communication, mutual exclusion, and synchronization. If semaphore primitives have been provided in the operating system for incorporation into user defined tasks, it would be a sensible economy to use them for the needs of the Central I/O Routine as well. Indeed, a semaphore structure is the way most I/O systems will go about controlling the access to scarce I/O equipment and administering the suspension and reactivation of tasks that necessarily goes along with this.

Semaphores are very powerful and useful, but somehow they seem to be a little hard to think about. There is an alternative. Now we are prepared to look at how MP/M-II handles the traditional problems of intertask communication, mutual exclusion, and intertask synchronization. The MP/M operating system makes use of a single data structure and its associated primitives for handling all of these situations. This solution is very elegant. The data structure that is at the heart of MP/M's method is a message queue.

Imagine a queue system with the following properties. The basic unit is a FIFO queue with two associated lists. The lists are called the Enqueue and Dequeue lists. The queue can hold a certain number of fixed length messages. The length of the message and the capacity of the queue are defined when it is created. In general, any task that knows the name of the queue can read from it or write into it.

As always, we can run into problems with the boundary conditions. When the queue is full and a task tries to write into it, there are two possibilities depending on what kind of write command was issued. If a so-called conditional write was used, an error message will be returned because the operation cannot be completed. If an unconditional write was used, then the current task will be suspended and control will go back to the dispatcher. The name of the suspended task will be placed on the Enqueue List for this particular queue. The purpose of this list is to record those tasks that tried to write onto the queue and were unable to because it was full. A complementary operation occurs if a task tries to read an empty queue. If a conditional read is used, an error message will be returned. If an unconditional read is used, then the current task will be suspended and placed on the Dequeue List associated with this queue.

Suspended tasks are marked "ready" again in the following way. Whenever a Write Queue Command has been successful, the operating system, as part of this command, will check the Dequeue List to see whether it contains the name of a task that should be reactivated. Similarly, whenever a Read Queue Command is successful, the system will check the Enqueue List for a task to reactivate.

MP/M includes operating system primitives to create, open, close, delete, read, and write to queues. These operations are reminiscent of files, except that the queue data structures reside totally in memory.

It is easy to see that the message queue is a very general communications device that can do anything a mailbox can do.

A variation on the queue data structure expands the mechanism so that it also can do anything a semaphore can do. A special kind of queue is supplied with the MP/M-II system. It is called a Mutual Exclusion Queue. It is just like any other MP/M queue with one exception—the nature of the message. Only one message is allowed per queue, and the message is of zero length. There are routines to manipulate the queue, but no message is actually passed. Does this seem a bit strange? An actual message is not important. What is important is the conditions under which the operating system will suspend or reactivate tasks that are using the Mutual Exclusion Queue.

System calls to read or write this queue accomplish exactly the same thing as calls to a Wait on Semaphore or Signal Semaphore Routine, except that the language is different. There is a one to one correspondence. In those places where it would be appropriate to call a Wait On Semaphore Routine, instead we can make a call to read a particular Mutual Exclusion Queue. In those places where a call to the Signal Semaphore Routine is appropriate, a call to write a particular Mutual Exclusion Queue will serve the same purpose. Instead of talking about the semaphore being raised (set) or down (reset), we talk about the queue message being available or unavailable. Task suspension and reactivation will be carried out in exactly the same circumstances no matter which mechanism is used.

The message queue mechanism can also be used to implement counting semaphores. The counting semaphore is a control construct that is frequently used to protect a shared piece of reentrant code if you want no more than 2 or 3 or n tasks to be concurrently using the code. The queue mechanism can be used for this purpose in the following way. You must define a queue that can hold n short messages. Once again, the message content doesn't matter, so the messages can be made of minimum length. At the start of the protected code there will be an operating system call to read a message off the queue. At the end of the protected code there will be a call to write the message back on the queue. What we are really doing in this case is using the messages to stand for sets of access rights to use the code in question. If the queue can be read, it means a set of access rights to use the code has been granted. If it can't be read, it is because all sets of access rights are in use. The calling task will have to wait until another task returns its access rights by writing onto the queue. A similar pattern of queue reads and writes can be used to control producer-consumer systems.

Thus we have seen that the message queue in MP/M-II can do anything that can be done with mailboxes and any kind of semaphore. It unifies these different ideas; it is easy to implement; and all in all it is a very elegant mechanism.

14.4 THE REAL TIME OPERATING SYSTEM NUCLEUS—VRTX

We will begin our discussion of existing systems for larger microcomputers by examining a real time nucleus, or kernel, as it is sometimes called. This is an example of a generic type of software which is a true multi-tasking system yet is also small and easy to understand.

The sophisticated functions found in today's instrumentation, communication, and control machinery are most often organized around an embedded microprocessor. The microprocessor orchestrates the whole operation. This is the realm of real time programming. Traditionally it has been hard to write programs for these applications. The operating system requirements have been relatively small—multi-tasking, interrupt handling, and ways to synchronize the tasks. But since the applications were so different, it was common for software designers to effectively write their own operating systems each time they put a new application up. This is specialized work, full of subtleties, and prone to errors. It has caused big cost overruns on many projects.

A solution to this problem is emerging. Several companies are now marketing what are essentially small, standardized operating systems that can easily be incorporated in equipment designs requiring an embedded processor. This software becomes the focal point for the whole system. It helps the programmer in the following way. Instead of writing a monolithic program that performs the tasks at hand and also coordinates and synchronizes them, the programmer merely writes a separate program for each task and uses the system calls in the operating system kernel to do the rest. This can significantly reduce the development time of complex real time software systems. It can also provide higher reliability because the commercial operating system kernels are small and well tested. If all the products from a given manufacturer who uses embedded computers are built around the same kernel, then he will in addition derive benefits from having a standardized system.

Much experience now exists in the computing community in the writing of small operating systems for real time applications. A surprising thing has happened. It turns out that most of the good systems were using a common set of mechanisms to support real time multi-tasking. So the logical next step was for some smart person to package these mechanisms in such a way that they could be easily interfaced to, put them in a read-only memory, and distribute the package as a general system component just like any other electronic chip. Several manufacturers are now doing this, most notably Intel. The operating system kernel we are going to focus on is VRTX, from a company called Hunter and Ready. It was one of the first of such operating systems, and it is typical of the so-called software on silicon technology.

VRTX is a kernel for the Zilog Z8000 sixteen bit processor. It consists of 22 independent subroutines distributed in a read-only memory. User programs can access these routines through a Z8000 instruction called a System Call.

The System Call instruction is a software interrupt. It provides a convenient way for a user program to call the operating system and request an operating system service. It works like most other interrupt schemes in that return information is placed on a stack and control branches to a particular place where there is a System Call Handler. This handler, of course, will be part of the operating system kernel. There's one other feature. The System Call Instruction contains eight bits that are used to number the call. Thus one can make 256 different system calls. Effectively, the CPU hardware places this identification number on the stack along with the return information. When the System Call Handler gets control, it can examine the identification number and then branch to a subhandler appropriate to the work being asked for. When the work is finished, a normal interrupt return takes control back to the original calling program.

The entire VRTX package takes up only 4 kilobytes worth of memory and supplies a surprising amount of functionality. Figure 14-9 summarizes the VRTX system calls. One of the things we can learn here is how functionality measures up against the amount of code necessary to achieve it. We know how big this system is. Let's see what it can do.

First we will examine task management. Dispatching is done on a priority basis with round-robin time slicing among groups of tasks that have the same priority.

VRTX uses a 52 byte task control block for each task. The maximum number of tasks that can run at one time, and thus the number of task control blocks, are set up when the system is initially configured. This information becomes known to VRTX through a small table of parameters and addresses that the user must set up and which the nucleus can use to know how it should interact with its environment. This is called the Configuration Table.

The task management functions are very simple. The *Create Task Call* finds a TCB, writes into it the priority, the identification number, and the starting address of the task, and marks it "ready." The input parameters to this call are the priority, the identification, and the starting address. The *Task Delete Call* removes a task descriptor from the list that the scheduler scans and it wipes out the associated TCB (accessed by task priority or by identification number) and returns it to the system. There is also a *Task Suspend Call* whereby any task can suspend any other task or group of tasks, including

Task Management
SC-TCREATE   Task Create
SC-TDELETE   Task Delete
SC-TSUSPEND   Task Suspend
SC-TRESUME   Task Resume
SC-TPRIORITY   Task Priority Change
SC-TINQUIRY   Task Inquiry

Memory Allocation
SC-GBLOCK   Get Memory Block
SC-RBLOCK   Release Memory Block

Intertask Communication and Synchronization
SC-POST   Post Message
SC-PEND   Pend for Message

Interrupt Servicing
UI-POST   Post from Interrupt Handler
UI-EXIT   Exit from Interrupt Handler
UI-TIMER   Timer Interrupt
UI-RXCHR   Received Character Interrupt
UI-TXRDY   Transmitter Ready Interrupt

Character I/O
SC-GETC   Get Character
SC-PUTC   Put Character
SC-WAITC   Wait for Special Character

Real Time Clock
SC-GTIME   Get Time
SC-STIME   Set Time
SC-TDELAY   Task Delay
SC-TSLICE   Enable Round-Robin Scheduling

Figure 14-9:   The System Calls in the VRTX Real Time Operating System Nucleus. The VRTX Real Time Nucleus provides the common core of mechanisms necessary to orchestrate multiple tasks within the framework of a responsive, event-driven system.

itself. The inverse of this is the *Task Resume Call* whereby any task can wake up any other task or tasks. There is a call whereby any task can change the priority of any other task. And finally, there is an *Inquiry Call* through which any task can find out the priority and status of any other task.

These are very basic task management operations. One is immediately struck by the fact that any task can do anything to any other. There is no implicit hierarchy of who can control whom. This would definitely not be a suitable design for a big time sharing system, but it is suitable for the type of applications VRTX is intended for. That is, by and large VRTX will be used in a dedicated real time system, where all the tasks are operating to achieve a common purpose. They will have all been designed by a common architect. Thus there isn't much need to protect the tasks from each other. Their interactions will have been well planned in advance.

There are two system calls to control memory allocation. When the system is configured, all the memory can be broken up into fixed size blocks. The system will know about this through its Configuration Table. Any task that wants a block of memory, for any purpose, will get it through the *Get Memory Block Call*. The address of a block to use will be returned if any are available. When tasks are finished with memory, they return blocks to the system for general use via the *Release Memory Block Call*.

You may be wondering how this call would be used. When VRTX starts up, a single user-supplied initialization task is empowered to run. It has the responsibility of creating any other tasks the user has designed and setting them up to run. Before a task is created, memory must be found for it. Hence, the Get Memory Block Call. The initialization routine will be making these calls. This will be especially important if tasks are created dynamically when the system runs, and if it will be impossible to tell how many tasks there are going to be below a certain maximum number. Another use for the memory allocation calls would be if the tasks are processing data from the outside world, and the arrival time and quantity of data cannot be planned for. In this case, the system lets the tasks request buffers from the common pool of memory as needed.

The VRTX intertask synchronization calls are quite primitive. They involve an unusual species of mailbox. It is possible to send a 16 bit nonzero message to a mailbox that can be located anywhere. There can be as many mailboxes as desired, and all tasks have equal access to them. The mailbox doesn't have to be created. The address for it can be specified as part of the call. A mailbox can only contain one message, but the sending task will not automatically be suspended if the box is already full. Instead, it receives a return code describing what happened, and it can take whatever action it deems necessary.

There is a *Pend for Message Call* whereby a task reads a mailbox. The task will automatically suspend if there is no message there, and it will automatically be reawakened when a message arrives.

The synchronization primitives don't do much. This is probably apppropriate for a small real time nucleus. We should remember that any of the more complicated synchronization structures, if they were desired, could be built by a user upon the foundation given by these primitives.

Interrupt handling is very straightforward in VRTX. It is possible to write interrupt handlers that don't touch VRTX at all. This must be done if high speed is necessary. A more common way to use the interrupt system is as follows. The responsibility for any particular I/O device will be split between a user task and a very simple interrupt handler also written by the user. They will be coordinated through a mailbox. The user task will start the I/O and then suspend through trying to read a mailbox with nothing in it. When the external device gives an interrupt to signal that it is ready to do something, the interrupt handler receives that interrupt and writes a message to the mailbox to wake the user task up. That is all it has to do. The user task continues from there. This is the reason for the *Post Message from Interrupt System Call*. This system is quite convenient, but slow, since effectively the operating system must redispatch the user I/O task on every interrupt.

The other system calls associated with interrupts are an *exit call* which returns from the interrupt, but also results in an immediate operating system task dispatch. This is useful. It gives a programmer the option of setting up an interrupt handler either to return to where control came from via a machine language return statement, or to go back to the dispatcher. What about the *Timer Call?* This is provided so that a clock interrupt handler, written by the user, will have a way to tell the system that the clock ticked.

VRTX also has some routines to support character by character I/O, since even in minimum configurations, it will be common to have at least a terminal interacting with the nucleus. The system will buffer the character stream. User programs can use the *Get and Put Character Calls* to send characters to the external device. The characters really go into the operating system buffers. So how do they get to the external device? At the interrupt level, the user must define handler routines to take care of the mechanics of a particular character-oriented I/O device. These routines can be very simple. They put characters into and take characters out of the operating system buffer by using two calls that are meant to come from interrupt handlers: *Post Received Character* (to the operating system) and *Post Transmit Ready* (i.e., get a character and send it). Tasks will be automatically suspended when they use Get and Put routines if other parts of the system are not ready.

The *Wait for Special Character Call* is unusual. It allows a task to go to sleep, until a special character, such as Control C, arrives in the character stream from the character I/O device being supported by the system.

The only other system calls involve the clock. They allow user tasks to set and read the time. They allow a task to suspend itself until a specified number of clock ticks have passed. And finally, there is a call to specify the length of the time slice for tasks of equal priority.

VRTX has been designed to allow easy incorporation into the software of any embedded processor application using a Z8000. The nucleus is wedded to the rest of the system via the Configuration Table, which we have mentioned in previous paragraphs. This is a data structure set up by the user describing the hardware configuration and the desired software configuration. The nucleus reads the Configuration Table and adjusts its activities accordingly. The table contains information such as the following:

1. Address and size of system data and stack area. The Task Control Blocks are kept here.
2. Size of the system stack.
3. Maximum number of tasks active at one time.
4. Address and size of RAM area for all the user tasks.
5. Stack size for user tasks.
6. Size of the block for memory allocation.

7. Address of the initialization task.

8. Address of the system interrupt trap area.

9. Addresses of routines for user supplied System Calls.

A real time nucleus is a pleasing thing to a systems programmer because it is small, modular, and easy to understand. It has become fashionable to design new operating systems around something like a real time nucleus even if a big, general purpose system is the target rather than an embedded processor. An operating system designed in this way consists of only about five components. There is the kernel, the interrupt handlers, some routines to implement a file system, some watch-dog routines called monitors, and a small collection of system tasks.

There is a monitor to control the access to every device or piece of code in the system that might be shared and have tasks competing to use it. A monitor is like a fence. The idea is to collect inside of it, in one place, all the code by which other tasks might gain access to a shared resource, i.e., the device or program associated with the monitor. The beginning and ending of a monitor will be guarded by semaphores so that the system can control the circumstances under which competing tasks can access the shared resource. Sometimes only one task at a time will be allowed to use the resource; sometimes more will be allowed, depending on circumstances.

The system tasks are programs that work in close cooperation with the operating system but compete for CPU resources in the same way user tasks do. An example would be a command line interpreter program that would provide an initial dialog with users at the terminal and bring programs requested by them into execution. All of these system programs, and indeed all user programs, are coordinated by making system calls to the kernel.

14.5 TREE ORIENTED FILE STRUCTURES: UNIX

The last sections of this chapter concern three powerful features that are found in the UNIX multi-tasking operating system developed at Bell Laboratories.

What is the best way to organize the file system on a multi-tasking computer? There seems to be no definitive answer to this question. However, there are many advantages in the solution embodied in UNIX. We will examine the distinctive UNIX approach to files in this section.

The UNIX file system is organized as an inverted tree. Each terminal node in the tree represents a file. Each nonterminal node is a directory. The scope of any given directory is just those nodes that lie below it in the tree. In this kind of structure, the basic way of identifying a file to the system is via a pathname. A pathname identifies a path through the tree from the root node to a particular terminal node. The pathname starts with the name of the root directory and then lists in order any other directories that are encountered on the way to the terminal node. Finally, the terminal node is listed. Figure 14-10 shows the layout of a small UNIX file system.

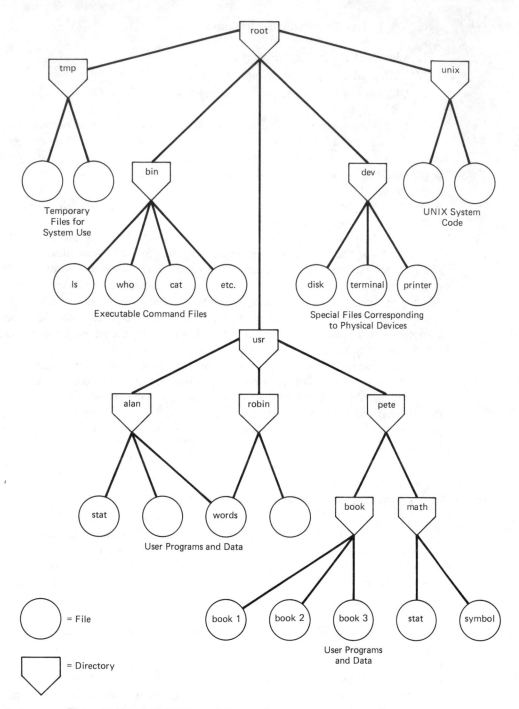

Figure 14-10:   A UNIX Hierarchical File System. UNIX files are the terminal nodes of an inverted tree. The interior nodes are the names of directories. Any file can be specified by a path from the highest level directory, through intermediate directories, down to the file itself.

Let's look at some examples. In all the examples that follow, file names and program names are given in lower case letters, because this is traditional in UNIX systems. The user named pete is writing a book. He has the separate chapters in files labeled book1, book2, etc. The most complete specification of the first chapter of the book is

```
/usr/pete/book/book1
```

The slash character at the beginning refers to the root directory. The file at any terminal node can be specified in a similar manner. In practice, a more concise specification is always used. When you sign on to the system, you will automatically "be in" your own system standard user directory. When pete signs on, any file references will always be searched for first, in the parts of the tree that are subordinate to the directory pete. Thus, another way to specify the first chapter in the book is simply to use

```
book/book1
```

Some other characteristics to note about the tree hierarchy are as follows. The same file can appear in many directories, if this is desirable; but each user of the file will see it as a different pathname. The two pathnames are referred to as aliases. For instance, these two pathnames refer to the same file:

```
/usr/robin/words
/usr/alan/words
```

It is also possible for two terminal nodes to have the same names, and yet clearly be different files because their pathnames are different. For instance, the following two file specifications refer to files with the same name, but different pathnames:

```
/usr/pete/math/stat
/usr/alan/stat
```

Some parts of a UNIX file system have special system uses. The subdirectory unix has system code in it. The subdirectory tmp is used for files that are dynamically created and destroyed by the system during the exchange of information between processes. The subdirectory bin contains utility programs that are normally included with a UNIX system. These are executable command files—programs that are executed just by specifying their names to the system. Finally, the files in the subdirectory named dev are special files. There is a physical device associated with each of them. Anytime the system wants to do I/O, it reads or writes one of these special files. Then underlying I/O drivers, which are not visible to the programmer, take over and use the information in the special file to do actual physical I/O operations.

There are several reasons for setting up the I/O system in this somewhat convoluted manner. For one thing it makes a complicated and varied process seem simple. A programmer, then, can communicate with any device that is on the system in one standard way—by reading or writing records to the associated file. It also makes possible a very powerful feature called I/O redirection, which we will discuss in a later section.

What are the advantages of the hierarchical file system? It is particularly good for cooperative projects. It is easy for anyone on the system to access any file in it if he has appropriate permission. He just specifies the file name. Thus data and programs can be exchanged between programmers. It is never necessary to have multiple copies of the same file between which errors may accumulate. If one programmer wants to make a file available to another, he will just tell him the pathname or allow him to create an alias so the second programmer can link to the file directly through his own directory tree.

It is also easy in a larger system to enforce uniform system-wide naming standards for all modules. The modules can be named according to a pathname that reflects the decomposition of a task in the manner of top-down design.

These are advantages of allowing a programmer to look "widely" through the file system. There are also advantages of "narrow" looking. A directory is like a window into the file system. By working within a specific directory, the programmer can control how much detail he sees. If pete is working on his book, chances are there will be times when he wants to see just the files that have to do with that and nothing else.

Hierarchical directories also offer a convenient way to control access to particular parts of the system. A user has to have appropriate permission to read any directory. We can easily create different directories above a group of files corresponding to the different classes of users who might be using the files.

The only disadvantage of the hierarchical system is that sometimes file access can be relatively slow. Each directory is a file. If we are dealing with a file hierarchy that is quite deep, then a number of files will have to be opened, and searched, and closed, before the system can identify the location of the desired file. UNIX handles this problem by creating a dynamic directory for every user that directly relates file names to locations for all files that the user is manipulating. This secondary directory means that a long search through the file hierarchy only has to be done once—the first time the file is referred to.

This elegant hierarchical directory scheme masks an underlying storage method for file data that is very simple. A UNIX file consists simply of a string of characters, with lines delimited by newline characters. The structure of files is controlled by the programs that use them, not by the system. Thus a user program might insert other delimiters in the character stream for its own purposes, but the system would treat these delimiters like any other characters.

There are UNIX operating system primitives to do the normal file operations such as create, open, read, write, position, and close. The create and open commands are given a fully elaborated pathname as one of their parameters. If the file does not already exist, these commands manipulate the hierarchical directory and create a place for it. If it does exist, its place in the hierarchy is found and a secondary directory is set up for fast access the next time the file is used.

File reading and writing are essentially sequential. Since a file is just a character stream, transfers can be done in reference to a pointer identifying a position in the stream. For instance, a user might ask to read 100 characters after the pointer. The system can be made to look as if it is doing random access, by using the position command. This can establish the pointer at any character position in the file.

14.6 *TREE STRUCTURED PROCESS INVOCATION: UNIX*

Tasks in the UNIX system are referred to as processes. New processes are brought into execution under UNIX in an unusual way. Everything starts with a single process for each user terminal. This is established when the system is turned on and initialized. Each of these processes may create other processes. These will now be called child processes, and the original will be called the parent. Each of the child processes may find it useful to spawn their own children, etc. A hierarchy like a genealogical family tree can thus develop relating all the processes in the system. At any time, all these processes may be executing concurrently, or selected ones may be suspended awaiting certain computational events.

Let's concentrate on the relationships between a process and its children. A new process can come into existence only by use of the fork system call. When a fork is executed, the process splits into two independently executing processes. It is very much like a single celled organism multiplying by binary fission. The program code in the child process is exactly the same as in the parent process. Also all files that were open for the parent process remain open for the child process as well.

The only difference is in the fork call. The code looks as follows in both processes:

```
processid = fork()
```

However, the result of executing the fork is for the call to return with processid = 0 in the child process, and processid equalling a number identifying the child process in the parent. Then in the code that follows this, there can be a test that allows control to follow different paths through the remaining instructions in the parent and child. This allows them to act as two different processes rather than as two copies of the same one.

There is another system primitive related to creating process hierarchies that we need to discuss. It is the execute command; and it supplies a mechanism whereby the child process can become differentiated from the parent. Here's how it works. There will be a program line following the fork that has the form

```
execute(file,arg1,arg2,  . . . ,argn)
```

Normally control will be such that this line is executed in the child process and not in the parent process. To maintain a biological analogy, this statement is like a brain transplant. The effect of it is that all the code and data in the process invoking execute are replaced from the file mentioned in the execute command. The arguments in the execute command are also made available for use by the child process. What stays the same under this mechanism is that all open files, the current directory, and any interprocess relationships are unaltered. So the execute command is how a child process can be spawned and then personalized to do work other than what was contained in the code of the parent.

Figure 14 11 shows the code for a parent and child process immediately after a fork. Notice that the code is exactly the same, but soon it won't be. The child process is about to do an execute command to differentiate itself from the parent. In this example,

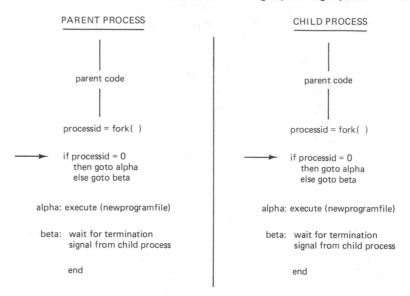

Figure 14-11: The Linkage Between Parent and Child Processes. This pseudocode focuses on UNIX process control. It shows the code for a parent and child process immediately after a fork has taken place. The arrows show where control is in each process as execution proceeds. The next thing that will happen is that the parent and child will follow different paths through the remaining code. The parent will suspend, and the child will get new code through the execute statement.

we have shown that the parent will wait for a signal that the child has completed execution. This means that whatever the code is that the child process receives from execute, this code must terminate by sending a signal to the parent (there is a system call for this).

UNIX is rather weak in constructs for interprocess communication and synchronization. These things tend to be more necessary in real time operating systems. The primitives that are available are provided as a way to synchronize within a given parent-child hierarchy. One way processes can communicate is through pipes. A pipe is a temporary file that one process writes into and another process reads. The ancestor of a hierarchy will usually establish the pipe. All the descendants of the process can use it because the forking process makes all the files of the parent available to the child, and a pipe is just a type of file.

The other kind of synchronization primitive is a system call that allows a parent process to suspend until a child process terminates. When the child process is through, all its resources are released; and a signal is given to the parent causing it to wake up and continue processing. We have already given an example of this primitive in Figure 14-11.

Which programs make use of the forking process? Any program can fork, since the fork is an operating system primitive, but it is most commonly done from the user interface program—the shell. The shell uses the fork mechanism as a way to start up commands and other user programs and to maintain hierarchical control over them.

Let's consider one more example of where tree structured process invocation would be useful. This example is from communications programming. The point we want to focus on here is that the fork capability allows processes to be created and destroyed dynamically to match the workload on the system. The number of active processes doesn't have to be preplanned.

Consider an application where one of the things a computer has to do is handle requests and store information that comes in over a network of telecommunications lines. At any time anywhere between o and n lines might be active and need to be attended to rapidly. This application could be set up in several ways. The calls could be queued and processed one at a time. But this would result in unacceptable service delays. The calls could be funneled through a single monolithic call handler that was set up to be able to respond to all possible permutations of service requests. This kind of program is difficult to write and difficult to debug. Or we could have a UNIX-like solution. That is, a process would automatically be started for each call that came in, and it would act as an independent entity, doing everything that was necessary to move that call through the system.

Let's flesh this idea out a little more. There probably would be a simple monitoring process that would look at the phone lines. When it detected a call, it would fork. The child process would then be customized as a call handler, via an execute command, and it would be turned loose on the call. If other calls came in, the monitor process would fork as many times as needed to make one call handler per call. A handler would release its resources and go out of existence whenever a call completed. This kind of arrangement divides the work modularly. It is easy to write and debug, since a single call handler only deals with one call. It also results in the system being full of call handling code (some of it will be reentrant) when there are many calls, and almost empty of that code when there are none. It is an elegant solution.

14.7 EMBEDDED COMMAND LANGUAGE INTERPRETERS: THE UNIX SHELL

The user interface in the UNIX system is very unusual and is probably UNIX's most powerful feature. The system has an interpreter, called the shell, that is built into it. The user and user programs generally interact with this interpreter rather than making direct contact with the operating system. Every multi-tasking operating system has somewhere within it a program called a command line interpreter. In many cases this is really little more than a program loader, but in UNIX, it has many other functions. The shell program has a language in its own right. It is every bit as powerful and about as hard to learn and use as other interpretive languages we have looked at, such as BASIC. However, the items the shell manipulates are not variables and arrays as in a BASIC program. Rather they are the names of programs and files.

The purpose of this section is to illustrate the main kinds of things an embedded command processor can do for you, and to give some idea of how to implement these things with an interpreter. We will first need to understand how the shell can activate commands using the fork primitive. Then we will consider how a command interpreter can take a very terse command syntax and expand it into a series of lower level commands suitable for an underlying operating system. The next thing we will look at is how the shell administers the UNIX I/O redirection scheme. Finally we will want to see what it buys to have an intermediate programming language standing between a user program and the operating system.

Since we are discussing the command interpreter, we need to make a short digression into what UNIX commands look like. The syntax for commands is as follows. The first word in the command line is the name of the command. It is also the name of an executable program file listed somewhere in the system directory. All things on the command line that follow the first word must be separated by spaces. The first fields after the command name are for switches. These are indicators that select options in the way the command will execute. Not all commands have them. For instance, the list command given as

```
ls
```

causes the names of all files in your current directory to be listed, one file per line. However, if you give the command as

```
ls  -l
```

(the switch stands for "long"), then, in addition to the name of each file, on each line there is the owner of the file, the date of creation, the access rights, and other information.

After the switches, if any, come the command's arguments, and then any files required by the command. For instance, the command

```
grep 'engineer' personfile
```

will output all the lines in the file called personfile which contain the string "engineer". In our present context, 'engineer' is a command argument and personfile is a file.

The last thing in a command should be fields that the shell will interpret as calling for I/O redirection. UNIX commands normally input from the keyboard and output to the screen. This is the default, but it's easy to do I/O redirection. The command

```
cat  f1  f2  f3
```

concatenates the three files and outputs the result to the screen. If we issue the command in a slightly different format, the system will create a file called temp and the output will be put there.

```
cat  f1  f2  f3  >temp
```

Figure 14-12 lists an assortment of the simpler commands that are associated with UNIX.

Now let's get back to how the embedded command language works. Here is the basic procedure whereby the shell can start a command into execution (programs look like commands to the shell). Most of the time, the shell is just waiting for the user to

ls	Lists the names of the files in a directory.
mv	Moves a file. It is used for renaming files or directories and for moving files into new directories.
cp	Copies one file to another.
rm	Deletes file(s).
cat	Concatenates one or more files onto standard output. Also, cat is often used to display the contents of files on the terminal screen.
pr	Prints files with title, date, and page number on every page with optional multi-column output.
mkdir	Creates one or more new directories. Note that there is no command to make a file. Files are created dynamically, when they are needed, by being named as arguments in commands.
wc	Counts lines and "words" (strings separated by blanks) in a file.
grep	This is a general purpose pattern matcher. Given a pattern as part of the command, it will output all lines from its input which contain that pattern.
sort	Merges and/or sorts files line by line on a variety of keys.
who	Reports what users are signed on to the system-one line of information per user.
ps	Reports on what processes are currently active in the system—a window into the system for performance evaluation.

Figure 14-12:   A List of Some Simple UNIX Commands. These are simple commands useful for examples and a good starting point for someone who wants to learn the UNIX system. UNIX is usually distributed with a great deal of software in the form of commands. There are many more standard commands than we have listed here, and some are very complex—compilers, interactive calculators, editors, text formatters, parser generators, and the like.

type a command. After the newline character ending a command line is typed, the shell analyzes this input. It puts the arguments in a form appropriate for the execute system primitive. Then fork is called. The child process, whose code, of course, is still that of the shell, attempts to perform an execute with the appropriate arguments. If successful, this will bring in and start execution of the program whose name was given. Meanwhile, the other process resulting from the fork, the shell itself, standing in the position of a parent, waits for the child process to finish. When the child process is about to terminate, it signals the parent. When this happens, the shell wakes up, types its prompt, and reads the keyboard to obtain another command.

A related shell feature we should mention is that it is possible for the shell to start up a child process, and then continue in execution itself to receive more commands from the user. This is known as placing a command (the child process) in the background. Whether the shell is to suspend or not is governed by a parameter that can be set as part of any UNIX command. This facility makes it easy for the user to start up a number of jobs at once from his terminal. For instance, he might be running a test version of a program that was under development. He could simultaneously be compiling a second version; and he might also be editing a third version of the program in response to the problems that had been discovered in earlier runs. Being able to control multiple concurrent programs in this way is a feature normally found only on very big systems.

The shell acts in some ways like a macroprocessor in that it provides a mechanism whereby a high level command will be replaced by a series of lower level ones that accomplish the same functions. There is nothing that is analogous to a macro definition. That is all implicit in the command language. However, the concepts of parameter substitution, expression expansion, and conditional interpretation are all important, as they are with macroprocessors.

Some of these concepts require shell programming to illustrate, and we will discuss them later. For now, let's consider an example of command expansion. Let's say we have a book with files named in the form chap1-1, chap1-2, chap1-3, chap2-1, chap2-2, chap3-1, etc. That is, there is a file for each subheading of each chapter. Let's say we wanted to print the first two chapters in the normal order of the book. This long command would do it:

```
pr chap1-1 chap1-2 chap1-3 chap2-1 chap2-2
```

but a simpler way would be to do it with

```
pr chap[1,2]*
```

What the shell will do is expand this expression into a number of arguments by looking in your directory and pulling out all names that begin with chap and that end with either 1 or 2 followed by any other string. So it expands the argument to the five arguments you would have had to type if you wanted to give explicit directions. UNIX programmers use this feature and related ones to give very terse commands that end up doing a great deal of work.

Another powerful feature administered by the shell is I/O redirection. What does this mean? Most programs that execute under UNIX are written to communicate with three files: a file for input, a file for output, and a file for error messages. As part of the process of setting a program into execution, the shell is able to indicate to the program specifically what file to use for input, and what ones to use for output and diagnostics. There are many possibilities. Any of these channels can be connected to a device, or a named file, or to another program that is producing or consuming data. This system is like an old-fashioned telephone switchboard where the operator plugs in cables to make specific connections. The shell is the operator.

Let's examine how such a system can be implemented. Briefly every program has logical slots that hold three descriptors for the three standard files which it should use for input, output, and error messages. Before starting up a command in the child process, the shell can give the program new descriptors for these files so that the input and output can come from anywhere. All normal programs that execute under UNIX read from the file pointed to by their input descriptor and write to the file pointed to by their output descriptor. They have no knowledge that the actual source or destination of the text is being manipulated at a higher level. The default case for I/O is that the slot for input will point to the special file corresponding to the user's keyboard. The slots for output and error diagnostics will point to the special file corresponding to the screen of the user's terminal.

Now we need an example. Normally the list command will list all files in your current directory onto the screen of your terminal. The list command is

```
ls
```

However, if you want the output of this command to go into a file, you just issue the command in a slightly different way.

```
ls  >filename
```

The arrow means the output goes into the named file. If the file doesn't already exist, the system will create it automatically.

A similar situation exists for input. If you use the print command alone,

```
pr
```

it will simply echo to the screen whatever you type on the keyboard. That is, it is taking its input from the keyboard. If you use it in the following way, it will take its input from a file and put it onto the screen.

```
pr  <filename
```

A related concept is the famous UNIX pipe arrangement. Pipes are a way that concurrent processes can communicate with each other. They are intermediate files that will be written into by one process and read from by another. The shell creates the pipe(s), via a system call, and then redirects the output from one process into the pipe and the input from another process out of the pipe. Pipes are unidirectional. One process writes, the other process reads. The drivers are smart enough to accomplish some interprocess synchronization. That is, a process trying to read an empty pipeline will go to sleep until there is something there to be read. A process writing into a full pipeline will go to sleep until some other process empties it out.

Let's look at an example, and then we will see how the basic I/O redirection mechanism can accommodate this extension. Let's say that the terminals on a system are numbered as tty1-tty100. Suppose we wish to generate a file with the names of all users who are on the low numbered terminals, say, terminals one through fifty. We need to remember three commands to do this. The *who* command will print a list of currently logged-in users. Its format is such that each line contains a user name, the terminal identification, and the sign-on time. Another command we need is *grep*, which is the pattern matcher built into UNIX. It can search a string for a match to a pattern that you supply as part of the command. And the last command we might use is *rm*, which is used to delete a file. A command sequence to do the job we want without pipelines is

```
who  >tempfile
grep  'tty[1-50]'  tempfile  >resultfile
rm  tempfile
```

We have had to explicitly form a temporary file that captures the output of the *who* command. Then we extract this file with *grep* to get the proper information. Then we delete the temporary file because we don't need it any more.

The pipeline facility was developed to do away with these manipulations on temporary files. It also allows the task you are trying to do to run as one entity rather than three sequential pieces. The same job can be done with pipelined I/O using

```
who  | grep  'tty[1-50]'  >resultfile
```

Nowhere is a temporary file named. The vertical bar tells the shell to use I/O redirection so that the output of *who* becomes the input to *grep*.

The shell implements this command construct as follows. It defines a temporary file of type pipeline and puts its descriptor in the place where the *who* command will look to find its output file. Then it forks a child process and starts up the who command in it. Next it places a descriptor for the same temporary file into the place where the *grep* command looks for a description of its input file. Then it forks a child process and starts up *grep* in the child process. Then the shell, which has acted as a parent process, goes to sleep awaiting a signal it will receive when the last process in the pipeline terminates.

Pipelines are not limited to two commands. Any number of commands can be strung together in this way. The shell essentially sets up all these commands to run concurrently. They are synchronized automatically because when the I/O drivers are working with pipeline files, they are smart enough to suspend a process that tries to read an empty pipe or one that tries to write a full one. There are complementary operations for waking up processes that have been suspended in the course of their use of the pipes. The reader should now notice the similarity in the operation of a UNIX pipe and an MP/M-II message queue.

Now we come to the final topic in this section, which is shell programming. It is possible to build up a series of shell commands, which act like a program, and invoke them by typing the name of this composite command. This apparatus is called a shell procedure. It does the same kind of thing a submit file or a command file will do in other systems. These things call lists of commands into execution one by one. However, the shell procedure is more powerful because of the programming features of the shell language. It is possible to flexibly control the system's passage through a stream of simple commands by using the conditional branches, case statements, and looping constructs that are part of the shell language. These are the normal control constructs of any programming language.

Let's consider an example in which the shell would execute the commands of a simple command file without any fancy programming. Examine the following command:

```
sh  file  [args]
```

Using the name of the shell itself in a command causes the shell to read and execute other commands that are in the file. The arguments in the command that we have shown are real parameters or real filenames that will be substituted for dummy parameters in the lines of the command file as those lines are processed. The dummy parameters must be indicated by $1, $2, . . . , etc. $1 will be matched with the first argument that comes in on the command line, $2 with the second argument, etc. For example, if the file called subset contains the line:

```
ls  |  grep  $1
```

then:

```
sh  subset  book
```

is equivalent to

```
ls  |  grep  'book'
```

What this configured command does is print out the names of all files in your current directory which contain the string 'book' as part of their name.

The real power of shell procedures is not in the simple sequential execution of a list of commands. Power arises through the use of the control constructs which allow the order of execution of the commands to be controlled just as they are in a more familiar programming language. The primary contructs are

```
if-then-else
the multi-way branch (case statement)
looping using all values of an argument list
looping while some condition is true
```

We will give one example that uses looping over a list. Imagine that we have an employee information file (called user/personnel) in which the lines look like this:

```
Tietjen     engineer      dept57  ×346
Marcellus   programmer    dept59  ×212
Madoff      statistician  dept02  ×250
Hammer      manager       dept59  ×315
Smith       salesman      dept61  ×248
Van Zee     programmer    dept59  ×212
 etc.
```

Let's say we want to make a general purpose procedure that can pull out lists of all the people in certain job categories. This procedure should be reusable by changing parameters. We also want to use it right now to make a list of all the programmers followed by all the engineers who are employed by this company. The shell procedure to do this will be called extract. The text of extract is

```
for  i
do  grep  $i  /user/personnel;  done
```

We can issue a command to print the desired list by using

```
sh  extract programmer engineer
```

The shell will parse the command line and recognize that it is being asked to do a command procedure called "extract." It will find the procedure. It will interpret the loop construct in the procedure to mean, for each of the arguments on the original command line, substitute them one by one into the do clause, and then execute the resulting command. Thus what will happen will be the same as if we had given these two simple commands in succession:

```
grep 'programmer' /user/personnel
grep 'engineer'   /user/personnel
```

Of course, the extract command can be used to form subsets of the personnel list in any other desired way, simply by changing the arguments given on the command line.

Many users prefer to write shell procedures instead of programs in the normal languages provided on the system. Why is this? First of all, it is easy to create the procedure because it is only text. It doesn't have to be compiled and linked; all you need is the editor. Secondly, the procedures are short and are never put in any form other than their source language. This means they are easy to find, understand, and modify. Finally, because of the fluidity of a UNIX system, it is easy to create a procedure on the fly, use it a few times, and then get rid of it. In other words, it is good for getting the job done now.

STUDY QUESTIONS AND EXERCISES

1. Outline a data processing application that could profit from being run under a single user multi-tasking operating system on a dedicated small computer.

2. Write 8080 code for a simple Dummy Task. The first location will be labeled DUMMY.

3. Is a Dummy Task necessary in a system that uses round-robin dispatching? Without a Dummy Task, what happens if no task is ready?

4. In the priority dispatching environment described by Figure 14-2, imagine that the system decided to increase temporarily the priority of Task D because higher priority tasks were hogging all the time. How would the dispatch list look when the priority was changed? How could the system keep track of when to reduce the priority back again to its original level?

5. During the task switch procedure, why is it necessary to put the resume parameters in the Task Control Block? Couldn't they just as well have been left on the stack?

6. Discuss how multi-tasking systems of the sort we described should be initialized so that when the system is turned on the time slicing operations will start properly.

7. Write a fragment of 8080 code that would be suitable for use at the end of the ACTIVATE routine where the resume parameters are restored and control is given over to the new task. Assume the registers are stored in the Task Control Block in this order: AF, BC, DE, HL. The first byte is in a location labeled REG. The Program Counter has been stored at location PROCNT in the Control Block, and the Stack Pointer is at location STKPNT.

8. Imagine that we wish to incorporate into a multi-tasking operating system the ability to suspend tasks for a certain number of ticks of the system clock. Suggest in detail how the design of our dispatching system could be expanded to encompass this feature.

9. Would it be feasible to link Task Control Blocks directly into a Dispatch List rather than having a separate descriptor structure which was linked and had pointers to the Task Control Blocks?

10. Operating systems are generally configured to a specific machine environment with the help of an interactive system generator program. The user tailors the operating system through a dialog with this program. This is necessary because the equipment and physical characteristics of installations vary so much from one place to the next. Write down the kinds of things the generator would want to know in order to produce a tailored operating system for a particular computer installation.

11. Write 8080 code for a round-robin dispatcher. There are 64 task descriptors in this particular system, each of which is eight bytes long. The block of descriptors starts at location DESBLK. In each descriptor, the first byte is the task number (0-255). The second byte is the status: 0 for running, 1 for ready, −1 for blocked. The last two bytes are a pointer containing the address of the next descriptor. Two bytes at location RUNTSK point to the descriptor of the current running task. What this subroutine should do, and all it should do, is return a pointer to the descriptor of the next task to run; and this should be returned in the BC register pair.

12. Rewrite Figures 12-10 and 12-11 to show how the CIO and CIH would be organized if they could use semaphores to control access to a system's I/O resources.

13. Give an example of a data processing application (other than those mentioned in the book) that could be profitably analyzed as a producer-consumer problem. Assume that two counting semaphores will be used to synchronize the application. Construct a scenario involving some pattern of buffer traffic that will demonstrate how the semaphores operate.

14. Write 8080 code for a subroutine called WAIT that performs the wait on semaphore function. The semaphores have just two states, and they have been created and initialized by some other routine. Upon entry, register B will contain the number of the semaphore (there may be several). The semaphore data structures begin at location SEMDATA and take up 18 bytes per semaphore. That is, a single flag and queue structure take up 18 bytes. The first byte is for the flag. The next byte is a count of how many tasks are queued. And then comes the queue itself. One byte is used per task, and it contains the task number. The queue has room for 16 tasks. Use SUSPEND and DISPATCH as discussed in Section 14.2 to block the current task if necessary.

15. Would it be possible to install a small multi-tasking kernel on a single chip microcomputer like the Motorola 6805 or the Intel 8051? What system features would a single chip computer need in order to be successful in making use of a multi-tasking system?

16. Assume that something like VRTX has been adapted to run on an Intel 8080 microprocessor system. There are 8 interrupt lines hooked up to this system, and they trigger the various Restart instructions with the aid of a Peripheral Interrupt Processor. This chip forces a Restart instruction on the data bus that corresponds to whatever interrupt line is active. Assume that an equivalent of the VRTX routine UI-TIMER can be executed by the 8080 code CALL TIMER. The clock interrupt handler for this system is to be located at location E000. Write this handler in 8080 code. Hint: it is a very simple routine.

17. This question asks you to write another VRTX style interrupt handler. Once again, assume a VRTX like system is running on an 8080 based microcomputer. One task in the system produces

and occasionally outputs strings of characters to a special I/O device. It is the only task that does anything with these strings and the only one that uses this particular I/O device. After the task outputs a character, it pends for a message that will appear in a 16 bit location called MAILA. A one appearing here means that another character can now be sent. A zero means not ready (or actually, no message). The device interrupts when it is ready for another character, and a Restart instruction routes control to a particular handler associated with the device. Write the handler. Code equivalent to UI-POST and UI-EXIT can be executed by using CALL POST and CALL EXIT. When using the POST Routine, the address of the mailbox should go in the BC pair and the 16 bit message should go in the DE pair.

18. Explain the various features of UNIX that would keep it from being an effective real time operating system.

19. Does a single user UNIX system make any sense? If so, what could you do with it that would not be possible on a single task system?

20. What advantages does tree structured process invocation bring to UNIX?

21. Ten people in your engineering department have recently written papers about various aspects of designing with microprocessors. The documents are on a common UNIX system shared by all the users. Another two papers are going to be sent to you as files over a communications link that is a standard part of your installation. The communications link can be accessed as if it were a file named comfile. You are going to collect these papers into a book. Explain how you could gather all the documents together into a single document or document structure by manipulating the directory and using I/O redirection. Explain how you could then print out the entire book-length document with a single UNIX command.

Appendices

A.1 LEARNING TO PROGRAM THE INTEL 8080 MICROPROCESSOR

It is likely that someone skilled in the programming of small computers will encounter and have to make use of a large number of computer instruction sets in the course of his career. Significant new computers seem to appear every year or so. The micro world is not like the comfortable milieu of the IBM 360/370, where it has been possible to get along using the same instruction set (with extensions) for upwards of 15 years.

Because change is a fact of life with small computers, it would be good to have a systematic procedure for learning about new machines. Learning a new machine means learning to function with its instruction set. We propose such a procedure here for those who are unfamiliar with the Intel 8080. The steps we are going to discuss should help to bring someone up to operating speed on this particular processor in a minimum of time, if he has had experience with assembler language programming for some other computer. For someone who knows no assembler at all, this article will probably not be enough, but it is a good place to start. There are many good references on assembly programming. One that fits in well with the approaches used in this book is Lance A. Leventhal's text, *Introduction to Microprocessors*,[1] particularly the first five chapters.

To get going quickly, we recommend the following steps:

1. Learn the programming model of the processor.
2. Learn the available addressing modes.

[1] Lance A. Leventhal, *Introduction to Microprocessors: Software, Hardware, and Programming*, Prentice-Hall, Englewood Cliffs, N.J., 1978.

3. Learn the most frequently used instructions in some important categories.

4. Do some simple programs.

5. Go back and learn the exotic instructions—the ones that won't be used much.

We will now show how to apply these steps to the 8080. Learning the programming model means learning the usage of all registers and any special locations in memory that act like registers or have other special properties.

To understand why the registers are the way they are, it is necessary to understand the 8080's external buses. Physically, the microprocessor is a 40 pin chip. Sixteen pins on the chip form the address bus, and thus the maximum addressable memory is 64 kilobytes. Eight of the other pins form a bidirectional data bus. Data is exchanged with the memory in one byte units over these lines. Most of the other pins on the processor are various control lines, which, taken together, can be thought of as the control bus.

Figure A-1 shows the 8080's registers. The machine has seven registers which are called A, B, C, D, E, H, L. These registers are general purpose. They all can hold 8 bit numbers, and there are instructions for moving data in and out of them. Some of the registers have additional special uses. The A register is an accumulator. It must hold one of the operands in any 8 bit arithmetic or logical operation, and it receives the results after the operation has been completed. There are additional instructions to move data in and out of this special register that do not apply to the other ones.

For some instructions certain pairs of 8 bit registers can be used together to form pseudo 16 bit registers. The H and L registers together are called the HL register pair. It is the most important of the pseudo 16 bit registers. One of its uses is as a 16 bit address pointer for getting at data in the memory.

The only 16 bit arithmetic on the 8080 is a 16 bit addition instruction. For this instruction, the HL register pair acts as a 16 bit accumulator. The other 16 bit operand in the addition comes from either the BC or DE register pairs. All arithmetic in the 8080 is done in 2's complement format.

What about the flags? These are five 1 bit registers which assume values that give information about the result in the accumulator after arithmetic and logical operations and a few other operations. The sign flag sets when the number in the accumulator is minus. The zero flag sets when the number in the accumulator is zero. The carry flag sets when an arithmetic operation generates a carry. The parity flag sets when the parity of the number in the accumulator is even. Lastly, the half carry flag sets whenever there is a carry out of bit position three. Remember that in the 8080 not all instructions set the flags.

The flags are used for conditional branches. Typically a program will use flags by having some sort of arithmetic or logical statement that sets the flags. This will be followed by one of several kinds of branching statements which will execute a branch if a designated flag is set. If it is not set, execution continues sequentially.

There are just a few special locations in the 8080 memory structure. The reset location, which is where control goes when the reset line on the CPU is asserted, is location zero. There are also eight restart locations which are associated with the 8080's interrupt system. The 8080 has a one byte subroutine call instruction called the Restart

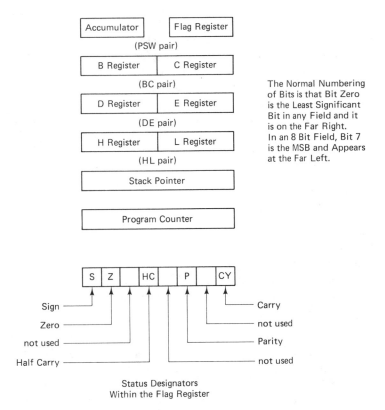

The Normal Numbering of Bits is that Bit Zero is the Least Significant Bit in any Field and it is on the Far Right. In an 8 Bit Field, Bit 7 is the MSB and Appears at the Far Left.

Status Designators
Within the Flag Register

Figure A-1:   The Intel 8080 Registers. The Intel 8080 microprocessor has seven general purpose registers (8 bits wide). Of these seven, the accumulator has many additional special uses. For instance, it holds one operand and the results in any arithmetic or logical operation. The H and L registers, concatenated together, can be used as a 16 bit address pointer or as a limited 16 bit accumulator for addition. A flag register reflects the results of arithmetic and logical operations. There is also a 16 bit stack pointer and program counter.

instruction. When used, it puts the return address on the stack, and causes control to branch to one of the restart locations (which one is specified in the instruction). The restart locations are

```
0000H
0008H
0010II
0018H
0020H
0028H
0030H
0038H
```

We also have to include the stack in our programming model. The 8080 has a 16 bit stack pointer (SP), which means the stack can be anywhere in memory. When items are pushed onto the stack, it grows in size toward the low numbered locations in memory. The stack pointer always points to the very last byte put on the stack. The only data the stack can accept are two byte units that come from pushing or pulling specified register pairs.

A final detail that we should perhaps note in the programming model is that the 8080 uses variable length instructions. They can be one, two, or three bytes long. The first byte is always an operation code specifying what is to be done. The second or second and third bytes are always pieces of data or addresses that fit in an 8 or 16 bit field.

Now we are ready to tackle step two of our procedure, the addressing modes. The addressing mode refers to the method used in a machine instruction to specify where its operands are or should be. The 8080 uses these addressing modes:

- Direct Addressing
- Register Addressing
- Register Indirect Addressing
- Immediate Addressing
- Implicit Addressing

Unfortunately, the instruction set is not very clean. That is, you can't use every mode with every instruction. So, for each instruction, you have to remember what modes it can use. We will give examples of all the modes. The mnemonics used in the following discussion are all from Intel standard assembly language.

In the Direct Addressing Mode, a 16 bit address is included as part of the instruction. Here is an instruction that specifies that the contents of the accumulator are to be stored at location 4000H.

```
STA  4000H
```

In the Register Addressing Mode, each register to be used is coded for with three bits of the operation code (there are only seven registers). These instructions are very short (1 byte) because at most 6 bits are used to address the registers. The following instruction shows how to move data into the H register from the B register.

```
MOV  H,B
```

Many data movement instructions have two operands. The normal 8080 convention in this case is that the first operand is the destination and the second is the source for the move.

In the Register Indirect Mode, one of the 16 bit register pairs is used as an address pointer, usually it is the HL pair. For instance, suppose the HL pair contains the number 2000H. Then the following instruction will move the contents of the C register into memory at the place pointed to by the HL pair.

```
MOV   M, C
```

M is always used to mean the memory location indicated by the HL pair. A previous instruction will have had to be executed to set up the HL pair properly before making this transfer.

In Immediate Mode Addressing, a piece of data is included as part of the instruction. Here is one way to load the HL registers. The instruction loads 2000H into this pair of registers.

```
LXI   H, 2000H
```

It is not necessary to state HL in the instruction. H is enough. Similarly, B stands for the BC pair and D for the DE pair in this instruction. LXI means load immediate.

Implicit Addressing is used in situations where the operand is always the same, so it doesn't have to be stated. It is implied. An example is

```
RAR
```

This instruction rotates the contents of the accumulator right by one bit. The carry bit is part of the rotation. It can be thought of as an extra bit adjacent to the MSB position in the accumulator. The accumulator is the only thing that can be rotated in this machine.

Now we are ready for step three, learning the most important instructions. Computer langauge is like human language in that 80% of the talking or programming can be done with a selected subset of the whole language. Our attempt now should be to learn the instructions in such a subset. Logically, the 8080 instructions seem to form five categories corresponding to the type of things the computer can do. We will pick the most important instructions from each category. The categories are

- Data Movement Instructions
- Data Transformation Instructions (Arithmetic and Logic)
- Input-Output Instructions
- Program Control Instructions
- Machine Control Instructions

See Figure A-2 for a good working subset of the language. There are some abbreviations you will have to understand in order to read the chart.

r	means a register – A, B, C, D, E, H, or L
rp	means a register pair – BC, DE, or HL
M	means the location in memory pointed to by HL
data8	means one byte of data
data16	means two bytes of data

Eight Bit Instructions   Sixteen Bit Instructions

1. *Data Movement*

MOV   r,r   MOV   r,M   MOV   M,r
MVI   r,data8   MVI   M,data8   LXI   rp,data16

STA   addr16   LHLD   addr16
LDA   addr16   SHLD   addr16

                                                   PUSH   PSW   POP   PSW
                                                   PUSH   rp   POP   rp

2. *Data Transformation*

ADD   r   ADD   M   ADI   data8   DAD   rp
SUB   r   SUB   M   SBI   data8
ANA   r   ANA   M   ANI   data8
CMP   r   CMP   M   CPI   data8
INR   r   INR   M   INX   rp
DCR   r   DCR   M   DCX   rp

3. *Input/Output*

IN   addr8   none
OUT   addr8

4. *Program Control*

JMP   addr16   none
CALL   addr16
RET
JC   addr16
  also JNC, JZ, JNZ,JM,JP,JPE,JPO
RST

5. *Machine Control*

EI   none
DI
HLT
NOP

Figure A-2:   A Useful Subset of 8080 Instructions. Learn these instructions to come
up to speed on the 8080 quickly and to be able to read the programming examples in
this book.

addr8   means a one byte address (port number)

addr16   means a two byte address

Note also that we have divided this chart into an 8 bit and a 16 bit side, since sometimes there are both kinds of instruction in each category.

In the *Data Movement* category we see many move instructions (MOV). They can use any combination of registers and the memory symbol as operands. There is also a move immediate instruction (MVI) which is used to fill an arbitrary register with 8 bits of data, or to fill a memory location that is pointed to by HL. The Store Accumulator instruction (STA) has a complementary load instruction (LDA) that works the same way. In fact, every store in the 8080 has a complementary load.

In the 16 bit category, there is the important Load Register Pair Immediate instruction (LXI) whereby 16 bits of data can be established in a register. The LHLD and SHLD instructions load and store to and from the HL pair with the data location being specified by a 16 bit direct address that is part of the instruction. PUSH and POP are the stack transfer operations. Only register pairs may be used, thus these are 16 bit instructions. PSW stands for Program Status Word. It means a 16 bit word formed by the flags and the accumulator.

In the *Data Transformation* category, the most important instruction is the Add instruction (ADD). One of the operands must always be in the accumulator. The other operand can be specified in three ways as is shown. The result will appear in the accumulator. The third form is an Add Immediate, (ADI) where 8 bits of data is part of the instruction. Note the change in the Add mnemonic. In general, the immediate instructions have different mnemonics from the base form to which they belong. The form of the Subtract instruction (SUB) follows that of the Add instruction. We also see three forms of the Logical And instruction (ANA). The deployment of operands and addressing modes are the same as for addition. Remember the pattern of these instructions. We will see that many others have the same pattern. We also need to include the Compare instruction (CMP) in this section. It is in every way identical to the Subtract instruction, except that the result is not used. It is not written back to the accumulator. The compare is used to set the processor flags before a program control instruction which will cause a branch depending on the state of those flags. Finally, we should note that there are instructions to increment (INR) or decrement (DCR) any register or any indirectly addressed byte in memory.

On the 16 bit side, the 8080 has a 16 bit addition operation (DAD) in which either the BC or DE pair can be added to the HL register, and the result left in the HL pair. There are also extended increment (INX) and decrement instructions (DCX) that work with any register pair.

The 8080 only has two *Input/Output* instructions. They cause the transfer of 8 bits of data between the accumulator and a numbered external register known as an I/O port. Programming is very easy. You just have to know the numbers and functions of the ports that have been designed into your hardware.

The *Program Control* section includes an instruction for a simple jump (JMP) to a 16 bit direct address (specified as part of the instruction). The Subroutine Call instruction

(CALL) works in the same way as a jump except that it puts a return address on the stack. The Return instruction (RET) takes the return address off the stack and puts it in the program counter so that it is the next instruction executed. The same return instruction is normally used to terminate subroutines and interrupt routines.

There are also conditional jumps. These work with the flags which presumably will have been given values on some previous instruction. The JC and JNC instructions cause a branch to a 16 bit direct address if the carry flag is set (1) or reset (0). The JZ and JNZ cause branches if the zero flag is set or reset. Note, the zero flag will have been set if the last arithmetic or logical instruction left a zero in the accumulator. The JM or JP instructions cause branches if the sign flag is set or reset. The sign flag, in those instructions that use it, is taken from the MSB position in the accumulator. The JPE and JPO instructions branch if the parity flag is set (even parity) or reset.

Finally, in the Program Control section, we have the Restart instruction (RST), which is very important for interrupts and which was discussed earlier.

In the *Machine Control* section, we have instructions to enable (EI) and disable (DI) the 8080's interrupt system. There is a halt instruction (HLT), which will stop all program execution until there is an interrupt or the machine is reset. Finally, in this category we have the NOP—no operation. Since it takes up four machine cycles in its execution, it frequently appears in code for timing purposes.

The foregoing instructions are sufficient to do a great deal of 8080 programming, and if you understand them you can read most programming examples in this book.

Let's consider a simple programming example to give you the flavor of 8080 programming. Figure A-3 shows a program that finds the minimum value in an array of 8 bit positive numbers. The array starts at 0201H. The number of elements in the array

Memory Address (hexadecimal)	Instruction (mnemonic)			Memory Contents (hexadecimal)
		ORG	0100H	; START CODE AT 0100H	
0100	START:	LXI	H, 0200H	; SET UP COUNT OF ELEMENTS	21, 00, 02
0103		MOV	C, M		4E
0104		INX	H	; POINT TO FIRST ELEMENT	23
0105		MOV	A, M	; USE AS A TRIAL MINIMUM	7E
0106		DCR	C	; COUNT ITS USE	0D
0107	LOOP:	INX	H	; GET NEXT ELEMENT	23
0108		MOV	B, M	; INTO REGISTER B	46
0109		CMP	B	; COMPARE WITH TRIAL MINIMUM	B8
010A		JM	ENDTST	; GO TO END TEST, OR	FA, 0E, 01
010D	SWITCH:	MOV	A, B	; USE A BETTER MINIMUM	78
010E	ENDTST:	DCR	C	; TEST FOR MORE ELEMENTS	0D
010F		JNZ	LOOP	; GO BACK FOR MORE	C2, 07, 01
0112		HLT			76
		END		; END OF THE ASSEMBLY	

Figure A-3: A Simple 8080 Program. This example program finds the minimum element in an array of positive 8 bit numbers. The array starts in location 0201H. The number of elements is given in 0200H. The answer is to be left in the accumulator. The code is to start at location 0100H.

is in location 0200H. The minimum element is to be left in the accumulator. The code is to be assembled so that this program will start at location 0100H.

The program begins by determining how many elements there are and by using the first element as a trial minimum. Then a loop begins. A pointer is set up that will be moved progressively through the array to single out elements that will be compared, one by one, with the trial minimum. If the element being pointed to is less than the trial minimum, it will become the new trial minimum. Each time around the loop, the count of elements is decreased by one. When the count reaches zero, the program stops this process, because all the elements have been examined.

Figure A-4 shows the rest of the 8080 instructions, the part of the instruction set that we haven't discussed yet. In the *Data Movement* category, first of all, we have instructions to do a store (STAX) or load (LDAX) of the accumulator according to a 16 bit address pointer in the BC or DE register pairs. Then there are several exchange instructions. XCHG will swap the DE and HL register pairs. XTHL will swap the top of the stack and the HL pair. SPHL will load the stack pointer from the HL pair. Finally, there are four rotate instructions. They rotate the accumulator left without carry (RLC), right without carry (RRC), left using the carry bit as part of the rotation (RAL), and right using the carry bit as part of the rotation (RAR). The mnemonics are backwards from what you would expect.

On the 16 bit side, we should expand our conception of Load Immediate (LXI), since this instruction not only loads register pairs with 16 bit data but also can load the stack pointer.

In the *Data Transformation* category, we see the mnemonics for some peculiar addition and subtraction operations. They are there for extended precision arithmetic. It is possible to do 16, 24, 32 . . . bit addition or subtraction by breaking the computation into a series of 8 bit operations and using the carry bit (borrow bit) to connect the subcomputations. The instructions for this are called Add with Carry (ADC) and Subtract with Borrow (SBB). There are also some more logical instructions. The Inclusive OR instruction (ORA) and the Exclusive OR instruction (XRA) use the accumulator and have operands in the same pattern as the other arithmetic and logical instructions.

Finally, there are a few miscellaneous instructions in this category. CMA complements the accumulator (1's complement only). STC sets the carry flag. CMC complements the carry flag. The DAA instruction is a special purpose operation. It should be used immediately after a normal addition instruction, if your operands have been expressed in BCD notation, and you want your answer to be expressed the same way.

On the 16 bit side, we should take note of some more operations that are possible with the stack pointer. The stack pointer can be added to the HL register pair (DAD). It can also be incremented (INX) or decremented (DCX) as a 16 bit unit.

There are no more *Input/Output* or *Machine Control* instructions.

Our final category among the less-used instructions is *Program Control*. The PCHL instruction loads the program counter from the HL register. It is thus a jump instruction with an indirect address. The 8080 instruction set also has many varieties of conditional subroutine calls (CC, CZ, etc.) and conditional return instructions (RC, RZ, etc.). These statements will do their work according to the way the flags are set. The notation is exactly parallel to the conditional branch instructions discussed earlier.

Eight Bit Instructions   Sixteen Bit Instructions

1. *Data Movement*

STAX rp   LDAX rp

                                                                      LXI   sp,data16

XCHG   XTHL   SPHL
RLC   RRC   RAL   RAR

2. *Data Transformation*

ADC r   ADC   M   ACI   data8   DAD   sp
SBB r   SBB   M   SBI   data8

                                                                      INX   sp
ORA r   ORA   M   ORI   data8   DCX   sp
XRA r   XRA   M   XRI   data8
CMA   STC   CMC   DAA

3. *Input/Output*
—

4. *Program Control*

PCHL
CC, CNC, CZ, CNZ, CM, CP, CPE, CPO
RC, RNC, RZ, RNZ, RM, RP, RPE, RPO

5. *Machine Control*
—

Figure A-4: The Less-Used 8080 Instructions. Learn these instructions, after you
digest the basic subset, in order to fill out your knowledge of what the 8080 can do.

A.2 CODES FOR DIGITAL COMMUNICATION

ASCII Code	Character	ASCII Code	Character	ASCII Code	Character
00	NUL	2B	+	56	V
01	SOH	2C	,	57	W
02	STX	2D	-	58	X
03	ETX	2E	.	59	Y
04	EOT	2F	/	5A	Z
05	ENQ	30	0	5B	[
06	ACK	31	1	5C	\
07	BEL	32	2	5D	]
08	BS	33	3	5E	$\wedge(\uparrow)$
09	HT	34	4	5F	$-(\leftarrow)$
0A	LF	35	5	60	\
0B	VT	36	6	61	a
0C	FF	37	7	62	b
0D	CR	38	8	63	c
0E	SO	39	9	64	d
0F	SI	3A	:	65	e
10	DLE	3B	;	66	f
11	DC1 (X-ON)	3C	<	67	g
12	DC2 (TAPE)	3D	=	68	h
13	DC3 (X-OFF)	3E	>	69	i
14	DC4	3F	?	6A	j
15	NAK	40	@	6B	k
16	SYN	41	A	6C	l
17	ETB	42	B	6D	m
18	CAN	43	C	6E	n
19	EM	44	D	6F	o
1A	SUB	45	E	70	p
1B	ESC	46	F	71	q
1C	FS	47	G	72	r
1D	GS	48	H	73	s
1E	RS	49	I	74	t
1F	US	4A	J	75	u
20	SP	4B	K	76	v
21	!	4C	L	77	w
22	"	4D	M	78	x
23	#	4E	N	79	y
24	$	4F	O	7A	z
25	%	50	P	7B	{
26	&	51	Q	7C		
27	'	52	R	7D	} (ALT MODE)
28	(	53	S	7E	$-$
29	)	54	T	7F	DEL (RUB OUT)
2A	"	55	U		

Figure A.5 ASCII Character Codes for Digital Communication. This code is an agreed-upon medium through which information can be exchanged between pieces of digital equipment—for example, a computer and a disk drive, or a terminal and a modem driven telephone line. Each character to be transmitted is coded as one byte. In this table these bytes are represented as hexadecimal numbers with the most significant bit set to zero.

Index to Tables
and Data Structures

Index

M

N

O